WHEN GOD SPEAKS
Reflections on the First Readings of the Sunday Lectionary

Archbishop Daniel E. Pilarczyk

ST. ANTHONY MESSENGER PRESS
Cincinnati, Ohio

Cover design by Mike Winegardner
Book design by Mark Sullivan

LIBRARY OF CONGRESS CATALOGING-IN-PUBLICATION DATA

Pilarczyk, Daniel E.
  When God speaks: reflections on the first readings of the Sunday lectionary / Daniel E. Pilarczyk.
    p. cm.
  ISBN 0-86716-623-1 (pbk. : alk. paper) 1. Bible. O.T.—Meditations. 2. Catholic Church. Lectionary for Mass (U.S.) I. Title.

BS1151.55.P55 2006
264'.02034—dc22

                                                    2005014533

ISBN-13 978-0-86716-623-1
ISBN-10 0–86716–623–1

Published by St. Anthony Messenger Press
28 W. Liberty Street
Cincinnati, OH 45202
www.AmericanCatholic.org

Printed in the United States of America.

Printed on acid-free paper.

06 07 08 09 10   5 4 3 2 1

CONTENTS

PART THREE—*Lent*

PART FOUR—*Easter*

PART FIVE—*Ordinary Time*

PART SIX—*Solemnities*

Introduction

Over the past forty years or so churchgoing Catholics have
become much more scripturally literate than they used to be.
This is due in large part to the lectionary, the book of readings
for Masses for Sundays and weekdays of the year.

In the Constitution on the Sacred Liturgy, published by the
Second Vatican Council in 1963, the Council fathers decreed:

> The treasures of the Bible are to be opened up more
> lavishly, so that richer fare may be provided for the
> faithful at the table of God's word. In this way a more
> representative portion of the holy Scriptures will be read
> to the people over a set cycle of years. (*Sacrosanctum
> Concilium*, 51)

In response to this directive, an expanded selection of readings
was published by the Holy See in 1969. It provided readings for a
two-year cycle for weekdays and for a three-year cycle for
Sundays. The new lectionary has been a gift that every member
of the church is or should be grateful for.

This book, *When God Speaks: Reflections on the First Readings of the Sunday Lectionary Resource* is a series of brief commentaries concerned with the Sunday cycle, specifically with the first of the three readings assigned to each Sunday in the three-year cycle.

The First Reading for each Sunday is generally from the Old Testament, that collection of sacred writings that records the relationship between God and human beings that prevailed before the coming of Christ, the universal Redeemer (cf. Vatican II, *Dogmatic Constitution on Divine Revelation*, no. 15 [*Divine Revelation*]). The Old Testament was *the* Sacred Scripture for the first generations of Christian believers. The church teaches that both Old and New Testaments were inspired by the Holy Spirit, and that the Old Testament, far from being a mere relic of antiquity, is part of the proclamation of the gospel, and serves to shed light on the gospel and helps to explain it (cf. *Divine Revelation,* no. 16).

During the early centuries of the church's life, readings from the Old Testament were a regular feature of the Sunday liturgy. By about the seventh century, however, the regular use of the Old Testament for the Sunday Scripture readings seems to have fallen into disuse. In the missal that was in use just before Vatican II (which also contained the Scripture readings for Mass), passages from the Old Testament were used on only three occasions: the feast of the Epiphany, Good Friday and the Easter Vigil.

Now we have readings from the Old Testament on every Sunday of the year (with the exception of the Sundays of Eastertime, as we shall see in a moment). During Advent, we have a series of selections from the messianic passages of the Old Testament. During Lent, the Old Testament readings offer God's people a brief review of the history of salvation. For feasts like

Epiphany and Corpus Christi, the First Readings have been chosen to fit in with the theme of the feast. Finally, in the thirty-three or thirty-four weeks of Ordinary Time, the Old Testament readings have been chosen for their harmony with the Gospel, to illuminate certain aspects of the Gospel and to highlight the unity between the Old and New Testament.

But there has also been another dynamic at work in these Sundays of Ordinary Time. As the introduction to the second edition of the lectionary puts it:

> Care has been taken to ensure that many Old Testament texts of major significance would be read on Sundays. Such readings are distributed not according to a logical order but on the basis of what the Gospel requires. Still, the treasury of the word of God will be opened up in such a way that nearly all the principal pages of the Old Testament will become familiar to those taking part in the Mass on Sundays. (no. 106)

Catholics were never discouraged by the church from reading the Old Testament, but the liturgy didn't do much to encourage them. Now we hear the Old Testament almost every week. Whereas in the pre–Vatican II list of Sunday and Holy Week readings there were only fourteen readings from the Old Testament (one of them being used twice), in the Sunday and Holy Week lectionary we use now there are no fewer than 160. The church has indeed provided "a richer fare" in setting before its people "all the principal pages of the Old Testament."

For the Sundays of Eastertime, the First Readings are not from the Old Testament but from the Acts of the Apostles. This book of the New Testament was neglected in the former lectionary. During the one-year cycle that was then in use for

Sundays, there were only three readings from Acts. In our current lectionary, there are twenty-three.

The church offers us First Readings from Acts during Eastertime for a number of reasons. First of all, there seems to have been an ancient Christian tradition of reading Acts at Easter. Second, one of the purposes of Acts is to record the reaction of Jesus' followers to his Resurrection. Finally, this series of readings provides an overview of the early history of the church that corresponds to the overview of Old Testament salvation history that was provided during the First Readings of Lent.

The purpose of this series of commentaries is to help people understand and assimilate the "richer fare" that Vatican II has provided for us. All too often the First Readings are either totally neglected in reflecting and preaching on the Sunday readings, or they are looked on exclusively as illustrating the Gospel. There's nothing wrong with looking at them that way, but each of these First Readings does have a meaning and a context of its own, and being aware of that will provide further enrichment.

In this series of commentaries I intend to set forth the following elements for each reading:

1. Context: How does the reading fit into the biblical book from which it is taken, and how does it fit into the liturgy of the day?
2. Content: What is the original, basic meaning of the text?
3. Connection: Does the reading relate to other readings in the liturgy?
4. Consequences: What does this reading at this place in the liturgy mean for my life of faith?
5. Conversation possibilities: Questions to help people

talk about the reading with the Lord, with themselves, or with each other.

There is still one more aspect of these readings, especially the Old Testament readings, that calls for some preliminary comment: These readings are rooted in a history—a long, complex, meaningful history. One of the principal ways in which God related to his people and taught them in Old Testament times was through history. He helped them to understand his will and their relationship to him through the social and political events they experienced. This history is a long one. If we posit that the history of God's chosen people as recorded in the Old Testament begins with Abraham (sometime about 2000 B.C.) and stretches to the time of the Maccabees (about 150 B.C.), we have almost 1900 years of history to deal with. (By contrast, the time period covered by the New Testament is less than 150 years.) History involves dates, and most people don't like to deal with dates. In order to make things a little easier, I am suggesting a bare minimum of five dates that you have to know if you are going to be able to make sense out of the Old Testament. I will refer to these dates, and the events they recall, in the reflections that follow. Here are the dates and the events:

c. 1250 B.C.: the Israelites enter the Promised Land after some years of wandering in the desert;
1000 B.C.: David becomes king of Israel and Judah;
721 B.C.: Samaria is overcome by the Assyrians and the Northern Kingdom disappears;
587 B.C.: Jerusalem is destroyed by the Babylonians and the leaders of the people are taken into exile;
515 B.C.: the Jerusalem temple is rededicated after the return of the exiles.

Familiarity with these dates and these events will enable the reader to put practically everything else in the Old Testament into appropriate perspective.

Assuming some familiarity with these dates, I think the best way for readers to use these reflections is to read the First Reading for the Sunday in their Bible or worship aid, then to read and consider what is offered here (perhaps with the text open alongside) and then pay special attention to the reading at the Sunday liturgy. For the Sundays in Ordinary Time it will be helpful to look over the Gospels as well. (Note that the translation used in the lectionary and as a basis for these commentaries is a somewhat modified version of the *New American Bible.*)

It is my hope that this series of reflections will serve its readers as an opening, an introduction, an overture to a deeper and better informed appreciation of the inspired word of God and of God's love for his people.

PART ONE
Advent

First Sunday of Advent (A)

Isaiah 2:1–5

Advent means "coming." It is a season in which we prepare to celebrate the coming of Christ at Christmas, and in which we remember the coming of Christ at the beginning of his public career. Advent is also a season when we look forward to his Second Coming at the end of time. This third Advent theme provides a kind of overlap or connection with the theme of the concluding Sundays of Ordinary Time.

For the first Sunday of Advent, the Gospels are about the Second Coming of the Lord. For the second and third Sundays they are about John the Baptist and Jesus' first public appearances. For the fourth Sunday of Advent, the Gospels are about the events that prepared immediately for the Lord's birth.

The Introduction to the lectionary (no. 93) implies that the Old Testament readings for these four Sundays have not, as a rule, been chosen to match the specific themes of the Gospel selections. Rather, they constitute a little series of their own, concerned with prophecies about the Messiah and the messianic age. Seven of the twelve Old Testament readings for the Sundays of Advent in the three-year cycle are from the book of the prophet Isaiah.

The prophet Isaiah is one of the giants of the Old Testament. He was active in the Southern Kingdom of Judah from about 740 B.C. until after 701 B.C. This was a turbulent time. It saw the destruction of the Northern Kingdom by the Assyrians and increasing hostility between the Southern Kingdom and the Babylonians. For part of this time, Isaiah was an important advisor to the king of Judah.

Isaiah was a man of deep spiritual influence, not only during his own lifetime but also after his death. In fact, Isaiah seems to have been the center of a school or community or tradition that was still proclaiming God's word in his way and his spirit some two hundred years after the end of the prophet's personal career.

What has come down to us as the book of Isaiah is really an anthology of prophetic poetry. Some of it is by the prophet himself. But much of it has its origins in the followers of Isaiah. Scholars generally divide the 66 chapters of Isaiah into three parts: chapters 1 to 39 (called First Isaiah) contain mostly Isaiah's own personal work; chapters 40 to 55 (Second Isaiah) seem to have their origin in the time of the exile, after Jerusalem had been destroyed; chapters 56 to 66 (Third Isaiah) are from the years after the Israelite's return from exile. It is all God's inspired word, and somehow it is all connected with Isaiah son of Amoz, but it is not all his own individual work. Being aware of the timing and origin of the various parts of Isaiah make it easier to understand the meaning of what we read.

This Sunday's reading is from the earliest part of the book, the part that contains the most of Isaiah's personal work. After a couple of introductory lines, the prophet proclaims that the Lord's house on Mt. Zion in Jerusalem would become a universal seat of authority, a source of clear and certain teaching for the whole world. People from all over would come to the Lord's mountain to receive guidance. From the Lord's mountain direction would go out that would result in universal peace and the destruction of the instruments of warfare. In the last verse, the prophet points out to the people of Judah that if pagan nations are going to respond so earnestly to God's guidance, how much more is it incumbent on God's own people to do so. "[L]et *us* walk in the light of the LORD!" (emphasis added).

This reading is more about the messianic age than about the

person of the Messiah and his achievements. But its message is clear and comforting: God has plans, plans for peace that include all the peoples of the earth. Something wonderful is going to happen and everybody will benefit from it.

There seem to be at least two important lessons for us in this reading that opens the church's year.

First of all, it is clear that the nations of the world have not yet beaten their swords into plowshares and their spears into pruning hooks. As a matter of fact, we spend a great deal of our resources in making ever more destructive swords and spears. We are still waiting for the final fulfillment of God's plan, still looking forward to the completion of what God had promised.

Secondly, it is God who will bring all this about. Consequently it is only when nations have accepted God's guidance that the community of universal peace will come.

We find it hard to imagine how all this will happen. Yet God's word tells us that it is coming. One of the reasons for taking Advent seriously is to renew our awareness of what God has in mind for us and our hope for its completion.

FOR REFLECTION AND DISCUSSION

How does God offer instruction to nations in our time?

Where do I see hope for universal peace in today's world?

First Sunday of Advent (B)

Isaiah 63:16b–17, 19b; 64:2–7

Advent is about the coming of God, the coming of God in the birth of Jesus, the coming of God in the beginning of Jesus' public ministry, the coming of God in the glory of Christ at the end of time.

During these four weeks, the Old Testament readings are selections about the Messiah and the messianic age. The term "Messiah" means "anointed," and originally it was used of the anointed king of God's people, specifically of David and his descendants. The king was appointed by divine command, a person of special holiness, an adopted son of God. His person was sacrosanct. He was divinely protected. He was a unique instrument of God's justice on earth. As the years went by, a gap became apparent between the ideals of this Davidic sonship and the concrete reality of the kings of Israel and Judah. And so these royal and religious prerogatives began to be applied to a hoped-for future king whose reign would be characterized by everlasting justice, security and peace. At the heart of the expectation of a Messiah is the idea that God intervenes in history to deliver his people from suffering and injustice. Christians see the fulfillment of this expectation in Jesus of Nazareth.

Our messianic reading for this first Sunday of Advent is from the third part of Isaiah. This part of Isaiah (chapters 55–66) preserves the messages of one or more prophets of the religious tradition of the eighth century Isaiah which were directed to the people of Judea after their return from exile in the last half of the sixth century B.C.

Our lectionary reading is a selection of verses rather than a continuous passage, but all the verses come from a single heartrending psalm of entreaty and lament. The returned exiles face a ruined city and a temple that has been destroyed. They voice this plea for God's intervention on their behalf. It is a prayer for a time of desperation, an anguished cry for the coming of the messianic age that God had promised.

The reading begins with the acknowledgment of God's care for his people: "You are our father and Redeemer." Next comes a petition: "Return. Come back to us like thunder booming out of the clouds with power that shakes the mountains." Then a confession of the people's sinfulness: "You have done wondrous deeds in the past for us, but now we are sinful. Our guilt has made us worthless in your sight." Finally, an appeal for God's intervention: "But you are still our father and you can make of us whatever you wish."

"We need you, God! We need your intervention to make something worthwhile out of this sinful people!" That's what the Israelites said as they struggled to find a life for themselves in their ruined homeland. That's the prayer that the church invites us to make our own as we begin a new liturgical year.

One of the most dangerous elements of the moral infection, the spiritual disability that we human beings have inherited, is a sense of self-sufficiency. We like to think that we can do things for ourselves. If we just get the right breaks we can bring meaning and fulfillment to our lives. If we are holy enough and virtuous enough and religious enough, God will have to recognize our worth and confer on us the happiness we deserve.

Wrong! For one thing, we are totally dependent on God. Our life, our faith, our talents, the support we receive from the people around us: It's all God's gift. It's all God's doing. We are the clay and God is the potter. We can no more direct our lives for ourselves than a lump of clay can decide what shape it is to assume.

Then there is our own personal sinfulness. We have all misused the gifts that God has given us. We have taken for ourselves what God intended us to use for others. Even what seems like a virtuous achievement is often defiled by selfish motives. "[A]ll our good deeds are like polluted rags..../ [O]ur guilt carries us away like the wind."

We need God's intervention to deliver us from our sorry state. We need a Messiah to bring us into harmony with God's will, with God's benevolence. The Messiah will indeed come at the end of time, but we also need the Messiah for our survival now.

FOR REFLECTION AND DISCUSSION

Where do I experience a need for God in my life?

What evidence do I see in my daily life of the Messiah's presence and work?

First Sunday of Advent (C)

Jeremiah 33:14–16

During the season of Advent, the beginning of the church's liturgical year, the First Readings for Sunday are more or less independent of the other two readings. While these First Readings do fit in with the general themes of the Advent season, they have not been chosen for their relationship to either of the other two readings. They are, rather, a selection from the Old Testament prophecies about the Messiah and the messianic age.

In Hebrew the word "messiah" means "anointed one" and is used to refer to anyone set apart for any special function—a priest, for example, or the king. When the chosen people's kingdom came under threat from foreign enemies, the term "messiah" began to be used to denote a future king of the house of David whose rule would be glorious, wise and secure, a ruler who would deliver his people from suffering and injustice. This shadowy anointed one was an image, an expression of the hope that God continuously offered to his people, even in their most difficult circumstances.

Today's brief Old Testament reading is from the book of the prophet Jeremiah. Scholars tell us, however, that it is not a product of the pre-exile prophet who is responsible for most of the book that bears his name. Instead, it seems to be part of a booklet inserted later into the prophecy of Jeremiah, after the rest of the book had been assembled. This booklet, from which today's reading is taken, seems to date from after the exile, when the Jews had begun to return to their land, at a time when the people were looking for a restoration of the Davidic monarchy. (Note that this section of Jeremiah, though probably not written by the great pre-exile prophet, is not, for that reason, any less inspired, any less the word of God.)

Today's short selection is an oracle of hope, a proclamation intended to rekindle positive expectations about God's plans for them in the hearts of those who had come back to their homeland. The voice of the Lord speaks of the days that are coming, an indefinite future, but a sure one. (God is not offering his hearers a calendar here, but encouragement.) Then God reminds them of the promise he had made to David (cf. 2 Samuel 7, 11–16) that the house, i.e., the family of David would rule God's people forever. When the time comes for that promise to be fulfilled, God says, a righteous descendent of David will appear who will do what is right in the land and bring security to God's people. Jerusalem, God's holy city, will be a sign of God's intervention in favor of his people, a sanctuary of salvation, safety and fulfillment.

These verses do not offer a detailed account of the Davidic messiah, nor specifics of the time and circumstances of his coming. But they do call us to hope, to confidence in the Lord's faithfulness to his promises.

We Christians believe that the messianic prophecies of the Old Testament were fulfilled in Christ (a word which means "anointed one"). He is the king sent to rule God's people. He is the bringer of salvation, safety and fulfillment. We believe not only that the Messiah has already been manifested in the earthly life of Jesus, but also that Jesus is still to come again at the end of time to bring his messianic mission to final completion. We don't know all the details of the earthly life of Jesus, nor the details of his Second Coming. But we know that he is God's Anointed One, the Savior, the Deliverer, and that God's promises will come to fulfillment.

Today's reading serves to remind us of the basics of God's messianic plans and calls the men and women of our time to hope and confidence, just as it called the men and women of post-exilic Jerusalem to hope and confidence.

We need to hear about God's messianic plans once in a while so we don't forget about them. It's easy to get so caught up in our daily round of work, in solving our own particular problems, in worrying about how we are going to carry out our responsibilities, that we forget that all this is taking place in a wider context, that our life, with all of its details and demands, is part of a larger plan that has already been initially fulfilled in the life, death and resurrection of Jesus and that will reach a final fulfillment when the Lord comes again in glory to put his final stamp of approval on the good we have done for him. We are called to be a messianic people. We are called to hope.

What part does hope play in my life?

Do I see any signs of the coming of Christ in the world around me?

Second Sunday of Advent (A)

Isaiah 11:1–10

Isaiah is a very important book of the Old Testament, especially for Christian readers. Apart from the Psalms, Isaiah is the book of the Bible that has the most chapters. It is cited in the Gospels more than any other book of the Hebrew Scriptures apart from the Psalms. In fact, Isaiah is sometimes called the fifth Gospel. It is the Old Testament book that is most used in the Sunday lectionary. There are no less than thirty-eight Sunday readings from Isaiah during the three-year Sunday cycle, which means that we hear from Isaiah on the average of once every four weeks. Slightly more than 13 percent of the full text of Isaiah appears in the Sunday lectionary, a higher percentage than any other Old Testament book. It's an important book of the Old Testament.

And today's reading from Isaiah is a very important section of the book for Christian readers. It is used not only for the Eucharistic liturgy of the second Sunday of Advent in year A, but also for Tuesday of the first week of Advent (every year), and for the office of readings for Christmas in the Liturgy of the Hours.

It's almost as if the church wants to be very sure that its members are well acquainted with this passage.

These ten verses provide a description of the Messiah and an account of the results that he would bring about. We don't know if Isaiah had any specific person in mind as he first proclaimed these words, but Christian believers have always understood it as referring to Christ Jesus and to the final outcomes of his saving ministry in our midst.

The passage begins with the Messiah's origin: a shoot from the stump of Jesse. Jesse was King David's father. This wondrous person would be a descendant of the family of the greatest king that God's people ever had. Even if the family of Jesse was no longer the flourishing tree it once was, the Messiah could spring forth even from a stump.

The next four verses describe the personal attributes of the messianic king. The Lord would be with him, conferring qualities reminiscent of those of King Solomon (wisdom and understanding), of King David (counsel and strength), of the prophets (knowledge and reverence in the presence of the Lord). He will be an instrument of justice, deciding wisely and fairly, taking particular account of the poor and the afflicted. He will be powerful enough to overcome the powers of evil. Integrity and faithfulness will be his trademark.

The next four verses speak of a new kind of world, a world in which there would no longer be violence and destruction, but in which all hostile forces would come together in harmony. The ruthlessness of nature would be changed into a paradise of peace. The garden of Eden would return. The young of the cattle, the young of the lion, the young of humanity would walk together without fear. There will be "no harm or ruin" in this messianic kingdom. The Lord's presence will cover the kingdom like water covers the seabed.

Finally, there is a concluding verse about the Gentiles. This offspring of David's family would be so glorious that people from all over the world will come forward to be part of his kingdom. (This attention to the rest of the world is a characteristic of

Isaiah. He has been called the prophet of universal salvation.)

Isaiah's message here is similar to that of last Sunday's opening reading: God has great plans, plans for peace and harmony. These plans will come to fruition through the life and work of this son of Jesse. He will exemplify virtue of every kind. He will do away with everything that is ugly and harmful on the earth. He will bring all nations together to live with him.

It's a glorious and idyllic picture that Isaiah paints for us here. All the evils of the earth will be confronted and dealt with by this wonderful person. The whole world will be changed. We believe that Christ is the fulfillment of what Isaiah spoke of. Through his life and teaching, through his self-gift on the cross, through the Father's acceptance of his mission everything is different. We now have possibilities that weren't there before, possibilities for goodness and justice, possibilities for peace and harmony. It has all come through our messianic Lord.

What Isaiah proclaimed has not all been brought to conclusion yet. There is still sin in the world, still evil and violence. But the word of the Lord assures us that what has been promised will come to pass. Our Christian faith leads us to trust in the promises of the Lord. Our Christian hope leads us to look forward to their fulfillment.

FOR REFLECTION AND DISCUSSION

What tensions do I see in the world that need messianic resolution? Do I hope for enough from God?

Second Sunday of Advent (B)

Isaiah 40:1–5, 9–11

This Sunday's First Reading is one of the best-known passages of the Old Testament. It is stately, yet intensely lyrical. It almost cries out to be sung. In fact, George Frederic Handel used most of these verses in the first part of his *Messiah,* and people who are familiar with the oratorio cannot read this Sunday's reading without finding Handel's melodies running through their memories.

These verses are at the very beginning of the second main section of the book of Isaiah, the part known as the Book of Consolation (chapters 40–55). These chapters are the work of one or more members of the spiritual school of Isaiah of Jerusalem and seem to have been written during the Babylonian exile.

God's people, or the most important part of God's people, had been carried off into a foreign land. The temple and the holy city had been destroyed. The Israelites found themselves in the midst of an alien culture. Their corporate identity was threatened. Everything that was important to them seemed to have been taken away.

Into this context of sadness and despair comes the voice of the prophet, a voice that speaks out the message of God, a message of comfort and of hope.

Our passage begins in the throne room of heaven. We hear the majestic voice of God giving direction to his messengers: "Tell my people Israel that their time of testing is over, that their sins are forgiven. Give them comfort."

Next comes the voice of one of God's messengers responding to God's command. The voice calls for a highway to be made so that God's people can get to where God wants them to be. It is to be a road that will enable them to pass through the difficult places with ease. What is being promised here is a repetition of the people's deliverance from Egypt. Just as God brought them out of slavery through the desert of Sinai in the exodus, so also God will deliver them from exile now.

Next the voice calls for Jerusalem to become the herald of God's good news. Even though the city may be in ruins now, it can still serve as an image of God's messianic kingdom and as an agent of God's loving plans for his people. The message is to be delivered from a high mountain, so as to be heard throughout the world.

The message is the good news of the presence of the Lord: "Here is your God!" The God that Zion announces will be a God of power, but also a God who rewards those who serve him, a God who cares for his people as a shepherd cares for his flock, treating the weakest and most vulnerable members of the flock with special attention.

To a weakened, discouraged, powerless people comes the message of God: The people will be liberated; God will come in glory; Jerusalem will be the herald of God's love throughout the world; God will take care of his people.

Mark used part of this text in the introduction to his proclamation of the good news of Jesus as we hear in this Sunday's Gospel (Mark 1:1–8). What Isaiah had said was pertinent to the mission of Jesus. What Isaiah said is also pertinent to our situation twenty centuries after the beginning of the mission of Jesus, twenty-six centuries after the Israelites' exile.

In many ways we are like the Israelites in exile. We live in a society that is foreign and even hostile to our most deeply held beliefs. The culture that surrounds us looks on religious dedication as basically irrelevant to human existence. In a society that treasures success, self-assertion, independence, we are called to build our lives on being subject to the Lord, on self-gift to God and neighbor, on humility. The world is constantly inviting us to travel paths different from the paths that a loving God has laid out for us.

And so the Lord speaks to us, "Don't be afraid. I will forgive your sins. I will lead you home. I will take care of you. I am with you now and I will stay with you. Take comfort in my presence." In this passage God's word proclaims fundamental messianic realities. No wonder people find this passage so memorable. No wonder they find themselves enveloped in music when they read it.

FOR REFLECTION AND DISCUSSION

In what ways do I find myself in exile?
What do I look forward to from the presence of God?

Second Sunday of Advent (C)

Baruch 5:1–9

The book of Baruch is a collection of poems that seems to have been written in the first or second century B.C. It is addressed to the members of the people of God who were still living outside the Promised Land, remnants of the exile that had taken place several centuries before. The general purpose of Baruch seems to be to encourage those who continued to live in dispersion outside the ancestral homeland (that is, in the diaspora) to be faithful to their identity, to stay in touch with their traditions, to continue to look forward to the final fulfillment of God's promises. The author wanted his readers to remain conscious of their religious roots in the midst of the pagan world in which they lived, a world in which they were being tempted ever more strongly to take on pagan ways.

The unknown author of this collection has assumed the name of Baruch, secretary to the prophet Jeremiah. The historical Baruch was long gone when this book of the Bible was composed, but its author wanted his reflections on the Jewish tradition, his message of reconciliation and hope to be seen as related to the classic prophetic tradition.

In the fourth chapter of Baruch, Jerusalem (the people of God) is personified as a widow who sorrows for her lost children. Then, in the chapter that constitutes today's reading, the prophet invites Jerusalem to put aside her garb of sorrow and dress up in her best clothes so that all the world could see what God has done for her. Her brilliance is to shine out through the whole world in the names that God has conferred on her: peace through integrity, glory through faithfulness to God. The Holy City is to welcome home its children as they return from exile. God will lower the mountains and fill up the gorges so the path of their return will be easy. After all, they are being led home in joy by the holiness and mercy of the Lord himself.

This reading continues the selection of messianic proclamations that began last Sunday and that we will continue to hear in our First Readings for the rest of Advent. Today, however, God's word presents to us not an individual messianic person, but a whole messianic context, an ideal homeland to which all of God's sons and daughters are called, a heavenly city made bright by the holiness of God, a goal toward which God helps them by smoothing out the obstacles that stand in their way. God's goodness and generosity are leading his scattered people to final security, richness, fulfillment, to the messianic kingdom that constitutes their real home.

These words of an anonymous sacred writer calling his people to faithfulness and hope in the midst of the pagan world in which they found themselves are also addressed to us. We are threatened by some of the same dangers that the diaspora Jews of the first and second century B.C. had to face.

There is a lot of comfort around us. We live in a world of ease and leisure that could very easily bring us to forget that we are not in our lasting home here. We are still on the road to something better.

The values that our world holds out to us—success, security, prosperity, personal comfort—are not the values that will bring us final happiness. We have to reject much of what the world offers us and strive to stay on the road that God invites us to walk, the road that leads to the heavenly Jerusalem, to the messianic kingdom in which God is everything for all of us. There our worth and value will consist in our sharing in the holiness of God. Our fulfillment will be our sharing in the glory of the eternal liturgy of heaven.

Sometimes the enemies of faith deride our struggle to stay on the track toward the heavenly Jerusalem by calling it "pie in the sky," and by suggesting that believers delude themselves with an imaginary future so they don't have to deal with a difficult present. Yet our quest for the messianic kingdom does not call us to reject the value and demands of our present existence, but to remain aware that the present is only the beginning. Of course our present world has value. After all, it was made good by a good God. But our faith calls us to remember that we are in a kind of exile here, that, in spite of the world's worth, it is not really our home. We're headed somewhere else, led by the Lord to a kingdom where God himself waits to welcome us.

FOR REFLECTION AND DISCUSSION

In what ways do I see my life as a journey?
How clear am I about where I am going?

Third Sunday of Advent (A)

Isaiah 35:1–6a, 10

The first thirty-nine chapters of the book of Isaiah are generally, but not exclusively, the personal work of Isaiah the son of Amoz. Scholars tell us that these chapters also contain some material from later times. That seems to be the case with the reading for this Sunday. It is a poem concerned with the return from exile, apparently written some 150 years after the time of Isaiah, though still reflecting his teachings about the Messiah and the messianic kingdom.

The reading is a message of comfort and hope addressed to those in need of liberation. It describes for the exiles in Babylon how things will be when God brings them home again.

The text as presented to us in the lectionary is divided into three parts. The first part describes the road that the returning exiles would travel. It would pass through desert country, to be sure, but God would beautify and refresh the country so as to make it pleasant and easy for the travelers. The desert will bloom. There will be singing along the road. Luxuriant growth will spring up, like the green on the mountainsides or the robust growth in the Valley of Sharon, along the Mediterranean. Traveling the road will be like seeing the very splendor of God.

The next section of the reading has to do with the travelers. The prophet encourages someone (perhaps the religious leaders of the people) to strengthen feeble hands, make firm the knees that are weak and to encourage the fearful to be strong. The assurance of God's presence and help would give the travelers the strength and courage they need to continue their journey of return. "God is coming to rescue and deliver you." When that occurs, every disability will be removed. The blind, the deaf, the lame, the mute will enjoy a fullness, even an abundance of power and energy.

Finally, a concluding summary: no more sorrow, only singing with joy when the return has finally taken place and the Lord's people return to their homeland.

Like last Sunday's First Reading, these verses have found a place of special importance in Christian prayer and teaching. For one thing, an expanded version of this reading is read each year on Monday of the second week of Advent. It is not often that the church gives us the same reading twice in the same week.

But there is more. Jesus himself seems to have been alluding to this passage (and others) to describe his own ministry when he was questioned by the disciples of John the Baptist as we hear in this Sunday's Gospel (Matthew 11:2–11). "Go and tell John what you hear and see: / the blind regain their sight, / the lame walk, / lepers are cleansed, / the deaf hear...." What the author of Isaiah had promised was already beginning to be brought to fulfillment through Jesus. The messianic kingdom had begun. God's people were on their way back home.

The messianic journey of God's people has begun, but it is not yet ended. We are not home yet. To a greater or lesser extent, we are still in exile. To a greater or lesser extent, we are all infirm, disabled, handicapped. But we have the words of Isaiah and the words and deeds of Jesus. They are not mere poetic effusions nor symbolic actions. They constitute God's own reassurance that the road we travel is not impassible, that the infirmities we bear are not incurable. Both the First Reading and the Gospel offer words of hope not just to the people of the sixth century B.C., nor just to the crowds of Jesus' time, but to us as well.

What's important for us is to remember that we are, in fact, still on a journey, that we are going someplace. Sometimes we are tempted to be content with what we have, to put down final roots where we are now. We content ourselves with our present life, its comforts, its consolations. We are inclined to settle down and make the best we can out of our life here in Babylon. We tend to forget that God has something more and better in store for us.

On the other hand, sometimes we realize that the here and now cannot be our final home, but we forget that God is willing to go to great lengths to bring us to where we belong. It's easy to get discouraged. It's easy to forget that God is interested enough in our journey to make the desert bloom and to make the lame leap like stags.

On this Sunday God's word reminds us to keep moving on our journey. But it also invites us to travel in hope.

FOR REFLECTION AND DISCUSSION

In what ways is my life a journey?

How does God make my journey more pleasant, safer, easier?

Third Sunday of Advent (B)

Isaiah 61:1–2a, 10–11

This Sunday's reading is from the third part of the book of the prophet Isaiah (chapters 56–66). This part of Isaiah seems to have been written by members of the spiritual community of Isaiah of Jerusalem after the Israelites' return from the Babylonian exile had begun.

The reading as presented in the lectionary is in two parts.

The first part (verses 1–2a) is spoken in the person of the author. The second part (verses 10–11) seems to be spoken in the person of Zion, that is, by the corporate person of the people of God.

In the first part, the prophet describes his calling and his role. He has been called to his task by being anointed by the Spirit of God. Generally anointing was an act of empowerment reserved for kings and high priests. Here anointing is used as an image of the prophet's being set aside and consecrated for a special work.

The prophet then lists three tasks to which he has been called, three gifts that God would give his people through the ministry of the prophet. The prophet has been sent to encourage those in need, economic need or spiritual need. He has also been sent to bring freedom from every kind of exile or imprisonment. Finally, he is to be a voice of reassurance by announcing the generosity of God, a generosity that would bring God's people to a final state of fulfillment and well-being.

In the second half of our reading, we hear the voice of God's people, reflecting on what God has done for them and what God would still bring to pass. It is a voice of rejoicing because God has gifted his people with life and holiness, because God has entered into a kind of marriage relationship with them. The people and God belong together, even as man and wife belong together.

But there is more still to come. God promises a state of holiness and thanksgiving and praise throughout the world. God's whole earthly creation will be a garden of goodness cultivated by its loving Lord.

Both parts of this reading are messianic, that is, they are concerned with the future that God has planned for his people, a future that would involve forgiveness, holiness, fulfillment, strength, liberation, completion. All the First Readings of the Advent season deal in some degree with God's messianic providence, since Advent is a time of preparation to celebrate the coming of the Messiah in the ministry and birth of Jesus and at the end of the world.

The first verses of the reading seem to hark back to the four "servant of the Lord" readings that are found in the second part of Isaiah. These are a series of poems that speak of the ideal servant of God, God's agent who would carry out God's will in a unique career of service. In fact, some scholars look on this Sunday's text as a fifth servant song. We Christians look on the servant songs as prophecies about Jesus Christ. This Sunday's reading, whether or not it should be counted as a servant song, is also about Jesus. In fact, Jesus refers this passage to himself when he is giving a description of his calling to his friends and relatives in Nazareth (cf. Luke 4:16 ff.). He is the anointed one who would bring healing and freedom.

The second part of the reading is concerned with the definitive messianic kingdom, the state in which God would take final and full possession of his people and through them lead the world to a harvest of justice and praise. Our vision of the people of God is cast in terms of the church. Although the church and the messianic kingdom are not simply coterminous, the church is the beginning of the kingdom and is the instrument that God will use to bring the kingdom to fulfillment.

In this reading, then, the author speaks of a prophet who has claims on the attention of his hearers and of a people who would be the agents of God's salvation and God's justice. We see here a proclamation of Christ and a foreshadowing of certain aspects of the church.

But this reading is about us, too. Because we are baptized, we share in the life of Christ Jesus, the unique servant of God. We are therefore called and anointed to bring glad tidings to the poor, freedom to captives, the announcement of God's favor. Moreover, because of our baptism we are also members of the church and so share the church's relationship with God as well as the church's mission to lead the world to justice and praise.

We are all somehow prophets of the Lord. We are all agents of God's kingdom.

FOR REFLECTION AND DISCUSSION

How do I see myself as called by the Lord?
What evidence do I see of God making justice and praise spring up in the world?

Third Sunday of Advent (C)

Zephaniah 3:14–18a

The prophetic career of Zephaniah occurred a generation or two before the destruction of Jerusalem. Zephaniah's prophecies seem to have been proclaimed about the same time that Jeremiah was beginning his prophetic ministry.

Zephaniah lived and spoke out for God in a time of religious degradation, a time when people prayed to sun and moon and stars, a time when the true worship of the true God had been pushed aside in favor of the worship of foreign deities.

In this context of idolatry and delusion, Zephaniah's theme was "the day of the Lord." By "the day of the Lord" Zephaniah meant a time of impending judgment for the kingdom of Judah and the nations that surrounded her. It was a time of catastrophe, destruction and doom that would come upon God's people and the people's neighbors as recompense for their sinfulness. The day of the Lord would be a time of rebuke for pride and rebelliousness not only for the enemies of God's people, but for that people itself. The prophecy of Zephaniah is a grim message of retribution. (It may be worth noting that the book of Zephaniah inspired the medieval *Dies Irae* sequence that we used to sing at funerals before the Vatican II reform of the liturgy.)

And yet, although the basic theme of the book of Zephaniah is doom, judgment and reproach, it concludes with songs of joy. It's as if the Lord cannot bring himself to offer his people only threats of punishment. He must also reassure them before the end that some of them, at least, have a better destiny in store for them. Universal wickedness will be overcome by God's joy in his people.

Today's reading consists of two small psalms of rejoicing (verses 14–15 and 16–18) from the last part of the book of Zephaniah. Their common theme is that, in spite of everything, the Lord is in the midst of his people. He has turned away from judgment, preserved the people from their enemies, and spared them further misfortune. There is no need for fear or discouragement because the Lord is with them. The Lord is happy because of his contact with his people. The Lord is so glad to be with them that he will sing for joy, the way people sing at community celebrations. (One translation of this passage has the Lord dancing with shouts of joy.)

The specific figure of a Messiah is absent from this reading, yet the words of the prophet engender an attitude of excited expectation. The problems and the threats, both theological and political, that faced God's people in the seventh century B.C. would give way to the presence of God singing and dancing for joy in the midst of his people.

But Zephaniah's message is also addressed to us. Like the people of his time, we live in a pagan world, a world in which the prevalent orientation seems to be attentiveness to the false gods of comfort and security and self-satisfaction. Power and achievement seem to be the goals that most individuals and most groups of people pursue. Those of us who strive to remain in touch with the Lord know that this kind of situation cannot endure, that there will come a time of retribution, a time when human sinfulness will reap the harvest that it has sown for itself. Deep in our hearts we know that the day of the Lord is coming.

Yet the prophet tells us today that retribution will not be the final stage of our relationship with God. For those who are faithful, the conclusion to it all will be a new time of favor when the Lord will sing and dance for the joy he takes in being in the midst of his people. One might almost say that the Lord is planning a final family reunion at which the music will consist of the joyfulness of God being present with us. The day of the Lord will conclude with God's celebration of his people, with God's celebration of us.

During this season of Advent we prepare to celebrate the coming of the Messiah to our human world in the birth of Jesus.

It was a sinful world to which Jesus came, and it is a sinful world in which Jesus' followers live today. Yet God's word assures us that sinfulness will give way to joyful celebration. The birth of Jesus marked the beginning of the end of God's loving plans for his human creatures. Today our reading directs our attention to the end of the end, when the purpose for the coming of Jesus will have reached fulfillment and we will all celebrate together in a sing-along with God, present in the midst of his people.

FOR REFLECTION AND DISCUSSION

Which aspects of the world are most distasteful or threatening to me? What signs of God do I see in the midst of his people here and now?

Fourth Sunday of Advent (A)

Isaiah 7:10–14

This Sunday's Old Testament reading may be the preeminent messianic prophecy of them all. It certainly is used often in the church's liturgy: on this Sunday every third year, on December 20th every year, on the Solemnity of the Annunciation every year, and as one of the options for the First Reading for Marian celebrations throughout the year. The church can't hear it proclaimed often enough.

Our reading brings us to the year 735 B.C. Ahaz was the young king of Judah and the kingdom was in crisis. The kings of Damascus and of Israel had formed a league to unseat him and put a new king in his stead. Ahaz is panic-stricken and has decided that he has to enter an alliance with the pagan king of

Assyria, the enemy of his enemies. Isaiah had already told him, in the opening verses of chapter seven, that this wasn't what God wanted from him. What God wanted was for him to do nothing, to wait out the crisis. God would deal with Damascus and Israel (as indeed he did just a few years later). But Ahaz isn't having any of that. He intends to go ahead with his own plans.

Now, in our passage, Isaiah addresses Ahaz again. Speaking in the name of God he says to him, "If you didn't believe me before, believe me now. Ask for a sign and I will give it to you. No matter what it takes to convince you, I'll do it so that you will have confidence in me." In a burst of arrogant hypocrisy, Ahaz says that he will not tempt God by asking for a sign. He didn't need any sign from God. His plans were already made. He preferred to depend on the Assyrians rather than on God. But God gives him a sign anyway. We can almost hear Isaiah shouting at Ahaz. A son would be born to the royal household. The dynasty would not be destroyed. The child would be called Emmanuel, which means "God is with us." God would continue to be with his people in spite of kings like Ahaz. There would be a glorious future, but Ahaz wouldn't be part of it.

In its original, historical setting, what Isaiah says is simply that a young woman would have a child who would be a sign of God's continued plans to be with his people. In spite of Ahaz's short-sighted political scheming, the house of David would survive. Scholars are not in agreement about whom Isaiah (and God) had in mind. As later generations reflected on the promise, however, they saw more in it than reassurance about Ahaz's successor. They saw it as the promise of the king *par excellence*, the Messiah. But at both levels, the basic message is the same. God has plans for the future, and the center of those plans is God's presence in his people.

Christians, of course, see Jesus Christ as Emmanuel, as the promised Savior of God's people. And in the mother of Emmanuel, we see the Virgin Mary.

This episode in the history of God's people describes our situation, too. We are always under threat from outside and from inside. Outside of us there are always forces at work striving to weaken and undermine God's people. Within our hearts there is always the tendency to work our own way out of our difficulties, paying lip service to the power of God, but conducting ourselves as if God really wasn't going to get involved. To us God speaks: "I will be with you in ways that you may not expect or understand. I have plans for you, plans for future greatness. I want to be with you and I want you to be with me." It is through Jesus that God carries out his plans. It is in Jesus that God gifts us with his presence. Jesus is Emmanuel and we are his people.

The message that this Scripture passage gives us is a message of reassurance. The angel of the Lord in this Sunday's Gospel (Matthew 1:18–24) quotes this passage to reassure Joseph in his bewilderment. And the nearness of God that the passage promises gives reassurance to us that we never have to face our trials alone because the Lord is with us always.

This reading teaches us that God wants to be our Savior. He wants to rescue us from our enemies. He wants to confer on us an everlasting value. He wants to preserve what he has made us to be for all eternity. God has plans for us, big plans, important plans. And those plans include God's ongoing presence in our life through our sharing in the life of his Son, Jesus, Emmanuel, God who is with us.

The child that was promised to Ahaz was an image of the child that has been given to us, the child whose birthday we celebrate on Christmas.

FOR REFLECTION AND DISCUSSION

Where do I look to gain understanding about God's plans?
How is Christ Emmanuel (God with us) for me?

Fourth Sunday of Advent (B)

2 Samuel 7:1–5, 8b–12, 14a, 16

This prophecy is one of the most important and influential texts of the whole Bible. It constitutes the basis for Jewish expectations of a Messiah and, therefore, the basis for the messianic elements in Christian belief.

It is about the year 1000 B.C. David has now become king of all the tribes of Israel. He has captured Jerusalem from the Jebusites who inhabited the region and has brought the Ark of the Covenant into the city. It seemed that there would be peace and quiet for a while.

This is where our text begins. There are three main sections as it has been edited for the lectionary.

First of all, David acknowledges his good fortune and tells the prophet Nathan that now he wants to do something for God. He wants to build God a house in the city so that the God of the Israelites will be housed among his people as were the gods of the other peoples in the area. Nathan told him to proceed as he intended.

Now God intervenes. First of all, God tells Nathan to unsay what he had told David. Next we have an extended passage that contrasts God with David. The passage is full of pronouns, and the contrast between them and their repetition is what gives these verses their strength. "Should *you* build a house for *me*?"

Then comes a whole series of I's, in which God reminds David of what God had done for him and what he would do in the future. "*I* took...you from the pasture.... *I* have been with you.... *I* have destroyed all your enemies.... *I* will fix a place for my people." There are no fewer than eight I's in these four verses. God wants to make it clear that David's success, past, present and future, has been the gift of God and no other.

Next comes the third section of the reading. Again the text uses contrast to underline God's point. God says, in effect, "You want to make a house [a temple] for me, but instead of that I will make a house [a dynasty] for you." God promises that David would have a successful heir who would enjoy God's favor. And then God adds the messianic promise: "Your house and your kingdom shall be made sure forever before me; your throne shall be established forever" (NRSV). The house of David would last forever. David's line would have an altogether special relationship with the Lord.

What God promised to David was quite extraordinary from at least two perspectives. First of all, at the time of this promise, David's kingdom was weak and fragile. Humanly speaking, there was no reason to expect that it would survive his death. Second, David himself did not prove to be such a great king. He would engage in adultery and murder; he would tempt God's providence by having a census to learn the extent of his military resources; there would be immense family problems. It wasn't the kind of reign that one would imagine God would bless.

Of course, David was succeeded by Solomon, whom God did permit to build a temple. Solomon's reign was the high point of the history of the Israelites. Wealth and territory and reputation: He had it all. But after Solomon things began to decline. The kingdom split into two parts. There were cycles of hostility between them. Finally each part was overcome and destroyed by enemies.

By the time the Babylonians destroyed Jerusalem in 587 B.C., God's promise to David must have seemed rather empty. It must have appeared that there was some mistake here, that God couldn't possibly have meant what he seemed to have said.

Yet the Israelites held on to God's promise, and eventually—a thousand years after David—the promise was fulfilled, though in a way that nobody could have imagined. The messianic king finally arrived, though born in circumstances that would have made a beggar blush, and the king was nobody less than God himself.

The New Testament applies this prophecy to Jesus several times. Gabriel quotes this passage in this Sunday's Gospel (Luke 1:32). It is cited in Acts 2:30 and in Hebrews 1:5. The earliest Christians saw Jesus as the fulfillment of God's promise to David.

Yet the messianic promise was not simply fulfilled in the past and is now done with. The promised heir of David's throne is still alive and still with us. And the kingdom that God promised would last forever is still here, not yet complete, but no less real for all that. The heir that God promised to David is our Lord, and the everlasting kingdom over which he reigns is the eternal community to which we trust and hope we belong. We are the beneficiaries of God's promise to David.

FOR REFLECTION AND DISCUSSION

How do these promises affect my life today?

Where do I see signs of the messianic kingdom?

Fourth Sunday of Advent (C)

Micah 5:1–4a

This fourth Sunday of Advent in year C is the only time the Sunday lectionary gives us a reading from Micah.

Micah was one of the earlier prophets whose work is preserved in writing. He was roughly contemporary with the prophets Amos, Hosea and Isaiah. His prophetic ministry seems to have taken place just before and just after the destruction of Samaria, the Northern Kingdom, by the Assyrians in 721 B.C.

He was a man of the country, without pretensions. He seems to have disliked the elegance of the city and to have been intensely aware of its vices. His prophecy attacks the exploiters of the poor, the fraudulent merchants, corrupt judges and priests. He himself was a poor person suffering with the poor, a spokesman for justice.

The written version of Micah's prophecy that we find in the Bible has arranged the prophet's pronouncements into a series of alternating passages of threat and promise. The passage that we hear today is from a section that speaks of future blessings that God will confer on his people, specifically about a future king who would bring lasting peace.

First of all, the Lord speaks through the prophet about the future king's birthplace: the village of Bethlehem, settled by the small clan of Ephrathah. It's a backwater place without much importance. But from this insignificant village will come the future king. Bethlehem's only prior claim to fame was that it was the birthplace of King David, and so the future king will have his origin in the deep historic roots of the family of David.

The people will have a time of suffering until the new king is born, but once his mother has given birth to him, they will gather again around their leader. He will be a firm leader, but a loving one, careful to look after his people. His strength will be from God and his greatness will reach over all this earth. His rule will be peaceful. In fact, he himself will be peace.

Chapter seven of the second book of Samuel records God's promise that David's family would rule over God's people gloriously and prosperously forever. As David's kingdom began to decline, as his heirs, generation after generation, proved themselves unworthy of their great ancestor, the expectation of the promised ideal king was pushed farther into the future. He would be God's anointed. He would be king over many nations. He would bring peace. And he would certainly come. The messianic expectations that God inspired his prophets to proclaim made his people into a people of hope. Every generation could aspire to the fulfillment of God's promise. David's descendant would come, because God had promised. He would bring eventual salvation to the people. He would deliver them from distress.

The special quality of today's messianic message from Micah is his emphasis on the humble origins of the coming king. Like David, he would come from a place that nobody would ever have expected to produce a king. The implication is that God doesn't need high-quality, cosmopolitan, pretentious human material in order to work his will. The messiah that everybody was waiting for would come out of nowhere.

When it was first proclaimed, this message would have helped Micah's readers keep their hope alive at a time of cultural and political decline. It reassured them that God's promise to David would be fulfilled, that God would be faithful.

As we hear Micah's message some twenty-eight centuries later, we are reassured that God's promise has been fulfilled. The

Davidic king has been born in Bethlehem, Ephrathah, born without fanfare and glitz, born to a life of faithfulness to God, born to give a shepherd's care to his flock. In the course of this unpretentious life of his, he would bring salvation to his people and deliver them from distress. In the final analysis, he would be their peace.

Jesus is the Messiah the prophets proclaimed. He was born in Bethlehem as Micah had foretold. He is everything that God's spokesmen, the prophets, said the Messiah would be. Because he still lives, he still offers salvation to his people. He still frees them from distress. He is still their peace.

The age of the Messiah has begun, but it is not yet finished. As Micah looked forward to the first coming of the messiah, we look forward to his continued presence each day and to his final coming when his kingdom will have reached completion.

FOR REFLECTION AND DISCUSSION

When have I been surprised by the quality of the instruments that God uses?

Where do I encounter the Messiah in my life?

PART TWO
Christmas

Christmas, Mass at Midnight (ABC)

Isaiah 9:1–6

Many details in the background of this passage are not clear, but scholars seem to think that it dates from between 733 and 722 B.C. During this time, the Northern Kingdom, Israel, had been invaded by the Assyrians. Many of its people were deported and much of its territory had been made into Assyrian provinces. Apparently the full and final destruction of Israel by the Assyrians (which would happen in 722 B.C.) had not yet taken place.

In those circumstances Isaiah of Jerusalem delivers this oracle of hope. Its occasion may be the birth of a child who would eventually become king, or the accession to the throne of a king who would thus be looked upon as God's son. Many scholars think that the person that Isaiah had in mind was King Hezekiah, and that the person spoken of here was the Emmanuel that Isaiah had already prophesied in 7:14 and 8:8. In any case, our text is clearly a messianic prophecy.

There are two main parts. The first part (verses 1–4) deals with a new dawn in the life of the people of Judah. This people has now been delivered from the oppressive dominion threatened by the Assyrians, an oppressive dominion that the Northern Kingdom had already experienced. The gloom that expressed the likelihood of foreign conquest was now dissipated. The people experienced a joy like the joy of harvest or the exhilaration of victory. The symbols of defeat—the yoke used to drive cattle, the sticks used to beat slaves—have been destroyed. It's almost a repetition of Gideon's stunning victory over the Midianites (Judges 7:15–25). The garments of war will now be fuel for the fire.

The reason for this new dawn is the child (or the new king). He will have authority and wisdom. He will be a warrior and a defender for his people, ever devoted to them, a bringer of peace. He will rule over the kingdom of David, presumably including what became the Northern Kingdom, forever. (Clearly Isaiah is alluding to the prophecy of Nathan in 2 Samuel 7.) All of this will be the result of God's enthusiastic care for his people.

What we have here is a proclamation of hope. An ideal king was coming, or is here. He is a king who possesses the qualities of all the great figures of his nation. This new king of the house of David in Jerusalem would bring hope and deliverance also to Israel, and there would be no end to his virtuous reign.

King Hezekiah was a better king than his father Ahaz, but he was far from being the messianic figure that Isaiah outlines in our text. If Hezekiah was the only king to whom this oracle of hope was to be applied, the prophecy certainly proved itself empty. But both Jewish and Christian tradition have seen this proclamation as also envisioning a later king, a ruler who would come in the final ages of God's care for his people, a ruler who would rule in the final kingdom of God.

We Christians believe that the figure that Isaiah announced was Jesus, the Christ. His birth in the middle of the night at Bethlehem was the beginning of a new day. It was a burst of light in the darkness. That seems to be why this particular text that begins with light was chosen to be read at the Mass that takes place in the middle of the night, when the dark is deepest. Jesus is the one who has been called to ascend the throne of David. He is the Prince of Peace. He is the source of ongoing joy and liberation and light.

The word that God speaks through his prophets is often fulfilled in ways beyond what the original hearers expected, probably beyond what the human authors understood. This reading was originally intended to bring encouragement to the people of a tiny nation, tiny even by the standards of the eighth century B.C. It was first delivered in circumstances that do not seem to have much relevance for us today. What it seemed to promise to its first hearers never really came to pass. Yet we still read Isaiah's words with reverence and gratitude twenty-eight hundred years later because we know that they are addressed to us. They remind us that God's plan of salvation for his people is a plan that God has been working on for a long, long time. They also remind us that, just as this prophecy was not fulfilled in the time of Isaiah, so it is not completely fulfilled even now. The Prince of Peace has indeed come once and is still with us now. But his definitive coming is still in the future. Not every boot that has tramped in battle has yet been burned. The final kingdom of judgment and justice has not yet been manifested. We still experience darkness.

But we also take joy in what the prophet has said, because we know that "the zeal of the LORD of hosts" will accomplish what has been promised to us.

FOR REFLECTION AND DISCUSSION

How does God give me light?

How do I experience liberation at the hand of God?

Christmas, Mass at Dawn (ABC)

Isaiah 62:11–12

God's deliverance of his people from the Babylonian exile did not mark the beginning of a period of ease and prosperity for those who returned to the land of Israel. Things were difficult in this land that had been neglected and abused for fifty years or so. There were social problems and political problems and economic problems. The people began to wonder whether they had misunderstood God's promises or whether God might have changed his mind about their future.

This was the situation to which the author of the third part of the book of Isaiah addressed himself. The last eleven chapters of this book are songs of return, prophetic utterances intended to offer encouragement and direction to the people. They were probably written soon after the return of first groups of exiles around 538 B.C.

The reading presented for this dawn Mass at Christmas is only two verses long, but it contains a wealth of comfort. It is a proclamation of the salvation of God's people (Zion), but it is addressed to the whole world. "Tell everybody (the ends of the earth) that God is coming as a savior." God comes to bring gifts to his people, rewards and recompense, presumably in response to their faithfulness, as an answer to their acknowledgment of their need for God, their need for salvation. But apparently, although the children of Israel are the primary addressees of the pronouncement, God's generosity is also addressed to the rest of the world as well: "They [the ends of the earth] shall be called... the redeemed of the LORD. And you shall be called...a city that is not forsaken."

God is coming with gifts for everybody. That's the message of the author of this part of Isaiah to the discouraged returnees. God hasn't forgotten them. The abundance of his blessings will be offered to the impoverished folk who were resettling Jerusalem. But the whole world needs to hear that God is concerned about them, too. The very ends of the earth will be called his "holy people."

This is an important pronouncement not just for the Jews of the sixth century B.C., but also for Christian believers celebrating the dawn of salvation in the birth of Jesus. God delivered his people from the darkness of their exile and brought them back to their own land and, through them, promised his blessings to the whole world. Similarly the birth of Jesus constitutes a dawn of renewed hope and encouragement to God's new chosen people. In Jesus, God presents "his reward" and "his recompense," reward and recompense not just for a small group of defenseless people living in a harsh corner of the world, but to all nations. The Savior comes for everybody. The Savior offers redemption to us all.

It is important to recall that what God comes to bring us is not wages or earnings. "Reward and recompense" are not meant literally here, as if we had done something important for which God now owes us a return. None of us—returned Jewish exile or twenty-first century Christian believer—has done anything that constitutes a claim on God. We are not able to do that. All of our potential, all of our energy, all of our purpose is already a gift of God. Perhaps we have striven to be faithful to God. Perhaps we have remained conscious of our need for God's ongoing care for us. Those are appropriate religious postures for us to take in God's presence. But they do not constitute a debt that God must now pay off. Whatever we have to offer God comes from God's generosity one way or another. Whatever we can give God is already his. We cannot deserve God's goodness. We can only respond to it.

In what does God's reward and recompense consist? In more of the same, in a further sharing of what we have already received: in a deeper and more fervent relationship with him; in an increased awareness of our need for God's goodness; in a deeper sense of gratitude for God's mercy and forgiveness. All that is what God brings to us as part of his saving and redeeming presence and action.

In a way, every day is Christmas for the believer because every day the Lord comes to save us. In a way, every moment is dawn, because at every moment the Lord's goodness and care shines into our lives anew. In a way, we are all still exiles because we have not yet reached our final heavenly dwelling place. But in a way, we are already delivered from exile because God has already made us holy. Our Savior has come.

FOR REFLECTION AND DISCUSSION

How has the Savior come into my life?

What "rewards" or "recompense" from the Lord am I conscious of in my life?

Christmas, Mass During the Day (ABC)

Isaiah 52:7–10

The second part of the book of the prophet Isaiah was written during the Babylonian exile. These chapters (40–55) are known as the Book of Consolation because in them the prophet proclaims words of encouragement and hope to the Israelites who had been carried off into the distant land of Babylon.

The verses chosen for this Christmas reading are part of a longer poem that sings of the deliverance of Jerusalem and that proclaims God as the Creator and Savior of his people. These verses seem to be the climax of the poem.

The prophet imagines a long train of returning exiles who are now approaching Jerusalem. They are preceded by outrunners who announce the good news of their coming. How wonderful their news! How beautiful, how blessed the feet that carry them forward to bring God's announcement! They bring glad tidings, they announce peace, they bear good news, they proclaim salvation. And the heart of their announcement is that the kingdom is being restored. It is not the restoration of a merely human kingdom led by sinful rulers, but the establishment of a new kind of kingdom in which God is in charge. "Your God is King!"

Now the sentinels who have been standing guard over the ruined Jerusalem, watching and waiting for news from afar, see and hear the messengers. They shout for joy as they begin to understand the message that the returning exiles proclaim. The Lord is restoring their nation!

Finally we learn how the Lord is going about restoring his people. He comforts his people and frees them from danger. He bares his arm to fight for them against all the nations of the world. The salvation that God bestows on them will be a sight for all the ends of the earth to see.

These verses have been chosen for use at Christmas because they foreshadow some of the people and events that we celebrate on this feast. The heralds of the returning exiles are mirrored by the angels who announce peace on earth, God's blessing for his people. The sentinels in Isaiah are recalled by the shepherds in the fields who receive the message of the angels, who glorify God for what they hear and see. And then there is the news itself: God comforts his people. He frees them from sin. He defends them from their enemies. All the nations of the earth will be included in these wonderful works of the Lord.

A message that had originally been addressed to a social and political situation in one small corner of the world becomes the expression of a whole new kind of salvation, a whole new relationship between God and his people. It is no longer a matter of God bringing the exiles back to their homeland, but rather of God himself entering our homeland and becoming one of us. "[T]he Word became flesh / and made his dwelling among us."

"Good news" is a kind of technical term in the Christian vocabulary. It is the translation of another technical term, the Greek word *euangelion* from which we get words like "evangelize" and "evangelist." Bringing and receiving good news is part of our calling as Christian believers.

We are all called to evangelize, to serve as heralds for the Lord, to proclaim the message of God's good will that the angels sang on the first Christmas. We don't need to be wide-ranging travelers like Isaiah's heralds nor heavenly beings like the angels. But we do need to be willing to share the good news of the Lord's love and care for his people, to let other people hear and know the glad tidings that give sense and direction and joy to our lives.

But we are also all called to receive the good news. The salvation that God offers us is not a series of propositions which, once learned, remain stored away in our minds and hearts. No, the salvation that God offers us is a relationship, a sharing in the life of our divine Lord, the risen Christ. It is a relationship that cries out to grow and deepen. It is a relationship that needs to be tended to and enriched. Because we are such limited creatures, we need constant reminders of the wonderful things that God has done for us, of the wonderful things that God still has in store for us. We need ongoing evangelization.

The liturgy is one of the major energy sources both of our proclamation of God's good news and of our ongoing reception of it. In the Scripture that is read and in the re-presentation of

Jesus' sacrifice of himself we learn both what we are to announce and what we are to receive and assimilate: God is King, the Word has been made flesh, Our Lord dwells in our midst.

FOR REFLECTION AND DISCUSSION
How does the birth of Christ constitute good news for me?
Where do I hear God's good news proclaimed most convincingly?

The Holy Family of Jesus, Mary and Joseph (A)
Sirach 3:2–7, 12–14

The feast of the Holy Family is a relatively recent addition to the church's liturgical calendar. Devotion to the home life of Jesus, Mary and Joseph as a model for Christian families had been common in Europe and French-speaking Canada since the seventeenth century. But it wasn't until 1893 that a liturgical observance of the Holy Family was established by Pope Leo XIII. The feast was intended to offer support to the family values that seemed threatened at that time. Of course, family values are still threatened today, so the feast of the Holy Family speaks to a contemporary need and the feast of the Holy Family is the feast of every good Christian family.

All three readings have been chosen to address the main theme of the liturgical observance: the relationships of family life—the family life of Jesus, Mary and Joseph, and the family life of each of us.

The First Reading for the feast of the Holy Family in year A is taken from the book of Sirach or Ecclesiasticus. Sirach was written about 200–175 B.C. in Jerusalem. At that time the homeland of the Jews was under the domination of the Seleucids, Hellenistic Greek rulers whose rule reflected the sophisticated and brilliant pagan culture of the time. It was a dangerous time for the Jews because what the pagan culture offered seemed so attractive. The author of Sirach seems to have been a wise and pious man who wrote in order to help his people maintain their traditional religious faith and moral integrity in the face of the temptations that surrounded them.

Our reading comes from near the beginning of the book. In chapter one Sirach offers an extended encouragement to the reader to pursue wisdom, that profoundly important quality that leads people to live as God intends us to live. The second chapter is about our duty to serve God and about what is involved in that service. Now, in chapter three, we have a little treatise about our duties toward our parents. The placing of this material so close to the beginning of the book seems to imply that our duties toward our parents are of immense importance to our life as children of God, second only to the pursuit of wisdom and to reverence for God. This portion of Sirach is a kind of extended commentary on the fourth commandment: Honor your father and your mother.

Our reading is divided into two parts. The first part gives positive direction about honoring one's parents. Our parents are given to us by God and represent God. Offering reverence and obedience to our parents brings the same rewards as offering reverence and obedience to God: the forgiveness of sins, long life, the blessing of children.

The second part of the reading is negative, what not to do. Don't be unkind to parents in their old age. Don't neglect them even if they are feeble in body and mind.

(The last line of the reading, "a house raised in justice to you," is unclear in meaning. In fact, there seem to be problems with the text throughout the reading. No two translations seem to be translating the same original. Maybe God provides these kinds of problems to give his Scripture scholars something extra to do!)

The lesson is clear: Our parents represent God. They must be treated with reverence and kindness and respect. This is an important lesson to have brought home to us occasionally. Sometimes we take our families for granted. We may not always be aware of the extent to which our parents make us what we are. The fact is that our basic attitudes toward God and the world and our fellow human beings are instilled in us by our parents. Our religious faith and our prayer life, our work habits and our priorities depend to a great extent on what our mother and father taught us, explicitly in their words and implicitly by their example. The way we speak and even the way we laugh are conditioned by our parents. They are primary channels of God's providence in our lives, and God calls us to acknowledge them as such.

But if parents are channels of God's providence for their children, so also are children channels of God's providence for their parents. All human beings sooner or later experience the need for care and affection and help and support, parents included. And children are the ones that God establishes as primary caregivers for their parents. Generous and thoughtful children are among God's basic rewards to good parents.

The presence and the action of God are part of every aspect of a holy family.

FOR REFLECTION AND DISCUSSION

For what am I most grateful to my parents?
How is my family a holy family?

The Holy Family of Jesus, Mary and Joseph (Optional B)

Genesis 15:1–6; 21:1–3

This reading is somewhat unusual in the wide spread of the chapters that make it up. The first part of the reading is from the beginning of the Abraham narrative in Genesis (chapter 15), while the second part is from near the end of the story of Abraham (chapter 21). Apparently those who prepared the lectionary wanted to offer for this occasion the story of the promise of progeny to Abraham and of its fulfillment. The fulfillment of the promise took a long time, and so the account of it stretches over some six chapters of Genesis. This day's reading gives us the beginning and the end of the story.

As our reading begins, God is speaking to Abram (whose name would only later be changed to Abraham). God had called Abram away from his ancestral home and had promised to make him the father of a great nation (Genesis 12:1 ff.). Now God repeats the promise of future greatness. Abram respectfully responds to God that if he is to be the founder of a great nation, he would have to have legitimate children. Otherwise, according to the practice of the culture in which he lived, if Abram died childless, his chief steward, Eliezer, would inherit everything. And no children seemed to be likely, given Abram's age and that of his wife Sarai. God assures Abram that he will not be without an heir. In fact, God takes him outside the tent, points up to the starry sky, and says that Abram's descendants will be as numerous as the stars. Abram takes God at his word. His total reliance on God puts him in a right relationship with God.

At this point there is a break in our reading. In the full biblical text, Abram now fathers a child from one of his slaves, and God again appears to Abram and changes his name to Abraham. God renews his covenant with Abraham and demands that Abraham's family observe circumcision as a sign of the covenant. Abraham is again visited by God and reassured that Sarah would bear him a child. God saves Abraham's nephew, Lot, from the destruction of Sodom and Gomorrah. Finally, in chapter twenty-one, our reading takes up again.

In accord with what God had promised, Abraham's wife Sarah finally bears him a child whom Abraham names Isaac.

There are two main lessons that God's word offers us in this text. The first is one that would have been obvious to the initial readers of Genesis: the importance of family. In the times of the patriarchs and for millennia afterward family was not merely the context in which human beings began life and were cared for and educated until they could begin to survive on their own. The family gave human beings their identity, their standing in society, their wealth, their dignity, their protection from enemies throughout their lifetime. A person without family was, for all practical purposes, a nobody. And a man and wife who were without offspring were looked upon as somehow under a curse. God's promise of progeny to Abraham was a promise to save him from oblivion.

The second lesson in our reading is the lesson of faith. Abraham trusted in the promise of God even when the promise was slow to be realized. Abraham believed that God's word would come to pass even though what God promised was seemingly impossible. His faith made him not only the father of God's chosen people, but also the father and model of all those who would trust in the other promises that God would make in Jesus.

Both of these lessons resonate with the feast of the Holy Family. First of all, the feast reminds us that one of the ways in which we are in touch with Jesus is through our shared human family. Though conceived by the Holy Spirit, Jesus was truly human. His life began in the context of family. In the bosom of his family, Jesus learned how to be a human being. In the family he developed his earliest and perhaps deepest human relationships. In adulthood Jesus was known by the family he belonged to, that is, as the son of Joseph and Mary. We are Jesus' relatives because we are members of the human family that he entered through the cooperation of his Virgin Mother. Family determines who Jesus is and also who we are.

Faith is also part of what we celebrate on this occasion. It was thanks to faith that Abraham became the father of a great people, both historically and spiritually. It was thanks to the faith and responsiveness of Mary that Jesus became a human being. It is thanks to faith that we are members of the family of Jesus, that we share his life.

The blessings of Abraham are our blessings, too.

FOR REFLECTION AND DISCUSSION

How has God blessed me?
What role does family play in my life?

The Holy Family of Jesus, Mary and Joseph (Optional C)

1 Samuel 1:20–22, 24–28

The First Readings for the Sundays of Advent were a series of more or less independent selections about the Messiah and the messianic age. For the feasts of the Christmas season, the First

Readings are chosen to harmonize with the themes of the feast, to help articulate what is being celebrated in each of them.

For this feast of the Holy Family, the Hebrew Scripture readings for each year are concerned with parents and children. In the reading that is presented for optional usage in year C, we hear about the birth of Samuel, one of the great, towering figures of the Old Testament.

Our selection is from the beginning of the first book of Samuel, which is part of the long series of historical books that begins with Genesis and carries through to the second book of Kings. These books received their final form during the Babylonian exile, but they were based on stories and writings that had been handed down for a long time prior to the exile.

To understand the text we hear in the liturgy, we need to know its context. Hannah was the wife of a pious husband, Elkanah. She had been unable to bear children. She was often taunted about her barrenness by Elkanah's other wife. On one of the family's visits to Shiloh (the principal place for worship in this early time of Israel's history), Hannah went off by herself to pray for a child. She promised that if God would give her a child, she would dedicate the child to God as a holy man, an ascetic (Nazarite) from the time of its birth. She moved her lips as she prayed and Eli, the high priest who was sitting nearby, thought she was drunk and rebuked her accordingly. She responded that she was only pouring out her troubles to the Lord. She returned home with her husband.

Our liturgical text presents the conclusion to this episode. Hannah conceives and bears a son. Mindful of her promise, she keeps the boy at home until his infancy is over and then takes him to Shiloh to present him as a gift for the Lord. Elkanah brings along appropriate food offerings. When the gifts had been offered, Hannah reminds Eli, the priest, of their prior encounter and makes the presentation of the child to the Lord. Samuel stays behind at the temple when his parents return home.

Samuel was a special child and a special person in the history of God's people. He had been born to a barren mother through a special intervention of God. He was dedicated as a Nazarite from his birth. He spent almost his whole life in the presence of the Lord at the Lord's temple. He was a priest and perhaps the earliest prophet. He was a leader of his people who brought them through a particularly difficult period of their history, as they moved from being ruled by a succession of charismatic tribal leaders (judges) to being ruled by kings. He identified the kings, and anointed them, and was the agent of God's direction for them.

A great man, indeed.

This reading harmonizes with the Gospel narrative of the finding of the child Jesus in the temple (Luke 2:41–52). Both stories are about parents and children, both about familial affection. But both are also about the temple, about the house of the Lord. Samuel grows up in the temple at Shiloh. Jesus gently rebukes Mary and Joseph for not realizing at once that they could find him in the temple. "Where else would I be if not in my Father's house?" he asks in effect. For both Samuel and Jesus there was another level of family beyond the realm of human parenthood. Each of them in his particular way belonged to the family of God. Each of them knew how to be at home with the Lord. We, too, are children of God in our particular way. Through our baptism we have been remade into the image of Christ Jesus, the divine Word of God. We live the life of Christ in a preliminary way during the course of our life here on earth. When this life is ended, we look forward to being brought into our Father's house for an eternity of togetherness with all those who have lived in Christ Jesus, with all those who are part of the final family of God.

In our life here and now we begin to learn how to live in the presence of the Lord. We learn to love and trust the Lord, to carry out his will, to look after our brothers and sisters in his family. Through prayer and openness to the presence of the Lord and attentiveness to his word, we become increasingly comfortable with him. We prepare ourselves for the stage when, like Samuel and Jesus, we, too, will be at home with the Lord.

FOR REFLECTION AND DISCUSSION

Where do I experience contact with the Lord?
Do I feel at home in the presence of the Lord? Why or why not?

Solemnity of the Blessed Virgin Mary, the Mother of God (ABC)

Numbers 6:22–27

The book of Numbers is the fourth volume of the Pentateuch, the collection of five books that stands at the beginning of the Old Testament and that constitutes the foundation for the history and the law (Torah) of the Israelites. The title of this fourth book of the Pentateuch comes from the accounts of the two censuses of the people that occur in its first and last chapters.

The first six chapters of Numbers are concerned with the organization of the people into an effective fighting force, including the duties of special groups of the Israelites such as the Levites (in charge of the cult of God) and the Nazarites (persons who dedicated themselves to a special religious rigor). At the end of the sixth chapter comes the blessing of Aaron that constitutes the liturgical First Reading for this day.

This was the formula the high priest and his sons were to use in calling God's blessing on the Israelites. Scholars point out that the pronoun "you" is singular in the original Hebrew, and thus the blessing is addressed to the people as a whole rather than to a collection of individuals.

These verses are said to constitute one of the oldest pieces of poetry in Sacred Scripture. The blessing is a poem of three verses or lines, each of which has two parts. It is a prayer for material and spiritual well-being.

"May the Lord bless you and keep you." To be blessed by God means to be granted all that God wants to confer on his people. Asking that God "keep" the people is to pray for the exercise and fulfillment of God's loving, ongoing providence for them.

The face of God means God himself and to ask that God's face shine on the people is to pray that God will look on them with favor. God's favor is "gracious," that is, it is an undeserved gift.

This idea is repeated in the opening of the next verse, where God's favor will result in God's gift of peace to his people. Note that, in the context of sacred Scripture, "peace" involves much more than the absence of war. It includes elements of fullness, completion, harmony and happiness.

Notice that each of the three verses calls for an action of God ("bless," "face shine," "look kindly") that results in something good for the people ("keep," "graciousness," "peace").

The final verse of our reading, and of chapter 6, is a kind of wrap-up sentence. The priests are to invoke God's name on the Israelites in these words. Invoking God's name "upon" the people means imprinting God's name on them, putting on them a seal of ownership. The Israelites are proclaimed to be God's property. That's why God will bless them. God's ownership of this people is precisely what constitutes the blessing.

Numbers is not one of the books of the Old Testament that is used frequently in the liturgy of Sundays and Holy Days. In fact, it is used only one other time in the whole three-year Sunday cycle. It is not inappropriate to ask why this particular piece of Numbers is used for this Solemnity of Mary, the Mother of God.

One reason that immediately suggests itself is that this day is also the day on which we celebrate the beginning of a new year. What better way to mark the new year than by asking God to protect us, to be gracious to us, to give us peace, to renew his lordship over our human existence?

The observance of World Peace Day, a kind of parallel observance that the popes have fostered over the last decades, also fits in with what the Aaronic blessing asks for.

But there may be a still deeper connection between our text and this day's liturgy. At the end of the Gospel (Luke 2:21), Luke tells us that on this day, eight days after the birth of Jesus, the name that the angel had given him was conferred on him through the Jewish rite of circumcision. "Name" links the Gospel reading with our reading from Numbers. Just as the Israelites would be constituted as God's people by God's name being invoked upon them, so also the new people of God would be constituted by the name of Jesus Christ. Christ's ownership of us is what makes us what we are.

There are always reasons for gratitude in the Christian life. On this day, it seems natural to be grateful for the new year that we begin. But it is also appropriate to be grateful for the other

blessings that God has given us, especially for the blessing of
sharing in the life and the identity of the people of the Lord.

FOR REFLECTION AND DISCUSSION
What blessings have I received from God?
What blessings do I seek from God?

Epiphany of the Lord (ABC)

Isaiah 60:1–6

Today's reading comes from the third part of the book of Isaiah.
This part of our Bible, the last eleven chapters that come under
the heading Isaiah, was written at the end of the Babylonian
captivity by an anonymous member of the spiritual posterity of
the great prophet who had lived some two centuries earlier.

Our reading seems to have its origin at a time shortly after
the return of the exiles had begun. Although one might have
expected that the people's liberation from captivity and their
homecoming would be a time of unalloyed joy, it was not so. The
number of those who returned from Babylon was a trickle rather
than a flood. Life in the homeland was fraught with partisan strife
and economic uncertainty. Discouragement was in the air. In
response to that, the prophet offers these words of hope to a
wavering community.

To this prostrate people, the Lord says, "Get up and be
bright!" There may be darkness everywhere, but God's people
would be a source of light, light that has its origin in the glory of
the Lord, that is, in the presence of the Lord. The brilliance of
God's people will offer radiance and direction to all the nations

of the earth. Jerusalem's sons and daughters who are still far away will now return home, coddled like babies in the arms of their nannies.

But there is more. Jerusalem's heart will be gladdened by the richness and variety of the gifts that God will bestow on her. All the wealth of the seafaring nations (like Phoenicia and Greece) would pour into her from the west. From the south and the east would come caravans of camels with luxury products from Egypt and Syria and Arabia. It will be like King Solomon's day once more! Yet the worth of what the caravans bring will be mere symbols of the praise of the God of Jerusalem that will come with them. Jerusalem, God's people, will be the spiritual center and the source of enlightenment of all the world.

This selection from Isaiah 60 is a precious passage in the church's liturgy. In fact, before the publication of the Vatican II lectionary, it was one of only fourteen Old Testament readings that were ever proclaimed in the Eucharistic liturgy. And now, when we have a great variety of Old Testament readings over our three-year cycle, we read this one each and every year on the feast of the Epiphany of the Lord, almost as if to say that you haven't really celebrated Epiphany unless you have heard this reading.

This passage, then, is more than a poem of extravagant encouragement to the depressed population of a sixth century B.C. hill city. It is a passage that the church has looked on as describing the future not of a political kingdom, but of the kingdom of God. Darkness will give way before the beauty and brilliance of God's kingdom. All nations will be illuminated by its brightness. People from all over the world will seek to become part of it. Every sort of riches from every quarter of the earth will be brought to the kingdom, not to bring it economic enrichment, but as a sign of the dedication of those who come from afar.

The kingdom of God, the messianic Jerusalem, of course, is Christ. He is the brightness of God who calls men and women from near and far to come and live in him. It is he who is worthy of the riches of the sea and the wealth of nations. It is he who calls forth the flash and fragrance of praise and adoration from peoples all over the world.

The feast of the Epiphany of the Lord is the feast of manifestation. On this day we celebrate the coming of the mysterious strangers from across the desert who had been following heavenly direction and who finally arrived at the source of the brilliance they had seen. The Savior, the Lord, the ultimate Jerusalem, the final kingdom was manifested to them. It was the beginning of the manifestation of God that Jesus would embody for the rest of his earthly life and that he and his church would continue for the rest of the life of the world.

In one way or another, darkness still covers the earth and thick clouds cover the peoples. Sin is everywhere and tomorrow won't necessarily be any better than today. But, in Jesus, God says to us now what the author of our reading said to the prostrate people of his time: "Get up and be bright! Take joy in the gifts that I am giving you. Be radiant in my light and in my life. The glory of the Lord shines upon you!"

FOR REFLECTION AND DISCUSSION
Where do I find darkness in the world around me?
Where do I encounter the glory of the Lord?

The Baptism of the Lord (A)

Isaiah 42:1–4, 6–7

The feast of the Baptism of the Lord marks the conclusion of the Christmas season and the beginning of Ordinary Time. It is a hinge observance that responds to two questions. What became of the Child born in Bethlehem? After an appropriate time he came to be baptized by John in the Jordan. And what then? He began to preach and teach and work miracles. This is the activity that is recorded in the Gospel readings that the church will give us throughout the rest of Ordinary Time.

The Gospel assigned for this Sunday is from Matthew, from whom we will be hearing for most of the rest of Ordinary Time this year. Toward the end of the reading Matthew tells us that the Spirit of God descended on Jesus and that a voice from heaven announced, "This is my beloved Son, with whom I am well pleased." These two elements from the baptism narrative are allusions to Isaiah's first servant song, our First Reading. The Isaian text provides the background on which we are to understand what God said and did at Jesus' baptism—and in the mission of Jesus.

This First Reading is from the second part of the book of the prophet Isaiah, chapters forty to fifty-five. While second Isaiah reflects the spirit of the eighth-century Isaiah, son of Amoz, it was not his personal work, but the work of one or more anonymous followers of Isaiah who wrote to console the Israelites during their exile in Babylon after the destruction of Jerusalem in 587 B.C.

In this section there are four passages of special intensity called the servant songs. These short poems describe a special servant of God, uniquely chosen by the Lord to carry out his will. The servant's mission would involve effort and suffering. It is not clear whom the author of these prophetic poems had in mind, but Christian tradition has seen the fulfillment of them in Jesus. The reading for this Sunday is the first of the four servant songs.

This reading describes who the servant is and how he will carry out his mission. God says, "I am pleased with this servant of mine and I have put my power into him. His mission is addressed to the whole world. But he's not going to go about his mission like some conquering general, laying down the law in the city square. On the contrary, he's going to be gentle and patient. He will attract all nations to himself by his compassion and gentleness."

In the second part of the reading God offers himself as a guarantee of the servant's work. "I have called you...I have taken you by the hand and kept you; I have given you as a covenant to the people, a light to the nations" (NRSV). It is God and no one else who is sending the servant to bring light to those in darkness and freedom to captives.

When Matthew records that the Spirit came down upon Jesus at his baptism and that the Father proclaimed that Jesus is the one with whom he is well pleased, it's almost as if he is telling his readers, "Go read the first servant song. Here is the one whom the prophet was talking about. In those verses from Isaiah you will find a description of the style of Jesus' mission, Jesus' agenda, Jesus' relationship with the Father. All this is what began to be fulfilled when Jesus was baptized by John."

This first servant song, like the other three, is a passage of almost unending richness and beauty. But there seem to be two main themes in what the prophet says.

The first is the theme of patience and mercy. The servant

(and Jesus) would not bring people to God by force. He will not threaten them and then crush them if they do not conform to his demands. He will have compassion on the weak and the wounded. He will work with the feeble resources they have. He is an agent of mercy, not condemnation.

The second main theme is the universality of the mission of the servant (and of Jesus). His ministry is for everybody, for the whole world. Nobody is to be excluded from the gentleness and mercy of this servant of God, of this beloved Son of the Father. Justice and enlightenment and guidance and freedom—that's what all the nations of the earth can look for from this chosen one whom God upholds.

This servant that Isaiah describes and this beloved Son that Matthew writes about is the same Lord whom we worship today, the Lord of mercy, the bringer of universal salvation. If our faith is to be healthy, it's important for us to be clear about who he is and what's he's here to do.

FOR REFLECTION AND DISCUSSION

Where do I see God exercising mercy?
How does my faith involve "the nations?"

Baptism of the Lord (Optional B)

Isaiah 55:1–11

If you attend Mass on every Sunday and weekday throughout the three-year cycle, including the Easter Vigil, you can hear all or part of this Sunday's reading proclaimed no less than ten times. The most extensive form is found on this feast of the Baptism of the Lord in year B and as the Fifth Reading of the Easter Vigil. Shorter versions are presented on the fifteenth, eighteenth and twenty-fifth Sundays of year A and on Tuesday of the first week of Lent. No passage of the Old Testament is read more frequently. One might say that it is the church's favorite Old Testament passage.

It comes from the last chapter of the second part of Isaiah, the section written during the Babylonian exile by one or more followers of the school of Isaiah of Jerusalem. That section of Isaiah is known as the Book of Consolation and seems to have been written to help the exiles maintain their confidence in God during the time of their greatest trial.

It is a poem about salvation and, as presented to us in the lectionary, seems to fall into four parts or paragraphs.

The first part is a call from God to his people. God offers them life if they will only come to him and listen to him. They don't need to pay for God's attention to them. The only requirement is that they hunger and thirst for him. It doesn't make much sense for them to expend their resources on things that cannot nourish them.

The second paragraph is about the covenant. God had made a covenant with David, promising him that his family and his kingdom would last forever (cf. 2 Samuel 7:12–16). David had been outstanding among the national leaders of his time. Now, in their time of humiliation, God promises to renew the covenant, and give his people a position of leadership among the nations of the world, not because of their inherent excellence but because of God's own generosity.

Now God calls the people to repentance. They are to turn to God for forgiveness. God assures them that he is near to them and that his generosity, his willingness to forgive, is far greater than they can even imagine. "[M]y thoughts are not your thoughts."

Finally God speaks of fruitfulness. Just as certainly as God's free gift of rain and snow enables humans to grow food and nourish themselves, so will God's word be fruitful. His promises to his people will not be in vain. God's generosity, his care for his people, his desire to forgive will as certainly come to fulfillment as the snow and rain carry out God's will for the fruitfulness of the earth.

What a wonderful way to conclude a book of consolation! One of the standard Scripture translations entitles this chapter "An Invitation to Grace." It could also be called a rhapsody of deliverance and salvation. It offers a synthesis of many of the most fundamental images and themes of the Old Testament: water, food, listening to God, David, covenant, repentance, God's graciousness, God's providence, God's desire to bring salvation to his people.

The feast of the Baptism of the Lord brings the Christmas season and the commemoration of Jesus' "hidden life" to a close and celebrates the inauguration of Jesus' ministry. Beginning with this feast, the liturgy will concern itself for the rest of the year with the proclamation of Jesus' public words and deeds.

Our Old Testament reading could be interpreted as the Father's agenda for the ministry of Jesus. Jesus is to bring nourishment and life to those who would believe in him. His followers don't need to qualify for his gifts. They only have to acknowledge their need.

Jesus would offer God's new covenant for all the nations. God's favor would not be confined to the earthly relatives of David, but would be extended to all those who were willing to accept fellowship with the greatest son of David.

Jesus would bring God's forgiveness to God's people. He would reach out to sinners, even to the point of giving his life for their salvation. Jesus would express the Father's love for those who had gone astray in a way as breathtakingly lofty "as the heavens are higher than the earth" (NRSV).

Finally, Jesus' mission was assured of success. His words and his actions would not remain void but would achieve for all ages what the Father had in mind for them.

This is a passage that is worth reading more than once!

FOR REFLECTION AND DISCUSSION

How am I responsive to God's generosity?

What effect does God's will to save all nations have in my life?

The Baptism of the Lord (Optional C)

Isaiah 40:1–5, 9–11

This reading, whose use in today's liturgy is optional, is the beginning of the second main part of the book of Isaiah. Chapters 40 to 55 of Isaiah were written in the sixth century B.C. by a member of the school or community of the prophet who had lived two hundred years earlier. This later prophet perceived that the Babylonian captivity was coming to an end and wrote to offer the exiled people a message of hope and encouragement. These chapters became known as the Book of Consolation.

The Book of Consolation, and our reading, begins with the voice of God speaking out in the midst of the community of heaven. (Note that, in the original language, the command to give comfort is in the plural; it is addressed to more than one hearer.) The Lord commands his angelic servants to offer comfort

72

to his people, to assure them that their time of servitude and subjection has now reached an end. The punishment that God has allotted for his people has been inflicted in full. Indeed, God seems to say that he has punished them even more than they deserve.

Now comes another voice, that of one of the heavenly retinue. It calls for the preparation of a kind of cosmic superhighway, straight and level, without obstacles, easy to move along. This road through the desert is for God to travel with his people, just as God traveled with them in their liberation from Egypt. What's happening here is nothing less than a new exodus! The happy outcome of the journey is guaranteed by the Lord and all the nations of the earth, all the Gentiles will see it and know that the Lord is here.

Then comes still another voice. Jerusalem/Zion/the company of the exiles is told to make its proclamation and praise audible to the whole people. They are to announce that God is here. God is present as a victor wielding his strength for the benefit of his people. But God is more than a conquering hero. He is also a careful shepherd who takes tender care for the needs of his flock.

This is a majestic and memorable passage of God's word. It cries out to be carefully proclaimed and attentively received. (Classical music enthusiasts will find themselves remembering the opening sections of Handel's *Messiah*.)

This sacred text tells us that God is coming to take care of his people, to rescue them from captivity. This is a message that is always true, whether it be addressed to an oppressed people of the sixth century B.C. or to Christian believers of today. God is always coming, and nothing can hold him back. We are all invited to take comfort in God's promise. We are all exiles. We are all far away from our final home. We are all on a journey through the desert, all headed for Jerusalem. Isaiah is speaking to us.

It's not hard to see why this Old Testament passage was chosen to adorn the celebration of the Baptism of the Lord. What the author of the Book of Consolation proclaimed to the exiles is also what John the Baptizer proclaimed to the people of his time. "The Lord is coming." Then we see Jesus publicly identified by the Spirit as the beloved Son of the Father. As Jesus begins his public life, God once more offers comfort to his people. God is present in their midst. Through Jesus, God will now begin to lead them—to lead us—once more to the new Jerusalem.

It is important for us to remember, however, that our call from the Lord is not just to receive the comfort that the Father offers us in Jesus. It is not just to move along with everybody else toward the final Jerusalem, as if we were baggage in the caravan of God. Our call is not just to open ourselves to the protection and the care of our shepherd and king. Our call is also to stand up on the heights and be heralds of God's good news. Because we are sharers in the life of Jesus through our baptism, we are not just to receive what he offers us but also to be agents of its further proclamation, to stand on the mountaintops and invite others to enter God's kingdom.

The baptism of Jesus marked the beginning of his public life. From now on he would not just be the Father's beloved Son, but would be the public voice of God speaking tenderly to Jerusalem and offering comfort to God's people. Thanks to our baptism, we, too, have a kind of public life in the Lord, a role in carrying out God's plan of repatriation for his people. We are the people of Zion, called as heralds to proclaim God's power and God's care to all the world.

FOR REFLECTION AND DISCUSSION

How do I proclaim the glorious presence of the Lord?

Do I see any obstacles in the road to the new Jerusalem?

PART THREE
Lent

First Sunday of Lent (A)

Genesis 2:7–9; 3:1–7

Lent is a season of preparation, preparation for baptism for the church's catechumens, preparation for the rest of us to celebrate the paschal mystery at Easter. "Paschal mystery" or "the mystery of Christ" is God's special, long term plan to make something worthwhile of us sinful human creatures. It is a plan that has been gradually made known in the process of revelation. But the Christian mystery is not just a body of information. It is also something that happened through the life, death and resurrection of Jesus. It is something that is still going on, something still being gradually accomplished through Christ and the Holy Spirit. The mystery of Christ is God sharing his life with us here and now so that we will be ready to live forever with Father, Son and Spirit in the life to come. The summary and peak points of Christ's mission of salvation were his death on the cross and his resurrection which we relive in a special way at Eastertime, and so the "mystery of Christ," "the mystery of salvation" is also called the "paschal mystery."

During these weeks of preparation to celebrate the paschal mystery at Easter, the church gives us a series of background readings from the Old Testament. These readings form a series in themselves, though there is occasionally some secondary linkage with the Gospel readings. The series deals with Old Testament salvation history, that is, with the unfolding of events that culminated in the coming of Christ.

On the first Sunday of Lent in years A and B, the Old Testament reading is about "primeval history," the period that stretched from creation to the Tower of Babel. On the second Sunday each year we hear about Abraham, on the third about

Moses, on the fourth about the chosen people in their own land. On the fifth Sunday the readings give us prophecies about deliverance and renewal in the wake of the destruction of Jerusalem and the exile that followed. This series of readings anticipates the Easter Vigil when the more lengthy Old Testament readings give us a more extensive account of salvation history.

This Sunday's reading is from the book of Genesis. Genesis is the first book we find when we open up our bibles. It deals with the beginnings of creation, of humanity, and of God's ongoing care for us human creatures. Genesis forms part of the Pentateuch, the group of the first five books of the Bible whose authorship had traditionally been attributed to Moses. Over the past century or so, scholars have learned that Genesis, like the other four books of the Pentateuch, is a compilation from several sources put into final form during the Babylonian exile, but reflecting the authority of Moses and no less inspired because they are an ingathering of various kinds of traditional material.

Our text is from chapters two and three and in them we see the beginnings of God's redemptive purpose. The reading begins with an account of creation, an account in which the human being is created first and the rest of creation is made for man's benefit and comfort. (Most of us are more familiar with the version of the creation story that is found in chapter one of Genesis. We read that version during the Easter Vigil.) But the man, together with woman that God had also formed, were not content with what God had given them. The serpent, representing all that is hostile to God and all that is harmful for humanity, convinced them that God wasn't being fair with them, that God was jealous of them in not letting them enjoy everything in the garden. The dialogue between Eve and the serpent provides a universal picture of temptation. Our reading stops as the two first humans realize that they have made a terrible mistake and that what seemed so appealing before is not worth what it has cost them.

The basic sin of Adam and Eve was the sin of pride, of being unwilling to acknowledge dependence. To try to get control of what God had set aside for himself, i.e., to be unwilling to let God be God and to be subject to God, is inherent in every sin. The desire to shove God aside and take the initiative for ourselves is part of every wrong that every one of us has done. We may not look on the bad we have done in precisely those terms, but the reality is there. We want to be in charge. We want to decide what is best for ourselves. We want to live our life our way. We want to be free of God whenever God seems to be getting in our way.

And that's where the history of salvation begins: with two disillusioned sinners standing shamefaced before God. Each of us has stood thus because we are sinners as they were. But each of us is also involved in God's plan of salvation as they were.

FOR REFLECTION AND DISCUSSION

What wrong choices have I made?

How do I experience sinfulness in myself?

First Sunday of Lent (B)

Genesis 9:8–15

With the season of Lent the church prepares for its annual reliving of the events of our salvation: the death and resurrection of Jesus. But God's plans for salvation, God's project of making something really worthwhile out of us sinful human creatures, did not begin with the life of Jesus. It was a project that had begun in the garden of Eden, right after the sin of Adam and Eve had cast humanity into separation from the life of God. God immediately set out to heal the separation. His plan was to restore these human creatures of his to the relationship that had prevailed before our first parents sinned. God's preliminary activity in carrying out the plan is what is recorded in the inspired books that we call the Old Testament. During the Sundays of Lent, we are given a series of readings from the Old Testament that offer us some of the highlights of the story of salvation. (At the Easter Vigil, we hear the story once again in a longer series of more extended Old Testament readings.)

In year B, the survey of salvation history begins with a reading from Genesis, the book that gives us the narratives of the oldest and most basic events of the relationship between God and us.

Just prior to our reading, God had cleansed the earth of its sinfulness through the flood. Everything had been destroyed except what was in the ark with Noah. Earth had now been restored to human supervision and human beings had been told once again to increase and multiply (cf. Genesis 9:1–7).

As our reading begins, God offers a kind of guarantee of his continued benevolence. He establishes a covenant with Noah and his descendants (i.e., with all of humanity) and with every other living creature that he would never again destroy the earth by flood.

Then he establishes a sign—for humanity, but also for himself. The rainbow would serve to remind God of the commitment that he had made. When clouds gathered and threatened to flood creation, God would see the rainbow and remember the covenant he had made.

A covenant is an agreement or contract, and covenants were among the most basic instruments that God used in dealing with his people to prepare them for salvation. Covenants involved a relationship based upon a commitment. In purely human covenants, both parties make a commitment and both parties benefit. God's covenants are somewhat different in that they arise exclusively from God's initiative and benefit only the human party. God and man do not enter covenants as equals.

In addition to the covenant with Noah, God also made covenants with Abraham, with Moses and the Israelites and with David. Sometimes there were signs to represent the covenant (the rainbow in the covenant with Noah, circumcision in the covenant with Abraham). Sometimes the covenant involved specific obligations (the observance of the law). Sometimes the covenant was simply proclaimed (the messianic covenant with David in 2 Samuel 7). But in every case, the covenant was a gracious commitment on God's part that established or strengthened a relationship with human beings. In every case, some response was expected, if only the acknowledgment of the kindness and generosity of God.

Jesus constitutes the final covenant between God and human creatures. Jesus is the final chapter in the history of salvation. Through our sharing in Jesus' life, death and resurrection, God links us to himself fully and finally. The initiative of the Father makes us into a new kind of creature. We cannot deserve to be remade into the image of the risen Christ. We can only respond to God's overtures and God's generosity. The sign of the covenant of Jesus is the Eucharist. Jesus' gift of his body and blood that is represented in the Eucharist expresses and strengthens our relationship with him. It constitutes, as the liturgy puts it, "a new and everlasting covenant," a relationship that will never wear out, that will never change.

As we begin Lent, we look forward to the Easter Vigil in which the church's new members will enter the Christian covenant by their passage through the water of baptism. The Christian theological tradition has seen Noah's passage through the flood as symbolic of baptism.

But we also set to work in renewing our attention to God's commitment to us. We who are already Christians do not need to reenter the covenant. But we do need to renew our response to it.

FOR REFLECTION AND DISCUSSION

What does God expect of us by way of response to the Christian covenant?

How well do I respond?

First Sunday of Lent (C)

Deuteronomy 26:4–10

During Lent, the Sunday First Readings are not chosen to harmonize with the Gospel readings. Nor are they a selection of detached readings on one theme, as they are in Advent. The opening readings for the five Sundays of Lent constitute a free-standing series which, each year, gives an overview of salvation history, of the way in which God dealt with his people, of how God revealed himself to his people by overseeing and participating in their history.

It is important to remember, however, that the history of salvation that is provided in the Old Testament is not just the story of a people that God happened to be interested in a long time ago.

Old Testament salvation history was a preparation for the salvation that would be offered to all the world in Christ, a salvation that would reach its climax in the Resurrection of Jesus. So, as the church prepares for Easter, it is appropriate to attend to the theme of salvation, salvation as offered by way of overture in the Old Testament, and salvation brought to fulfillment in the New.

For the first Sunday of Lent in year C, the church gives us a reading from Deuteronomy. This book of the Old Testament is a law code, a summary of the religious directives first expressed in Exodus, Leviticus and Numbers. Its purpose was to teach the people how to live in the land the Lord had given them. The laws are set forth in the form of discourses put into the mouth of Moses.

Our reading comes from near the end of Deuteronomy. Moses is portrayed as instructing the people how to make the offering of their first fruits. He says, in effect, "You are to come to the Lord's altar and present the priest with your basket of products of the land. Then you are to acknowledge before the Lord that you belong to a family or nation that was originally without land or prosperity, that God took an interest in you, brought you to good times in Egypt, then delivered you from there when things got difficult and brought you to the fruitful land you now inhabit. An awareness of all this is what has brought you to express your gratitude to the Lord for what the land has yielded for you. It is all a gift from the Lord. Then you are to bow down in worship of the Lord."

There are several levels of teaching in this passage. First of all, as an instruction on how to make the offering of first fruits, it is a reminder that the first products of the soil each year belong to God because the land from which they come is God's. The ceremony described here is an act of religious submission to

God. Bowing down in the Lord's presence at the end of the declaration is a sign of this submission.

The ceremony is also a call for the expression of gratitude. The householder is to acknowledge all that God has done for him and his family, leading them out of poverty and insignificance, exercising works of "terrifying power, with signs and wonders" on their behalf, then leading them into a fertile land and giving them these products of that land to enjoy.

But perhaps most important of all, the rite described here is a declaration of religious identity, an expression that the one presenting the first fruits is what he is because God has been interested in and involved with him and his family. Originally they were a marginal people, but once God became involved with them they became a nation with a promise, a destiny, an identity provided by the Lord. This reading is a kind of Old Testament *credo* in which the faithful householder gives voice to the fundamental realities of his religious faith.

This passage constitutes a survey of the basic outlines of the history of God's relationship with his people. We will hear further expositions of this history in greater detail in the overture readings in the next few Sundays, but most of it is somehow already here in this reading from Deuteronomy.

This passage is about us, too. As part of our observance of Lent, we are called to remind ourselves of our dependence on God, of the gratitude that we owe to the Lord for everything we are and have. We are also invited to enliven our consciousness of our religious identity: that we are loved by God, that God's love has given us the opportunity to share his own life in Jesus, that we assimilate and receive what God offers us not by earning it or achieving it, but by accepting it as God's gift. We have all been resourceless wanderers. And now we are God's people in Christ.

How have I experienced God's providence in my life?
How do I express my religious identity?

Second Sunday of Lent (A)

Genesis 12:1–4a

The second Sunday of Lent brings us the second chapter of
salvation history, of the account of the execution of God's plan of
salvation. Last week's overture reading was from the first large
section of Genesis, what scholars call the primeval history. That
section (the first eleven chapters) is about sin and destruction,
about the slide of humanity into an ever-deepening pool of
alienation from God.

With chapter twelve a new section begins. It lasts for about
fourteen chapters and gives us the story of Abraham, a single
individual who would become a family and ultimately a nation
which would serve as God's instrument for the salvation of the
whole world.

As a preface to the story, at the end of chapter ten, we learn
that Abram's father, Terah, brought Abram and his wife Sarai and
his grandson Lot away from the splendid metropolis of Ur (in
present-day Iraq) to Haran, a city to the northwest of Ur. They
were on their way to Canaan. Then Terah died. That's about all
we know about Abram when his relationship with God begins.
He was not particularly prominent, not particularly important.

Without any warning or prelude God calls Abram (whose
name God would later change to Abraham). God tells him to
leave everything and go to the place to which God would lead

him. Now comes God's promise. God would make Abram great. A great nation would arise out of him. God would care for Abram and defend him from his enemies. Abram would become a blessing for all the world. "So Abram went, as the LORD had told him" (NRSV).

There are several things worthy of comment in this short reading. First of all, the pronoun "I" occurs no less than five times. God is the main agent here, the lead actor. What happens is God's initiative and would be carried out by God's power.

Likewise, "bless" and "blessing" occur five times in our reading. What is going to develop is a good thing, a wonderful gift, something that Abram would treasure. Abram himself will prove to be a gift to the rest of humankind. People all over the earth will look on Abram as someone particularly graced and favored by God and when people want to wish good to one another, they will say, "May you be blessed as Abram was."

It's all God's initiative. It's all God's doing. It's all God's gift. Why? Nobody really knows except that it is clear that God wanted to bless and save his human creatures and decided to do it through the instrumentality of this unknown man from Ur of the Chaldeans who happened to be living in Haran.

And what did Abram do? He obeyed. This landless and childless alien sets out in response to God's order. He had no itinerary, no map, no destination. He left everything behind— security, homeland, kinfolk—in pursuit of the fulfillment of God's promise. He put himself totally at God's disposal.

What we have here are the two basic elements of salvation history. The first is the initiative and generosity of God, which we have already seen in last Sunday's reading. God did everything for Adam and Eve. God called Abram to be a blessing for the whole world. Nobody deserves these gifts from God. Nobody can say that God owes us anything. But God is generous. He blesses us in the present and promises us greater gifts still to come. It's all God's idea. It's all God's doing. The history of salvation is the story of God's outreach to his human creatures, the story of God's initiative of blessing.

The other basic element of salvation history is human response. God does not force his gifts on anybody. He offers. And the extent to which God's offer is accepted is the extent to which God's plan of salvation is brought to fulfillment. Adam and Eve rejected God's offer of happiness in paradise. They wanted something else. Abram had trust and confidence in God's promise. He was submissive to God's will. He accepted what God offered him, even when that acceptance involved leaving everything he had.

We have all been the objects of God's initiative. We have all been offered blessings beyond calculation. And we have all been invited to respond. Life, faith, family, talents, bodily health: all these are God's gifts. They all constitute God's call. And the way we respond to what we have been given constitutes our answer to God's call.

Sometimes responding to God's call, doing what we know God wants us to do with our gifts, can be difficult, demanding, even frightening. But we have the example of Abram to teach us where trust and confidence can finally lead.

FOR REFLECTION AND DISCUSSION

How much do I trust God?

Has my trust in God ever cost me anything?

Second Sunday of Lent (B)

Genesis 22:1–2, 9a, 10–13, 15–18

This Sunday's reading continues the survey course in salvation history that the church gives us in the First Readings during Lent. On the second Sunday of Lent each year we hear about Abraham. In this year B we hear about Abraham's call to sacrifice his son, Isaac.

For this lenten Sunday we have an abridged version of the narrative. This shorter version omits many of the details that occur in the full text of Genesis and limits the text to the bare essentials. At the Easter Vigil, this text is also read, but in its full, uncut form. (This narrative is one of only five Old Testament texts that are read more than once in the course of the three-year Sunday cycle.)

The first sentence of our reading clearly announces the purpose for what happens: God intends to put Abraham to the test.

So God speaks to Abraham. God had already spoken to Abraham many times in the course of their relationship, but this time, instead of encouragement and promise, God makes a demand: "Offer up your son Isaac to me in sacrifice."

It's important to note that Isaac was essential for the fulfillment of God's covenant with Abraham. Abraham was to be the father of many nations, and this was to take place through the son of Abraham and Sarah. Now God seems to be telling Abraham to cut the link between himself and the future that God had promised.

The second part of the reading, as edited for this Sunday, tells us how another command came from God as Abraham was preparing to fulfill the first command. God's messenger, seeing

Abraham's willingness to obey, calls on him to spare the boy. Instead of Isaac, Abraham offers God a ram that happened to be nearby.

Now, in view of Abraham's willingness to obey, God repeats his promise of progeny and universal blessing that would come through Abraham (and Isaac). God had tested him and he had been found submissive to the Lord.

There are several levels of significance in this narrative as Genesis presents it to us.

First of all, the story was meant to teach its Israelite audience that God does not accept human sacrifice. Sacrificing a child to the local divinity was not unusual for the Canaanites among whom the Israelites lived. It seems clear that sometimes Israelites who had slipped into idolatry engaged in this practice, too. The story of the averted slaying of Isaac was meant to teach God's people that human sacrifice was not an acceptable religious practice for those who worshiped the one true God.

But more importantly, the narrative of the sacrifice of Isaac was meant to offer the reader a stunning example of the obedience of Abraham, of Abraham's trust in God, of Abraham's response to the covenant that God had entered with him. It's important for us twenty-first century readers to realize that the main point of the story is not what Abraham must have thought about sacrificing his son, but what Abraham thought about God. Abraham knew what God had promised him. Abraham knew that Isaac was part of the promise. But Abraham also knew that God's commands could not be contradictory to one another. Abraham's willingness to carry out God's command was a sign that, against every human sentiment, against a seemingly irrational demand on God's part, Abraham believed that God knew what he was doing. Abraham gave evidence that he knew and accepted that. Isaac was deeply important to Abraham. Isaac was essential for the fulfillment of what God had promised. But the command of God had to be more important than either. Abraham accepted that and acted accordingly. The result was a reaffirmation of the promise and an example of dedication and obedience for all believers in all ages to come.

There is a third level of significance in our narrative. Christian writers have seen the narrative of the sacrifice of Isaac as a prefiguring of the sacrifice of Jesus, done to death because of his faithfulness and obedience to his heavenly Father.

God is not a cruel master who calls for painful acts of obedience from his servants in order to satisfy his own divine egoism. God is the realist who brings his children, through the demands of obedience and sacrifice, to a deeper awareness of how things really are. Responding to God's covenant is not always easy. But Abraham's response resulted in a deeper relationship with God for him and in an example of faith for all of us.

FOR REFLECTION AND DISCUSSION

Have I ever been tested by God?

Who or what is most important in my life?

Second Sunday of Lent (C)

Genesis 15:5–12, 17–18

Genesis, the first book of the Bible, is about beginnings, about the beginnings of creation and of human history in chapters 1 to 11, and about the beginnings of God's special relationship with his chosen people in chapters 12 to 50. This special relationship that we call salvation history begins with God's association with Abraham. It's only fitting, therefore, that one of the lenten First Readings each year (when we get a survey of salvation history) be about Abraham.

When God first called Abraham to leave the land of his ancestors, God promised him a great name and many descendants. God said he would make Abraham a great nation (cf. Genesis 12:1–3, a reading we hear on the second Sunday of Lent in year A). Note that at this time in this culture, success and prosperity consisted in family and land. To be promised a large family and vast areas of land was to be promised great blessings indeed. Now, some years later, Abraham is still without an heir and he is an old man, still wandering in a land not his own. At the beginning of chapter 15, God speaks to Abraham in his tent, repeating the promise to give Abraham great blessings. Abraham gently reminds God that so far he has no son, no heir, and that therefore any prosperity he might have would be without any long-term benefit to him. This is where our passage begins.

God takes Abraham outside the tent and shows him the starry heaven. "That's how many descendants you will have," God promises. Abraham accepts God's promise with trust, and God accepted this trust as an appropriate response to what he had promised.

But there's more. God is not content just to make promises. Now he enters into a formal contract with Abraham. God binds himself to faithfulness with a legal agreement. That's the meaning of the strange proceedings that follow. God tells Abraham to split certain animals and line up the halves in two rows. Abraham then falls into a deep sleep in preparation for something awesome that is about to happen. While he is in this religious trance, God's presence, symbolized by the smoking cookpot and the flaming torch, walks between the split carcasses. This was how people made a legal contract in those days: the contracting parties passed between the parts of the slain animals and called down upon themselves the fate of the victims if they should violate the agreement. In this case, however, it is only God who walks between the parts because it is only God who initiates the contract and agrees to be bound by it. At the end of our reading, the content of the contract is enunciated: "To your descendants... I give this land from the river of Egypt [the Nile] to the Euphrates." God had entered into a formal contract with a human being to give him all that a human being could desire.

(The birds of prey that swoop down on the carcasses are omens of the misery that awaited Abraham's descendants in Egypt before the exodus. God speaks of this in the verses that are omitted from our lectionary reading.)

God's people begin with God's initiative. For no particular reason, God decided to look after one man in a special way. God promises to make him the father of many nations, to give him land and riches of imperial dimensions. But God not only promises. He binds himself with a contract. Abraham now has a legal claim on what God had said he would give him. The whole further history of Old Testament salvation, the whole further history of the people of Israel will be an account of how God fulfilled the promise and observed the covenant.

But God expected a response from Abraham. It wasn't that God expected Abraham to earn or deserve favor. It was rather that God looked for faith and trust. Abraham did have faith in God's promise. He did trust that God would observe the covenant that he had made, in spite of the fact that what had been promised and guaranteed by covenant was, humanly speaking, beyond realization. And that faith and trust made him pleasing to God.

This narrative of God's covenant and Abraham's response is not just an account of a one-time occurrence in the history of humanity's relationship with God. It is the story of each of us. Just as God approached Abraham with undeserved generosity, so God in Christ has approached each of us with generosity. And just as God looked to Abraham not for efforts that would enable him to deserve God's blessings but for faith, trust and receptivity, so God looks to us not to earn his attention, but to accept it.

Abraham is the father of God's chosen people. He is also our father in faith, teaching us what a relationship with God involves.

FOR REFLECTION AND DISCUSSION

What have I been promised by God?

How do I respond to God's overtures to me?

Third Sunday of Lent (A)

Exodus 17:3–7

Our survey course in salvation history continues. On the first Sunday of Lent we heard about the very beginning of the story of God's love for his human creatures—the story of the first sin that infected every human being and made salvation necessary. Last Sunday we heard about the call of Abraham, the founder of the people and its first shepherd. We learned how God brought him out to a new country, a new mode of life. On this third Sunday we hear about the second great shepherd of God's people, about the leader that brought God's people out of Egypt, the guide who found them a formless collection of tribes and who, under God's guidance, made them into a people with a land of their own. It's impossible to talk about salvation history without talking about Moses.

This Sunday's reading shows us the Israelites in the first months after their departure from Egypt. Pharaoh had been persuaded to let them leave Egypt, and then changed his mind. The people escaped Pharaoh's chariots and charioteers, passing dry shod through the Red Sea, thanks to the intervention of God through his servant Moses. The Egyptians were destroyed as they attempted to catch up with the Israelites. Moses led the people on. As God's agent he provided the people with drinkable water at a place called Marah. Then, in response to the people's demands for bread and meat, God sent them manna and quail to eat.

This Sunday's reading shows us Moses and the people in crisis once more. As they move through the wilderness, they are thirsty again and there is no water. They demand that Moses do something. After all, it was he who had brought them so rashly (as they now thought) out of Egypt. Moses turns to the Lord. "What shall I do with this people?" He is afraid that they will kill him. God instructs Moses to take the staff he had stretched over the Red Sea. With this rod he was to strike the rock in front of them, and they would have water. Moses did as he was instructed and, sure enough, there was water for these quarrelsome people. They called that place "Massah and Meribah," "test and quarrel," and they remembered what happened there for a long time. They had quarreled with the Lord and put the Lord to the test.

There are several things worthy of note in this episode in the history of Moses' role in the salvation of the people.

First of all, God tells Moses to use the same staff to strike the rock that he had used to make the Red Sea open up. The point here is not that the staff was endowed with magical powers, but rather that what God would now do was part of the same plan that brought the people out of their Egyptian slavery.

Second, the primary issue here is not so much the people's thirst as their doubt about the wisdom of God's plan for them. "Why did we have to leave Egypt? Why didn't God leave us alone back there where we were at least a little more comfortable?" When God's providence makes demands on people, they are inclined to think that God really doesn't know what he is doing. They complain. They want to be liberated from what is really God's generosity toward them. The Israelites in the exodus were world-class complainers. Like Adam and Eve—and most of us at one time or another—they wanted to be in charge and couldn't understand why God wasn't doing things the way they would have preferred.

Third, this episode in the exodus looks forward to God's continued generosity toward the dozens of generations still to come. Just as God saved and refreshed his people in the desert by giving them water, so also God continues to save and heal and refresh people today through his gift of water, this time through the water of baptism. God still looks after his people, only now it is not in response to physical thirst, but in response to their thirst for eternal life. For the Israelites in the desert, water meant life. For God's people of today, water is the vehicle through which we receive eternal life.

Any number of passages from Exodus could have been used to introduce us, in this overview of salvation history, to the great Moses who brought God's people out of Egypt and led them as a people into the land that God had promised to Abraham. The editors of the lectionary chose this passage, a passage about water, a passage that ties in with the Gospel (John 4:5–42). Jesus and the

Samaritan woman dialogue about living water and about how to get it. Jesus gradually leads the woman to understand who he is and what he offers her. Just so, Moses in the desert strove to bring his people to understand, through the gift of water, the firmness and complexity of God's plan for them and the extent to which God was willing to go to bring them to their final home.

FOR REFLECTION AND DISCUSSION

In what ways does God provide for me?

When and why have I grumbled at God's providence for me?

Third Sunday of Lent (B)

Exodus 20:1–17

On the third Sunday of Lent, our lectionary survey course in Old Testament salvation history brings us to Moses, the contact agent between the Israelites and God, their leader out of slavery, their great spiritual father and lawgiver.

In this year B Moses is not mentioned by name, but the reading gives us the commandments that Moses received from God on Mount Sinai. These commandments would constitute the required response to God's covenant with the people that would soon be formalized. The Pentateuch gives us the Ten Commandments twice: here, at the beginning of the people's sojourn in the desert, and again (in Deuteronomy 5:6–21) as they prepare to enter the Promised Land.

This reading is rather long as Old Testament Sunday readings go in the lectionary, seventeen verses. The average length of Old

Testament Sunday readings is just short of six verses. One gathers that those who prepared the lectionary thought that the Ten Commandments were important enough to demand a full, unedited presentation (although the lectionary does give a stripped down version of the reading that can be used if necessary).

Just before our reading begins, Moses had been called into the presence of God. He had gone up and down Mount Sinai several times to get God's instructions and to prepare the people for the majestic manifestation of the Lord. Then God delivers his commandments to Moses, commandments that would serve as the grounding for their moral identity as a people, commandments that would keep them aware of God's covenant with them.

The commandments begin with a brief prefatory statement of God's right to make demands on the people of Israel. "I am your God who brought you out of Egypt. That's why I have the right to look for some response from you."

Then follow the Ten Commandments, the first three (or four) being concerned with Israel's relationship to God, the others with the Israelites' relationships with one another.

First the most basic command of all: "You shall have no other gods before me" (NRSV). The Israelites were not to have many gods as did the Egyptians from whom they had fled and the peoples who would surround them once they had entered the Promised Land. The Israelites were to worship only the God who had rescued them from slavery. Later, as the relationship matured between God and the Israelites, it would become clear that there simply was no other God but the God of the Israelites.

They were not to make images that claim to represent God. It was important for the Israelites to be aware that God is beyond human representation. Moreover, images of gods tend to be transformed into gods themselves, and become occasions for idolatry. (Catholics look on these first demands as one commandment, while others look on them as two. Consequently there are two ways of numbering the Ten Commandments.)

God insists on these basic signs of reverence because he is "a jealous God," one who demands exclusive allegiance, a God who punishes the wicked and offers mercy to the faithful.

Next come the commands about reverence for God's name and about the observance of the Sabbath. These three (or four) initial commands would constitute the religious identity of the Israelites. They would be able to be seen as God's people to the extent that they observed these directives.

Then come the other commands that deal with the Israelites' relationships to one another. Basically they call for mutual reverence in human relationships and for respect for the property of others.

The Ten Commandments set forth the demands of any relationship with God. They enunciate the people's duties toward God and toward one another. They were to be learned and constantly remembered. That's why there are ten: so that the people could count them off on their fingers.

The Ten Commandments apply to us, too. They each provide material for self-examination and repentance during the season of Lent. But the most basic and important of all of them is still the first commandment, the prohibition of idolatry. Most of us tend to look on idolatry as something that only primitive people engage in, natives in grass skirts dancing in front of a statue. But idolatry is more pervasive than that. Whenever people make a creature more important than God, they are engaging in idolatry. Lots of twenty-first century people practice idolatry when they center their lives around comfort or success or money or security or self-indulgence. It is possible that even some who count themselves as believers may be idolaters without realizing it.

FOR REFLECTION AND DISCUSSION
Which commandments call for most attention from me?
Have I ever practiced idolatry? When and how?

Third Sunday of Lent (C)

Exodus 3:1–8a, 13–15

After Abraham, the next greatest personage in Old Testament salvation history is Moses. As Abraham was the father of the people, so Moses was its liberator from slavery.

Neither was a very likely candidate for carrying out what God intended. Abraham, called to be the father of a great people, was an old man when God promised him progeny, a nomad when God promised him a stable patrimony of land. Moses had been saved from death as an infant and brought up in Pharaoh's household, but his intervention to defend one of his people from being beaten by an Egyptian resulted in his having to flee the country (cf. Exodus 2:11–15). When our reading begins, Moses is a fugitive both from the Egyptians and from his own people, hardly the sort of person one would expect to be called to engage in diplomatic negotiations with Pharaoh or win the confidence of his oppressed fellow Israelites. Yet Moses is called.

We hear his story and the story of the liberation of the Israelites from their Egyptian slavery in the book of Exodus. Exodus recounts that portion of salvation history that runs from the birth and vocation of Moses through the people's escape from Egypt to their acceptance of a contractual relationship, a covenant with God.

As our reading begins, Moses is a fugitive in Midian, a desert area down on the Sinai Peninsula. He has married a Midianite woman and is looking after his father-in-law's flock when the Lord calls his name. The Lord presents himself as "an angel" in a flaming bush. (God would not present himself in his own form since human beings would be destroyed if they saw his true majesty, and fire was one of the ways in which God manifested himself, as we saw in last Sunday's reading.) As Moses approaches the bush, God calls his name and tells him not to come any closer. The presence of God makes the place holy, and the holiness of God is more than humans can bear.

Then God identifies himself: "The God of Abraham, of Isaac and of Jacob." This was the God who had entered a covenant with Abraham and who had watched over Abraham's descendants. This was the God of Abraham's people who had been active on their behalf for centuries. God now tells Moses that his care for his people continues and that he intends to rescue them from slavery and lead them into a prosperous homeland. (In the verses omitted in our lectionary reading, God tells Moses that he, Moses, is to be the people's leader in this endeavor. Not surprisingly, Moses tries to beg off, but God will not take no for an answer.)

Now Moses raises the identity issue. "What is your name so I can tell the Israelites?" God's answer is unclear and somewhat equivocal: I AM. (In the Semitic culture knowing a person's name gave one power over that person. God does not want to make himself subject to human beings in that way.) God tells Moses that he wants to be known by this ambiguous name, but also as the God of Abraham, Isaac and Jacob. God would be identified by his relationship with his people.

As this reading has been edited for liturgical use, its main point is that God presented himself to Moses and wanted to be known by Moses and the people Moses would lead. In a way one could say that this passage constitutes a basic, essential act of divine revelation.

Revelation is not a matter of God telling us a collection of truths that we are to accept. Revelation is not primarily God letting us in on his plans for us. At the deepest level, revelation is God making God's self known to us, letting us know how he chooses to relate with us, teaching us how we are to relate to him. Revelation is about relationship.

When God entered the covenant with Abraham, the real issue was not children and property. The real issue was God reaching out to Abraham. When God tells Moses that he will help him free the Israelites, the real issue was not emancipation. The real issue was God manifesting himself to his people and demonstrating his love for them. And when we speak of Christian revelation, we probably think of the truths of our faith, but what it all boils down to is God presenting himself to us in Christ Jesus and inviting us into a definitive relationship with himself—Father, Son and Spirit.

Moses begins his leadership task by getting to know God. It's the essential foundation for everything else. That same foundation—getting to know God—is what gives stability and meaning and purpose to every aspect of our life as Christian believers.

FOR REFLECTION AND DISCUSSION
How does God reveal/manifest himself in my life?
In what ways do I know God?

Fourth Sunday of Lent (A)

1 Samuel 16:1b, 6–7, 10–13a

During these weeks of Lent, our First Readings have introduced us to a series of personages who are of fundamental importance for the story of God's salvation of his people: Adam and Eve, Abraham, Moses. On this day we meet still another personage, one who would bring God's people to unprecedented prosperity, prestige and security in the land that the Lord had given them. This Sunday's reading introduces us to David.

As our narrative begins, Saul is ruling God's people. Saul was their first king, a king chosen by God at the urging of the people who wanted to be ruled as the neighboring nations were ruled. God gave them a king, but Saul was not satisfactory. He was cruel and unpredictable, often unfaithful to important directives from God. God makes clear to the prophet Samuel that Saul would need to be replaced.

As our reading opens, God sends Samuel to consecrate a new king. He was to go to Bethlehem, to the family of Jesse. In verses omitted in the lectionary reading, Samuel prepares the sacrifice of a heifer, and calls Jesse and his sons to the banquet that would follow. He is on the lookout for the one who would be chosen by the Lord to become king. Jesse presents seven of his sons to Samuel but, in spite of appearances, none of these is the one that God had in mind. Finally Jesse sends for the youngest son, David, who apparently was not thought important enough to be invited to the sacrificial banquet to begin with. This turns out to be the one that the Lord had in mind. Samuel performs the ritual anointing with oil and the Spirit of the Lord took possession of David to lead him forward to the destiny that God had in mind for him.

David became a great warrior, a unifier of his people, a singer of unforgettable songs for the Lord, a monarch who, with his successor Solomon, brought the Promised Land to the highest point in its political and economic life. Here was the fulfillment of the promise that God had made to Abraham (cf. Genesis 15:18–21). In later times, when the peak period had passed, the Israelites looked forward to another king, another anointed one, the Messiah, who would be for the people of his time what the charismatic David had been before.

There are several important lessons for us in the story of David and of his rule over the land promised to Abraham.

First of all, we note that David was not among the likely candidates that were presented to Samuel that day in Bethlehem. In fact, he wasn't likely enough even to be brought forward with his brothers at first. God often chooses the unlikely to carry out his purposes. This is to demonstrate that it is the Lord who is the primary agent in getting his will done. If God decides to use human instruments, he is obviously free to do so, but often, in choosing the least likely, God reminds us that what's important is not human talent and ability, but the will and the power of the Lord.

Second, David did not insure God's continued care for him by his personal holiness. To be sure, David loved the Lord, but David was also a sinner. He was conniving, lustful, cruel, selfish, vindictive. Yet, somewhere deep in his heart, he continued to be in love with God, and God continued to be in love with him. The story of David and his brilliant reign over God's people is the story neither of skill nor of sanctity on the part of God's instrument. David's is the story of God's providence triumphing in spite of human limitation.

Then there is the land. Land and offspring had been part of God's promise from the beginning. At last, by means of God's work through David, the people had land and prosperity greater than they ever expected. But it didn't last. Soon after Solomon's death, the kingdom began to disintegrate and, in spite of occasional spurts of well being, it gradually declined into insignificance. It wasn't that God's promise to Abraham couldn't be fulfilled. It was rather that the land God promised, the land God secured for the people, was only the symbol of another kingdom, another kind of homeland. Through their history, God seems to have been trying to teach the Israelites that what they possessed was only a symbol, only a beginning. The kingdom of David would last forever, but it would be a different kind of David, not a tribal warlord but a suffering servant. And it would be a different kind of a kingdom, not a land flowing with milk and honey but a state in which everyone would be nourished and enlightened and enlivened by the eternal Spirit of the Lord.

FOR REFLECTION AND DISCUSSION

In what ways have I been called by God?

How is God involved in the history of today's world?

Fourth Sunday of Lent (B)

2 Chronicles 36:14–16, 19–23

The two books of Chronicles are not the best known or the most quoted books of the Bible. Nor are they much used in the liturgy. In fact, this reading is the only time that either book of Chronicles is used for a Sunday reading throughout the three-year cycle. For a long time Catholic Bibles entitled these two books the books of Paralipomena, "leftovers."

Yet Chronicles are far more than collections of otherwise unused material. They are an overview of all sacred history from Adam to the destruction of Jerusalem. They are a reworking of other books of the Bible (e.g., Samuel and Kings) plus the addition of other material. They present the history of salvation, but from a slightly different religious perspective than the other books of the Bible.

Written about 400 B.C., i.e., after the exile, they teach that the greatness and worth of the people would no longer be found in political or economic power, but in the careful worship of God, in corporate reverence for the temple, in an ongoing consciousness of the people's connection to David, the religious giant whose relationship with God set the pattern for the religious consciousness of all Israelites. The general theme of Chronicles is not messianic expectation, but cultic exactitude. For the author of Chronicles, what was important was not the messianic savior still to come, but the contemporary opportunities for relating to God in post-exilic Judah.

This Sunday's reading is from the very end of the second book of Chronicles. Over the past Sundays we have selections from the history of the growth of God's relationship with human beings: Noah, Abraham, the law given to the people by Moses. Now we read about destruction, the destruction of Jerusalem and the end of the political importance of God's people.

As the lectionary presents the reading to us, it is in three parts. The first part deals with the immediate causes of the catastrophe. The leaders of the people, including the priests, neglected authentic temple worship. God sent spokesmen to them, like the prophet Jeremiah, but the leadership rejected and scoffed at them. Finally the situation had reached the point of no return. "[T]here was no remedy."

In the second part of the reading, the text, in a few lines, tells of the destruction of the temple and of Jerusalem itself. The Chaldeans (i.e., the Babylonians) then carried everybody of any consequence off into exile as enrichment for their captors. Their exile would last as long as the Babylonian empire would exercise supremacy in what we call the Middle East.

The author gives Jeremiah the last word. Jeremiah had prophesied that the land would be laid waste and would experience seventy years of inactivity, a kind of long Sabbath consequent to the kingdom's defeat. (Actually, the exile lasted from 587 to 538 B.C., fifty years rather than seventy. However, scholars point out that it was seventy years from the beginning of the exile to the rebuilding of the temple, and that the number seventy is often used to signify an indeterminately long period of time.)

Finally comes the beginning of the next period of the history of God's people. The Persians unseat the Babylonians as the dominant power and their king, Cyrus, sends the exiles home to rebuild the temple. A new era begins.

As this text is presented to us here, we learn in just a few verses about some major turning points in the history of God's relationship to his chosen people. Everything that was sacred and important to the Israelites—temple, city, economic resources, political independence—was taken away. Even the land that God had promised to Abraham was no longer theirs. And they had brought it all on themselves. Yet that wasn't the end. Out of the blue comes Cyrus the Persian, a pagan whom God used to bring the people back home. It is true that the Jews would never again be the political and social power that they had been in the good old days of David and Solomon. But God would be in touch with them in a new way. Rather than a people of large armies and vast areas of dominion, they would be a people whose uniqueness lay in their worship of God, a worship centered in the renovated temple, but rooted in the dedication to God proclaimed by religious giants like Moses and David. Catastrophe had yielded to hope.

This double turning point in the history of the Israelites—from independence to defeat, from defeat to restoration—teaches us that God always loves and cares for his people, even when the people are unfaithful, even when everything seems lost.

FOR REFLECTION AND DISCUSSION

What have been the turning points of my life?

Where do I see hope in present day political and religious circumstances?

Fourth Sunday of Lent (C)

Joshua 5:9a, 10–12

The three-year cycle of the Sunday lectionary gives us only two readings from Joshua. One is from an early section of the book (this Sunday's reading from chapter 5), the other (for the twenty-first Sunday in Ordinary Time in year B) from its very last chapter. Both readings are about faithfulness: the first about God's faithfulness to his people, the second about the need for the people to be faithful to God.

Joshua was the successor of Moses as leader of the Israelites, and the book of Joshua is concerned with the Israelites' conquest of the land that God had promised them. Like the preceding books of the Bible, Joshua is the result of a long and complex process of editing: putting order into historical memories that had been handed down orally or in writing over an extended period of time.

Our reading from chapter 5 shows us the Israelites encamped in the Promised Land, having just crossed over the Jordan River into the land's boundaries. They pause, as it were, to express who and what they were one more time.

The theme of this episode is expressed by the Lord at the beginning of the passage: "Today I have rolled away from you the disgrace of Egypt" (NRSV). The Israelites are no longer subject to the humiliating position they had experienced in Egypt, slaves in a foreign land. Nor were they any longer landless wanderers in the desert. They were now God's free people entering their very own land.

Then, as an expression of their identity as God's people, they celebrate the Passover. This Passover celebration in the new land served as a rite of closure of the process of their liberation from Egypt. On the night they fled from Egypt, they had carried out the Passover ritual in accord with God's command. Then came forty years of wandering in the wilderness, during which they apparently did not celebrate the feast, perhaps because they were without the makings for the unleavened bread. Now they had found grain in their new land and they could again do what they did as they began their journey so long ago.

As if to emphasize this aspect of closure, God no longer sends them manna to eat. It's not necessary any longer because they are now in a position to look after their own needs. The land that God was giving them would provide their food from now on.

There were still many challenges ahead of the Israelites. They had to finish taking possession of the land. Then they had to learn how to live in it in accord with the covenant they had entered into with God. Centuries of history still lay ahead of them, centuries that would bring some successes and many failures. But crossing the Jordan into the land that God was giving them marked the end of an era. Their time of wandering was over. A new epoch was beginning.

This reading is about faithfulness, God's faithfulness. God had promised family and territory to Abraham. God had promised delivery from slavery through Moses. Now, as the Israelites are encamped on the west bank of the Jordan celebrating Passover, all these promises have been fulfilled. A numerous people descended from Abraham and freed from servitude are now beginning to take possession of the land to which God has brought them. God has proved faithful.

What began with Abraham was now drawing to a conclusion. But it is only an interim conclusion. God had in mind for them much more than the gift of land and population. The gifts that God had promised to Abraham and Moses and which were now being delivered were symbolic of a relationship, a relationship between God and this people. God intended the relationship to grow and deepen. As the years went by, the people would want to settle down to enjoy the milk and honey that God had given them, to take their part in the affairs of the world as one nation like all the others. But God would not let them do that. He keeps reminding them in all kinds of ways that he wants them to have more, that he wants them not just to possess *things*, but to enter into an intimate personal relationship with him.

The extension and clarifying of God's promises reaches its final stage in Jesus. God becomes one of us to enable us to become like him, to share not in milk and honey but in the personal life of God.

God is faithful, but God's faithfulness involves much more than we are inclined to expect.

FOR REFLECTION AND DISCUSSION

How have I experienced God's faithfulness?
How have I responded to God's faithfulness?

Fifth Sunday of Lent (A)

Ezekiel 37:12–14

In the course of the lectionary's overview of Old Testament
salvation history over the last four weeks, our overture readings
have presented us with Adam and Eve, with Abraham, with
Moses and his people in the desert, with David and the land that
God had promised his people. On this Sunday we encounter
another basic element of salvation history: the future.

This Sunday's reading is from Ezekiel. The prophet Ezekiel
belonged to a priestly family in the sixth century B.C. Because of
his prominent position among the people, he was deported to
Babylon in 597 B.C., ten years before the final destruction of
Jerusalem. In Babylon he was called by God to a prophetic
vocation in 593 B.C. He was in Babylon, dutifully pronouncing
the message of God, when the Babylonians finally destroyed
Jerusalem and the kingdom of Judah in 587 B.C.

Chapters 33 to 39 of Ezekiel seem to have been proclaimed
during and after the final siege of Jerusalem. The Israelites in
exile were losing their hope. They looked upon themselves as
nothing more than dried up bones, with no life and no future. In
the first part of chapter 37, God brings Ezekiel to a plain filled
with dry bones and empowers him to bring the bones back
together and to put sinews and muscles on them and make them
come alive again and stand upright, "a vast army."

In the second part of chapter 37, from which our reading is taken, God explains the raising of the dry bones. "Even if you were dead and dried up like heaps of dry bones," God says, "even if you are utterly dead and buried, I will bring you up out of your graves and make you live again. I will bring you home, not because you are a saintly and obedient people, but just because I am God and this is what I have decided to do."

What we have here is an oracle of hope. God promises a future to this exiled and dried up people. It is not because of their merit, either individually or collectively. It is simply because God is generous and has long-term plans for the children of Abraham and Moses and David. God will never allow them to dry up and blow away, never allow them to settle down into their graves forever. On the contrary, God will bring them to where he wants them to be in spite of the situation in which they find themselves, in spite of what they have suffered. God's plan for his people always includes a future. The story of their salvation is never quite ended. However desperate the situation, God will breathe life into his people again. No matter what happens, God will take care of them.

This reading from Ezekiel teaches us about the concluding stages of salvation history. There will always be life. There will always be rescue.

The long Gospel reading for this fifth Sunday of Lent in year A (John 11:1–45) is about the resurrection of Jesus' friend Lazarus. In raising Lazarus from the dead, Jesus not only demonstrates his power over life and death, but also suggests that what Ezekiel had foreseen for the whole people was beginning to be brought to fulfillment by him. The subject matter of this long Gospel reading and this short overture reading is not the Christian doctrine of individual immortality and resurrection from the dead, but rather the determination of God to make his people live, no matter what their particular circumstances might be.

There are all kinds of death in the world around us: death of the body, death of the spirit, death of our common aspirations. We are invited in dozens of ways to forget about a future sharing in the life of the Lord and settle for comfort, satisfaction, security, power, immediate individual fulfillment. When people learn from their experience that such goals are not satisfying, they tend to dry up and curl into their graves. Why bother? Why struggle? Nothing makes much difference.

Yet in these readings from Ezekiel and from John, God's word reminds us that there is always life in store for us. If we accept what God offers us, we will experience resurrection, a return from disillusion and disintegration. We will be restored to vigor. We are called to look forward to resurrection, not just the one final resurrection at the end of time, but to repeated resurrections as we experience the repeated interventions of God in our lives.

Death and destruction for God's people are never the last word. The history of salvation, corporate and individual, is the history of resurrection. And the history of salvation is not over yet.

FOR REFLECTION AND DISCUSSION

Where do I see death in myself, in the church, in the world?
How have I experienced resurrection in my life?

Fifth Sunday of Lent (B)

Jeremiah 31:31–34

In this year's series of lenten Old Testament readings we have heard quite a bit about covenant. We heard about God's covenant with Noah, about God testing Abraham's loyalty to their covenant by asking him to sacrifice his son, about the Ten Commandments which would be part of the children of Israel's response to the covenant that God made with them at Sinai, and, finally, about the seeming dissolution of the people into exile when their response to the covenant was so deficient as to amount to a rejection of it.

On this Sunday, we hear about covenant again. This time the sacred writer is not dealing with God's outreach in past covenants, but about a new covenant, a different relationship that would come in the future and that would never need modification or change.

This Sunday's reading is from the section of Jeremiah's prophecies that is called the Book of Consolation, chapters 30 to 33. This is a collection of the comforting pronouncements that Jeremiah had made throughout the course of his prophetic career. It does not seem possible to determine at exactly what time each portion of these chapters was first proclaimed.

Our reading is composed of four verses from chapter 31. Each verse contains the phrase, "says the LORD." This repetition is probably intended to underline the importance of what is being said and to guarantee that the prophet is proclaiming God's word and not his own.

The first verse announces the coming of a new covenant between God and his people. In the next verse God says that this new covenant will be different from the one offered to the people when they left Egypt, the covenant that they eventually rejected.

The difference, our third verse says, will be that the new covenant through which God enters a relationship with his people will be written on the hearts of the people (not on stone tablets).

Finally, this covenant still to come will involve deep personal knowledge of the Lord and the definitive forgiveness of sin.

This passage has been called the highest peak of Jeremiah's spirituality. Yet what Jeremiah says here about future relationships between God and the people is not totally without parallel. Ezekiel (36:26 ff.) speaks of God's putting a new heart and a new spirit within his people. In Isaiah 55:3 (from the time of exile) God promises to renew an everlasting covenant with his people. Similar promises are in Isaiah 59:21 and 61:8 (from the time after the exile). But Jeremiah's proclamation has found a special place in the hearts of Christian believers.

What God promises in this new covenant is a new and deeper level of relationship between himself and the people. This covenant will not be able to be broken as the old one was. It will not be an agreement that calls for merely external observance or formal compliance. It will not be political or legalistic. Rather, it will be a matter of the heart, a covenant that people will observe because of what is within them rather than because of external pressures. It will be shared not so much by the teaching of detailed prescriptions from generation to generation as by the covenant participants showing by way of example what it means to be in touch with the Lord. The newness of the new covenant consists to a great extent in its interiority. It's a matter of the heart.

Matthew (26:28), Mark (14:24) and Luke (22:20) all recount Jesus' institution of the Eucharist at the last supper. Each of them shows us Jesus speaking in terms of covenant. As Luke has it, "This cup that is poured out for you is the new covenant in my blood" (NRSV). What Jeremiah had foretold, Jesus now brings to fulfillment. His suffering and death would constitute a sacrifice that would mark the beginning of a new relationship, a new covenant between God and human beings. This new covenant would consist in what the Christian tradition has come to call grace.

This new relationship is not a kind of contract between God and humanity as other covenants had been. It is not a matter of God looking out for us and of our observing certain formalities to express our acknowledgment of God's goodness. No, the new covenant consists in our sharing in the life of God, in our accepting the life of the risen God-man Jesus Christ into our hearts and minds and extending it into our life and our world. It's not primarily a matter of learning things or doing things. It's rather a matter of following our hearts, hearts which are no longer just ours but which are also the dwelling place of the Lord.

FOR REFLECTION AND DISCUSSION

How do I experience God's law in my heart?

How does the covenant nature of the Eucharist influence my Eucharistic devotion?

Fifth Sunday of Lent (C)

Isaiah 43:16–21

The reading for the fifth Sunday of Lent brings this year's overview of Old Testament salvation history to a close. As is the case in years A and B, so in year C our reading offers the theme of renewal and restoration. Salvation history is future-oriented.

This Sunday's reading is from the second main part of the book of Isaiah, the part called the Book of Consolation. The Israelites to whom the writer addresses God's message are exiles in Babylon. What God had promised Abraham and Moses, what God had brought to fulfillment under Joshua was now lost. Jerusalem and its temple had been destroyed in 587 B.C. The leaders of the people had been carried off into a foreign country, and had been kept there for several decades now. Yet that is not the end. God still has further plans for his people. God will bring them home again. That's the recurrent theme of chapters forty to fifty-five of Isaiah.

This Sunday's reading begins with the prophet reminding the people of the exodus experience, that community-founding event when the Israelites were set free from slavery. The prophet mentions God bringing them through the sea on dry land. He recalls God beguiling the soldiers of Pharaoh into destruction, all "extinguished, quenched like a wick" (NRSV). That had been the people's finest hour, a time they would always remember.

"Well," God says, "you can forget all about that. That's over and done with and I'm doing something new and different. It's already starting."

Just as God formerly made a path out of Egypt for his people through the water, now water would mark out their path home from Babylon through dry land. To get home again from Babylon, they would need to cross the Syrian desert. God would make a way for them and provide water for them to drink in the badlands. Jackals and ostriches, signs of desolation and destruction, would now give honor to God. God will bring the people home again and make them his people so that they can give him praise.

There are two themes inherent in this reading. One is the exodus theme. God never allows his people to remain in privation and slavery. Just as God freed Abraham from being childless and landless, just as God liberated the Israelites through the leadership of Moses, just as God brought them into the Promised Land under Joshua, so God would bring them home again from exile. God keeps delivering his people. Exodus, coming out of deprivation and oppression, is a recurrent pattern in salvation history.

The second theme suggested by this Sunday's reading is that salvation history is future oriented. No single intervention of God is final, not even the unforgettable intervention of his rescuing them from Egypt. God is always doing something new. He brought his people out of Egypt. He would bring them out of Babylon. That to which they returned from exile was not a mere restoration of what had been before they were carried off into Babylon. It would prove to be a new kind of existence, no longer as a politically powerful nation, but as a nation with a deeper and wiser relationship with God. Eventually this history of God's saving concern for them would lead to a whole new concept of kingdom, a kingdom based not on human wealth and military resources, but on the ever increasing dominion of God. The ultimate stage of Old Testament salvation history for the Israelites would begin when yet another prophetic spokesman for God began to preach about the presence of the kingdom of God in their midst. The something new that God began among the exiles in Babylon would reach its conclusion in the kingdom proclaimed by Jesus.

In Jesus a new era of salvation history begins. The family and the nation promised to Abraham, the freedom promised to Moses, the liberation promised to the Babylonian exiles have all been brought to fulfillment through the life and ministry of Jesus. But there is still a further future. God is still doing something new. God is leading us through the desert of the present into the ultimate, final, timeless kingdom. There all of us together, united into the one family of Christ, freed from sin, will enjoy our heavenly homeland. Then there will be no more development of salvation history. There will only be the eternity of the kingdom in the life of the risen Lord where we will be, once and for all and forever, the people God has formed for himself to announce his praise.

FOR REFLECTION AND DISCUSSION

What do I look forward to from God?

What part does the future play in my day-to-day relationship with God?

Palm Sunday of the Lord's Passion (ABC)

Isaiah 50:4–7

The free-standing lenten series of First Readings concerned with Old Testament salvation history has now come to a close. For Palm Sunday of the Lord's Passion and for Easter Sunday the First Reading has been chosen to harmonize with the second reading and the gospel in the observance of the day.

The reading for this Palm Sunday is from the fiftieth chapter of the book of Isaiah, that part of the book written during the exile by one or more followers of the tradition of the eighth-century prophet. This reading is from one of the "suffering servant songs."

The "suffering servant songs" are poetic productions of

extraordinary intensity. They speak of a unique Israelite, completely consecrated to God's will who, though innocent, is called to suffer as part of his vocation.

As is the case with all great poetry, there is more than one level of meaning in these songs. Probably no single interpretation expresses their full significance. Scholars and literary critics have spent great energy trying to discern who the servant is actually intended to be. That is one of the key questions to understanding the meaning of the poems. Some say it is the prophet/writer himself, suffering rebuff from his own people for being too optimistic, too open to welcoming sinners and Gentiles into the embrace of God's providence. Others say that the servant is God's people seen as a collective, who, though pardoned of their sinfulness and now innocent, are nonetheless called to suffer for the sake of others. Others see the servant as an embodiment of the great figures of Israel's history—Abraham, Moses, Jeremiah— the ideal Israelite who somehow brings about universal salvation. The richness of the possibilities is one of the fascinations of these writings.

This Sunday's reading is an excerpt from the third of these four poems. (The whole poem will constitute the First Reading for Wednesday of Holy Week.) The prophet presents himself as a speaker who faithfully proclaims God's word of energy and encouragement to the weary. He is careful in listening to what God says to him and has not refused to accept it. He is patient when he is mistreated and persecuted, though subject to the greatest of human indignities. Finally, he is confident that God will protect him from final disgrace, that God will make him strong in bearing his sufferings.

Whatever the significance of the four servant songs may be in their original context, Christian believers have seen them as referring to the suffering of Jesus (and, by implication, to the Christ-like suffering that goes with being a follower of Christ). It is for that reason that they are read on Monday, Tuesday, Wednesday and Friday of Holy Week, all four of them, each year. They provide a modality in which Christian believers can look upon the sufferings of their Lord, a modality already prepared many centuries before the actual passion and death of Jesus.

The use of a portion of the third song as the First Reading for Palm Sunday each year is to provide a preview for the whole of Holy Week. In these verses the church invites us to recall the ministry of Christ, a ministry of teaching and speaking comfort to the weary ("a well-trained tongue...a word that will rouse them"). The reading also speaks of the faithfulness and obedience of Jesus ("he opens my ear...I...have not turned back"), a faithfulness that would bring Jesus to his death. In the course of mistreatment and persecution he would be patient ("I gave my back to those who beat me..."). But in the end God will intervene to bring his Christ to glory ("I am not disgraced... I shall not be put to shame"). These are all themes that we will encounter in the course of the days that lie ahead during Holy Week: Jesus condemned for his teaching, refusing to back away from his faithfulness to the Father, putting up with scorn and pain and even death without complaint, and, finally, brought to Resurrection in which all the dedication and faithfulness and suffering are touched with the glory of a new life, a life that all those who open themselves to Christ would be called to share. Jesus is the true, the ideal Israelite, the new Abraham, the new Moses, the new Jeremiah, the founder of a whole new people whose suffering for the sake of others would bring them a new life and a new identity. Everything that we hear each year from the various proclamations of God's word on Palm Sunday and throughout the rest of Holy Week is an exposition, a clarification, a development of what we hear in this overture.

FOR REFLECTION AND DISCUSSION

What role has suffering played in my relationship with God?

What sources of confidence do I experience in my life?

PART FOUR
Easter

Easter Vigil, First Reading

Genesis 1:1—2:2

The Easter Vigil is the longest single activity in the Roman
liturgy. In its fullest form, it is intended to begin at dusk and to
conclude about dawn. It's an all-night event. In most parishes the
Vigil does not last that long (because not all the readings are
proclaimed), but it is nonetheless a lengthy ceremony. Its
celebration at night and its length are part of its significance. The
Vigil liturgy calls us to relive the long history of salvation, that
began at creation itself and that is still in the process of
fulfillment. We gather to express and experience the salvation
brought by Jesus. We do this through the symbolism of light
overcoming darkness, a protracted and mysterious process. The
Vigil is intended to give us an unhurried opportunity to foster
gratitude for what God has done for us over the centuries and to
increase our awareness of how salvation has come to pass in our
midst.

There are nine readings in the Easter Vigil, some of them
significantly longer than we are used to in the regular Sunday
liturgy. The Easter Vigil is not something that one goes to if one
is in a hurry! Seven of these readings are from the Old Testament.
Of these, at least three should be used, the rubrics say, although
the church's preference is that all of them be read. At the
beginning of the Liturgy of the Word, the celebrant invites the
people "to listen attentively to the word of God, recalling how he
saved his people throughout history and, in the fullness of time,
sent his own Son to be our Redeemer."

It all starts with creation. In the long First Reading from the
first chapter of the book of Genesis we hear the fundamental
narrative that is presupposed by everything else that follows in

the Bible and in the history of salvation. None of it makes sense unless we are clear about creation. (Note that there is a second account of creation that approaches the same realities in a slightly different manner in the second chapter of Genesis. We hear some of that version of creation on the first Sunday of Lent in year A.)

The reading we hear at the Vigil is a passage of Scripture that most people are more or less familiar with, but there are a couple of elements in it that call for comment before we look at its general meaning.

The order of creation that is presented in Genesis 1 shows us God bringing things forth from nothing in their order of dignity and worth, with man being the last created and therefore having the greatest dignity. Note that in verse 26 ("Let us make man") the word for "man" does not mean a male human being but human beings in general ("male and female"). This explains the sentence that follows: "Let them have dominion..."

There are still other patterns in God's creative activity. In the first three days God builds a stage of heavens, water and land. In the corresponding second group of three days God provides actors for the stage each in turn: specific lights for the heavens, fish and sea creatures to fill the sea; animals for the dry land. Another pattern is in the way the activity of each day is described: God said, let there be, there was, God saw that it was good, that's how the day passed beginning with evening. God's creative undertaking was not haphazard. God worked methodically, as all good craftsmen do.

What we have here is not a scientific account of how our particular planet came to be, but rather a theological statement, a profession of faith. This reading shows us one transcendent God, almighty, existing before the world he created, a world over which he alone exercises final control. The narrative is calculated to arouse in the reader an optimistic outlook on the world in which each element serves a divine purpose. God saw that what he did each day was good. Each day brought new goodness. The climax of God's creative activity was (and is) humanity, men and women who were like God, whose similarity to God included their dominion over all creation. At the same time, these human creatures were dependent on and were meant to be subject to God.

Here, then, is the stage and here are the actors on which the drama of salvation would be played out. In a good world in which God himself took satisfaction, the creature in charge was given directions. The way in which those directions were carried out, or were disregarded, would constitute the history of the world that God had created. Here was the beginning of it all.

The ultimate conclusion of what God did "in the beginning" was the new creation brought into being by the faithfulness of Christ and inaugurated by his Resurrection, the event that constitutes the focal point and the goal of the Easter Vigil.

FOR REFLECTION AND DISCUSSION

How and where do I experience the goodness of creation?
How do I exercise dominion over creation?

Easter Vigil, Second Reading

Genesis 22:1–18

The story of the testing of Abraham has already been heard in an abridged form as part of the Lenten survey of the history of salvation on the second Sunday of Lent in year B. The reading we hear during the Easter Vigil is the full, uncut version. Its length reminds us that the Vigil is supposed to be an extended communal reflection on the care of God for his people. Every detail is included for our instruction. (It is true, of course, that the lectionary offers a shorter form of this reading for the Vigil, but the clear intent of the liturgical action is to favor extension rather than short cuts.)

After years of faithful waiting, Abraham at last has a son, Isaac. It was now clear that God's promises of progeny were being fulfilled. Through Isaac, Abraham would indeed be the father of many nations.

Now comes a new command from the Lord, a chilling directive that seemed to undermine everything that Abraham had been promised. "Sacrifice your son, your uniquely precious one, on a mountain that I will show you."

The story unfolds with careful detail: how many servants went along, what Abraham carried with them, how long it took to get to where God wanted them to be. Now Abraham and Isaac separate themselves from the servants, who apparently have no idea what is going to take place on the mountaintop. Neither does Isaac. We can almost hear the childish tenor of his voice as he asks his father about the victim for the sacrifice.

When they have arrived at the appointed place, Abraham prepares to carry out the sacrifice. Suddenly there is a voice from heaven that commands him to stop and that expresses God's blessing for Abraham's faithfulness. The promise of progeny is repeated, to be fulfilled through this same uniquely dear son that Abraham was willing to sacrifice at God's behest. A ram serves as a victim in Isaac's place.

Human sacrifice was not unheard of in the culture in which Abraham lived. In fact, it continued to be practiced for centuries after this time. The original point of this narrative seems to have been to teach the people that such a practice was not in accord with God's will.

But there is a deeper meaning in the story as well. It is intended to show once more the firmness of Abraham's faith in God's promises. The important part of the promises was not the means through which they were to be fulfilled—the uniquely precious Isaac—but God's will to bless Abraham. This is not a story that is primarily concerned with Abraham and his son. It is primarily concerned with Abraham and God. It is a story about faithfulness: the faithfulness of Abraham and the faithfulness of God.

Even when God's will seems totally incomprehensible, even when it seems to contradict what God has already provided and seems totally incompatible with the future that God had guaranteed, God's will is still to be obeyed.

The story of Abraham's sacrifice is the climax of the whole story of Abraham, our father in faith. It is the great moment of test, a test not imposed so that God could learn about Abraham's faithfulness, but so that Abraham could learn still again that God's promises were irrevocable.

But there is still another dimension of this story that arises out of the Easter Vigil context. Again from this perspective, the issue is faithfulness, a many-sided faithfulness. Jesus' faithfulness to his father brought him to suffering and death. And just as Abraham was willing to sacrifice his beloved only son out of faithfulness to God, so also God himself was willing to permit the sacrifice of his only Son Jesus resulting from Jesus' faithfulness to the Father's plan for our salvation. But it was a faithfulness that also brought about the Resurrection. Just as Isaac was delivered from dying, so Jesus was delivered from death. God's promise of salvation moved toward fulfillment in spite of the most definitive and irreversible of human realities, the reality of death.

As Jesus' disciples returned to Jerusalem after Jesus had died, they must surely have shared the emotions that Abraham experienced as he led his son up the mountain: everything seemed undone, all that he had hoped for was ruined; there was no way that what had been promised could come to pass; it was all over. But the followers of Jesus, like Abraham, discovered in due time that what they thought was the end was only the beginning.

FOR REFLECTION AND DISCUSSION

What sacrifices has God asked of me?
In what ways have I trusted in God?

Easter Vigil, Third Reading

Exodus 14:15 – 15:1

The Easter Vigil is intended to be a lengthy event, a whole night's reflection on being saved. That's why the lectionary gives us so many readings. Yet the liturgy does allow us some leeway. While we are encouraged to read all seven of the Old Testament readings, we are permitted to reduce the number to three if circumstances warrant that abridgement. However, under no circumstances whatsoever is this reading from Exodus to be omitted or shortened. It is the most important of the designated Old Testament readings.

The importance of this reading over all the others is that it deals most directly with the main themes that the church celebrates in the Easter Vigil. First of all, it deals with the rescue of the children of Israel from the power of their Egyptian oppressors. This is the central event of the Passover experience, the event that Jews would celebrate forever as a basic, constitutive element of their national consciousness. But the passage through the Red Sea also symbolizes the exodus of Jesus from death into a new life of Resurrection. Finally, the Israelites' passage through water also images the passage through water that is the sacrament of baptism, the constitutive event of our Christian existence. These verses from Exodus deal with all this in one way or another. They are the salvation narrative *par excellence.*

The narrative can be divided into seven sections or paragraphs. (As we go through the reading, we should note the recurrent phrase, "chariots and charioteers." It occurs five times in our passage, and serves as a kind of recurrent drumbeat to remind us that God was matched here against the mightiest war machine of the age.)

The first section of the narrative, verses 15 to 18, shows us the Israelites' state of mind. They are panic-stricken, but God reassures them by means of his instructions to Moses, by reassuring him and the people that he was going to teach the Egyptians a lesson.

Next we see the preparations for what was to happen. The cloud of fire that had been leading the Israelites now goes behind them and turns dark to hide them from the Egyptians.

Then Moses carries out God's instructions. The sea divides, a dry path is formed and the Israelites "marched into the midst of the sea on dry land."

The Egyptians follow, but the Lord threw them into a panic and they turned back in retreat.

In response to the Lord's command, Moses now reverses

what had been done before. The sea that had opened at Moses' behest now closed over the Egyptians and, in spite of their efforts to get away, "[n]ot a single one of them escaped."

Now comes a summary, or epilogue, which recaps what had happened and describes how the Israelites reacted to it. So "[the people] feared the LORD and believed in him and in his servant Moses."

Last of all, our reading leads into what scholars call "The Song of the Sea," or "The Song of Moses," a poetic celebration of what the Israelites had experienced. (Some scholars consider this canticle to be the oldest written text in the Bible.) It celebrates God as a warrior chieftain coming in battle to the rescue of his people.

In this reading, God is revealed as lord and savior, protecting and freeing his people from oppression through a miraculous intervention that surpasses all human hope and capability. It was an intervention that was essential for the establishment and continued existence of God's people.

But God's action at the Red Sea is not just something that concerned the Israelites. It also symbolizes the Father's rescue of Jesus from the waters of death. Even as the Israelites marched through the sea on dry land, so also Jesus came through the waters of death into a new kind of life, a life that still continues.

And each of us has experienced the same thing in baptism. Even as baptism symbolizes and brings about our sharing in the death and resurrection of Jesus, so also baptism associates us with the saving of God's first chosen people by means of their passage through water.

These are the basic acts of salvation that make us who and what we are. But there are still other saving acts of God. God preserves each of us from harm each day because each of us is precious to him. Threatened though we may be by devastating chariots and charioteers, God still brings us through the waters around us safe and dry shod.

FOR REFLECTION AND DISCUSSION

How have I been rescued by God?

What difference has baptism made in my life?

Easter Vigil, Fourth Reading

Isaiah 54:5–14

In the first three readings of the Easter Vigil we hear about God's actions: the creation of a good and well-ordered world, God's faithful care for Abraham and his future, God's liberation of his people from slavery in Egypt. These three readings are from the first two books of the Old Testament.

The next four readings are from the prophetic books of the Old Testament. In them we hear God speaking to his people. Through the agency of his spokesmen over the centuries, God addresses his people about forgiveness, generosity, wisdom and purification.

All seven of these readings are intended to foster awareness of and gratitude for the salvation that God has offered to us. These Old Testament readings are followed by the reading from the Letter to the Romans in which Saint Paul speaks of baptism and life in Christ. Last of all comes the Gospel account of the Resurrection of Jesus.

This fourth Old Testament reading is from chapter fifty-four of Isaiah, the second last chapter of the second section of Isaiah, which runs from chapters 40 to 55. These chapters were written by one or more followers of the spiritual school of Isaiah of Jerusalem to bring consolation to the Israelites in the midst of their Babylonian exile.

Here God is offering forgiveness to his people. The text uses three images to express what God wants to say.

First of all, the people of Israel are looked upon as God's spouse, an image that is also used in the prophecies of Hosea and Jeremiah. Israel was a wife who had been forsaken by her husband, cast off, presumably for unfaithfulness. Now the Lord calls her back. He had been angry and turned away from her, but now he takes pity on her "with great tenderness,... / with enduring love."

Next God likens the present situation to the days of Noah, when the waters receded and God promised never again to punish humankind with flood. Even so God now swears that he will no longer be angry with his people. He will have mercy on them. "[M]y love shall never leave you."

Finally God compares the people of Israel with its holy city, Jerusalem. It is a battered city now, but God will restore it. From top to bottom God will adorn it with precious stones. No part of the city will remain without embellishment. And the people who live within it will receive guidance and direction from the Lord. It will be a city of peace and justice, forever freed from oppression, incapable of being destroyed.

What we have here is a love song in the context of sorrow and separation. The people had turned away from God over the years. They had incurred punishment for their sins, the punishment of exile that seemed to be tantamount to the dissolution of the nation. But now God speaks of his love for them. In spite of their sinfulness, in spite of their unfaithfulness, in spite of what seemed like the destruction of their world, in spite of the demolition of their holy city which they had brought on themselves, in spite of all that, God loves them still. God promises to take them back into his love and care, to clothe their city in precious stones, to defend them from any further danger. He will once more be their lover as well as their Lord.

There is no question here of the suffering of the innocent. The Israelites deserved everything that had happened to them. They had been grossly unfaithful. They had rejected God's prophets. They had turned away from the Lord. But now God assures them that he loves them in spite of all that they had done.

Loving somebody in spite of what they have done is what it means to forgive, and that is precisely what God is doing here. When someone has injured me and asks for my forgiveness, I am not being asked to make believe that no wrong was done. I cannot pretend that there was no hurt, no damage, no pain. No, I have to acknowledge all that. It's real. But at the same time, I must love the person who inflicted the harm on me. I have to acknowledge that there is good in that person that remains in spite of the injury that the person did to me. I must want to find ways to do good to that person. I must forgive. Forgiveness means "loving in spite of."

And that's what God does for the Israelites in this reading. In spite of their faithlessness God offers them love and care and protection. And that's what God does for us, too, in the salvation he confers on us through the risen Jesus.

FOR REFLECTION AND DISCUSSION

How has God shown his love for me?

For what have I been forgiven by the Lord?

Easter Vigil, Fifth Reading

Isaiah 55:1–11

The Vigil's long series of extended readings about salvation continues with another reading from the second part of the book of the prophet Isaiah. Attentive Mass-goers will recognize this reading because it is used so often during the course of the liturgical cycle. But each time it occurs, it has a slightly different tonality. These different tonalities are the result of the interplay between this extraordinarily rich Old Testament text and the New Testament context that it illustrates.

On the feast of the Baptism of the Lord in year B, for example, our text serves as a descriptive preview of the public ministry of Jesus. The early verses of the reading, which describe God's banquet, are used to lead into Mark's narrative of the feeding of the five thousand on the Eighteenth Sunday in Ordinary Time in year A. Just a few weeks earlier, on the Fifteenth Sunday, the last verses of this reading highlight the vitality of God's word which is the subject of that Sunday's Gospel parable of the sower and the seed.

Here, in the Easter Vigil, the reading occurs in a context of salvation: how God has prepared salvation for his people, what salvation means, what salvation involves. In this context the motif that seems to surface most clearly from our reading is the motif of generosity.

In the first two verses the text speaks about generosity and life. God will provide water for the life of his people, and grain and wine and milk. Whatever they need for their nourishment will be given to them, given without cost, given in abundance. God calls them not just to survival, but to a feast.

The next three verses are about God's covenant. God will

restore the agreement he made with David, but it won't be just between God and David's people any longer. It will be wider and deeper than that, freely extended to every people of every nation. In his generosity, God spreads his arms wide to include everyone.

Then comes generosity in forgiveness. God doesn't deny the sinfulness of his people. Nor does God pretend that their sins are not grievous. It is all real, but so is God's forgiveness. God presents himself to this nation of exiles arrayed in mercy, generous in forgiving. God assures the people that his will to forgive is far beyond what they can even imagine.

Last of all, God speaks of energy and growth. Just as surely as rain and snow have their effect on the earth, "making it fertile and fruitful," so God's word brings about the effect for which God sends it forth. It cannot be void or fruitless. It will necessarily bring about what it promises simply because it is God's word, a word of power, a word of generosity.

This reading teaches us that God doesn't do things in a half-hearted way. If God gives nourishment, it is in the festal proportions of a banquet. If God offers a covenant, it is to everybody without exception. If God offers forgiveness, it is to an extent and in a degree that is beyond human comprehension. What God's word promises is what God's word delivers as surely as the rain makes things grow. And it's all free. You don't have to deserve it and you can't buy it. Always and in every way, God is generous.

This dimension of generosity that is characteristic of God's relationship with the Israelites in the Old Testament is also a prefigurement of the salvation that Christ brings to us.

First of all, salvation in the Lord Jesus is free. There is no way we can deserve it or earn it or pay for it. It comes to us as grace, as a freely given gift.

Salvation involves being nourished by God, not just getting enough to survive on, but being fed with the Body and Blood of the Lord himself. Who could ever have expected that?

Salvation also involves participation in a community that includes all the world and all the ages. There is no cultural or ethnic limit to the inclusivity of God's care for us.

Salvation includes forgiveness, the gift of God's love in spite of any evil that we may have done. When God says that our ways are not his ways, he is not talking about his majesty and might but about his mercy.

Then there is life and growth. Ongoing life, unerring growth, more abundant than we have any right to expect, more fruitful than we can imagine.

God is generous. The salvation that we celebrate in the Easter Vigil comes to us not in teaspoons but in buckets.

FOR REFLECTION AND DISCUSSION

How have I experienced the generosity of God?

How is generosity part of my response to God's generosity to me?

Easter Vigil, Sixth Reading

Baruch 3:9–15, 32— 4:4

The book of Baruch is used only twice in the three year Sunday cycle, once here in the Easter Vigil and once on the second Sunday of Advent in year C. The historical author of this book is not known, but it is attributed to Jeremiah's secretary, Baruch. The book seems to be addressed to Jews living outside their homeland. Living outside the holy land was something that would have been familiar to the historical Baruch who lived at the time the Babylonian exile began in 587 B.C. The book that we have, however, seems to have been written about 150 B.C. in order to encourage Jews living in the diaspora (i.e., outside of Palestine) to remain faithful to their Jewish religion and culture at a time when hellenistic Greek culture was threatening their ethnic identity.

The reading from Baruch that the church gives us for the Easter Vigil consists of the beginning and the end of a hymn of praise in honor of wisdom. In general, the Jews looked on wisdom as obedience to God's will, as knowing how to make sense of one's life and live in a way that was pleasing to God. More specifically, the Jews looked on the Mosaic law that God had given them as the essence and incarnation of wisdom.

Our reading is in three parts. First of all, the author reminds his readers of their situation. They are living amid Gentiles, in foreign lands in which they can easily incur religious defilement, in a situation in which it is easy for them to forget about God and God's gift of wisdom. The author calls on them to search for wisdom so that they will be able to find meaning and direction for their lives.

In the verses of the original text that are omitted from our reading, the author insists that it is only in God that wisdom can be found: not among mighty rulers of old, not among the experienced and educated who have traveled the world, not among the primeval giants that walked the world at the beginning of creation.

Now we return to our lectionary text. It is only in the creator that wisdom is at home. God associated wisdom with his creative powers in producing the world and what dwells in it, in calling forth the stars with their brilliance that give glory to God.

It is this wisdom, God's own intimate knowledge, the expression of God's own life, that God has given to his people.

God offers wisdom in the form of the Mosaic law to all those who will accept it. It is the source of life and splendor. It constitutes the glory of God's people. The reading concludes with an exclamation: "Blessed are we, O Israel; / for what pleases God is known to us."

Like all the other readings of the Vigil, this one has to do with salvation. It gives us still another perspective in which to understand what it is we are celebrating as Easter approaches.

Just as salvation is rooted in the goodness of creation, just as it involves God's faithfulness and deliverance and forgiveness and generosity, so also salvation involves wisdom. Salvation involves God extending his heart and his mind to us—his wisdom, in the person of his Son Jesus.

In the final analysis, Jesus is the wisdom of God that Baruch speaks about. As Saint Paul would tell the Romans a century or so after the composition of the book of Baruch, "Christ is the end [the purpose] of the law so that there may be righteousness for everyone who believes" (Romans 10:4, NRSV). Jesus embodies and offers to us everything that the law was meant to bring, everything that was included in the concept of wisdom.

In the last section of this Old Testament reading, the author says, "[A]ll who cling to her [to wisdom] will live, / but those will die who forsake her." Immediately after that, in the responsorial psalm, we sing out together, "Lord, you have the words of everlasting life." This response is directed primarily to what God's word has told us in the reading. Wisdom brings life and God offers us wisdom. But we Christians recognize this response refrain as coming from the Gospel according to John (6:68) and as referring to Jesus. Jesus is the life that God had promised to his people. Jesus is the wisdom that gives meaning and direction and worth to the community of those who believe in him.

This reading teaches us that wisdom is the innermost heart of God. It teaches us that only God can provide his people with wisdom. In the context of the Vigil, it also teaches us that Jesus is the wisdom of God and that worth and salvation can only be ours to the extent that we accept the wisdom that is Christ Jesus.

FOR REFLECTION AND DISCUSSION

How/where do I experience the wisdom of the Lord?

How/where do I find wisdom in creation?

Easter Vigil, Seventh Reading

Ezekiel 36:16–17a, 18–28

Ezekiel was deported from Jerusalem to Babylon in 597 B.C. This was what one might call a preliminary deportation of some prominent citizens as part of a peace settlement between the Israelites and the Babylonians. It was not the final settlement, however. The Israelites soon rebelled against their Babylonian masters and the result was the total destruction of Jerusalem and the deportation of almost everybody of any significance whatsoever in 587 B.C.

Ezekiel's prophetic career began soon after he arrived in Babylon, before Jerusalem had fallen. For the first years of his ministry, his preaching consisted mostly in reproaches addressed to his fellow exiles, reminders of the sinfulness that had brought them to where they were. God also instructed Ezekiel to prepare the people for the worst, for the final destruction of Jerusalem which the exiles were convinced could never come to pass. After

the devastation did come to pass, Ezekiel's prophetic task
changed. Now he was to speak to the people about salvation,
about how God would care for them and eventually bring them
home again. This last Old Testament reading in the Easter Vigil is
from the later part of Ezekiel's ministry. It is a promise of renewal
and restoration.

Our reading is in three parts. The first section begins by
reminding the Israelites of their previous sinfulness before they
had been carried off into Babylon. It was their sins that elicited
God's anger and that led God to disperse them in exile. But even
in exile they did not bring honor to God. The Gentiles among
whom they lived looked on them with dismay. "These are the
people of the LORD, yet they had to leave their land."

So now, in the second part of our reading, God promises to
bring blessing on the Israelites, in spite of their sinfulness, in spite
of the disgrace that they have brought on their Lord. It is not for
their sakes that God does this, but for the sake of God's own
name, to vindicate himself and his glory in spite of the
worthlessness of his people. By his generosity God would assert
the holiness of his name even though his own people had
profaned it in the midst of the Gentiles. This is an initiative of
God's goodness, not something the people have come to deserve.

In the last section of the reading God reveals to the people
what he plans to do for them. God will bring them home again.
He will sprinkle clean water on them to purify them of the
uncleanness they have contracted. He will give them a new heart
and a new spirit to replace the sinfulness that had brought them
to disaster. They will live a new kind of life, a life of careful
observance of God's will. God will restore them to the land of
their fathers. God will embrace them once more as his own.
"[Y]ou shall be my people, and I will be your God."

The ultimate fulfillment of these promises of God's comes to us in the sacrament of baptism. Before our baptism each of us was a foreigner to God, eking out a difficult existence in a land far removed from what God had provided for our first parents, mired in sinfulness and self-seeking. We were in exile. Then God washes us with the water of his love. Our sinfulness is taken away. We begin to live in a whole new way, at a whole new level. We begin an existence that consists in our taking part in the life of God. It's what God had in mind for all of us from the beginning. God brings us home. We are no longer strangers and exiles, but members of God's family. "[Y]ou shall be my people, and I will be your God."

The Easter Vigil is a kind of annual homecoming celebration for the Christian community. At the heart of it is the baptism of new members of the community, women and men who now become part of God's household. But the Vigil also serves as a homecoming for those who have already been part of God's family.

Through the extended readings from God's word we recall the basics of our family history, a history that begins with God's joyous act of creation and which unfolds over thousands of years. This family history of ours involves God's faithfulness. It involves deliverance. It involves God's forgiveness and generosity and wisdom. It involves God bringing us home at last to where we belong. Most important of all, as our family history moves into the New Testament, we recall that it involves the risen Christ and our participation in his eternal glory.

During the long hours of this gathering of the Christian family, we remember who and what we have been. We remember who we are. We remember what God intends us to be forever.

How has the history of salvation unfolded in my life?

How does the history of salvation continue to unfold among God's people?

Easter Sunday (ABC)

Acts of the Apostles 10:34a, 37–43

This Sunday's First Reading is pivotal. From several different perspectives it expresses a turning point, a turning point in God's relationship with his chosen people, a turning point in the meaning of salvation and liberation, a turning point in setting the mood of the Sunday liturgical celebration.

The reading is from the Acts of the Apostles, that book of the New Testament that teaches us what happened after the Resurrection: how Jesus' risen life was expressed and shared with his earliest disciples, and then how it was carried throughout the whole world. We will be hearing from Acts for the whole season of Easter because, one way or another, every word of it is somehow connected with the resurrection of Jesus. Today and in the weeks ahead, Acts replaces the Old Testament in establishing the atmosphere in which the Sunday liturgy is to be celebrated.

The reading for Easter Sunday (which the church presents to us each year in the three-year cycle) is itself pivotal in the structure of the book. Up to this point, the story of the community of believers has been concerned with proclaiming the news of Jesus' resurrection only to the Jews, at first in Jerusalem, then in Judea and Samaria. But now a change occurs, a monumental swerve that would make the whole church different. Peter has seen a vision in which he is told to eat ritually unclean food and accept the hospitality of the Gentile Cornelius. This was new. Jews didn't eat food like that and didn't associate with the Gentiles. Peter knows that something different is going on. When he gets to the house of Cornelius, he learns that God had directed Cornelius to send for Peter and to listen to what he had to say. Peter now realizes that God wants to include everybody in the people called by Christ, and so begins to tell Cornelius and his household about Jesus. That discourse is what constitutes our reading.

The public proclamation of Jesus' messiahship, Peter says, took place in the context of his baptism by John. Jesus carried forward the messianic program by healing the sick and freeing the possessed. The apostles witnessed all this themselves. But then his enemies put him to death like a criminal. (Deuteronomy 21:22 prescribes that executed criminals should be "hung upon a tree" as a warning to others.) But then God brought Jesus back from the dead. He was seen by chosen witnesses who ate and drank with him. They understood that the risen Jesus was Lord of everything, living and dead. Jesus commissioned them to testify to his lordship. It was now clear also that the prophets had in advance been testifying to him, too, and that *everybody* could receive forgiveness for their sins through belief in him.

This discourse constitutes the beginning of the evangelization of the Gentiles. The rest of Acts will be concerned with carrying forward that evangelization.

There are three lessons of importance here. The first is that Jesus is the anointed one of God whose earthly ministry of healing and salvation was certified and validated by his resurrection from the dead. Jesus' Resurrection was not just something nice that happened to him, but a turning point in the story of salvation. It identified him as the one anointed Messiah of God.

Second, there were witnesses—witnesses to his life and to his return from the dead, witnesses empowered to testify to his ongoing messianic mission. The prophets of the Old Testament, in looking forward to the Messiah, were witnesses to Jesus, too. All these witnesses continue to testify today.

Third, the saving power of Jesus that is attested to by his Resurrection and by the testimony of his witnesses is not addressed to Jews alone, but is meant for "everyone who believes in him." Cornelius and his household, to whom Peter had been sent, represent the whole wide world, called to share the life of the risen Christ.

All of this is what we celebrate on Easter. All of this is what the Acts of the Apostles will continue to teach us during the Sundays of the Easter season. In this reading for Easter day we hear it all, as delivered by Peter in the house of Gentiles under the direction of the Holy Spirit.

It's important that there be witnesses, people to tell about Jesus and the meaning of his life and death and resurrection. If there had been no Peter to testify to what he had experienced, the good news of salvation might never have gotten to Cornelius.

All of us who are believers have had some contact with the risen Lord. And so all of us are also called to be witnesses to him.

FOR REFLECTION AND DISCUSSION

Who has served as a witness to the risen Christ for me?

How do I give witness to Jesus? How could I give better witness?

Second Sunday of Easter (A)

Acts of the Apostles 2:42–47

During the Sundays after Easter, our First Readings come from the Acts of the Apostles, the sequel to the Gospel according to Luke. This is the only time in the church's year when we do not have an Old Testament reading on Sunday.

These selections from Acts are a kind of extension of the survey of salvation history in the Old Testament that we read during Lent. During Lent we heard about God's original plan for salvation, how he worked through Abraham and Moses and others, how he brought his people to the Promised Land, how he promised them protection and fulfillment in times to come. Then we have the pivotal event of Easter, when Old Testament salvation history reaches its completion and a new history of a new people begins. "What happened then?" That's the question that Acts answers.

The selections from Acts form a series on their own, distinct from the Second Readings and Gospel readings. They are not strictly chronological. That is, these readings do not always give us events in the order in which they happened or are presented in Acts, nor do they cover the whole of Acts. They are all from the first half, in fact.

This series of readings seems to have been put together to provide the faithful of today with an idea of what went on in the early church, how things began to unfold after Jesus' Resurrection and Ascension. Each Sunday of the three-year cycle has its particular theme. On the second Sundays of Easter of years A, B and C we get a little overview, a summary of the state of affairs in the Jerusalem church. On the third and fourth Sundays we have sermons by the apostles or other spokesmen for the church. (About one-third of Acts consists of speeches or sermons.) For the fifth Sundays, the theme is the Christians' call to service and for the sixth Sundays it is the growth of the church.

This second Sunday of Easter in year A offers us one of the summary passages. It acts as a wrap-up of Luke's Pentecost narrative. This passage describes the atmosphere in the church after the Spirit had come and Peter had delivered the first public Christian evangelization.

Luke lists four central characteristics of the early Christian believers in the first verse of our reading, and expands upon them in the verses that follow.

First of all, they listened attentively to the teaching of the apostles. The apostles had known Jesus, and hearing what the apostles had to say about Jesus brought the early believers into touch with him. Like Jesus, the apostles did "many wonders and signs" that served to carry forward the mission of Jesus.

Second, they devoted themselves to the common life. They spent time together and took joy in their community. Luke tells us that they had all things in common and helped community members out as needs arose. This could mean that everybody gave over to the community everything that he or she possessed and depended fully on the community for sustenance. It is more likely, however, that people maintained ownership of resources, but made them available to care for particular needs.

They were also devoted to "the breaking of bread." Scholars wonder whether this is a deliberate and clear reference to the Eucharist, but it certainly refers to something more than an ordinary meal. It was a gathering that was characterized by "exultation and sincerity of heart," attitudes appropriate for dining with the Lord.

Finally, there was prayer. These early Christians met for prayer every day in the temple. There was as yet no separation between Jews and Christians, and the Christians seemed simply to have united themselves with the daily public prayers of the temple.

"And every day the Lord added to their number those who were being saved." This seems to be an allusion to baptism, the fundamental encounter with Christ that is not otherwise mentioned in this passage.

Apostolic leadership, care for one another, sharing in the supper of the Lord, praying: these were the elements that characterized the church at its earliest times. It was a time of joy and generosity and glad contact with the Lord. It was a time of fervor.

That primitive Christian community is the same church of which we are members. Over the centuries we have taken on lots of extra baggage. We express our contact with the Lord in somewhat different ways. But we are still dependent on the apostles, still reaching out to one another, still "breaking bread," still a people of prayer—and still joyful and still eager to praise the Lord.

FOR REFLECTION AND DISCUSSION

How do I express my participation in the life of the church?
Where do we express care for one another in our parish?

Second Sunday of Easter (B)

Acts of the Apostles 4:32–35

The First Readings' overview of salvation history that began with the first Sunday of Lent continues in these Sundays of Eastertime, but with a difference. The First Readings in Lent were from the Old Testament and dealt with God's relationship with humanity before the coming of Christ. In Eastertime, the readings are from the New Testament and deal with the Christian covenant, the relationship with God instituted by Christ that would last for the rest of human history and persist into eternity.

However, the readings for these Easter weeks do not provide a full history of the people of the new covenant. They only deal with its beginnings. They are selections from the first half of the Acts of the Apostles. There is quite a bit more about Christian salvation history contained in Acts that the liturgical readings do not present to us. For that matter, there are many other aspects of the Spirit's work in the early church in the other books of the New Testament that are not set forth in this Easter series of First Readings. It's not, therefore, the whole history of the young church that the lectionary intends to give us during these weeks, but only the initial trajectory, a taste of how things were at the beginning.

Each year, the second Sunday of Easter gives us an overview of the young church. The next two Sundays provide samples of apostolic preaching. The fifth Sundays deal with the call to Christian service, while the sixth describe the growth of the church. The seventh Sunday of Eastertime (where the Ascension is celebrated on Thursday) deals in various ways with the sending of the Spirit.

This Sunday's reading from Acts is one of the three summary passages that Acts gives us. (The other two are Acts 2:42–47 and 5:12–16.) These passages describe the chief characteristics of the Jerusalem community. They are initial progress reports on the life of the early church.

Our reading from chapter four is about unity. The Greek of

the first sentence stresses "one": "The community of believers was of *one* heart and mind…" (emphasis added). The text goes on to describe two elements of this unity.

One was the community of possessions. It does not seem to be the case that all private ownership was renounced in the early church, but that individual possessiveness was seen as incompatible with Christian faith. The needs of the brothers and sisters were more important than personal resources.

The other element of unity that our passage highlights is the central authority of the apostles. Peter and John have just defended their faith in the presence of the Sanhedrin. Now we see them bearing witness through miracles ("[w]ith great power") in the midst of the community. The material gifts brought to the community were placed at their feet, a gesture that acknowledged their power and authority. The apostles were in charge. They oversaw the oneness of the community.

The church community of today is still one. The pope and the bishops extend the ministry of the apostles. Their teaching and their leadership hold the community together.

But the generosity of the faithful contributes to the unity of the church, too. The continued care of one believer for another, the willingness, indeed, the necessity that people experience to be of service to those members of the community who are in need are manifestations of the same Spirit of Christ that enlivened the infant church in Jerusalem.

One of the most encouraging factors of Catholic Church life in our time is the growth of stewardship. Catholics continue to learn that support of the church is not just a matter of paying the bills. It is a matter of sharing ourselves, our time, our talent, our economic resources with others because we are called to be Christ for one another. In the practice of stewardship, Christ looks after Christ. It is the one Lord who inspires and directs the giver and the same Lord who is acknowledged in the needs of the receiver. Stewardship is an acknowledgment of the oneness of the risen Lord and of the oneness of the Lord's community of faith.

Apostolic faith and consistent sharing: Today God's word teaches us that these are what makes the church one.

FOR REFLECTION AND DISCUSSION

How do I experience the unity of the church?
What threats to the unity of the church am I aware of?

Second Sunday of Easter (C)

Acts of the Apostles 5:12–16

Salvation history and the story of Jesus' ministry did not end with the Resurrection of Jesus. In fact, their final phase only begins with the Resurrection. In the weeks that follow Easter, the First Readings for Sunday recount the early years of that final phase. They recount the beginnings of the church.

These weeks are the only time in the Sunday liturgical calendar in which there is no reading from the Old Testament. Instead, the lectionary follows an ancient Christian liturgical practice and gives us a series of readings from the Acts of the Apostles. Each year we get a semi-continuous series of readings from Acts that offers a description of the young church in capsule form. The passages are chosen not to teach about every aspect of the church's beginnings, but to express themes and incidents that are consonant with the joyful Easter season.

The passage that we have for this second Sunday of Easter in year C is a summary passage that gives us a thumbnail sketch of how things were in the Jerusalem church during those earliest times of the apostles' ministry.

The apostles were accustomed to gather in the part of the Jerusalem temple known as Solomon's Portico. They were well known for bringing about cures and other wonders. Most people seem to have been afraid to come too close to the apostles, either because of the divine power that they perceived in them, or because they were afraid of getting involved in the tensions that were already growing between the apostles and the Jewish religious authorities. Yet the people esteemed the apostles and became believers in great numbers: "Yet more than ever, believers in the Lord, / great numbers of men and women, were added to them."

The people's faith in the apostles' power was so great that they were eager to have their sick touched even by Peter's shadow. Word about the cures had spread to the towns outside Jerusalem, and country folk in large numbers came into town to have their sick cured of ills of body, mind and spirit.

Here we have a vignette of the church as it was in its earliest days: the apostles gathered as one in the context of the Jewish temple; wonders of healing; continuous and impressive increase of membership. That's how it was in the beginning. Some of this changed rather quickly. Some of it has persisted to our own times and will persist as long as the church is church.

One thing that would soon change, or at least be clarified, would be the church's relationship to Judaism. One of the most fundamental questions the early church's leaders had to face was whether a person had to become Jewish in order to be a follower of Christ. In last week's pivotal reading (which comes later in Acts than this Sunday's reading) we saw how Peter was led to welcome Gentiles into the church on non-Jewish conditions. Much of the rest of Acts will concern itself with the implications of extending the salvation of Christ to the Gentiles. It would not be long before peaceable gatherings of the apostles in Solomon's Portico would become unthinkable.

As regards miraculous healing, we still have that in the church. Christian religious shrines all over the world are decorated with the crutches and braces of those who have been healed there. But much more frequent are the healing of mind and soul that take place in the church's sacraments: strengthening of the spirit in the Eucharist, deliverance from sin in the sacrament of reconciliation, spiritual (and sometimes physical) energy and comfort conferred in the sacrament of the anointing of the sick. Christian salvation history continues to proclaim concern for the weak, the injured, the vulnerable. It no longer takes place through the shadow of an apostle, but through the sacramental words and actions of the ordained ministers of the Lord—and elsewhere also.

Finally there is the reality of ever-increasing vigor of Christ's life in the church. Every diocese celebrates the Rite of Election each year, a gathering in which those who have not been baptized are elected for reception into the Catholic Christian community at Easter. It's generally a crowded ceremony. This Sunday's reading from Acts offers us an important insight into becoming a member of the church. Our text does not say that great numbers of people decided to associate themselves with the apostles, nor that the apostles persuaded many to come in. It says that "great numbers . . . were added." Scholars tell us that "were added" is a theological passive, that is, it refers to God's action. It is God who brings people into the community. That's how it was then, and that's how it is now.

In what ways have I found healing in the church?
What leads people to seek membership in the church?

Third Sunday of Easter (A)

Acts of the Apostles 2:14, 22–23

There are six discourses in Acts that deal with the Resurrection of Jesus and its messianic significance. Five of them are attributed to Peter and one to Paul. Excerpts from five of these discourses constitute the First Readings for the third and fourth Sundays of Easter throughout the three-year cycle. We have already heard from the remaining one—Peter's speech to Cornelius and his family—on Easter itself.

This Sunday's reading is the central portion of Peter's discourse on Pentecost, the first public proclamation of the meaning of the Resurrection and therefore the inaugural proclamation of the church. (We will hear the ending of this speech next Sunday, together with the reaction of those who heard Peter.)

Peter's point in the verses that we hear is that the Resurrection of Jesus is the identifying sign of his messiahship. Through a complex kind of rabbinic argumentation Peter relates the messianic prophecies to the life of Jesus. He demonstrates that Jesus is the successor promised to David, the Lord who is established at the right hand of God, the channel through which the Holy Spirit of God would be sent into the world.

In order to grasp the force of Peter's argumentation, we need to be aware of certain presuppositions that would have been taken for granted by those that Peter addressed: 1) that David was the author of all the psalms; 2) that David was somehow God's "anointed"; 3) that God had promised to David an unending dynasty through his descendants; 4) that what is spoken of in the psalms refer either to their author (David) or to his descendant, the Messiah.

Our passage begins with a verse of introduction that shows us Peter as the spokesman for all the apostles addressing the full Jerusalem public. Now comes the speech itself. Peter first outlines the public career of Jesus. Jesus worked miracles as everybody knows. But then he was killed by the populace who used the agency of the Romans for this purpose. God allowed this to happen because it was part of the divine plan. But now Jesus has risen from the dead because God wanted him to be alive forever.

Next comes the scriptural argumentation that would demonstrate the meaning of the Resurrection. Peter quotes from Psalm 16. Here the author (David) speaks of seeing the Lord always, of dwelling in hope, of being liberated from decay and corruption, of having been shown the paths of life. But, says Peter, this can't refer to David himself since everybody knows that David died. He was not liberated from corruption. All Peter's hearers would have been acquainted with David's tomb! Therefore, in view of the fact that God had promised David a messianic successor whom he (David) would have been able to foresee thanks to his prophetic gifts, it must be that David is referring to this successor as the one who would not see corruption. Jesus did not see corruption (having risen from the dead). "We ourselves have seen the risen Christ," Peter says. Consequently, Jesus must be the Messiah that David looked forward to. In brief, Peter's argument is that the Messiah has come, and it is Jesus. Jesus' messianic identity is demonstrated by his Resurrection, as was foreseen in David's prophetic psalm. This risen Jesus has been reunited to the Father and will serve as the channel to bring the Holy Spirit to all those who are willing to receive the Spirit.

Most twenty-first century Americans probably find Peter's approach to be rather complicated. His use of Scripture seems strange. We certainly don't accept the presuppositions about the psalms that Peter and his audience shared. But the central idea of his message is still valid: Jesus is the promised Savior of humankind and his Resurrection serves not only to demonstrate his divinity, but also to provide an avenue for continued contact between humanity and God, between sinners and the Spirit. The Messiah promised to David, the anointed king who would reign forever, is the risen Christ that we know and love.

God's plans are not short-term. They are not short-term in their coming to be. God's plans for our salvation stretch back all the way to Adam and Eve. They reach out through Abraham and Moses and David to the life and ministry and death of Jesus. God's plans are not short-term in their fulfillment, either. The death and Resurrection of Jesus open the way to the final fulfillment of the world. God's plans are not yet fully implemented, but when they are, we will see that they involve proclamation and prophecy and resurrection and the coming of the Spirit, the very things that Peter spoke about in that inaugural address on the first Pentecost.

FOR REFLECTION AND DISCUSSION

What does Christ's resurrection mean to me?

How do I proclaim the risen Christ?

Third Sunday of Easter (B)

Acts of the Apostles 3:13–15, 17–19

The First Readings on the third and fourth Sundays after Easter give us some samplings of apostolic preaching. This Sunday we have part of Peter's first public discourse since Pentecost.

Peter and John have just encountered a lame beggar in the temple. He has asked them for money, and Peter has responded that they have no money, but he would give the man what he had. Peter orders the lame beggar to stand up. He helps him rise and the man finds that he is cured. In a heart-warming description of the scene, Luke shows us the man "walking and leaping and praising God." A crowd gathers in the Portico of Solomon, and Peter begins to explain who is responsible for what had happened. "What has happened here," Peter says, "is not a result of the power or the holiness of John and me. It is due to the power of the risen Jesus."

Now our reading begins. Peter tells the crowd that the source of the miracle they have seen is no one less than the God with whom they are already familiar, the God of Abraham, of Isaac, of Jacob, of our ancestors. This God has exalted Jesus by raising him from the dead, the Jesus whose ministry the people of Israel had refused to accept. This people had allowed the Holy One of God to be executed, unwittingly to be sure, by the Romans. But now God has reversed the judgment of condemnation that was levied against Jesus and raised him from the dead. Peter testifies to the Resurrection of Jesus: "[O]f this we are witnesses."

Now Peter shifts from blaming to excusing the people. What they did, they did through ignorance. But now it is time to "[r]epent, therefore, and be converted," that is, to turn to God by acknowledging Jesus as Lord. What had happened to Jesus was not accidental or arbitrary, but was in accord with the Father's divine plan for salvation. The suffering of the Messiah was long ago foreseen by the prophets. (Peter seems to be alluding here to the servant songs in Isaiah 52 and 53.) Ignorance may have been enough to excuse the people's first rejection of Jesus, but now, given the missionary proclamation of the apostles, the miracles occurring in Jesus' name, and the apostles' testimony to the Resurrection of Jesus, there was no further excuse under the rubric of ignorance. Their sins could be forgiven only by accepting Jesus as the Messiah sent by God.

This reading is more than just an account of the early preaching of the apostles. It is also a challenge to us and calls for a response from us.

Just as there are two aspects of the narrative of Peter's preaching recorded here—the apostolic testimony and the people being addressed—so also there are two aspects to what is called for from us.

First of all, like the members of the crowd that gathered in Solomon's Portico after the cure of the lame beggar, we, too, are called to acknowledge Jesus as our Lord and Savior. The life and mission and suffering and death of the Messiah were foretold for us through the Old Testament prophets. In addition, we have had the preaching and the testimony of the apostles and their successors for more than two thousand years now. We cannot claim ignorance. We cannot plead that we didn't know about God's plans for our salvation, about the ministry of Jesus, about his death and resurrection. We have had plenty of opportunity to know about Jesus and to respond to his overtures to us. Consequently, we are called to ongoing repentance and conversion so that our deficiencies in recognizing and responding to the salvation offered by the Lord Jesus can be healed and forgiven.

But we are not called just to repent and receive and respond. We are also called to proclaim the truth and the reality and the presence of the Lord Jesus. We are called, all of us, to proclaim the Lord even as the apostles did. Not all of us are deacons or priests or bishops or professional church ministers. But, thanks to the vocation we have received in baptism and confirmation, we are all called to proclaim the salvation that the Lord has won for the world. This means giving witness to the presence and action of Jesus in our lives. It means standing up for the teachings of Jesus in a world that seems to find such teachings increasingly irrelevant. It means extending ourselves to be recognized as a follower of the Lord in a society in which the public profession of religious belief is looked upon as bad form.

We are all limited and sinful persons who need to hear the proclamation of the apostles. We are all followers of the apostles who need to carry forward their proclamation of the salvation offered by the risen Lord.

FOR REFLECTION AND DISCUSSION

When have I ever refused to recognize or accept Jesus, even out of ignorance?

How do I give testimony to the risen Jesus?

Third Sunday of Easter (C)

Acts of the Apostles 5:27–32, 40b–41

Speeches are one of the main literary means that Acts uses to carry forward the story of what happened after Easter and how the church developed. This is an instrumentality that is also used by pagan historians like Thucydides and Livy. These speeches do not claim to present the exact words that were spoken on a given occasion, as if they were a stenographer's transcript. Rather they present in general outline what was most likely said, given the circumstances. We have already heard one speech of Peter's (from chapter 10) on Easter Sunday. On this third Sunday of Easter, as we continue the semi-continuous reading of Acts that began last Sunday, we have another.

Last week (Acts 5:12–16) we heard about the high regard in which the apostles were held and about the ever-increasing numbers of those who professed faith in Jesus.

However, prior to this the apostles had already fallen afoul of the authorities. They had cured a lame beggar, had been hauled before the religious leaders to explain themselves, and had been ordered not to teach any more in the name of Jesus. Peter replies that they cannot keep silent about Jesus (Acts 4:5–20).

In view of the apostles' continued activity in Solomon's Portico, they are arrested again, miraculously liberated by an angel, and then recaptured by the temple police (Acts 5:17–26). This is where our reading begins.

The high priests remind the apostles that they have not obeyed the injunctions that were previously imposed on them. They continued to teach "in that name" (i.e., in the name of Jesus) and had caused turmoil in the city by putting the blame for Jesus' death on the Jewish leaders.

Peter replies that they can't do anything other than what they are doing because they are doing what God commands. The religious leaders had indeed killed Jesus, putting him to an ignominious death, but God ("[t]he God of our ancestors," the same God we all claim to honor) had brought him back to life and certified him as the Lord and master, as the bringer of redemption and salvation. In support of his message, Peter invokes Jewish law (Deuteronomy 19:15) that says that truth is to be established on the word of two or three witnesses. As witnesses to the truth of what he has just said, Peter offers himself and the other apostles as a kind of composite eyewitness, but also offers the testimony of the Holy Spirit of God who would be recognized by those who are in touch with God.

Then comes what is by this time almost a chorus in a song. The Jewish religious leaders tell the apostles once again not to preach any more in Jesus' name, and the apostles, once more, go on their way totally unfazed by the orders that they had been given.

There are two items that seem to call for comment in this reading. The first is the term "the name" or "the name of Jesus."

Sometimes, as early in this Sunday's reading, the author of Acts shows us the enemies of Jesus using "the name," seemingly as a way to avoid having to pronounce his proper name. In these contexts, "the name" is a term of disdain.

More commonly, however, it is the followers of Jesus who use "the name," "his name," or "the name of Jesus" as a refrain to denote the presence and the power and the person of Jesus. It expresses the reality of Jesus. It serves as the authorization for the apostles' activity. People are baptized in the name of Jesus. Miracles are worked through it. It offers salvation. The followers of the Lord preach the name of Jesus and suffer for it. It is a reverent and, at the same time, a uniquely Christian way to speak of the Lord Jesus and to call upon him. We still conclude many of our liturgical prayers "in the name of," that is, in the power and the authority and through the intercession of "Jesus the Lord."

The second item that calls for comment in our reading is the duality of witnesses that Peter offers for what he says. There is the testimony of the apostolic eyewitnesses, but there is also the testimony of the Holy Spirit. This is called for by the demands of the Jewish legal system, to be sure, but it is still necessary in the life of the church today. The church teaches with the authority of the apostles and continues their mission. But the church's teaching also involves the Holy Spirit. It is the Spirit who gives life and vigor to the teaching. Without the Spirit, the apostolic word becomes mere formulas. Without careful apostolic teaching, the Spirit becomes uncontrolled enthusiasm. Authentic Christianity demands both.

FOR REFLECTION AND DISCUSSION

Where do I perceive the Holy Spirit at work in the church?
How do I relate to the name of Jesus?

Fourth Sunday of Easter (A)

Acts of the Apostles 2:14a, 36–41

This Sunday's reading is from the same chapter as last Sunday's and gives us the ending of Peter's speech on the first Christian Pentecost.

After the same introductory verse as in last Sunday's reading, we hear Peter drawing to a conclusion. (Note that the lectionary text omits verses 34 ff. which again demonstrate Jesus' messiahship through a quotation from the psalms.) Peter's bottom line is a call to awareness. He invites the people to "know for certain" that Jesus is "both Lord and Christ." That is, Jesus is both agent and extension of God and also the promised ruler of the house of David. "But instead of welcoming him, you crucified him," Peter tells the people.

In great fear they ask Peter and the other apostles what they are to do. Now comes more good news. In spite of their rejection of Jesus, they are to be given a second chance. First of all they must repent. That is, they must change their idea of Jesus. They are to share the conviction of the apostles that Jesus is the Lord. Then they are to be baptized, that is to undergo the ritual washing that would signify their acceptance of Jesus. This acceptance of Jesus in baptism would bring about the forgiveness of their sins, both their personal sins and their involvement in the corporate rejection and killing of Jesus. As a result of that, they would receive the Holy Spirit as the apostles had received the Spirit earlier on that Pentecost day and as the Holy Spirit had been promised to God's people and their children. (This last assurance refers back to the very beginning of Peter's speech, to a part not presented in the lectionary readings, in which Peter had told the people that what they were seeing in the apostles was the beginning of the gift of God's power and energy to his people that had been promised by the prophet Joel long ago.) But even more, the Spirit would ultimately come not only on the Jews but also on "whomever the Lord our God will call." Here we have an indication of the call of the Gentiles that constitutes the subject matter of the succeeding chapters of Acts.

Peter brings his address to a close by urging his hearers to separate themselves from "this corrupt generation," that is, from the people who had crucified Christ, the people with whom God had expressed his dissatisfaction in Deuteronomy and Psalms (cf. Deuteronomy 32:5 and Psalm 78:8). Those who wished to be saved had to cut themselves off from those who refused to accept Jesus.

Finally, we see the outcome of Peter's discourse. About three thousand persons were baptized, the beginning of a new chosen people.

What we have in this reading is not just a historical narrative, a remembrance of what was said and what happened on that first Christian Pentecost a long time ago. We also have God's inspired word offering us direction for our own faith life.

Granted, we have already accepted Christ as Lord and Messiah. We have been baptized. But that doesn't mean that we no longer have need for repentance. Repentance is not just sorrow for sin, but an ever-renewed dedication to the Lord Jesus. None of us, not even the greatest saint, can say that we have fully and definitively accepted everything that Christ offers us in faith. Our heart is always in need of further change. Our awareness and understanding of Jesus must be continuously in a process of deepening. We can never say that we know the Lord well enough, that we have received all we need from him, that our relationship with him is all that it could or should be. We are always being called to a deeper relationship with the Lord, to repentance.

And like those first Jews who accepted baptism in response to Peter's call, we, too, have to separate ourselves from the "corrupt generation" that surrounds us. The world in which we live is a world that proclaims that religious faith isn't really important, that self-satisfaction is the most important thing in life, that expending effort in pursuit of goodness is wasted effort. We can't afford to let ourselves buy into ideas like that.

Moreover, this corrupt generation is dangerous. It's easy to find ourselves attracted by the comfort and self-fulfillment that it offers. It's easy to be charmed away from the path of the Lord. And the corrupt generation is not tolerant of those who reject its offerings. It looks on those who accept Jesus as Messiah and Lord as outsiders, as critics, as accusers. Every Christian martyr has tasted the hostility of the surrounding world. And every disciple of the Lord is called to be a witness, which is another word for martyr.

FOR REFLECTION AND DISCUSSION

Is repentance part of my life?

How do I relate to the corrupt world around me?

Fourth Sunday of Easter (B)

Acts of the Apostles 4:8–12

This Sunday's First Reading comes almost immediately after last Sunday's text in Acts. Last Sunday we heard Peter addressing the crowd that had gathered after he and John had cured the lame beggar in the name "of Jesus Christ of Nazareth." At the end of that speech (Peter's second public discourse) the religious leaders of the people, including the Sadducees, arrested Peter and John because they were proclaiming the resurrection of the dead. The Sadducees were priestly aristocrats who vigorously rejected the whole idea of resurrection. The apostles were kept in custody overnight and the next day were brought before the "leaders, elders, and scribes . . . and the whole high-priestly class." These religious leaders demanded to know from the apostles how they had brought about the cure of the lame beggar.

This is where our reading begins. The lectionary gives us the entire text of this, Peter's third post-Pentecostal speech.

First he addresses the question of the cure. "If the issue is how this blind beggar was cured," he says, "it was in the name of Jesus, through his power. You crucified him and the Father raised him from the dead." Note that there is no attempt to diminish the guilt of his hearers on the grounds of their ignorance as was the case in Peter's prior discourse. Now he was dealing with the leaders, not the ordinary people!

Next Peter addresses a much more basic issue than the cure of the lame beggar. He speaks of the meaning of this Jesus. He first cites Scripture to describe what the leaders had done and what the outcome of their doing was. The stone that the builders had rejected had become the cornerstone. This is a verse from Psalm 118 and describes the good fortune of the nation of Israel which other nations had looked down on. But Peter here invokes it as a prophecy about Jesus.

Then comes the sweeping proclamation: "There is no salvation through anyone else." If you are not saved by Jesus, you are not saved at all.

Our reading stops here, while the text of Acts goes on to describe how the religious leaders reacted to this breathtaking assertion that Peter had made. The editors of the lectionary obviously want us to pay attention to what Peter had said.

Peter is giving us the basic Christian good news, namely that Jesus had risen from the dead and that Jesus is the only source of salvation for us human beings. Salvation is an appropriate thing to think about during the Easter season, because Jesus' Resurrection identifies him as the Savior sent to us by God.

Salvation means at least two things. First of all, being saved means being delivered from threat or danger. A drowning person is saved from death by the lifeguard. "Saved by the bell," we say after a narrow escape from harm. The life, death and Resurrection of Jesus and the life of the risen Jesus that we share through baptism save us from all sorts of threats and dangers. Without the example, the teaching and the ongoing life of Jesus we would be overwhelmed by the natural inclination to selfishness that we all share. Our propensity to sin would get the upper hand. We would surely go under if we were not saved from ourselves by the Lord Jesus.

Saving also means recognizing or conferring worth on someone or something. When we clean out a closet, we throw some things away because they are of no further value. But other things we save. "Save that. It's too good to throw away." We save money because it can serve us in all kinds of ways. Likewise, when we say that Jesus saves us, we mean that he confers a worth on us that makes us precious to him. It's not because of what we are or what we have achieved that we are important to God, but because of what the Lord Jesus has conferred on us, a share in his own risen life. That's what constitutes our salvation.

Of these two meanings of salvation, the second is the more fundamental. Being saved means being made into a new Christ. That's where our worth comes from. That's what liberates and protects us from threat and danger.

It's clear that, if salvation means being enlivened by the life of the risen Jesus, then, as Peter so clearly said, "[t]here is no salvation through anyone else."

There are all sorts of false salvations, false ways in which people seek to find worth and defend themselves from hurt and harm. But there is only one true salvation: the Lord Jesus that the apostles proclaimed at the beginning and that the church proclaims even now.

FOR REFLECTION AND DISCUSSION

What does being saved by the risen Christ mean to me?

How have I sought salvation elsewhere than in Christ?

Fourth Sunday of Easter (C)

Acts of the Apostles 13:14, 43–52

In our semi-continuous reading from the Acts of the Apostles, we now fast forward eight chapters, from chapter five to chapter thirteen. At this point in Acts, we are at a different stage of the church's early history and a new personage has entered the narrative. The faith is being proclaimed far beyond Jerusalem, indeed far beyond the boundaries of Israel. And the main character from now on will be Paul of Tarsus, preacher of the word par excellence.

Our reading begins with Paul and his traveling companion, Barnabas, in Antioch in Pisidia, west of the Taurus mountains in present day Turkey. Here they enter the synagogue on the Sabbath.

At this point, in the full text of Acts, comes a long section that the lectionary text omits. It is probably left out so that the reading wouldn't be excessively long, but if one is not aware of what is in the omitted section, it's hard to make sense out of what follows in the reading. Having been identified as itinerant preachers, Paul and Barnabas are invited by the presider to offer the congregation any words of exhortation they might have. Paul speaks for some twenty-five verses. He offers a recap of salvation history, concluding with the proclamation of Jesus as the fulfillment of all God's promises and as the source of salvation, a kind of salvation that the Jewish Mosaic law could not provide.

Now we return to the lectionary text. As that session of the synagogue service broke up, Paul and Barnabas were invited back for the following week. They had already made some converts among the Jews and the Gentiles who had been converted to Judaism.

The following week brought a still bigger crowd. The leaders of the Jewish community tried to contradict what Paul preached. Presumably they would have attacked Paul's teaching about Jesus as Christ and savior, as the fulfillment of the Scriptures, as risen from the dead, as the source of a new kind of salvation.

Paul and Barnabas counter these attacks boldly, telling the Jews that they had now had their chance and had proven themselves unworthy of it. Now the good news of salvation in Jesus would be presented to the Gentiles. They cite one of the servant songs from Isaiah that suggests that God intends them to bring light and salvation to the Gentiles.

The Gentiles who were present were delighted (literally, "began to rejoice") over Paul's promise of eternal life for them, and many more people came to believe. The Jewish leaders, however, ganged up on Paul and Barnabas and had them run out of town. So they "shook the dust from their feet" as Jesus had commanded (see Luke 9:5) and went on to the next town rejoicing.

The issue being addressed here is the central issue of the early church: whether you had to become a Jew in order to benefit from the salvation offered by Jesus. The practice of Paul and his colleagues in their apostolic journeys was to approach the Jews first as having the first claim on what God had provided. Only after their refusal did the apostles turn to the Gentiles, apparently first to the Gentiles who had already embraced Judaism, then to those who were pagans pure and simple. Paul is known as the apostle to the Gentiles, but he generally starts off being an apostle to the Jews first.

Paul's ministry seems to have been characterized by boldness and joy. In this Sunday's reading he and Barnabas "spoke out boldly" when the synagogue leaders attacked them on that second Sabbath of their visit. Throughout Acts Paul always speaks up, no matter what the circumstances. Over and over again Acts shows him to us disputing heatedly with the Jews before he brings his message one more time to the Gentiles. Maybe Paul's example tells us something about how we should share our faith. It's not something we need to apologize about. It's a gift that we should be willing to communicate to others—boldly.

In this Sunday's reading we also hear about joy. The Gentiles were filled with joy when they heard what Paul and Barnabas had to say. The preachers themselves were "filled with joy" even as they were being hounded out of town. Sometimes believers give the impression that their faith is a great burden: a complex of rules and regulations, a long list of things that you have to believe. That may be part of faith, but it's certainly not the main part. Christian faith is the conviction that God loves us in spite of our unworthiness, that God wants to free us from our sins, that God wants to bring us to an eternity of happiness. The appropriate response to that is gratitude—and joy.

FOR REFLECTION AND DISCUSSION

> *How do I proclaim the gospel?*
> *To what extent do I find joy in my life of faith?*

Fifth Sunday of Easter (A)

Acts of the Apostles 6:1–7

This Sunday's reading continues the series that might be called "episodes from the early church." On the second Sunday of Easter we saw a short summary of the state of the earliest times of the church. On the third and fourth Sundays of this year A we heard two selections from Peter's evangelical discourse after the coming of the Holy Spirit on Pentecost. On this fifth Sunday we see the church dealing with some of its earliest inner tensions.

Our text begins by telling its readers that the community was in a state of continued growth. Yet not everything was peaceful and quiet. There were groups in the community that found it hard to get along together. These groups were two. The Hellenists were Jewish Christians, presumably born outside of Palestine, whose native language was Greek. The Hebrews were Jewish Christians who were native to Palestine, who spoke Aramaic, and who read the Scriptures in Hebrew. In all probability, there were cultural and practical differences between these two groups beyond the use of different languages, things like attitudes to temple worship, for example, and the matter of openness to contact with Gentiles. They were all Christians but there were differences between them.

What caused their differences to come to a head was a very practical matter. Apparently there were daily distributions of food for the poor, specifically for widows, overseen or carried out by the apostles. Now a complaint is raised by the Greek speakers, that their widows were not being cared for as carefully as the Hebrew widows were. The apostles perceive that something has to be done. They call the people together (Hellenists and Hebrews alike). It seems to be taken for granted that something has to be done differently, but the apostles say that they can't take on any further responsibilities for feeding the widows. Their responsibility is leading the community in prayer and in preaching. Increased demands for material care would have to be taken care of by somebody else. So the apostles propose a new level of ministerial service in the church. In conjunction with the community, they choose seven men who would be called to dedicate themselves to the service of the widows, Greek widows as well as Hebrew. All those chosen for this service have Greek names and presumably were Greek speakers. The apostles prayed over them and laid hands on them, a customary Jewish way of designating a person for a task and invoking divine blessings and power.

Our text continues with another statement about the ongoing increase of membership in the church. It may be that, by this general statement, Luke intended to suggest that the extension of the apostles' ministry to the seven men was pleasing to God and in accord with God's plans for the church.

There are many things worthy of notice is this episode of early church history. One is that what we have here is an example of how increased needs call for increased and innovative structures. A new level of ministry arises out of the Greek widows' needs. It was no longer just the apostles who had responsibility for the well-being of the community. Others could be called, too.

Another important lesson here is that tension in the church is not new. From the earliest days various groups in the church have had trouble getting along, but, under the leadership of the apostles, these tensions are resolved in a way that leads to the betterment and strengthening of the community.

In addition, this Sunday's reading teaches us that there are different levels of ministry in and for the church. The apostles had their role to play, which they realized they should not give up to play another role. They were to pray and preach. Others were to "serve at table." That doesn't mean that all the apostles were better than everybody else, but only that different persons could carry out different kinds of service.

Finally, this reading also teaches us that tensions can be resolved and that their resolution can promote greater unity in the church. It wasn't necessary for the Greeks to stop being Greeks, or the Hebrews to stop being Hebrews. What was necessary was that all of them have their needs attended to in the context of the one Christian community and in the service of the one Lord Jesus. This initial lesson in dealing with diversity would prepare the Christian community to deal not just with different kinds of Jews, but even with Gentiles all over the world. One might say that the decisions taken in today's episode constitute cornerstones of the catholicity of the church.

FOR REFLECTION AND DISCUSSION

What productive tensions have I experienced in the church?
What service do I provide to the community of faith?

Fifth Sunday of Easter (B)

Acts of the Apostles 9:26–31

On the third and fourth Sundays of Easter each year, the First Readings give us some samples of apostolic preaching. On the fifth Sundays we see examples of service to the church in its early days.

On this fifth Sunday of Easter of year B we encounter one of the most important participants in the life of the early church, one of the major contributors to Christian salvation history: Paul of Tarsus.

Our reading is from the ninth chapter of Acts. Paul (or Saul as he was first known) has already appeared earlier in the story. In chapter seven we see him watching over the cloaks of those who were stoning Stephen after Stephen's run-in with the Greek-speaking Jews of Jerusalem. In chapter eight Saul sets about trying to eradicate the early church. In the first part of chapter nine Saul encounters the risen Christ who empowers him to be an apostle. Saul preaches the gospel of Jesus for some three years in Damascus until the Damascus Jews mount a plot against his life. His friends get him out of town by lowering him over the city walls in a basket. This is where our reading begins. The year is about A.D. 39

Saul now arrives in Jerusalem. The Christians were not glad to see him because they remembered him as a persecutor and apparently were unaware of what had happened to Saul since he had left Jerusalem some three years previously. They wanted nothing to do with him. Barnabas, a kind and generous member of the Jerusalem Christian community who would serve the early church in important ways, steps forward as Saul's guarantor and chaperone. He persuades the apostles that Saul has indeed seen the Lord and that the Lord has spoken to him. Now Saul is welcomed into the community and becomes an enthusiastic preacher of the word.

But things were not quiet, at least not for long. Saul enters into controversy with the hellenists—Greek-speaking Jews who had been the object of Stephen's preaching and who had ended up killing him. Now they go after Saul. (The literal meaning of the Greek is "they kept trying to kill him.") The other Christians (who doubtlessly remembered what the hellenists had done to Stephen and the persecution that had followed Stephen's martyrdom) hurried Saul down to the seaport of Caesarea where they put him on a ship that would take him home to Tarsus.

Now follows another little summary passage. Under the

guidance of the Holy Spirit, the church began to grow and become strong. It was at peace throughout Judea, Galilee and Samaria.

Paul seems to have been a stormy sort of person. He had only been a Christian for a short time and it had already been necessary for his friends to get him out of town on two different occasions. As the later chapters of Acts tell us, getting out of town in a hurry became a regular feature of his ministry. His letters, which form such a large part of the New Testament, show us a passionate man who could be tender and loving toward his friends, but stern toward his disciples who needed correction, and almost violent toward those he considered to be a danger to the faith. If nothing else, he was zealous.

Barnabas was zealous, too, but in a different way. He first appears in Acts in chapter four laying at the feet of the apostles the proceeds from the sale of a piece of property. In this Sunday's reading he appears as a go-between who brought Paul and the Christian community into trust and friendship. Later he would be sent by the Jerusalem church to Antioch to investigate the large number of Gentile converts there. He and Paul made several missionary journeys together. At first Barnabas seems to have been the leader, but at a certain point Paul takes over. Eventually they part company as a result of a quarrel.

Two zealous men, two dedicated preachers of the gospel, two dedicated servants of the early church, and two very different human beings. Yet each had very important contributions to make to the young Christian community. What would the church be today if there had been no Saint Paul, no letter to the Romans, no letters to the Corinthians? What would the church be today if Barnabas had not brought Saul into communion with the apostles, if he had not encouraged the conversion of Gentiles, if he and Paul had not been willing to undergo the hardships of first-century travel in the back country of Asia Minor?

All of us are called to serve the church in one way or another. It's part of our baptismal responsibility. But we don't for that reason all have to be the same sort of people. The church needs Pauls and the church needs Barnabases and the church needs each one of us.

FOR REFLECTION AND DISCUSSION

Is turmoil always harmful to the church? Why or why not?
How do I deal with people I find troublesome in the church?

Fifth Sunday of Easter (C)

Acts of the Apostles 14:21–27

After Paul and Barnabas had been driven out of Antioch in Pisidia, as we read last Sunday, they traveled on to Iconium, then to Lystra. They were expelled from both towns thanks to the activity of Jews from Antioch. They went on to Derbe. This is where this Sunday's reading begins.

Paul and Barnabas made a considerable number of converts in Derbe. Then they decided that it was time to return home. They turned around and went back to the cities where they had previously preached: Lystra, Iconium, Antioch in Pisidia. This was not the easiest nor the safest route back to Antioch in Syria. They could have kept going east, then south to Tarsus (Paul's home town), and on to Antioch in Syria where they had started from. Instead, they chose to provide further pastoral attention to the new churches they had founded, despite the risk of being mistreated again. The route they chose to go home was an expression of their sense of missionary responsibility and courage.

When they revisited these communities, Paul and Barnabas did two things. First of all they strengthened the believers in these cities by preparing them for persecution. They assured the converts that having to suffer for their newfound faith was not a sign that the faith was erroneous or misplaced. On the contrary, having to suffer was simply part of the process of entering into the kingdom of God that Jesus promised.

Paul and Barnabas also appointed "elders for them in each church." There was to be a definite structure in these early Christian communities, and the structure was determined by the apostolic missionaries. The apostles decided who would be in charge, and then entrusted these leaders to the care of the Lord.

Our text records the final stages of their journey, and finally brings the missionaries back home to Antioch in Syria. It was there that the Lord had inspired the community to send Paul and Barnabas on this first missionary journey (cf. Acts 13:1–3). Now they were ready to report to the assembly how they had fared, to render an account of what had happened as a result of the mandate they had received from the Lord and the local church. What had happened was something that they probably had not expected. God "opened the door of faith to the Gentiles." They had learned in their travels that it was possible for pagans to enter the kingdom, seemingly in large numbers and not just by way of exception. This had not been an achievement of Barnabas and Paul. It was God who had brought it about.

This must have been a surprise to them all. There had already been sizeable numbers of Gentile Christians in Syrian Antioch (cf. Acts 11:20–21). But the leaders of the church in Jerusalem seem to have looked on this as an unusual situation that called for special attention (cf. Acts 11: 22–26). When Paul and Barnabas were set apart for the work of the Spirit, they did not direct their efforts primarily to the conversion of pagans. They concerned themselves with the Jews in the cities they visited, and it was only when they were rejected by the Jews that they turned their attention to the Gentiles. It was almost as if God was driving them out of the synagogues and into the arms of the pagans.

Their experience on this journey, however, did not solve once and for all the question of whether a person had to become a Jew in order to be a Christian. There would be still further discussion and discernment about it as we will see next Sunday.

The appointment of elders for these new communities by Paul and Barnabas was an early stage in the establishment of what some today refer to as "the institutional church." The converts were not to be left on their own to express their faith as they chose. There would be leaders appointed and structures laid down by the missionaries to keep the community firm on the foundations the apostles had laid.

But there is more. The authoritative appointment of presbyters by the apostolic missionaries was to be a sign of the relationship of these new churches with the wider church.

Association with the traveling missionaries served to keep the local church oriented beyond itself, aware that there is a universe of faith beyond the particular congregation and that they were part of that church universal.

Sometimes people today get impatient with the structures of the church. They think we would be better off letting each member relate to the Spirit on his or her own, that all leadership should be identified and directed by the local community. There were probably people in Derbe and Iconium who thought that way, too. But Paul and Barnabas didn't. Apparently the Holy Spirit didn't, either.

Have I ever had to suffer for the kingdom?
How do I relate to the church universal?

Sixth Sunday of Easter (A)

Acts of the Apostles 8:5–8, 14–17

This sixth Sunday of Easter brings us still another chapter in the history of the young church. Soon after the choosing of the seven helpers for the Apostles that we heard about last Sunday, a persecution of Christians broke out in Jerusalem. One of the seven, Stephen, had been arrested. His accusers said he had been preaching against the temple and the Jewish law. He was brought before the Sanhedrin, condemned and stoned to death. These events were followed by a persecution, apparently directed toward the Greek-speaking Jewish Christians who fled into the countryside around Jerusalem and into Samaria.

This Sunday's reading is concerned with another of the seven, Philip, and his activities in Samaria where he had gone to escape the persecution.

Samaria was an area north of Jerusalem. In times past it had been part of the Northern Kingdom of Israel. The Northern Kingdom had been definitively overcome by the Assyrians in 721 B.C. The Assyrians deported most of the Israelites and brought in Gentile settlers to populate the land. The Samaritans of New Testament times, therefore, were a mixture of descendants of Israelites and foreigners. They had some connection with full-blooded Jews and observed a kind of stripped down Judaism, but the Jews of New Testament times looked on the Samaritans as half-savage heretics. It is to these people that Philip brings the good news of salvation when he is driven out of Jerusalem. In the process of evangelization Philip works miracles, driving out unclean spirits and curing the crippled. These are the same kind of miracles that Jesus had worked in his public life, and the results of Philip's preaching were like the results of Jesus'. People paid attention to his words and his works and found "great joy" in the fact that the salvation that Jesus had proclaimed to the Jews was now being offered to them, too. In the verses omitted in our reading, the text says that "men and women alike were baptized" (NAB).

Now comes, as it were, the second chapter of this Sunday's narrative. Word got back to Jerusalem that the Samaritans (of all people!) "had accepted the word of God." They had been baptized, but had not yet received the Holy Spirit. (At this time the coming of the Holy Spirit on a new member of the church seems to have been an observable phenomenon.) So the apostles in Jerusalem sent Peter and John to Samaria. They imposed hands on the Samaritan converts who thus received the Holy Spirit.

This narrative makes two important points. First of all, it describes another step in the spread of the faith. Last week we saw certain tensions of diversity being resolved by the institution of a new level of ministry. Both Hebrew-speaking Jews and Greek-speaking Jews were to be fully accommodated in the Christian community. Now comes another stage. Thanks to the circumstances of the persecution in Jerusalem, the Christian gospel is presented to the half-caste Samaritans, who receive it with joy and who are gifted with the Holy Spirit just like full-fledged Jews in Jerusalem. Later on in chapter 8 of Acts, Philip will baptize a pagan who was a sometime-practitioner of Judaism. Finally, Paul would bring the faith to Gentiles who had no connection whatsoever with Judaism. As the story of the church unfolds in Acts we see the Christian community gradually becoming universal, that is, catholic. This is one of the main themes of Acts.

The second important point in this reading is the involvement of the apostles. Their coming to Samaria was not so much a matter of providing certain services that Philip could not perform. It was rather a case of their ratifying or certifying what Philip had done. Bringing the Samaritans into the fold of the church was a revolutionary thing to do. By showing us the apostles playing a role in the event, Luke assures his readers that the gradual spread of the faith into ever-new contexts was in accord with the will of Christ. It wasn't a one-time aberration perpetrated by an offbeat enthusiast, but was an important happening sanctioned by the highest leadership of the church.

Our First Readings on these Sundays of Eastertime show us episodes in the life of the church that are still going on: the faith spreading throughout the world, and the successors of the apostles exercising leadership and direction in the name of the Lord.

FOR REFLECTION AND DISCUSSION

What part do Christians of other cultures play in my experience of the church?

How is the ministry of present-day apostles(the pope and bishops) part of my faith life?

Sixth Sunday of Easter (B)

Acts of the Apostles 10:25–26, 34–35, 44–48

One of the most difficult and divisive questions that the early
church had to face was whether it was necessary to be a Jew in
order to be a follower of Christ. It wasn't so much a matter of
whether those who were born Gentiles could become members
of the community of Christian faith, but whether Gentiles who
wanted to become members had to agree to observe the Jewish
requirement of being circumcised and to follow Jewish dietary
laws. The Holy Spirit led the church to the resolution of this
question, and Luke, the author of Acts, records the steps through
which the Spirit led the young Christian community. The
church's liturgy brings these steps to our attention in the First
Readings of the sixth Sunday of Easter.

In year A we hear about the first approaches in the
evangelization of the Samaritans. Samaritans claimed to be
Jewish, but the Jews considered them to be outside the pale.
Preaching to the Samaritans, therefore, was going beyond the
limits of conventional Judaism. In year C we have Paul and
Barnabas giving an account of their missionary activity among
the Gentiles to the church leadership in Jerusalem. The reading
for year B falls chronologically between the other two. It is
concerned with the reception into the church of the Roman
Cornelius, a Gentile, together with his household.

The Cornelius narrative was important to Luke, so important
that he tells it twice, once in chapter 10, again in chapter 11. Our
reading is an abridgement of chapter 10. Before our reading
begins, Cornelius, a Gentile, though well-disposed to the Jews,
had had a vision in which an angel had ordered him to send for
Peter. Peter, meanwhile, had had a vision whose import was that

Jewish dietary requirements need no longer be observed. No food (and by implication no human being) was any longer profane or unclean. As Peter's vision ended, the emissaries from Cornelius arrived and invited Peter to come back to Cornelius's house with them. Peter agrees.

At the beginning of our reading, Peter has arrived at Cornelius's house and Cornelius prostrates himself before Peter. He obviously expected some kind of heavenly being. Peter refuses to accept this kind of honor.

In the full text of the narrative, Peter now shares the import of his vision with Cornelius, and Cornelius tells Peter his own experience.

Now Peter begins a long evangelizing sermon, of which our reading gives only the theological core. "[I]n every nation whoever fears him and acts uprightly is acceptable to him." No groups or classes were to be excluded *a priori*.

The lectionary reading omits the rest of Peter's sermon and brings us to the climax of the narrative. The Holy Spirit comes upon the whole group assembled there. It was clear that God was pouring his gifts out on these Gentiles even as he had poured them out on the Jewish apostles at Pentecost. They were, thus, obviously fit for baptism, and Peter orders that they be baptized immediately.

Peter would go back to Jerusalem and have to tell the story all over again in order to convince the Christian community that he had acted properly in allowing these Gentiles to be baptized.

It's difficult for us to realize what a breakthrough the baptism of Cornelius and his household must have been. For centuries the Jews had looked on themselves as a specially chosen people, and they were. Now this small group of Jesus' disciples had experienced Jesus' death and resurrection. They had received the

Holy Spirit as Jesus had promised. They must have looked on themselves as a specially blessed group—of Jewish people. The idea that the salvation brought by Christ Jesus might be directed to outsiders as well as Jews seems not to have occurred to them at first. In fact it took direct intervention of the Spirit on more than one occasion followed by decades of in-house controversy for the early Jewish Christians to understand that God was exercising his generosity to all his human creatures without exception.

Today we see the breadth of God's generosity not just in the acceptance of Gentiles into the church, but also in the church's catholicity. Every race and people is welcome. The Spirit is foreign to none.

FOR REFLECTION AND DISCUSSION

How have I been surprised by the generosity of God in my life?

How is the presence of the Spirit manifested in the church of today?

Sixth Sunday of Easter (C)

Acts of the Apostles, 15:1–2, 22–29

This Sunday's reading brings us to the end of the semi-continuous series of First Readings from the Acts of the Apostles that the church provides for the Sundays of Eastertime.

Paul and Barnabas had now returned from what subsequent generations would call the first missionary journey. They had not had great success in bringing Jews to profess faith in the risen Jesus, but their approach to the Gentiles had been fruitful beyond their wildest dreams. It seemed clear that the salvation brought by

Jesus was not directed to Jews alone, but also to Gentiles, and, indeed, without their having to embrace Judaism in the process. The hand of God seemed to have been at work in all this.

But it wasn't going to be quite so simple (here is where our reading begins). Some Jewish Christians came to Antioch from Jerusalem. They claimed that Paul and Barnabas were wrong. They said that the only way a person could be saved was to be ritually circumcised and to observe the whole Mosaic law. In other words, you couldn't be a Christian unless you also became a Jew. After lots of strife and discussion, the community decided to send delegates to the apostles and elders in Jerusalem for an authoritative answer to this matter.

In the full text of Acts there now follow some twenty verses in which we hear Peter recalling to the assembly his experience with Cornelius, Paul and Barnabas describing their adventures on their journey, and James pointing out that the prophets had foretold that the Gentiles would come to the Lord.

Now the lectionary text resumes. Special representatives were sent back to Antioch with a letter from the Jerusalem community. The letter served as a summary of the discussions that had taken place. The letter pointed out that it was not the authorities in Jerusalem who had sent the troublemakers to Antioch. The persons who now brought the letter were the official representatives of the apostles. They would repeat orally what was written in the letter. The Gentiles were not obliged to become Jews. All they had to do was refrain from eating meat that had been sacrificed to idols (which could signify participation in idol worship), from eating blood and meat that contained blood (since blood signified life and life belonged to God alone) and from unlawful marriage (e.g., between close relatives).

These stipulations were not a matter of bringing Judaism in by the back door. Rather, they were prescriptions that were already called for by the book of *Leviticus* for Gentiles who had contact with Jews. They were the minimal observances that all Gentiles were expected to practice if they wanted to live in peaceable contact with Jewish people. It was a matter of social sensitivity rather than theological requirement. The Gentiles could remain Gentiles as long as they didn't disregard the feelings of the Jews with whom they would be associated in the Judaeo-Christian community.

These decisions (which the Jerusalem apostles and elders perceived were the will of the Holy Spirit) were among the most important events of the early church.

First and foremost, they established that the Christian community of faith would not be a subdivision of Judaism. People all over the world could become members of the community without being subject to the details of Jewish observance. From the moment of these decisions, the faith community would be different. The church would now be universal, i.e., catholic.

However, this was not brought about by means of a simple disregard for Jewish people who had become followers of Christ. Gentile believers didn't have to become Jews, but they still had to be respectful of the religious and social feelings of their Jewish brothers and sisters. The principle that was established here was that not everything in the church is equally important. Sometimes there has to be compromise on nonessentials for the unity of the church.

These decisions didn't solve everything right away. Saint Paul would spend a lot of energy in the years to come working out their implications. But they did set the church on a totally new path, one that we still follow today.

This series of readings from Acts has shown us the church growing from a timid group of people huddled together on Solomon's Portico to a religious force open to the whole world. The power of God was at work in all this. The power of God is still at work in the church now.

FOR REFLECTION AND DISCUSSION

What accommodations to the sensitivity of other believers does the church call for today?

In what elements of Christian faith and practice must there be conformity among believers?

The Ascension of the Lord (ABC)

Acts of the Apostles 1:1–11

The reading from Acts assigned for the observance of the Ascension of the Lord is of particular interest in at least two ways. First of all, it is one of the handful of First Readings that is read on a specific occasion each single year of the three-year cycle. It is a reading so important that the church insists that everybody hear it every year. The reason is clear. This reading gives us the most extensive treatment of Jesus' Ascension, the most detailed account of what we are celebrating. It is, as it were, the "constitutive reading" for the feast.

The second way in which our reading is particularly interesting is that it constitutes a linkage between the gospels and the rest of the New Testament. At the end of Luke's gospel (24:50–53) we have one account of Jesus' ascension. Here, in *Acts*, the second volume of Luke's two-volume work, we have another.

These narratives of the ascension of Jesus serve as a kind of overlap, therefore, between the story of Jesus' earthly life and ministry that is told in the gospel and the story of the church that is told in Acts, a story that constitutes the background for the whole rest of the New Testament.

The reading that is provided in the lectionary is in three parts, three paragraphs, as it were.

First of all, Luke very deliberately links this new work that he is beginning with his Gospel. Each is dedicated to the same individual, Theophilus. Luke reminds Theophilus, and us, what the Gospel had been about: the ministry and teaching of Jesus up to the end of his earthly association with his chosen apostles.

Next comes a section about Jesus' general activity during the time between his Resurrection and his Ascension. He strengthened their faith in his Resurrection and he taught them still more about the kingdom of God, which had been one of his main themes during his public life. He told them also that they were to be attentive to a further development: the coming of the Holy Spirit, who would give them a new relationship with God.

The third section is concerned with a specific occasion: the day of his Ascension. After all that Jesus had said about the kingdom, the disciples still seemed to think that the coming of the kingdom was to be a political event which would restore self-rule to Israel. Jesus—one more time!—tries to redirect their thinking. What they were to look for, he said, was not a political upheaval, but the power of the Holy Spirit which would make them witnesses to him "in Jerusalem, throughout Judea and Samaria, and to the ends of the earth." In these words, Luke is giving us a kind of table of contents for the rest of Acts, a preview of how the preaching of the gospel would unfold.

Then comes Jesus' departure. A cloud took him from their

sight. In Sacred Scripture clouds are often the sign of God's presence. Jesus returns to his Father. The apostles seem to have been taken aback, and stood there looking up into the sky. Then two men in white appear, like the ones who had appeared to the puzzled women after Jesus' Resurrection (cf. Luke 24:4). These heavenly messengers tell the apostles to pull themselves together, and comfort them with the assurance that Jesus would come again, just as surely as they had seen him going away. As our passage closes, we are left with the apostles waiting, as Jesus had commanded, for what would happen next.

The Ascension is a kind of interim stage that marks both an end and a beginning. It marks the end of Jesus' physical, earthly presence and the beginning of the age of the church. Jesus' personal instruction of the apostles has now been concluded. They haven't grasped particularly well what he had tried to teach them about the kingdom, but now his Spirit would take over in a new beginning. And that Holy Spirit would guide and protect the community of faith, the church, from now own. The Spirit would continue to be with the church as its members carried out Jesus' behest to give witness to him. That age whose beginning is marked by the Ascension of Jesus is still going on. The task of giving witness to the risen Lord is still the mission in which we are all engaged as members of Christ and agents of the Holy Spirit.

But there is another way in which today's liturgical celebration involves a beginning and an end. We see the apostles poised for the beginning of the church as Jesus ascends to heaven. But we also see them alerted to the church's end, to the return of Christ when the church's mission will have been completed. The life, death and resurrection of Jesus come to conclusion in the church, the church of which we are a part. The church will find conclusion in the return of the risen Christ in glory, a return to which we, also, look forward.

FOR REFLECTION AND DISCUSSION

Who witnesses to the risen Christ to me?

To what extent is Jesus' return in glory an element of my spirituality?

Seventh Sunday of Easter (A)

Acts of the Apostles 1:12–14

In the general calendar of the church, this seventh Sunday of Easter is the Sunday between the celebration of the Ascension of the Lord (observed on the Thursday after the sixth Sunday of Easter) and the solemnity of Pentecost. In most dioceses of the United States, however, Ascension Day is transferred to the following Sunday, and thus supersedes the observance of the seventh Sunday of Easter.

In those dioceses where Ascension Day is still observed on the Thursday, the liturgy of the seventh Sunday of Easter serves as a kind of bridge between Ascension and Pentecost.

As is the case in all the Sundays of the Easter season, the First Reading on the seventh Sunday each year is from the Acts of the Apostles. In year A, the verses of the reading are the verses that follow immediately upon the narrative of Jesus' Ascension into heaven.

At the beginning of the ascension narrative (Acts 1:4), Jesus had told his followers (gathered on the Mount of Olives) not to leave Jerusalem. Now, having been encouraged by the heavenly beings in white garments to be confident of Jesus' return, the disciples make the half-mile walk back to town. Our brief reading then tells us where they went, who was there and what they did.

They went back to "the upper room where they were staying." This may have been the same room in which they had gathered to eat the Passover dinner with Jesus, their last supper with him. It may also have been the house of Mary, the mother of Mark, that is referred to later in Acts (cf. 12:12). In any case, they were all together in the same place. (Scholars point out that the history of the early church that Acts offers us is structured in concentric circles: first the presence and preaching of the disciples in Jerusalem, starting in the upper room, then in Judea and Samaria, then among Gentile sympathizers, and finally among all the nations of the world. Their limitation to Jerusalem was only by way of beginning.)

The company consisted of the eleven leaders, whom we refer to as apostles, listed by name. Also present were "some women, / and Mary, the mother of Jesus." In addition there were "his brothers," blood relatives of Jesus whose exact relationship with him is not known. What we have here is a kind of membership roster of the infant church. There were probably other believers in Jesus around town, but this was the core of the Christian community. By the time Acts comes to an end in twenty-seven more chapters, this tiny group of women and men will have developed into a worldwide body of believers.

Gathered together in this way, "[a]ll these devoted themselves with one accord to prayer." As they looked forward to the coming of the Spirit that Jesus had promised (cf. 1:5) they spent their time in communion with God. This atmosphere of prayer seems to have been characteristic of the infant church. When

Luke gives a summary of their earliest days after the coming of the Spirit (Acts 2:42, NAB), he notes that they devoted themselves "to the breaking of the bread and to the prayers."

This is the last explicit mention of Mary, the mother of Jesus, that the New Testament gives us. It is her last appearance, as it were, but an appropriate appearance: as a member of the believing community, engaged in watchfulness and prayer, open to the next events in the history of salvation in which she has already played such an important role.

This reading is obviously intended to direct our attention to the coming of the Holy Spirit on Pentecost that will be remembered and celebrated next Sunday. Our reading seems to cry out for the phrase, "to be continued" at its close.

But the continuation will be not only the account of the coming of the Spirit in Pentecost that comes in the next chapter. The continuation is also the life of the church, a life of togetherness in community, a life of ongoing prayer, a life of openness for the gifts of the Lord.

This Sunday's little vignette of life in the infant church is not only a nugget of interesting historical information. It is also a pattern for the church's life in the centuries to come. It is a design that we Christians of today are called to follow: togetherness with other believers, including Mary the mother of Jesus; ongoing dedication to communion with God in prayer; watchfulness for what the Lord has in store for us.

FOR REFLECTION AND DISCUSSION

What role does prayer play in my membership in the church?
What am I looking forward to from the Lord?

Seventh Sunday of Easter (B)

Acts of the Apostles 1:15–17, 20a, 20c–26

This reading from Acts is chosen for this Sunday between Ascension Day and Pentecost because the events recounted here took place during the days after Jesus had ascended into heaven but before the coming of the Holy Spirit on the first Christian Pentecost.

The followers of Jesus are gathered together. In the verses that immediately precede our reading (Acts 1:13 ff.), we saw a small group gathered in the upper room, newly returned from witnessing the ascension: the eleven apostles, some women, Mary, the mother of Jesus, and his brothers. Now, some days later, it is a larger group, about a hundred and twenty. Perhaps Luke means for us to understand that the infant church had already begun to grow.

Peter gets up to speak to the assembly about Judas. First of all, he reassures them that Judas's betrayal of Jesus was not something that happened outside the foreknowledge of God. On the contrary, Judas's membership in the group of the twelve was the result of God's doing. He was "allotted" a share in the apostles' ministry. In addition, Psalm 109:8 long ago spoke of a wicked man being replaced in office by someone else.

It was now time to see to the replacement. The reason why Judas had to be replaced was so that the apostolic college would be restored to its full complement for the coming of the Spirit. Jesus seems to have looked on this group of twelve followers as the core of a new people, as representing and renewing the twelve tribes of Israel out of which God established his people after the exodus. The twelve apostles were to replace the twelve tribal patriarchs of old to establish a reconstituted Israel. In addition, Jesus had told the apostles at the Last Supper (Luke 22:30) that, when the kingdom came at last, they would "sit on thrones judging the twelve tribes of Israel" (NRSV). The number was important and had to be maintained.

Peter lays down the criteria for Judas's replacement. It was to be one of the men who had been with Jesus from the beginning of Jesus' public life until Jesus was taken up to heaven. These requirements were important because the new apostle (together with the original ones) acted as a witness to the Resurrection of Jesus, and only someone who knew Jesus before his death could witness that the risen Jesus was the same one who had preached, worked miracles and died on the cross. It wasn't just the number of apostles that was important, but their experience as well.

In response to Peter's instructions, they put together a short ballot of two names and asked God to indicate which of these two was the one destined to join the apostolic college. Some means had been determined ("lots") by which God could express his choice, and God chooses Matthias over "Joseph called Barsabbas" (NRSV). Matthias takes his place with the other eleven apostles. We hear nothing more about him in the New Testament, which may suggest that his importance consisted in his enumeration among the twelve rather than in any personal contributions he may have made to the life of the young church.

There seem to be two lessons for us in this little story from the early church. The first is that, from the very earliest days of the Christian community, there were distinct structures. The twelve apostles were a group different from the other members of the church. This is not to say that they were holier or more skilled in preaching and teaching than the other early Christians. It is to say that they were different, that they had a role to play that was not the same as the role of others who believed in Jesus.

And the preservation of this special group, this distinct structure was important enough to engage the attention of the entire Christian community and to call for a direct intervention from God.

The second lesson from this reading is that Peter was in charge. There was no question of who spoke for the community, who was to see to it that the will of Jesus would be followed. It was Peter, just as it would be Peter who spoke publicly in the name of the other eleven after the coming of the Spirit on Pentecost (cf. Acts 2:14). The leadership role didn't fall to him because he was the most intelligent, certainly not because he was the most faithful. It was simply that he was the one chosen by the Lord for this office.

Even at a time of waiting in the history of the embryonic community, the church was not without life. Even before the Holy Spirit brought the church to full birth, there were apostles and there was Peter.

FOR REFLECTION AND DISCUSSION

What qualities do I have that make me eligible to be a follower of the Lord?

How does God choose apostles today?

Seventh Sunday of Easter (C)

Acts of the Apostles 7:55–60

The story of Saint Stephen, the first martyr, takes up two whole chapters (six and seven) in the Acts of the Apostles. The story begins with the appointment of seven men (including Stephen) to help the apostles. Stephen soon distinguishes himself through his disputes with foreign-born Jews about the relationship between Jesus and the religious culture of Judaism.

Stephen is brought before the Sanhedrin and is asked to explain himself. He explains at great length in a speech that runs for some fifty-three verses, the longest of any of the speeches in Acts. His presentation involves a kind of survey of God's providence for his people beginning with Abraham, including God's liberation of the people through Moses. But the people turned from God and rejected Moses as well as the prophets who came after him. As regards the temple, Stephen says that it is a man-made building that God does not really need. The whole world is God's. He doesn't have to have an address in Jerusalem. By way of conclusion, Stephen points out to the members of the Sanhedrin that the people they represent have been disobedient and irreligious from the beginning. They have habitually killed the prophets that God sent for their salvation and finally have murdered the greatest of God's spokesmen, Jesus. God's gift of the law to the people has become totally irrelevant, twisted into something that God never intended, practically disregarded in all its most crucial elements.

Stephen has accused the Jews of being failures throughout the whole history of their relationship with God. Now, he says, the killing of Jesus has changed everything and a new level of association has begun between God and human beings, an association mediated by Jesus, an association in which the Mosaic law is no longer relevant. It's no wonder the Jews dissolved into rage and set about executing Stephen as a blasphemer.

This is where this Sunday's reading begins. Stephen says that he can actually see Jesus in heaven, standing at the right hand of God, i.e., in a position of supreme authority and honor. The anger of the members of the Sanhedrin reaches a new height. They carry Stephen out of town, strip off their outer garments, and set about stoning him to death. In these last moments of his earthly life, Stephen prays as Jesus prayed on the cross. He asks for forgiveness for his persecutors (cf. Luke 23:34) and, as Jesus had commended his spirit to the Father (cf. Luke 23:46), so Stephen commends his spirit to the Lord Jesus.

The story of Stephen is an important component of the history of the early church as Acts hands it on to us. For the first time we have the proclamation that faith in Jesus has implications that put ancestral Judaism into a new position of relativity that makes its continued validity questionable. With the story of Stephen, Luke brings the Jerusalem phase of his history of the young church to a conclusion. From now on, the focus of the narrative will be increasingly wider until, when Acts reaches its conclusion, we have the Christian faith being proclaimed at the farthest ends of the earth.

But why is this reading presented for this Sunday between Ascension Day and Pentecost? Apparently because it offers testimony to the reality of Jesus' Ascension. Twice in two verses we hear that Stephen saw Jesus in heaven "standing at the right hand of God." Jesus' Ascension into heaven is not some sort of pious story. It is real. The Jesus that Stephen saw at the right hand of God is the same Jesus that the apostles had followed, the same Jesus that they had seen going up into heaven from the Mount of Olives.

But what Stephen saw does more than offer reassurance that Jesus is now in heaven after the conclusion of his earthly life. The glorious vision of the Son of Man also signifies Jesus' approval and affirmation of what Stephen had just said to the Sanhedrin, i.e., that the promised Messiah had finally come and that his coming involves a new relationship between humanity and God. It's as if Jesus appears in order to confirm Stephen's analysis of what Jesus' life had meant, of what Jesus' life still means now.

We are all called to give witness to the risen Christ, to proclaim the kingdom that Jesus taught. This Sunday's reading, offered as we remember the liturgy of the Ascension and look forward to the celebration of Pentecost, serves to assure us that the Jesus we remember from the past is still in touch with us now.

FOR REFLECTION AND DISCUSSION

How/where do I experience Christ in glory?

What part does the presence of the risen Christ play in my spirituality?

Pentecost Sunday (ABC)

Acts of the Apostles 2:1–11

This Sunday's reading is like the reading for Ascension Day: it is a "constitutive" reading which gives the scriptural foundation for the feast that is being celebrated, and so it is read for this liturgical celebration in each of the three years of the lectionary cycle.

Luke begins his narrative by giving us its religious context. It was the Jewish feast of Pentecost, the Feast of Weeks, when the Jews offered thanks for the wheat harvest, but also celebrated the gift of the law to Moses on Mount Sinai (and thus the formal religious establishment of God's people).

The apostles were all together when a great noise filled the house where they were, just as a great sound had accompanied God's arrival on Mt. Sinai (cf. Exodus 19:16). There was fire, too, just as God had come down onto Mount Sinai in fire to give the law to Moses (cf. Exodus 19:18). This time the fire was in the form of tongues, because the gift that God was now giving would be a gift of speech. The apostles were being empowered to speak with the tongue of God. And speak they did, in all sorts of different languages.

Now Luke turns our attention from the apostles to the people of Jerusalem. A large crowd gathered, Jews from all over the world, some of whom may have been permanent residents of Jerusalem, some pilgrims come to celebrate the Feast of Weeks. They didn't know what to make of it all. The apostles were speaking in everybody's native language! Now comes a list of all the places they were from. It reads like a survey of the geography of the ancient world. Practically any place you could think of was represented there. But although the languages were different and the homelands were many, they all heard the same thing: the apostles speaking of "the mighty acts of God."

In this second chapter of Acts, our reading leads into an extended speech of Peter about what God's mighty acts were (verses 14–40). In that Pentecost sermon, Peter sets forth how Jesus constituted the fulfillment of what the prophets had preached, how he was the Messiah that had been promised, how he had been rejected by the Jews, how it was necessary to be baptized in his name in order to be saved. These were the saving achievements of God that opened up vast new horizons of faith.

The lectionary does not give us this first apostolic sermon as part of our reading. But in the introduction to the speech that we do hear on Pentecost, there is still a wealth of teaching, teaching about the church.

First of all, what we hear about the events of that day teach us that what the apostles were proclaiming was something new. It was a new law, the law of Jesus, and a new people, the people of Jesus. Yet the giving of this law and the founding of this people was a sort of remembrance, indeed a repetition of the giving of the law and the establishment of the people that their ancestors had experienced on Sinai. The church remains rooted in the experience of the Jewish people, and still looks to the story of God's care for them as the story of God's care for us.

What happened on that first Christian Pentecost was clearly under the direction of the Holy Spirit. So is the church today.

That first public proclamation was an exercise of the ministry of the word. Notice how often words like "speak," "proclaim," "hear" appear in our reading, not to mention the fiery tongues! The church today is a community of preaching, of speaking out the mighty acts of God in all the languages of the world.

This initial proclamation was carried out by the apostles. Their successors, the bishops of the church, are still responsible for what the church proclaims today.

What the apostles had to say was addressed to people from all over the world. From day one, the church was universal. It is still universal, i.e., catholic, today.

Finally, the events of that first Christian Pentecost took place in an exclusive context of Judaism. The people were from all over the world, but they were all Jews, Jews by birth or by conversion. This would change. There would be development in the apostles' awareness of the church. In fact, the whole rest of Acts is the story of how the church grew and changed from being a Jewish sect to becoming an all-embracing community. The church of today is the same church that had its beginning on that Pentecost day in Jerusalem, and so it is a church that is still growing and developing.

FOR REFLECTION AND DISCUSSION

How have I experienced the Holy Spirit working in the church?
Where do I see growth and development in the church?

PART FIVE
Ordinary Time

Second Sunday in Ordinary Time (A)

Isaiah 49:3, 5–6

Each year the Sundays of Ordinary Time present a semi-continuous reading of one of the Gospels: Matthew in year A, Mark in year B, Luke in year C. The Gospel of John is distributed throughout other parts of the year. We hear from John on three of the Sundays of Lent and on five of the Sundays of Eastertime. In year B the Gospel readings are from John on Sundays 17 to 21, in part to make up for the relative brevity of Mark's Gospel, in part to insure that the eucharistic discourse of Jesus in John 6 gets heard in the course of the cycle. The second Sunday in Ordinary Time in all three years also offers us readings from John. These readings are concerned with the first public manifestations of Jesus and so continue the theme of the feast of the Baptism of the Lord. They also present episodes from John (Jesus' baptism, the call of the first disciples, the wedding at Cana) that are important for us to hear.

This Sunday's First Reading and Gospel are connected not by a quotation in the Gospel from the Old Testament reading, as was the case last Sunday and will be the case next Sunday. Rather, on this Sunday the connection is a single word: *world*.

In the Gospel, the Baptist points to Jesus as "the Lamb of God, who takes away the sin of the world." In the Old Testament reading we hear about God's servant who would bring salvation to the ends of the earth.

This reading, like last week's reading, is from Second Isaiah, that part of Isaiah composed during the exile to offer comfort to the Israelites who had been carried off to Babylon. Last week's reading was from the first of the four Servant Songs that form such an important part of Second Isaiah. This week's reading is from the second of these important prophetic poems that Christian readers have always read as applying to Christ.

Last week's reading showed us the Lord describing his servant. This Sunday's reading shows us the servant proclaiming what the Lord had said to him. The mission of the servant was foreseen long ago by God, before the servant was even born. He was to be an agent of God's glory in bringing God's people back to their homeland. He would act with the strength of God and be glorious in God's sight. But all that wouldn't be enough for the servant to do. The servant's mission would extend far beyond his countrymen to be "a light to the nations," and to bring the salvation that God offers "to the ends of the earth." (Note that at the beginning of the reading God seems to refer to the servant as a collective, as the whole people of Israel, while a few lines later God looks on him as an individual human being.)

This worldview that we find in this Old Testament reading is not a rare or unusual teaching. It occurs often in Isaiah (in last week's reading, for example), as well as in Micah (4:1–3), Jeremiah (12:15–16), Zephaniah (3:9–10) and in some of the psalms. God wanted his people to be ready to share in extending his love and care to all his human creatures, not just to the offspring of Abraham he had chosen for the beginnings of his saving plan. Nobody was to be excluded.

The fact that God's servant seems to be both an individual and a collective at the beginning of our reading seems to suggest that the task of leading all the Gentiles to the Lord would be a responsibility for the whole of God's people.

The Baptist proclaims Jesus as the Lamb of God who takes away the sins of the world because Jesus is the servant of God that the author of Isaiah had foreseen in the Servant Songs. The saving mission of Jesus would be the saving mission of the servant in Isaiah. Jesus would be a light to the nations, his mission reaching to the ends of the earth.

But just as our Isaiah text refers to the whole people of Israel as the servant, so also the mission of Jesus is not confined to his personal activity. His people, his church is called to share in his mission. That means us. We are all called to help Jesus take away the sins of the world. We are all called to be a light to the nations and bring salvation to the ends of the earth.

One is inclined to wonder how good a job we do on that aspect of our calling. We tend to look after our own salvation, to pray for and care for only those who are close to us, to be interested only in what we are familiar with and understand. One is inclined to wonder how well we carry out our responsibilities as God's servants, as extensions of the mission of the Lamb of God who takes away the sins of the world.

FOR REFLECTION AND DISCUSSION

How wide are the horizons of my faith, hope and love?
How do I contribute to the salvation of the world?

Second Sunday of Ordinary Time (B)

1 Samuel 3:3b–10, 19

For the thirty-three or thirty-four Sundays of Ordinary Time, the lectionary gives us two series of more or less continuous readings from the New Testament. The second readings are from the apostolic letters of the New Testament. The Gospel readings are from a single evangelist (Matthew, Mark or Luke) for the whole series of weeks during each liturgical year (with the exception of the second Sunday whose Gospel is always from the Gospel of John and also excepting a few weeks in year B when we hear from John's Gospel commenting on Mark's narrative of the feeding of the multitude).

The Old Testament readings, however, are not in a series of their own. They have been chosen to correspond with the Gospel reading, to introduce it, to illustrate it, to show how the gospels are rooted in God's relationship with his first chosen people.

Today's reading, from the first book of Samuel, is in harmony with the Gospel reading from the first chapter of John in that both readings are concerned with vocation. They are about God's calling people to help carry out his plans for his people.

Samuel was a very important person in the Old Testament. He had been born to a woman, Hannah, who had previously been unable to bear children. She and her husband visited the shrine at Shiloh where the ark of the covenant was kept, and Hannah prayed for a child. She promised that, if she bore a child, she would give the child exclusively to the Lord. She did conceive, and as soon as it was possible to separate child and mother, Hannah turned the child, the young Samuel over to Eli, the priest of the shrine. Eli would raise Samuel and teach him the ways of the Lord.

In this Sunday's reading we read about an important event in Samuel's life: his call to be an agent of the Lord.

Samuel is awakened by someone calling his name. He thinks it is Eli, the priest, but Eli says it was not he who had called. This happens a second time, then a third. By the time the call has come for the third time, Eli realizes that it is the Lord who is calling the young Samuel and tells the boy how to respond. The call comes again, now for the fourth time. (God is insistent!)

Samuel answers as Eli had instructed him: "Speak, for your servant is listening." In the verses that are omitted in our lectionary reading, God tells Samuel how he will punish Eli and his sons for their lack of reverence and humility in their service to the shrine. There follows a general statement about Samuel: the Lord was with him and all of his words found fulfillment.

Samuel turned out to be a pivotal figure in Old Testament history. He was God's agent in leading the people from being a kind of tribal league to being a single people under one king. He was the link between primitive Israel and a more sophisticated kind of government ruled by people like David and Solomon. He has been described as the last of the judges and the first of the prophets. It was for this that God called him.

In the Gospel reading (John 1:35–42) we see Jesus calling his first followers. These men, too, would have important things to do in God's kingdom. They would become Jesus' apostles, not because of their personal talents or inherent excellence, but just because they had been called by Jesus.

Sometimes people tend to think that being called by God is a rare and special occurrence, reserved in the past for people like Samuel and the apostles, or for those destined for priesthood or religious life in our own time. There are special vocations, to be sure, callings that pave the way for extraordinary works in carrying out the Lord's will. But there are more general callings as well, initiatives that God undertakes not just through prophets and apostles and priests and sisters, but through more ordinary men and women, more ordinary circumstances.

We are all called to be alive, to be gifted with faith, hope and love, to live out a human existence that is not exactly like anybody else's human existence. All this happens to us not through our own initiative, not because of our own worth, but simply because God calls us. If God had not called us, we would not exist, we would not be members of the community of faith, we would not have any purpose to our lives. And it's not just to the big things that God calls us. Every little intervention of God in our lives, every blessing that we receive, every danger, great or small, that God averts from us is part of God's calling. God has plans for each of us, even as God had plans for Samuel and the apostles. It's up to us to be attentive to God's action in our lives. It's up to us to listen.

FOR REFLECTION AND DISCUSSION

In what ways have I been called by God?

How do I listen to God?

Second Sunday in Ordinary Time (C)

Isaiah 62:1–5

Ordinary Time began last Monday. The first Sunday of Ordinary Time is replaced by the celebration of the Baptism of the Lord, so this Sunday is the initial Sunday of Ordinary Time, although it is named the second Sunday.

Ordinary Time is a series of thirty-three or thirty-four weeks in which the Sunday Gospel readings are generally a semi-continuous series from one of the first three gospels. Our overture readings from the Old Testament are chosen to correspond in some way to the gospel selection.

The second Sunday in Ordinary Time is something of an exception, however, in that the Gospel reading in all three years is not from one of the synoptic Gospels, but from the Gospel of

John. Each of these readings centers on the manifestation of the Lord, which is the major theme of the feast of Epiphany. It's as if the church can't quite let go of the celebration of Epiphany, and carries it over for one more Sunday. The Old Testament readings for each year, however, do follow the general pattern of correspondence with the Gospel.

This Sunday's First Reading is from the third major section of the book of Isaiah. The author is addressing the people of Jerusalem, now returned from exile yet needing reassurance in the face of the difficulties that they were facing. Chapters 60 to 62 have been called "songs of return," poems of encouragement to instill confidence and hope in those who had recently come back from exile.

The prophet feels compelled to speak. He can't keep silence until Jerusalem's bright future shines forth like the dawn. He expresses God's intent for the restoration of Jerusalem in three images.

The city will be a crown or a diadem, held in the hand of the Lord, an artifact precious to the Lord, an adornment that will add splendor even to the majesty of God.

Second, the city will be given a new name, that is, a new state of worth and happiness. The Lord will no longer allow his people to be called "Forsaken" or "Desolate." From now on its name will be "My Delight," and "Married."

This second new name leads in to the final image of God's care for his beloved. The Lord is so captivated by his people that he will enter into marriage with it. He had constructed the city, and now he would make it his spouse. God will find happiness in his people the way a bridegroom finds happiness in his bride. God and Israel would be as close as man and wife.

This last image that the Old Testament author uses to

describe the glorious resurgence of Jerusalem is what links our First Reading with the Gospel reading, i.e., with the narrative of Jesus' first miracle at the wedding feast of Cana (John 2:1–11).

The association of these two readings seems intended to teach us that God likes to deal in the atmosphere of weddings. Just as God promises in the First Reading to bring worth and happiness and reassurance to his people by making the people his bride, so in the Gospel we see Jesus beginning his public life, revealing his glory for the first time in the context of a wedding celebration.

Weddings involve love and joy, family and friends, hope in future fruitfulness, music and dancing, special food and drink (and lots of it at Cana!). Weddings are times to enjoy being together with those we love, with those who love one another. If ever human beings expect to have a good time, it's at a wedding.

And just as God encouraged his people who had returned from exile by promising them the joy of a wedding, a wedding with himself, no less, so Jesus gives the first public announcement of his kingdom by providing a guaranteed good time in a situation that could otherwise have been socially catastrophic.

Jesus seems to be saying that he has not come to let people be embarrassed, to stand back and watch them try to deal by themselves with a difficult situation. No, Jesus is here to share in the festivities and to make sure the festivities go off as planned. He wants to be part of the celebration of love and family and friends and fruitfulness and future. Human worth and human happiness are important enough for him to work miracles to insure.

During the Sundays that follow, we will see and hear Jesus proclaiming the kingdom. In this Sunday's Gospel, and its corresponding reading from Isaiah, we are given one of the kingdom's basic themes: God loves his people and will do whatever it takes to care for them and make them happy.

FOR REFLECTION AND DISCUSSION

What aspects of the heavenly kingdom of God are particularly appealing to me?

What signs of celebration do I find in the earthly community of faith?

Third Sunday in Ordinary Time (A)

Isaiah 8:23—9:3

The book of the prophet Isaiah is the most commonly used book of the Old Testament in the Sunday lectionary, being read some thirty-eight times in all. This is the fourth Sunday in a row that we hear from Isaiah. This Sunday's reading is from the first part of the book, most of which was written personally by Isaiah, son of Amoz late in the eighth century B.C.

In the Gospel reading for this Sunday (Matthew 4:12–23), Matthew recounts the beginning of Jesus' public life. Jesus' ministry begins in Galilee, north of Jerusalem. The evangelist describes Jesus' initial public actions and words with an eye to one of the messianic prophecies of Isaiah. It is this prophecy that constitutes the First Reading for this Sunday.

In order to understand what the prophet is proclaiming, we need to be aware of the historical and cultural circumstances to which he is referring. In 732 B.C. the Assyrians invaded the Northern Kingdom of Israel. They did not utterly destroy the kingdom on this occasion. That would come later, in 721 B.C.

For now they contented themselves with annexing three districts of Samaria and making them into provinces of Assyria, introducing Assyrian (i.e., pagan) colonists. The districts comprised the territory that had historically been assigned to the tribes of Zebulun and Nephthali when the Israelites first entered their Promised Land. Also included was a portion of Galilee, which already was home to many non-Israelites. These territories seemed to be headed for a future of dark paganism.

It is to this situation that Isaiah speaks. Isaiah is situated in the Southern Kingdom, and seems to be looking forward to a new king of Judah. Our text may refer to a king still unborn, still to arrive. It could also be directed to celebrating the enthronement of this new young ruler of God's people. In the verses that follow our reading, Isaiah addresses the king to come as "Mighty God" and "Prince of Peace." Whomever Isaiah may have had in mind originally, Christians have understood this proclamation to refer to Jesus, the Messiah and universal liberator.

The timing in our reading is a bit unclear, due in part to the fact that the tenses of Hebrew verbs tend to be vague, and in part to the fact that the prophet seems to be looking back to the past from a point in the future. What he speaks of as past from his point of view is still to come from the point of view of the reader.

There are four parts to what Isaiah proclaims in this reading.

First of all there will be change. The humiliation inflicted on the territory of Zebulun and Nepthali will be reversed. Galilee, now filled with Gentiles, will be glorified.

Next the prophet promises light. Darkness will be dispelled. Those who lived in gloom will experience great illumination.

And there will be joy, joy like farmers experience when they have brought in a good harvest, joy like soldiers feel when they have overcome a rich enemy and sit dividing up what they have captured.

Finally, there will be liberation. This conquered people will no longer be subdued like beasts of burden, no longer subject to the beatings of their masters. Things will be like they were "on the day of Midian," when Gideon, with just a few men and against every expectation overcame the nomadic Midianites who were plundering and oppressing the people. (See Judges, chapter 7.)

By quoting this section of Isaiah, Matthew is telling his readers that Jesus was the Prince of Peace that the prophet was talking about, that Jesus would reverse the depredations of the enemies of God's people, that Jesus would bring light and joy and liberation. He was the bringer of the messianic kingdom.

Jesus is still the bringer of light and joy and liberation today, for us. His teaching leads us and enlightens us. His presence brings us joy.

And he liberates us. We may not be under the heel of a foreign oppressor. We may not have to experience the corporal punishments of slavery. But we are limited and constrained by our sins, by our inherited inclinations to selfishness, by the wounds and weakness we have inflicted on ourselves. We live in an atmosphere of hostility to the Lord and his kingdom. All this Jesus overcomes, as definitively as Gideon overcame the Midianites.

The Jesus that Matthew presents in this Sunday's Gospel is the Prince of Peace who brings light and joy and liberation.

FOR REFLECTION AND DISCUSSION

Where do I find oppression in my life?

How have I experienced liberation by the Lord?

Third Sunday in Ordinary Time (B)

Jonah 3:1–5, 10

This Sunday's reading is from the book of Jonah. This is the only time in our three-year Sunday cycle that we hear from this book of the Bible.

Jonah is counted as one of the twelve minor prophets, but this book is different from the books of the other eleven minor prophets and different from most of the other books of the Old Testament. It is not a collection of oracles pronounced by the prophet. Instead, this author (whose name we do not know) gets his message across by telling a story, a fable about a difficult man named Jonah.

The book seems to have been written in the fifth century B.C., but the story is set in a time several centuries earlier. Its setting is a time when the most powerful nation in the Middle East was Assyria, a kingdom that was cruel and ruthless toward its enemies, squeezing out tribute and wealth from those it defeated in order to build splendid cities like Nineveh. In many ways, the Assyrians were the Huns, or perhaps the Nazis, of the ancient world.

Once upon a time God called a man named Jonah and told him to go preach repentance to the Assyrians in Nineveh. Jonah did not want to preach to the Ninevites, and so he tries to run away from God. Instead of heading east into Assyria, he books passage on a boat headed west to Spain, about as far away from Nineveh as one could get. God sends a storm. The ship is destroyed. Jonah ends up in the sea where he is swallowed by a whale. After three days God rescues Jonah from the belly of the whale and sends Jonah again to preach repentance to the Ninevites. This time Jonah obeys God and goes to Nineveh, although he is still not enthusiastic about delivering God's call to salvation to these terrible people.

This is where our reading begins. Jonah set out and went to Nineveh, according to the word of the Lord. It was a great city, the text says, fifty or sixty miles across! Jonah begins to walk through this metropolis proclaiming a brief but clear message, that in forty days (a rather long and generous time line) Nineveh would be destroyed. All of a sudden everybody repents. The city of Nineveh is saved because, thanks to the Ninevites' change of heart, God revises his plans and does not bring destruction on it.

The lesson of our reading, and of the book of Jonah, is that God's compassionate mercy is wider and more generous than we are inclined to expect. Indeed, it is wider and more generous than we are inclined to think is appropriate. Can God love even the Assyrians? Jonah didn't seem to think that God should, but God did, in spite of what Jonah thought.

The reading has been chosen to prepare us for the first part of this Sunday's Gospel (Mark 1:14 ff.). There we find Jesus beginning his public life, proclaiming the gospel of God: "The kingdom of God is at hand. Repent and believe in the gospel." It's quite a short message, like Jonah's. And, as it unfolded in Jesus' public life, it proved a troubling message for some. Many of the religious leaders of Jesus' time thought he was too soft on sinners. They were disturbed that he spent so much time with bad people, with the politically and socially incorrect, with those who didn't pay adequate attention to the ritual observances that distinguished good Jews from the rest of corrupt humanity. They were unable to believe that the Father's compassion was as wide-ranging as Jesus seemed to be saying. They wanted to put limits on God's mercy. Jesus' message was precisely the opposite: there are no limits to the compassion of God.

We need to hear this message of Jonah and of Jesus with some regularity, because we can easily find ourselves trying to reduce the scope of God's goodness. We are inclined to think that God only offers salvation to nice, good people (like ourselves!). But that's not the way it is. God loves all of humankind, and offers his salvation to all sorts of unlikely people and proclaims that love and salvation through his Son, Jesus. Jesus loves and wants to forgive Nazis and Communists, those who practice genocide and those who oppress the poor, child abusers and murderers. There is no crime that is too great for Jesus to forgive. There is no group that is too wicked for Jesus to bother with. Jesus loves wild liberals and rock-bound conservatives, Republicans and Democrats. Jesus' most basic message is that the Father's desire to give and to save is universal, that his merciful compassion is unlimited.

It all comes from God's goodness. It's all a manifestation of God's generosity.

And to try to limit God's generosity is to slander our heavenly Father.

FOR REFLECTION AND DISCUSSION

Whom am I inclined to exclude from God's mercy?

Do I find the breadth of God's mercy comforting or challenging?

Third Sunday in Ordinary Time (C)

Nehemiah 8:2–4a, 5–6, 8–10

This Sunday is the only time in the three-year cycle that we have a reading from the book of Nehemiah. Nehemiah and its companion volume Ezra deal with the period after the exiles had been permitted to return to their homeland from Babylon by the king of Persia. Ezra was a priest, learned in the law, and Nehemiah was the civil governor, appointed by the king to oversee the small province of Judah. These two short books give an account of Ezra's efforts to restore the religious life of the nation and Nehemiah's efforts to make it possible for the people to live a viable life as a nation among other nations.

The event described in this Sunday's reading seems to have taken place sometime in the middle of the fifth century B.C. The temple and the walls of the city have been restored. Now it is time to restore the religious and civic identity of the people in the context of God's law. What we hear described in this reading is a renovation of the covenant between God and his people. This renovation is brought about by a solemn public reading of the law, i.e., of some portion of Scripture that provided authoritative guidance for the life of the Jewish community. The purpose of the reading was to reassert the identity of the people, to defend them from allowing themselves to be assimilated into the culture of the pagan peoples who surrounded them, to make them clearly nothing less than the people of God.

Our text shows us Ezra and Nehemiah gathered together in front of a full assembly of the people: "the men, the women, and those childeren old enough to understand." Ezra read the law of Moses out to them, standing on a high wooden platform so the people could see and hear. The people performed acts of reverence to the law and to the scroll on which it was written. Ezra read out the law and, with the help of the Levites who were there, interpreted it to the people. (It is not clear whether the interpretation offered by Ezra and the Levites was some sort of commentary on the text or was a translation from Hebrew into

Aramaic, the language the people spoke by that time.) As the people heard what was being proclaimed, they began to respond with tears, perhaps because they realized how imperfectly they had been observing God's law. But Ezra and Nehemiah and the Levites urge the people not to weep but to rejoice. In fact, they were to go home and engage in a full-fledged celebration, with special food and drink, with special attention to the poor. God's law was not intended to bring them sorrow, but peace and happiness. Their strength would consist in rejoicing in the Lord.

The connecting theme between this reading from Nehemiah and the Gospel reading from Saint Luke (1:1–4; 4:14–21) is the use of Sacred Scripture. In the Old Testament reading we see the proclamation of Scripture passages bringing about among the people a joyful new awareness of their identity as God's people. In the Gospel reading we see Jesus quoting from the book of Isaiah to proclaim his own identity: the anointed of God sent to bring good news and freedom. Scripture helps us to understand and to express who and what we are.

Sometimes we are inclined to look on Scripture as a collection of writings concerned with what happened a long time ago, a gathering of more or less interesting accounts of the way things used to be: the story of creation, the main events in the life of Jesus, what the prophets preached about, the problems that Saint Paul had to face. The books of the Bible are indeed that, but they are much more.

For one thing, they contain the fundamentals of our faith. They are the touchstone for the rightness of what we profess as children of God and followers of Jesus. If something is presented for our acceptance that is contrary to Scripture, we know immediately that it cannot be true. Moreover, our faith is not a matter of signing on to a list of ancient propositions. Our faith is our ongoing relationship with the Lord, and the Scriptures are the safeguard of that faith and that relationship.

For another, the Scriptures are addressed to us. What God communicated to the early Christians through the evangelists, God also wants to communicate to us, here and now. The way that Ezra and Nehemiah dealt with the difficulties of the returned exiles has something to say to us. The letters that Saint Paul addressed to the Corinthians are also addressed to us.

We must not allow ourselves to forget that Sacred Scripture makes us what we are and keeps us aware of who and what we are.

FOR REFLECTION AND DISCUSSION

What role does Scripture play in my faith life?

What elements constitute my identity as a believer?

Fourth Sunday in Ordinary Time (A)

Zephaniah 2:3; 3:12–13

The prophet Zephaniah carried out his prophetic ministry about 625 B.C. His seems to have been the first voice of prophecy in some seventy years, since the time of Isaiah, son of Amoz. Zephaniah was an older contemporary of Jeremiah, Nahum and Habakkuk.

Zephaniah spoke for God in a time of religious disintegration. Idolatry was rife. People tended to rely on their own resources and to forget about the Lord. The fundamental theme of Zephaniah's prophetic proclamation was the sinfulness and destructiveness of human pride.

This Sunday's reading consists of two small excerpts from Zephaniah's prophecy. The first excerpt, from chapter two, is preceded, in the full text of the Bible, by the threat of the Lord's anger. The second excerpt, from chapter three, is preceded, in the full text, by God's promise to remove the proud from the midst of the people.

Our lectionary text is about humility. Those who seek humility, who observe the law in submission and seek justice will be sheltered from the anger of the Lord. The humble will be saved by the Lord in the day of judgment. They will become a people conspicuous for truthfulness and honesty. They will take care of their flocks in peace and security. Zephaniah's message in these three verses is very clear and simple: be humble and you will grow in virtue; be humble and you will prosper.

This is the same message that we hear Jesus proclaiming in the Gospel reading for this Sunday (Matthew 5:1–12a). The Sermon on the Mount is about humility. Being poor in spirit, being sympathetic to the sorrows of others, being meek and merciful and clean of heart, acknowledging our need for righteousness from God—all these spiritual attitudes are varieties of humility. And the rewards promised for them—membership in the kingdom, comfort, mercy, inheriting the land, becoming children of God—are all specifications of what God had promised to the humble in the words of Zephaniah.

Jesus' teaching was and is uniquely his in many ways. Yet it is deeply rooted in what God has already taught his people in the Old Testament. This Sunday's Gospel reading, the beatitudes, gives us what we might call Jesus' platform speech, an outline of what he would proclaim throughout the rest of his public life. But the First Reading shows us that some of the principal elements of what Jesus taught had already been in the mainstream of the Israelites' spirituality for six or seven centuries. The sermon on the mount constituted the first act of Jesus' teaching career. The words of Zephaniah provide the overture for what Jesus would teach. They offer the basic themes that Jesus would expand and make his own.

The humility that Zephaniah called for from the people of his time, the humility that underlies everything Jesus said in his platform speech is a basic element of any relationship with God. Humility does not mean groveling self-abasement, rolling in the dust before God, denying that we are of any worth whatsoever. An attitude like that really gives no honor to the creation that God took such pains to make good. Rather, humility is an attitude of awareness of need. We are subject to God and dependent on God. We are never going to amount to anything if all we have to work with are our own limited human resources. We need God to make sense out of our earthly lives. We need God to bring us into lasting worth. Whatever we are that is of any value is a gift from God. Humility means acknowledging that need for God, that dependence on God. Humility is not a denial of our worth, but a sense of realism about where that worth comes from.

Pride, on the other hand, involves an unrealistic self-sufficiency. It involves trying to make it on our own. The proud person does not want to admit that he or she is dependent on the Lord. The proud person may give lip service to the sovereign lordship of God, but in practice behaves as if he or she were the one in charge. Pride has been around for a long time, ever since Adam and Eve decided that they didn't want to be subject to God and they could manage quite well on their own.

Jesus' basic message in the Sermon on the Mount is the same as the message of Zephaniah: be humble and you will prosper, acknowledge your need for the Lord and the Lord will give you everything you really need.

God's urgent message to the Israelites of the seventh century B.C. was, "Be humble." That was also the message with which Jesus opened his public ministry. And it's a message that the Lord addresses to us today.

FOR REFLECTION AND DISCUSSION

Am I humble?

In what ways do I recognize my need for God?

Fourth Sunday in Ordinary Time (B)

Deuteronomy 18:15–20

Deuteronomy is one of the most often used books of the Old Testament in the Sunday liturgical cycle. Only Isaiah, Genesis, and Exodus are read more frequently.

Deuteronomy is the fifth and last book of the Pentateuch, that collection of Scripture that constitutes the Torah, the basic law that provided direction and inspiration for every conscientious Jew.

Deuteronomy is presented as a speech of Moses addressed to the people after forty years of wandering in the desert, just before they entered the Promised Land. Although it is founded in the teachings that God gave to Moses, the final version of the book that has come down to us represents a compendium of the law that seems to have been put together about 622 B.C. as part of the religious reform that took place under King Josiah. However, it also contains material that had come into the mainstream of the Kingdom of Judah from the Northern Kingdom of Israel after its destruction a hundred years previously.

The section of Deuteronomy from which this Sunday's reading is taken has to do with the officials who would exercise authority in the Promised Land. These included judges, priests and kings. There would also be spokesmen for God—the prophets. Just before our reading begins, God tells the Israelites through Moses not to pay attention to the fortune-tellers and soothsayers that they would find in the land the Lord was giving them.

Now God tells them that, instead of soothsayers and fortune-tellers, he would send them a prophet (i.e., a spokesman) like Moses, someone from among their own kin. To him they were to listen. This would be a continuation of God's care for the people at Sinai (Horeb) when he agreed to speak to them through a mediator rather than directly (cf. Exodus 20:19–21). This prophet would have God's words in his mouth and would proclaim the words and the will of God, just as Moses had done. The people were to listen to him on pain of punishment from God. If anyone pretended to be a prophet who had not been commanded to speak by God, or who spoke in the name of other gods, that person would die.

While Moses speaks only of a single prophet here, it seems likely that the text was meant to refer to all those who would be called to succeed Moses as proclaimers of God's word. He is teaching the children of Israel about the religious institution of prophecy, an aspect of religious faith that would play an important role in the implementation of God's will for his people. Moses was not to be the only spokesman they would have from God. There would be others who would come after Moses and who would continue the intermediary role that Moses had played. God would not leave his people uninstructed. He would continue to provide direction for them. He would apply the demands of his law to succeeding contemporary situations.

The Jews of Jesus' time seem to have been looking for this promise to be fulfilled by one special emissary of God. In the Gospel of John we find them wondering whether Jesus might be "the prophet" (cf. John 1:21, 6:14, 7:40). In fact, Jesus was indeed the prophet *par excellence,* the spokesman for God that surpassed all others. The Acts of the Apostles show us Peter and Stephen applying the words of Moses about "the prophet" to Jesus (cf. Acts 3:22, 7:37).

In this Sunday's Gospel reading (Mark 1:21–28) we see Jesus at the beginning of his public ministry teaching with confidence, with authority, like an authentic spokesman for God. He was providing to the people of his time what God had guaranteed through Moses: ongoing instruction, direction about God's will in the circumstances of the time. Just as God blessed the people through the ministry of the prophets over the centuries of the old covenant, so in Jesus God blessed the people through the final, most definitive prophet of all, Jesus. God would not leave his people uninstructed. He would continue to provide direction for them.

After Jesus had finished his earthly ministry, he provided for continued instruction and direction for his new chosen people through the Holy Spirit in the context of the community of faith that we call the church.

Moses, Jesus, the Holy Spirit, the church: all have been instruments of the teaching of the heavenly Father, all have been gifts of the Father. God has always provided for his people, in different ways and different times, a prophet like Moses. He still does today.

FOR REFLECTION AND DISCUSSION

Who are the prophets among God's people today?
How can authentic prophets be identified?

Fourth Sunday in Ordinary Time (C)

Jeremiah 1:4–5, 17–19

Jeremiah was the archetypal prophet of doom. His prophetic call
came in 626 B.C. and he served as a spokesman for the Lord until
after the destruction of Jerusalem in 587, a career of more than
forty years. During those years the kingdom of Judah went
through one religious reformation, three wars, three exiles and
five kings. The kingdom went from one of the brightest periods
in its history to the darkest. Jeremiah preached faithfulness to the
covenant and confidence in God. In response, his own kinfolk
rejected him. At various times he was in public disgrace, suffering
arrest and imprisonment. At the end of his life, his own people
carried him away into Egypt where (according to Jewish folk
tradition) he was murdered. Many Christian thinkers have seen in
Jeremiah a foreshadowing of the suffering Christ.

The passage that we hear on this Sunday is from the
beginning of the book of Jeremiah and gives an account of
Jeremiah's calling to be a prophet. We find similar vocation
narratives in the books of Amos (7:14–15), Isaiah (6:1–13) and
Ezekiel (1:4–3:15). They serve to establish the prophet's
credentials as a representative of God.

Our passage begins with the Lord's reassurance to Jeremiah
(and his readers) that Jeremiah's prophetic vocation had been part
of God's providential plan long before Jeremiah was even born.

Moreover, he was not to be a spokesman only to the people of Israel, but to all the nations.

In the verses that follow in the biblical text, Jeremiah protests that he is not equipped to be a prophet. The Lord replies by assuring the young man that he would have the strength he needed from the Lord and gives him an overview of the message he would be asked to deliver. These verses (1:6–16) are omitted in the lectionary reading.

In the second half of our reading, the Lord again assures Jeremiah that he will be strong enough to stand up to all opposition, "against Judah's kings and its princes, / against its priests and people. / They will fight against you," the Lord says, "but not prevail over you."

This Old Testament reading seems to have been chosen to correspond to this Sunday's Gospel reading (Luke 4:21–30) on two counts. The first is that the ministries of both Jesus and Jeremiah were directed not just to their own countrymen, but to all the nations of the world. This is the meaning of Jesus' response to his neighbors' expectations that the home-town boy who seems to have made good would want to show what he could do in his native place. Jesus answers that his mission is wider than backwater Nazareth, even as the missions of Elijah and Elisha were. The folks at Nazareth, not surprisingly, don't like being told that they're not as important as they think, and they try to do away with Jesus.

Now comes the second link with the Jeremiah passage. Jesus got away from those who were trying to kill him. God provided strength and defense for his Son even as he had promised to provide strength and defense against all comers to his prophet Jeremiah six hundred years before.

The message of these two passages is, first of all, that God's love and concern is not focused only on a portion of his human creatures. He extends his word and his salvation "to the nations," to all women and men no matter how distant they may be from what we might consider God's home terrain. Nobody is foreign to God.

Second, both prophet and Messiah are under the protection of the Lord. Because they are ministers of God's word, God sees to it that the hostility that is directed against them will not have the last word. God cares for them throughout their ministries, and even though both die ignominious deaths (Jeremiah allegedly murdered by his own people and Jesus put to death as a criminal), their mission lives on, Jeremiah's in the inspired word of God and Jesus' in the risen life that all his followers share.

In some way or another, each of us shares the experience of Jeremiah and Jesus. We have all received God's calling to life, to faith, to witnessing God's truth in our individual human contexts. And we know that, although our own human strength will not be enough to carry out the mission we have received, we can be confident that God will extend his help and protection to each of us, no matter how numerous or how powerful our opposition may be.

FOR REFLECTION AND DISCUSSION

How have I experienced the Lord's call in my life?

In what context have I experienced God's protection in the face of opposition?

Fifth Sunday in Ordinary Time (A)

Isaiah 58:7–10

Last Sunday the Old Testament reading laid down a general principle which the Gospel reading clarified and expanded in greater detail. On this fifth Sunday in Ordinary Time the relationship between the readings is reversed. The Gospel (Matthew 5:13–16) gives the principle ("You are the light of the world" [NRSV]) while the Old Testament reading offers the specifics about the meaning of the principle.

The Old Testament reading is from that third part of Isaiah which reflects the Isaiah tradition as it was proclaimed by the time the exile was over.

The situation of the returned exiles was not a happy one. Many Israelites chose to stay behind in Babylon rather than uproot their families again. Those who returned to the Promised Land had a hard time of it. The land to which they returned was a only a small portion of what had once been the kingdom of Judah. Social and religious abuses sprouted up. Jews sold each other into slavery. Men divorced their wives to marry foreign women. Religious observance declined into formalism. They were in no particular hurry to get the temple rebuilt. This is the general context of this Sunday's reading.

The reading comes from near the beginning of third Isaiah. Its date is sometime between 538 B.C., when the return from exile began, and 515 B.C., when the temple was finally rededicated. The prophet is addressing the fasts that the returnees engaged in. He tells them that their problem is not that they are not religious, but that their exercise of religion was missing the point of it all. Fasting is not about doing without food and then expecting God to be pleased. Real fasting involves putting into

232

practice the compassionate justice of God.

This is where our reading begins. As the passage is given to us in the lectionary, it is composed of two parts, each in a kind of conditional structure: "If you do this, that will happen." The first section (verses 7–9a) is the longer of the two.

God tells his people that if they take care of their brothers and sisters in need, their light will break forth like the dawn, their wounds will be healed, they will be surrounded by the splendor of God and will be able to live in confidence, thanks to God's presence in their midst.

The same lesson is repeated in the second part of our reading (verses 9b–10). If they do away with oppression and falsehood, feed the hungry, care for the afflicted, there will be light in the darkness for them and the gloom they have been experiencing will give way to the brightness of noon.

The practice of true religion, which involves compassion for those in need, will result in light, that is, in vitality, energy, a sense of direction and joy. And the light will be not just for the practitioner of true religion, but for those who come in contact with the compassionate person. The darkness of their social and political situation will give way to the warmth and illumination that God offers in response to true religion, to healthy faith.

In the Gospel Jesus tells his disciples that they are the light of the world, brightness destined for the enlightenment of the world, a standing invitation to others to give glory to the heavenly Father. But he doesn't say in what their brightness consists, what it is that illuminates the world around them. We find that in the Isaiah passage.

By choosing as our introductory reading this passage from Third Isaiah, the church teaches us at least two things. One is that being "the light of the world" does not consist in standing around looking religious. It involves caring for those who have need of our help, getting our hands dirty in the pursuit of prosperity and justice for the world around us. That's what makes us bright and surrounds us with the glory of God. That's how we help enlighten the world. The other thing this pairing of Scripture passages teaches us is that Jesus' preaching carried on a tradition that was already some five hundred years old. That's why Jesus could say, immediately after this Sunday's Gospel passage, that he had not come to do away with the prophets, but to fulfill them.

Third Isaiah does not tell his readers that religious observances are useless. Rather, he says that unless our observances involve compassion and generosity, they are not really religious at all.

FOR REFLECTION AND DISCUSSION

Does my life bring light to the world?
To what kinds of action does my faith lead me?

Fifth Sunday in Ordinary Time (B)

Job 7:1–4, 6–7

The book of Job is one of the great literary masterpieces of the Bible. It addresses some of the deepest questions of human existence, questions like the suffering of the innocent and how God can be just while seeming to allow misery to prevail in the lives of good people.

We don't seem to know much about the background of the book of Job. Its author is unknown. We're not sure when it was written. Scholars think it was between the seventh and the fifth centuries B.C.—a rather wide span of time! It is written in story form, a story about a good and a prosperous man who loses everything in a series of tests from God. His friends try to explain what is happening to him by contending that he must have done something wrong. Job insists that he has not done anything wrong, and it is this that sets the stage for a marvelous intervention from God toward the end of the book. In several chapters of breathtakingly beautiful poetry, God, speaking out of a whirlwind, enunciates the lesson of the story: human beings cannot understand God's ways and they shouldn't try. God's mind and God's will absolutely surpass human capabilities. Our finite human mind cannot probe the depth of divine omniscience that governs the world. At the end of his long discourse, God restores to Job and his family everything that had been taken away, and they all live happily ever after.

In spite of its high literary quality and the important questions it addresses, Job is used only twice in the three-year Sunday lectionary cycle: once on this Sunday and again, seven weeks from now, on the twelfth Sunday of Ordinary Time in this year B.

The reading for this Sunday is based on Job's sufferings, but is a description of the burdens that, at one time or another, afflict almost every human life. We are not in charge of our lives, Job says. We are like slaves or employees of a demanding master whose whole life is taken up carrying out somebody else's orders. Our misery doesn't cease. When we go to bed, we get no relief from our misery, no rest through the long night hours. Our days go by quickly and without hope. At the end of the reading comes a short prayer for mercy as Job asks God to remember how wretched and transitory his life is.

Job's reflection on the miseries of human life provides a background for the healing work of Christ that we hear about in this Sunday's Gospel reading (Mark 1:29–39). Mark shows us Jesus confronted with a whole panorama of women and men afflicted with various kinds of human burdens: Simon's mother-in-law sick with fever, then the faceless, shuffling crowds that come after nightfall, people afflicted with all kinds of maladies—physical, psychological, spiritual. It seemed like everybody in town was there. For one reason or another these people steeped in misery all needed the healing touch of Jesus.

These two readings teach us that God is well acquainted with human misery, even as human beings are well acquainted with the burdens of their existence. But there is a difference in the direction in which each reading points us. The book of Job leads its readers to humility and trust in the power of God, but it is a God of mystery and detachment, before whom human beings must stand in silent awe. The Gospels, on the other hand, tell us the story of Jesus, a human being like ourselves who knew human misery from within. Jesus dealt with the burdens of humankind with the healing power of God, but also with the compassion of one who was himself vulnerable and acquainted with grief and infirmity. Jesus does not manifest himself as the God of the whirlwind, but as the Lord on whom human misery has a special claim.

Both ways of portraying God are valid and true, and both need to be taken into account as we relate to God. God's ways are not our ways. God's providence far surpasses our capacity to understand. We dare not run the risk of thinking of God as somehow just like us, only bigger. God is utterly and totally different from us and we overlook that at our peril.

At the same time, God is concerned with us because, through

Jesus, we are God's brothers and sisters. It is right for us to turn to the Lord and ask for help, confident that we are addressing a compassionate Lord, personally acquainted with our griefs and infirmities.

God does not expect us to overlook our infirmities or pretend that our sufferings do not exist. Through his teachings in Sacred Scripture he leads us to acknowledge him both as almighty Father whose plans we cannot fathom and yet also as compassionate brother, anxious to heal.

FOR REFLECTION AND DISCUSSION

What have been the greatest sufferings in my life?
How have I experienced the healing power of God?

Fifth Sunday in Ordinary Time (C)

Isaiah 6:1–2a, 3–8

Last week our overture reading gave us the story of the call of Jeremiah. This week we have the call of Isaiah.

Isaiah's prophetic mission unfolded during the second half of the eighth century B.C., a half century that saw the destruction of the Northern Kingdom in 721 and Jerusalem under siege by the Assyrians in 701, a siege which ended in miraculous deliverance. Isaiah received his prophetic vocation about 740 ("In the year King Uzziah died."). He seems to have survived the siege of 701, but the date of his death is unknown. He was a national political figure in his time as well as being a poet of genius.

This calling narrative is a very important part of Isaiah's career because this call was what gave Isaiah the right to speak in God's name.

While Jeremiah's call in last Sunday's reading seems to have come through hearing God's word, Isaiah's comes through a vision. He sees God seated in majesty in the heavenly temple. God is greater than the temple, just the train of God's garment being enough to fill up the temple. Around God, ministering to him, are awesome angelic creatures. These creatures proclaim the ineffable otherness of God. "Holy" means separated from that which is profane, and God is thrice holy. Armies obey him ("Lord of hosts"). His brilliance overflows the earth. Then it seems that even God's own heavenly temple is not great enough to stand up under the force of the praise that God receives. "[T]he frame of the door shook." The smoke that Isaiah saw filling God's temple would remind his readers of the clouds that surrounded God on Mount Sinai (cf. Exodus 19:16–19).

Isaiah is filled with fear because he knew that those who saw God would die because of their unworthiness to be in contact with him. Isaiah acknowledges his unworthiness. It is not a specific sin that he laments, but the impurity that is inherent in the human condition. His very humanity endangers him in the presence of God.

Now one of the awesome heavenly creatures who carry out God's will brings a purifying coal from God's altar and touches Isaiah's lips with it. This touch of God's power removes his unworthiness and impurity. He is now separate from the profane, now fit to speak God's word.

It is time for Isaiah to begin his mission. In response to God's call for a messenger, Isaiah now presents himself. "[S]end me!"

This is a breathtakingly beautiful passage. It gives us a glimpse of the heavenly glory of God, but also reminds us of our human limitation and our unworthiness to stand in the presence of God. We human beings are filled with sin and wickedness, totally other than the thrice holy God, foreign to God's presence. Yet human beings have stood in the presence of God. They have been purified by his touch. They have been sent to do God's work and bear God's message.

What happened to Isaiah happened again in Jesus' calling of his disciples, as we hear in this Sunday's Gospel reading (Luke 5:1–11). After the miraculous catch of fish, Peter and those with him realize that they are somehow in the presence of God. They are afraid because they are conscious of their sinfulness and unworthiness. The reassuring words of Jesus ("Do not be afraid.") give them the confidence to respond to his call. "[T]hey left everything and followed him." The setting is different in the two narratives, and the mode of reassurance and purification is different (gentle words instead of a burning coal), but the basic story is the same: In spite of their unworthiness, God calls human beings to do his work. He sees to it that they have the equipment they need and waits for them to respond to his invitation.

The story of Isaiah and the story of the first disciples is the story of each of us. None of us is worthy of the Lord's attention. We are all sinful, of unclean lips and living among a people of unclean lips. Yet God purifies us, not with a burning coal but with the waters of baptism. We are equipped to carry out God's mission, to proclaim God's message. Then God waits to see how we will respond to the calling we have received.

Sometimes Catholic Christians don't realize that they have been called, like the first disciples of Jesus, to engage in God's work. People tend to think that their membership in the church is an authorization to receive God's attention instead of a call to disseminate it. Being sent by God is something that happens mostly to bishops and priests, they think. The fact is that every member of the church is called to carry out the loving mission of the Lord. We are all apostles. We are all prophets. We have all been sent.

FOR REFLECTION AND DISCUSSION

Where and how have I experienced the majesty of God?
What mission have I received from the Lord?

Sixth Sunday in Ordinary Time (A)

Sirach 15:15–20

Sirach seems to have composed the book that bears his name sometime between 200 and 175 B.C. This was when hellenistic culture was making inroads among the Israelites, but still prior to the Macchabean uprising. The book was originally written in Hebrew, then translated into Greek after 132 B.C. The original Hebrew text was lost somewhere along the way, and for many centuries only the Greek version was known. As a consequence, Sirach is not considered a canonical book of the Old Testament by most Protestants, who accept as inspired only those Old Testament books that can be found in the Hebrew Bible.

Sirach is a collection of short essays whose common purpose seems to be to demonstrate that real wisdom is to be found in the traditions of Israel, not in the secular philosophy that underlay hellenism. Many of these brief essays are concerned with morality. For this reason, Sirach was often used as a source for moral teaching for catechumens in the church, so much so that the book is also known as Ecclesiasticus, the church book.

This Sunday's excerpt from Sirach is from a part of the book which is dealing with God's involvement in human decision making. If it is the case that God is the cause of everything, is it therefore the case that God is the cause of human sin?

That's the question that the author is addressing as our passage begins. The answer is that God is not responsible for sin. Human beings are responsible for sin because they have a free will. They can make choices about whether or not they want to obey what God has commanded, and the choices that they make will have consequences, consequences that involve life and death, good and evil.

The second half of the reading is about God's involvement in human freedom. God knows what human beings do. He understands what they are up to. But if humans sin, it is not because God instructs them to do so, nor does God give permission for humans to do wrong.

It has been said that this passage is the clearest statement in the Old Testament about human free will. Yet it is not a complete theological treatment of that quality which is among the most mysterious elements of creation. Free will is not something that human beings can ever fully explain, nor something about which God has chosen to offer a complete explanation. Yet it is real and it is important. Free will determines what kind of life we live and the consequences that will arise from that life.

This little lesson about free will seems to have been chosen as this Sunday's overture reading because it provides a theological background for the Gospel reading. In that long selection from Matthew Jesus is teaching about the commandments and about how we are supposed to observe them. In other words, Jesus is telling us how we are to exercise our free will.

Jesus first tells his hearers that he has not come to do away with God's instructions to his Jewish people. He is not doing away with the commandments, but fulfilling them. That is, Jesus is calling his disciples to go beyond the letter of the law, to intensify their dedication to the purpose for which the law had been given. Some Jewish religious leaders of Jesus' time seem to have specialized in legalistic interpretations of the law that led people to do as little as possible by way of authentic observance. Jesus says that that's not good enough.

Next Jesus shows what he means with examples from the law. He cites commandments that have to do with murder, adultery, divorce and perjury. In each case he teaches that mere minimal observance of the letter of the law is not adequate. God expects more than that from human freedom. Our will is supposed to reject not just what the law is directed against, but also the smaller preliminary choices that lead to violation of the commandment. Moreover, as regards the last two examples Jesus offers, the law itself permits what is at best only tolerable and should not therefore be seen as a guide to life-giving obedience.

Human freedom and law are the subject of much misunderstanding among human beings. Some think that freedom means that we can do whatever we want. Some wonder whether there really is any such thing as human freedom, or whether our choices are somehow predetermined by heredity or other factors. Some see law as nothing but constraint, as mere limitation on our freedom. Some see in law the sole guarantee of happiness, as if living up to the letter of what we have been commanded is all that's required.

Human freedom is real. When exercised properly, it is a reflection of the wisdom of God.

FOR REFLECTION AND DISCUSSION

What role does law play in my life?

In what ways do I exercise my free will?

Sixth Sunday in Ordinary Time (B)

Leviticus 13:1–2, 44–46

Leviticus is the liturgical book of the Old Testament. It gives regulations for proper worship and offers direction for the holiness of the nation and for individual, personal holiness. The basic principles that are set forth in Leviticus have their origin in Moses and in the first years of God's special relationship with Israel at Mount Sinai. But the book that has come down to us in the Pentateuch has been enriched during the centuries when Israel was ruled by kings, and still more during the period after the Babylonian exile. Given its technical nature and the fact that the liturgical life prescribed in this book is no longer exercised, it is not surprising that Leviticus is used only twice in our three-year Sunday cycle of readings.

Chapters 11 through 14 of Leviticus have to do with ritual uncleanness. Chapters 13 and 14 deal particularly with the uncleanness that comes from leprosy. There are, therefore, two points at issue in our reading from chapter 13: ritual uncleanness in general and the Israelites' medical response to the disease of leprosy.

Ritual uncleanness was a kind of religious pollution that resulted from a disruption of the divine order that God had put into the world. It generally involved mixing things together that belonged apart. Thus, for example, shellfish are unclean because they live in the ocean but crawl like land animals. Lepers were ritually unclean because they had two colors of skin. These seemingly unnatural combinations were seen as indications of the presence of evil, and so could have no part with the God of creation. Ritually unclean people were excluded from participating in the communal worship of the nation because they were not worthy to approach the divine. They were also excluded from ordinary social contact with other Israelites because of the evil that afflicted them.

But there is also a medical or hygienic dimension to uncleanness, at least the uncleanness associated with leprosy. The leprosy that Leviticus deals with seems to include various kinds of skin blemishes. It is not the same thing that we call leprosy today. These diseases were thought to be somehow contagious, and so people who suffered from them were to be quarantined to prevent the spread of the disease. They were not to have contact with other people.

In this Sunday's First Reading we learn how leprosy was to be identified and some of the social strictures that accompanied it. Those with skin blemishes of any kind were to present themselves to the priest. The priest would determine whether the sores constituted leprosy. This was a religious decision, not a medical one.

In the second paragraph of our reading, we learn how the leper was to conduct himself. His torn garments and bare head would indicate that he was a person in distress. He was to shield his upper lip so that his breath would not contaminate others. He was to announce his state of uncleanness so that others would not come near him. He was not to be allowed to live with the community.

This reading provides the background for this Sunday's Gospel (Mark 1:40–45) in which we see Jesus healing a leper. This poor outcast presented himself to Jesus and Jesus did the unthinkable. He touched him! Jesus voluntarily made contact with this unclean person, and, by his touch, made him clean again. The man's burden is lifted and, once he has taken care of the religious formalities, he can rejoin human society.

It is interesting to note the repetition of words in the two readings. In the Old Testament reading we hear over and over again the word "unclean." In the narrative about Jesus, the repeated word is just the opposite: "clean."

The lesson that Jesus' action offers us is that nobody is so unclean, nobody is such an outcast that Jesus will not bother with them. Even a person who inspired horror in most of Jesus' contemporaries, the leper—religiously unclean and potentially contagious, condemned to spend his life in solitude lest others might become like him through contact with him—even this man qualifies for the compassion of Jesus.

The first chapters of the Gospel of Mark, which we read during this year B, address the mystery of Jesus. They respond to the question, "Who is this man?" In this Sunday's reading we learn that this man is one whose care for the outcast knows no limits, one to whom the ordinary ritual constraints do not apply.

FOR REFLECTION AND DISCUSSION

Who are the "unclean" people in our society?

Where/how does Jesus exercise his healing mission today?

Sixth Sunday in Ordinary Time (C)

Jeremiah 17:5–8

This reading from Jeremiah is part of a series of short paragraphs in chapter 17 having to do with the true and the false Israelite. The question that is addressed here is what we are to trust in, how our lives are to be oriented if we are going to be truly responsive to the Lord.

This is the sort of question that is dealt with in the wisdom books of the Old Testament, but which has its place in the teaching of the prophets as well. The wisdom tradition (in the wisdom books and in the prophets) is aimed at teaching people how to conduct their lives in order to obtain true happiness. It is concerned with the art of living well, with true and lasting success.

This Sunday's passage from Jeremiah is very simply yet carefully structured. There is one curse and one blessing, each accompanied by a single comparison. The two halves of the passage are of equal length, as if to offer two stone tablets of the same size, one teaching what is bad, the other what is good.

The negative tablet comes first. If you trust in human beings, if you concentrate exclusively on the here and now, you are headed for self-destruction. You are of no good to anybody. You are like a bush in the desert that never grows and never bears fruit, but just stands there in the infertile earth.

The positive tablet is about the person who trusts in the Lord. This person is like a tree planted near running water whose roots go deep into the earth and is able to withstand difficult circumstances yet still bear fruit.

Jeremiah's message has relevance for Christian believers of today. We need God. If we try to get through life on our own, we are going to end up disappointed because we are simply not equipped to bring about success for ourselves. We will end up accursed, consigned to destruction not by the will of an angry Lord, but by our own unwillingness to acknowledge our dependence and need for him. If we affirm our need for God, we end up fruitful and filled with life, able to withstand any adversity.

In this passage Jeremiah is giving expression to one of the most basic and important secrets of success, to a fundamental paradox that enables us to direct our lives toward the success that God intended us to enjoy. That secret, that paradox is that the less we depend on ourselves, the better the service we do for ourselves; the more we depend on the Lord, the better our chances of making something worthwhile out of ourselves. This was an important lesson for the civic leaders of Jeremiah's time who looked for security in political and military expertise. It is an important lesson for us who are imbued with a culture that prizes individual achievement and honors the self-made man (or woman).

It was an important lesson in the teaching of Jesus, too. Our Jeremiah passage was chosen for this Sunday to illuminate the Gospel (Luke 6:17, 20–26) which gives us the inaugural discourse of the Lord, the Beatitudes. This first public teaching of Jesus is really a development, a revised version of what Jeremiah had to say some six centuries earlier.

The structure is the same: a contrast between those who are blessed and those who are cursed, except that in Jesus' sermon the blessed come first and the cursed later.

The fundamental content is the same, too. Jesus calls blessed those who are unable to make it on their own, those who have only God to rely on: the poor, the hungry, the sorrowing, the despised and excluded. All these will flourish like Jeremiah's tree beside the waters. On the other hand, those who have plenty of money, who don't have to worry about where the next meal is coming from, who are free of sorrow, who are highly regarded by their peers will end up deprived of it all, shriveled up like the barren bush in the desert. One wonders whether Jesus had the Jeremiah passage in mind as he spoke to the crowds of his time.

These two passages set side by side remind us that God's message to his people has been a consistent message. The basics of a successful, blessed life as set out by Jeremiah are parallel with the basics of a successful, blessed life as taught by Jesus. Both teach that no human being is self-validating, that it is dangerous to try to be successful on our own. Both teach that our final worth depends on our acknowledgment of our need, on our willingness to be dependent. The wisdom of God is unchanging.

FOR REFLECTION AND DISCUSSION

To what extent is self-sufficiency a value in my life?
How do I express my dependence on God?

Seventh Sunday in Ordinary Time (A)

Leviticus 19:1–2, 17–18

The book of Leviticus is a very important book of the Old Testament. It is the third volume of the five-volume collection known as the Pentateuch. It offers a collection of rules of conduct for God's people, rules of ritual and legal purity. Its latinized Greek name, Leviticus, comes from the fact that the book deals with the activities of the Levites, priests from the tribe of Levi.

But Leviticus is more than a book of rubrics. It is also a handbook of holiness, a guide for living a life that is in accord with God's will for the members of his people.

In spite of its prominence in the Old Testament and in spite of its fundamentally important subject matter, holiness, Leviticus is read only twice in the three-year Sunday cycle (and only three times more in the weekday readings).

This Sunday's brief reading contains the two most quoted verses of Leviticus (verses 2 and 18) and provides a kind of summary of the teachings of the whole book.

First of all, God calls us to holiness. In a context like this, holiness does not mean being observant of certain standards of personal behavior, keeping certain rules. Rather, holiness means being like God. "Be holy, for I, the LORD, your God, am holy." We are called to nothing less than likeness to God. Moreover, holiness is not a calling for a select few, but for the whole Israelite community. God wants an entire populace that is like him.

Our lectionary reading now skips fifteen verses and gives us directions about what holiness means in the context of our relationships with our brothers and sisters.

First of all, we are not to bear hatred toward our brother or sister. We are not to seek revenge or hold a grudge against anyone. If it is necessary to point out another's wrongdoing, we must carry out that responsibility in a way that does not involve us in wrongdoing.

Next we hear about loving our neighbor. Nothing less is called for than loving our neighbor to the same degree and for the same reasons as we love ourselves.

Our passage concludes with the rationale, the ultimate foundation for these commands: "I am the LORD." The reason why we must not hate or harm our neighbor, the reason why we must love our neighbor as ourselves is because that's the way the Lord treats our neighbor. God is our Lord and master, and God wants us to be like him, holy, forgiving, and loving.

These few verses of Leviticus serve as the foundation for the reading from Matthew's Gospel that we hear on this day (Matthew 5:38–48). It is as if Jesus is giving an extended commentary on the teaching of Leviticus, a commentary that carries the Old Testament teaching to new dimensions of generosity.

The teaching about an eye for an eye and a tooth for a tooth was given to the Israelites to put a limit to retaliation. The punishment was not to exceed the harm done. But for Jesus that's not good enough, even as the teaching of Leviticus is not good enough. You can't just refrain from doing harm to someone who has harmed you. Jesus calls us to do good in return for harm, to give more than is asked.

In the next paragraph of the Gospel, Jesus quotes our passage from Leviticus ("Love your neighbor") and adds what seems to have been a popular addition ("and hate your enemy"). Jesus uses this bit of folk wisdom to teach still more about loving. Not only are we to love our neighbor, but we are to love our enemy as well. That's what God does and that's what God wants us to do. Our generosity toward both friends and enemies is to be modeled on God's generosity, a loving generosity that includes both bad and good, both just and unjust.

What might be called the fundamental theme in both readings is the same: be holy, be perfect as the Lord is holy and perfect. The Old Testament reading provides the principles on which Jesus' teaching is based, but the application of the principles is Jesus' own. Jesus' teaching broadens the demands of Leviticus. That which applies to friends and brothers and sisters in the Old Testament is directed toward enemies and persecutors in the New. From Jesus we learn that our heavenly Father is even more loving than he had revealed himself to be to Moses.

FOR REFLECTION AND DISCUSSION

How do I express love for my neighbor?
How do I go about loving those who are hostile to me?

Seventh Sunday in Ordinary Time (B)

Isaiah 43:18–19, 21–22, 24b–25

This reading is from Isaiah's Book of Consolation, chapters 40 to 55, written during the Israelites' time of exile by one or more of the spiritual descendants of the eighth century B.C. Isaiah of Jerusalem. These prophetic poems seem to have been intended to provide hope and encouragement to the Israelites as God prepared for their return to the land that had been theirs.

Our reading for this Sunday is one of only five or six readings from the whole Old Testament that are used more than once in the three-year Sunday cycle. The verses that make up the first half of this Sunday's reading are used in the First Reading for the fifth Sunday of Lent in year C.

As our text has been condensed for use in the lectionary, it falls into two parts. The first part calls the Israelites to look forward to new wonders of deliverance from the Lord. There is no need to look back to the exodus from Egypt as the great intervention of God on behalf of his people. God is getting ready to do something new and better. Just as God brought the Israelites through the waters of the Red Sea on dry land, so God will bring them back home through the desert that will be fed by gushing rivers. (The words "The people I formed for myself / that they might announce my praise" do not seem to form a grammatically complete sentence. There seems to have been some omission or oversight when the text was edited for the Sunday liturgy.)

The second part of our text voices God's reproaches against his people. They have not honored God or taken pleasure in him or called upon him. Instead, they have offended him by their sinfulness. Yet on his own initiative, God will forgive their sins. God and no one else will wipe away their iniquities.

The *New American Bible* entitles chapters 43 and 44 of Isaiah "Promises of Redemption and Restoration." What we have here is a proclamation of salvation on God's part, an announcement that God's care for his people is not just a matter of the past, but something that still continues in the present. God will love his people even though their sinfulness has made them unworthy of his love. God's salvation of his people involves ongoing renewal, a newness that is never exhausted.

This reading from Isaiah is intended to serve as a lead-in to this Sunday's Gospel (Mark 2:1–12). There we see Jesus involving himself with the same three basic elements that we found in our First Reading: salvation or rescue, the forgiveness of sin, and newness.

Jesus starts with the most important thing: he forgives the man's sins. This approach teaches the spectators (and us) that the man's relationship with God is far more significant than anything else. It is only as a kind of afterthought, when he sees the scepticism of the scribes, that Jesus frees the man from his physical burdens and enables him to walk once more. The crowd perceives the newness of what is going on here as they acknowledge, "We have never seen anything like this."

In rescuing the man from sin and sickness, in dealing with him in a new way that people had never experienced before, Jesus is fulfilling once again the promises that God made through Isaiah to the Israelites in Babylon. God had kept his word once already in bringing the people safely back out of their exile, but that first fulfillment of his promises was only the beginning. God likes to do new things for those he loves. Our Gospel shows the power of God at work in a new way in Jesus, yet in a way that reflects what God had promised to his people six centuries earlier.

Another aspect of these two readings that needs to be highlighted is the gratuity of God's interventions. God does not rescue the Israelites from their Babylonian exile because they are good and faithful people. On the contrary, they are a sinful people and God makes no bones about reminding them of their sinfulness. Yet on his own initiative, just because he wants to, God takes away their sins. "It is I, I, who wipe out, / for my own sake, your offenses."

It's the same with Jesus in the Gospel. The paralytic is not some kind of hidden saint who has been misjudged all this time. The paralytic is a sinner who doesn't deserve Jesus' attention at all. But Jesus forgives him anyway, and does away with his physical illness besides.

God likes to do new things for his people, surprising things, things beyond what people expect. But certain things about God are always the same, and one of those unchanging qualities of God is the generosity of his mercy.

FOR REFLECTION AND DISCUSSION

How have I experienced newness from God in my life?
From what situations of exile has God freed me?

Seventh Sunday in Ordinary Time (C)

1 Samuel 26:2, 7–9, 12–13, 22–23

The first book of Samuel is concerned with the life and works of the prophet Samuel and with the first two kings of Israel, Saul and David. We read about the birth of Samuel on the feast of the Holy Family, earlier this year. In the chapters that follow the story of Samuel's birth, we find him called to a greater closeness with the Lord. He becomes a spokesman for God at a time when it seemed likely that the Philistines might well overrun God's people. In response to the clamor of the people for a king, Saul is identified and anointed as king by Samuel. Soon the defects of Saul's character become more obvious and his popularity is overshadowed by that of David. David is a young man from a tiny village who had made a name for himself through his military capabilities and his one-to-one combat with Goliath, the Philistine champion. Saul becomes jealous of David and wants to do away with him.

As this Sunday's reading begins, David is on the run from Saul. He and his followers are many times outnumbered by Saul and his men. David has learned where Saul and his troops are encamped and steals into their camp. He finds Saul asleep, surrounded by sleeping guards. David's companion, Abishai, offers to kill Saul there and then, but David will not allow it out of reverence for the sacred anointing that King Saul had received. Instead, David takes the pitcher of water and the spear (signs of life and safety) which had been near Saul and retreats to the other side of the valley. From there he calls out to those who were supposed to be guarding Saul, rebuking them for their faithlessness. He invites them to retrieve the pitcher and the spear, proofs that he had really penetrated Saul's camp and that he had refused to take advantage of his nearness to Saul to do him harm. He proclaims his respect for the Lord's anointed.

This story highlights the virtues of David. For one thing, it shows him as a magnanimous and chivalrous warrior, unwilling to take advantage of an enemy when the enemy was found in a vulnerable state. According to the standards of the time, David had every right to kill Saul as he lay there sleeping, but he refused to do so. His inherent nobility would not allow him to make use of his advantage.

But there is another aspect to David's virtue. He is not just a fair fighter who won't harm somebody who is down. He is also a man of reverence who refuses to show disrespect to the sacred anointing from the Lord with which Samuel had made Saul king. To kill Saul would have been to undo the work of God, and David's religious instincts would not allow him to do that.

When we read the Gospel for this Sunday (Luke 6:27–38), we see Jesus setting forth a level of generosity and respect that surpasses David's. "Love your enemies and do good to them. Be merciful. Don't condemn. Forgive." These words are not addressed just to charismatic young warriors and gallant knights. They are addressed to everyone who would be a follower of Jesus. We are all supposed to be generous to our opponents as David was to his.

The reason why Jesus can call us to these levels of kindness and unselfishness is similar to the reason why David spared Saul, but much more embracing. David looked on Saul as a sacred person because he had been called by God and anointed with holy oil by God's representative. Our enemies, those who hate us and treat us with unkindness are sacred persons, too, not because of an anointing with sacred oil, but because of an anointing with God's love. Each and every person is uniquely precious to the Lord, not because they have been called to special dignities in the world, but simply because they are creatures of a loving Father. Every human being is sacred because every human being has been touched with the hand of God. Each and every human being, therefore, has the right to be treated not just with respect but with reverence as well. We may never do harm to the Lord's anointed.

David is one of the most appealing personages in the Old Testament. He is respectful, loyal, generous, devout. When it's time to fight he is a good fighter. When it's time to pray, he knows how to conduct himself in the presence of God. When he has sinned, he is quick to turn to God for pardon. He would become a great king leading his people to levels of peace and prosperity that they hardly ever again enjoyed. In this Sunday's reading, we see David at his best. Then Jesus calls all of us to a still higher level of virtue and dedication.

FOR REFLECTION AND DISCUSSION

What is the relationship between reverence for others and forgiving them?

How have I experienced giving and receiving forgiveness?

Eighth Sunday in Ordinary Time (A)

Isaiah 49:14–15

This Sunday's reading is from the second part of Isaiah, the part that was written during the Babylonian exile. The two verses that the lectionary offers us are part of a long hymn about the liberation and restoration of God's people.

The hymn, a long lyrical love song put into the mouth of God, appears in 49:8–26. Most of the hymn is composed of God's invitation to his people to take heart and look forward to the time of God's favor. "They shall not hunger or thirst ... For he who has pity on them shall lead them.... I will soon lift up my hand to the nations, and raise my signal to the peoples.... I will contend with those who contend with you, and I will save your children." What we have here is God singing a great aria of his unending love to his people, assuring them of his care for them in spite of their present seemingly desperate situation.

But about a third of the way through the poem, where our reading begins, we hear an intervention from the people (Zion). They are convinced that God has walked away from them, that he doesn't remember them any more. But God will not allow sentiments like these to interfere with his love song. "Can a mother forget her infant?" God asks. "Obviously not. But even if that were possible, I will never forget you."

Our reading is composed of only two verses, yet it is a profoundly moving expression of God's unfailing love for Israel.

Zion is a name for Jerusalem, perhaps originally limited to the most ancient part of the city. As time went by, it became the name for the whole city, the dwelling place of God as king. Then the term was applied to the community itself, as is the case here in our text.

The point of our short reading is very clear and unforgettably moving: it is absurd to think that a mother could forget her infant. But the idea of God forgetting Zion is even more absurd than that. (It is worth noting that this image of God as mother shows us that female experience as well as male can serve to help describe God.)

In this passage God's word is teaching us that God's love for us surpasses the deepest of human affections. It's hard to imagine any way in which God could more memorably or more effectively tell us how much he loves us.

This is not to say that pain and sorrow and sadness are unreal or irrelevant. God's people were suffering in Babylon. They were experiencing powerlessness and oppression and scorn. From any reasonable human perspective their situation was desperate. No wonder they thought that God had forgotten them. But all this is secondary. God's love for his people is infinitely stronger than the most painful suffering. It may well be that God allows suffering to afflict his people—individually or corporately—in order to make them attentive to the working of his love when his plans become more clearly perceptible. We may think in our sorrow that we have been forgotten by God. But it may be that we have simply not yet been able to grasp the infinity of his love for us, a love that can exceed all pain and sorrow and disappointment and fear. In fact we are never alone, never forsaken, never rejected by God who loves us more than mothers love their children.

This reading, like the First Readings for the last few Sundays, seems to have been chosen to lay down the basic principles that Jesus, in the Gospel, would then comment on and expand and apply to our human experience.

On this Sunday, the Gospel (Matthew 6:24–34) is concerned about needless anxiety about our human needs. Jesus tells his disciples not that they don't need to look after their needs, but that they don't need to be anxious about them. If God takes care of the birds and the flowers, he's certainly not going to overlook his beloved humans. Men and women may sometimes think that God has forsaken or forgotten them, and that they have to make up for God's apparent deficiencies by extra attention and more intense concern on their part. Jesus, in the Gospel, says that that kind of worry is characteristic of pagans. The heavenly Father, in the reading from Isaiah, says that God can not forget about his people any more than a mother can forget about her children.

Each reading conveys the same basic message. God will never overlook us. He can't, because he loves us so much.

FOR REFLECTION AND DISCUSSION

How have I experienced God's love?

What part do suffering and sorrow play in my life?

Eighth Sunday in Ordinary Time (B)

Hosea 2:16b, 17b, 21–22

Of all the prophets whose writings have been preserved for us in the Old Testament, only Hosea was from the Northern Kingdom. His ministry unfolded between 750 and 725 B.C. We do not know whether he lived to see the destruction of Samaria by the Assyrians in 721 B.C.

Most of Hosea's preaching was directed against the people's involvement in the Canaanite cult of Baal, an idolatrous religion that seemed to have a special appeal to the wealthy and the worldly during the prosperous decades in which Hosea exercised his ministry. In delivering his message, Hosea's most fundamental metaphor is marriage. The people of Israel were God's bride. But they were an unfaithful bride who abandoned her husband in order to take up the life of a prostitute. (Note that cultic prostitutes were part of the religious practice associated with the worship of Baal.)

In this Sunday's reading God addresses an unfaithful Israel, a people who has abandoned God and given herself over to other gods. But our reading is not an oracle of threat and blame. It is rather a kind of love song that God sings to his beloved, unfaithful though she be.

God will take back his adulterous spouse. He will carry her off into the desert on a kind of second honeymoon "and speak to her heart." They will be together as they were in the good old days in the time of the exodus. Israel was faithful then (at least most of the time), before she was corrupted by the ways of Canaan.

Then God speaks of the bridal gifts that he would confer on his bride. First of all, their marriage will be forever. It will involve right and justice, love and mercy, faithfulness and the experience of intimacy (knowledge) with the Lord.

This reading tells us that God is madly in love with his people. God has every reason to walk away from his adulterous bride. She has been unfaithful in many ways and for a long time. But God does not walk away from his beloved. He takes her back and offers to spirit her away to where they had first been happy together.

It doesn't make much sense for God to be this generous to this kind of a bride. But God's association with his people is not something that can be explained in rational terms. God is in love with her and God acts like somebody who is head over heels in love. That's all there is to it. No more need be said. No more can be said.

Note that the qualities that God promises to bestow on his bride are qualities that are characteristic of God himself: eternity, righteousness, justice, mercy, steadfast love. This is to say that God loves his people so much that he wants to confer on them his very own personal attributes. His gift to his unfaithful yet beloved bride is to remake the bride into God's own image, to make the bride live as God himself lives.

This Old Testament reading provides background for this Sunday's Gospel (Mark 2:18–22). There we see Jesus comparing himself to a bridegroom, a bridegroom whose presence brings joy to everyone connected with the wedding.

Read in the light of Hosea, Jesus' use of the bridegroom image is filled with richness. For one thing, it hints that Jesus is more than another religious teacher. If he is a bridegroom, might he not be *the* bridegroom, the divine bridegroom who would wed a whole people to himself?

If Jesus is a bridegroom, he is also a lover, one who reaches out passionately to draw his beloved ever closer to himself. And the beloved to whom Jesus reaches out is the community of those who believe in him. Jesus reaches out to his church. Jesus reaches out to us. We are the ones with whom the Lord wants to run off into the desert.

If we are to see a parallel between the Jesus of the Gospel and the Lord who speaks through Hosea, we can also see a parallel between what the bridegroom of the Old Testament and the bridegroom of the New Testament offers to the beloved. Just as the Lord in Hosea offers to remake his adulterous people into his own likeness, so also Jesus offers to remake those who believe in him into himself. When we are espoused to the Lord through baptism, we begin to share the very life of the Lord. This is what we call grace. What God had promised to his first chosen people has been fulfilled in us.

FOR REFLECTION AND DISCUSSION

How does Christ express a husband's love for his church?
In what ways has God taken me back from unfaithfulness?

Eighth Sunday in Ordinary Time (C)

Sirach 27:4–7

Sometime between 200 and 175 B.C. a respected teacher, Jesus son of Eleazar, son of Sirach, who lived in Jerusalem, prepared, in Hebrew, a collection of essays and aphorisms. The purpose of his undertaking was to encourage his fellow Jews to be faithful to the traditions of Judaism in the face of the hellenistic philosophy that was rampant at the time. About fifty years after that, the grandson of this Jesus translated the book into Greek. Over the passage of time the Hebrew text was lost and the book was known only in the Greek translation.

The first-century Jewish scholars who determined which books were to be considered sacred rejected everything not written in Hebrew, and so did not include Sirach among their sacred writings. Some fifteen centuries later the Protestants followed the same criterion for determining the contents of the Old Testament. However, the book of Jesus ben Eleazar, ben Sirach (or simply the book of Sirach) was always recognized by the Catholic Church as inspired and canonical. In fact, it became a major source of ethical and moral teaching for the church, and so became known as Ecclesiasticus, i.e., the church book.

Much of Sirach (or Ecclesiasticus) is composed of collections of proverbs or axioms, wise sayings that sometimes remind one of the material that comes at the end of the articles in *The Readers' Digest*. Our reading for this Sunday is a selection of four such sayings that come from a section of Sirach that is concerned with personal integrity in the life of the community. All four of these aphorisms are concerned with human speech.

(There seems to be a difference of opinion among the translators about the second half of verse five. The lectionary translation has "so in tribulation is the test of the just," while the Jerusalem Bible has "the test of a man is in his conversation." This latter translation seems to fit better with the context.)

Each of the first three sayings is a comparison. A person's faults appear in his or her speech just as useless material is left behind in a strainer. A person's conversation tests the person just as firing tests a piece of pottery. Speech reveals what is in a person's mind just as fruit reveals what kind of care the tree has had. The fourth saying is more direct. Don't judge somebody until he or she speaks, because it's from their speech that you learn what people really are.

All four of these proverbs make the same point, i.e., that speaking involves risk. It reveals our innermost character. Hence we should be careful in our speech.

Jesus makes the same point, and even uses some of the same sort of illustrations in the second part of this Sunday's Gospel (Luke 6:39–45). In fact, one could say that Jesus is simply recasting in his own words what Sirach had already taught two centuries earlier. The fruit of a tree tells what kind of a tree it is. The way a person speaks tells what kind of a person he or she is. This sort of adaptation of older material is what Jesus had in mind when he said (cf. Matthew 5:17) that he had not come to abolish the religious traditions of the Jews but to fulfill them.

The point about the revelatory character of our speech became part of standard Christian behavioral instruction. We find it again in the Letter of James (3:2, NAB) where the author says that "[i]f anyone does not fall short in speech, he is a perfect man."

Good fruit, good tree. Good speech, good person. Be careful how you speak because in your speech you are showing what you are.

Probably each of us has had the experience of saying something we wish we hadn't said. Part of the desire to retract may be that we didn't speak quite exactly and now have to explain that we really didn't mean what we said. It didn't come out right.

But sometimes we regret what we have said because what we have said shows facets of ourselves that we would just as soon have hidden, aspects of character that are real but are not the parts of ourselves that we want to advertise. "What must they think of me? It just jumped out of my mouth. I said what I really think but I didn't want to. Now I have to work at erasing the bad impression I have made."

All this is not hypocrisy. It is simply a matter of being aware of the perils of communication. An important aspect of speech is that it is a test on the basis of which we form our judgments about other people. And also a test on the basis of which other people evaluate us.

FOR REFLECTION AND DISCUSSION

What judgments have I formed on the basis of what people have said?

Has what I have said ever gotten me into trouble?

Ninth Sunday in Ordinary Time (A)

Deuteronomy 11:18, 26–28, 32

This is the first appearance of the book of Deuteronomy in the Sunday lectionary. Deuteronomy is a book of the Old Testament that is much used in the church's liturgical life. In fact, there are only three books of the Old Testament (Isaiah, Genesis and

Exodus) that are used more frequently in the lectionary for Sundays and Solemnities.

This book of the Bible is part of the Pentateuch, that collection of five books with which the Old Testament begins and which Jews have looked on as the basic law of God, the constitutional writings of Judaism. Deuteronomy is presented as a long series of reflections offered by Moses to the people just before their entry into the Promised Land. However, scholars tell us that, although the basic teachings of Deuteronomy may go back to the time of Moses, the book as we now have it is probably the product of a later time, perhaps of the seventh century B.C.

Deuteronomy is an exposition of and a commentary on the law, on the agreement that God had made with his people, an agreement that gave them their corporate identity, a covenant that established them as his own particular people.

This Sunday's reading comes from the end of an early part of the book that consists of a general introduction to the Law and therefore to God's expectations of his people. After this part of the book there comes a series of fourteen chapters that deal in greater detail with the particulars of the law.

Our reading is constituted of five verses from the last half of chapter eleven. As these verses are presented to us in the lectionary, they offer four fundamental and general directives about God's law and its observance.

First of all, the law demands our constant awareness. It is not to be something to which we give our attention occasionally, but as much a part of us as our heart and soul. The directive about binding the provisions of the law at wrist and forehead led pious Jews of Jesus' time to write out verses of the law and tie them to their arms and heads. These items of religious observance were called phylacteries. (Used in the right spirit, they could be authentic expressions of religious faith. Used for purposes of self-aggrandizement, they could degenerate into instruments of hypocrisy.)

Next, God offers a blessing to those who obey his law. This is followed by God's threat of a curse on those who do not obey his commands, especially as regards not offering worship to false gods.

Finally, a general directive: "Be careful to observe all the statutes and decrees that I set before you today."

God's law is to be part of our ongoing life. Being a member of God's people is not just a matter of having been born to the right parents, nor even of keeping a set of particular rules. Being a member of God's people involves accepting God's law into our very hearts and minds, letting ourselves be made into godly people.

But this does not imply passivity. Observing God's law involves making choices. Each member individually and the people as a whole are called upon to decide who and what they want to be, to decide their future. God offers options. Some choices bring blessing because they open us up to receiving what God wants to give us. Other choices bring destruction, not because they provoke an irascible God but because they separate us from God's care and direction.

Idolatry is a constant threat to God's people, both past and present. We tend to think of idolatry as the worship of the golden calf in the desert soon after the Israelites had left Egypt. But there is also contemporary idolatry: putting comfort before everything else, making the acquisition of wealth the main interest of our life, situating our own wants and desires at the center of our human existence, giving quasi-religious reverence to athletes or political leaders. All that is idolatry, and all that brings a curse on those who practice it.

This reading sets the theme that Jesus expands on in the Gospel (Matthew 7:21–27). There Jesus makes clear that merely giving lip service to what God asks will not bring us entry into the kingdom. We have to do the will of the Father, to listen to the words of Jesus, to act on them. That's how we make our choices. That's what determines who and what we are.

FOR REFLECTION AND DISCUSSION

How have I ever served false gods?
What choices do I make in my daily life?

Ninth Sunday in Ordinary Time (B)

Deuteronomy 5:12–15

We last heard from the book of Deuteronomy on the fourth Sunday of Ordinary Time in this year B. That reading portrayed Moses teaching the children of Israel about the officials who would exercise authority over them once they had entered the Promised Land. It comes from the longest part of Deuteronomy, an extended commentary on the details of the law.

This Sunday's reading, on the other hand, comes from an earlier section of the book, a section that offers the general principles of the covenant between God and the people and that gives a kind of survey course in the basic demands of God's law.

In our chapter five, Moses is dealing with the most basic and most embracing part of God's law: the Ten Commandments. In our reading we hear Moses reiterating the third commandment: Remember to keep holy the Lord's day.

The Israelites are to keep the seventh day of the week holy, and they do this by abstaining from work on the Sabbath. But it is not just the Israelites themselves who are to refrain from working on the Sabbath. So are their slaves and their animals. So are the foreigners who live in their midst. They are all supposed to spend the day in rest.

The purpose of this rest, the reading tells us, is remembrance. The whole land is to take advantage of this recurrent day of freedom from work to remember the slavery that they had experienced in Egypt and to recall their deliverance at the Lord's hand. That's the purpose of observing the Lord's Sabbath.

The observance of a weekly day of corporate and individual rest is one of the most characteristic practices of the Jewish faith. The Jews put the origin of the practice at the very beginning of time, when God himself rested on the seventh day of creation. Consequently, observing the Sabbath was an act of godliness. It was a deliberate act of the imitation of God. That's why the Sabbath is holy.

Like most religious practices, this one has several dimensions. The basic dimension is reflection and remembrance. This is the day on which God reflected on his work of creation, when he looked over everything that he had created and took pleasure in its beauty and goodness. It was also the day when the Israelites were called to reflect and remember, to reflect and remember how God had rescued them from the Egyptians and how God's "strong hand and outstretched arm" had brought them to the land he had promised them. The Sabbath observance was part of Jewish identity, and so was the remembrance of the wonderful works of God, starting at the very beginning of things.

The other dimension of the Sabbath is rest. The whole community was to refrain from effort and exertion. As time went on, a great body of detailed teaching arose about exactly what was or was not a violation of the Sabbath rest. But the purpose of the rest was clear. It was to be a reminder of the power of God, the power that brought about creation, the power that led the Israelites out of slavery into their own land, the power that would take care of them without their own works and efforts. The people could afford to rest a whole day every week because their God was so powerful and so loving and so caring. Thus the Sabbath was not just an obligation. It was also a gift.

This reading provides the background for the Gospel (Mark 2:23–3:6). In the Gospel we see that God's law seems to have been distorted to the point that some Jews of Jesus' time thought that the casual plucking of grain as the disciples walked through a field was a violation of the Sabbath because it constituted harvesting. Likewise, working a miracle on the Sabbath was a violation because you weren't supposed to practice medicine on the Sabbath. Jesus responds to these excesses not by teaching that the Sabbath isn't important, but by teaching that the Sabbath is not something that God needs, but something that human beings need. As a result, the Sabbath law has to be interpreted in a way that is in accord with its humane purpose.

We Christians have our Sabbath, too, but on the first day of the week, Sunday, rather than the last. Most of us probably think that our Sabbath obligation is to go to Mass. That's part of it, of course, but we, too, are called to observe the Sabbath in rest and reflection. There is plenty to reflect on, plenty to be grateful for. Sunday rest is particularly important in our culture in which we have so many opportunities for doing and going and enjoying that, if we're not careful, we may find ourselves so busy that we simply don't have time for the Lord.

How do I observe our Christian Sabbath?
What gifts does the Sunday observance offer to me?

Ninth Sunday in Ordinary Time (C)

1 Kings 8:41–43

Most of the church's liturgical calendar is governed by the date of Easter, which can be as early as March 22 and as late as April 25. The dates for the beginning of Lent (and therefore for the end of the first annual part of Ordinary Time), for Holy Week, for Ascension and for Pentecost (and therefore for the beginning of the second annual part of Ordinary Time) are all determined by the date of Easter. While the weekdays of Ordinary Time begin again on the day after Pentecost, the Sundays of Ordinary Time that come after Easter do not begin to be observed until after the feasts of Holy Trinity and Corpus Christi. When there are only 33 (instead of 34) weeks in ordinary time, a whole week, including Sunday, simply drops out of the calendar. As a result of all this, there are some Sundays in Ordinary Time that are rarely observed. The ninth Sunday in Ordinary Time in year C is one of these. The last time it was celebrated was in 1989, and it will not occur again until 2043.

Yet the readings for this Sunday are not of small significance. In fact they deal with one of the most fundamental questions of the Christian faith.

Our Old Testament reading is from the eighth chapter of the first book of Kings. This chapter deals with the dedication of the Temple of Solomon in about 960 B.C. The first part of chapter eight speaks of the ritual of the dedication and then gives us an account of Solomon's address to the people on this occasion. Then comes an intensely moving prayer that Solomon addressed to the Lord. Solomon's prayer extends from verse 22 to verse 52. Beginning at verse 31, Solomon addresses to the Lord a series of petitions, prayers for the forgiveness of sinners, for God's help in time of drought and famine, for victory in war.

Our reading comes from this part of Solomon's prayer. It is a prayer for foreigners. Solomon asks for God's kindness for those who were not Israelites but who, because they had heard about the power and might of the God of Israel, would come to pray in the temple. Solomon prays that God will answer the prayers of the foreigners so that they, too, like the Israelites, would reverence God and acknowledge the presence of God in the temple that Solomon had built.

In the history of Israel's relationship with God, there was always a kind of tension between the Israelites, who were the main focus of God's care, and the foreigners, who were not. God often warned his people to beware of getting involved with the Gentiles. They, the Israelites, were different because God was their God in a way in which he was not the God of the Gentiles. At the same time, as it became gradually clearer that there was only one God, it became clearer that the Israelites' God was somehow the God of the rest of the world, too. Hence there is a recurrent universalist theme in the story of God's relationship with his people. Under certain conditions, foreigners could be allowed to live in the land of the Israelites. They could even become members of the people if they were willing to observe the Mosaic law. There would come a time when all the world would worship at God's temple in Jerusalem, Jew and Gentile alike. The God of Israel would be acknowledged as the God of all peoples.

This is the sort of thing that Solomon is presented as praying for in our reading.

The Gospel (Luke 7:1–10) shows the encounter between Jesus and the Gentile Roman centurion. This foreigner asks a favor of Jesus. In the course of asking he voices his conviction that Jesus could do what he asked without having to come to his home. Jesus grants the request and expresses his satisfaction at the deep faith of the centurion. A foreigner asks and God grants. It's almost as if Luke included this episode in his Gospel to demonstrate that the prayer of Solomon was now being answered.

The question of the foreigners became one of the most difficult issues in the early church. Did Gentiles have to become Jews in order to be members of the community of Christ? This is the question behind the Acts of the Apostles and behind most of the writings of Saint Paul. The answer is no. Gentiles don't have to become Jews. What they do have to do is accept the life of Jesus that is offered to all women and men of every race and nation through baptism. That's what constitutes their salvation. That's what makes them members of the community.

The new people of God, the church, welcomes strangers and outsiders because it is catholic, because it is the final fulfillment of what Solomon prayed for.

FOR REFLECTION AND DISCUSSION

What experience have I had with "foreigners"?
What gifts have "outsiders" brought to the church?

Tenth Sunday in Ordinary Time (A)

Hosea 6:3–6

The prophetic career of Hosea unfolded in the Northern Kingdom of Israel some twenty or thirty years before that kingdom's final destruction at the hands of the Assyrians in 721 B.C. When Hosea began to speak out for the Lord as prophet, the kingdom was enjoying a time of prosperity and plenty, at least for the upper levels of the society. This prosperity rested on the backs of the poor who were enslaved and oppressed. Although sacrifices were still offered to the Lord God and although ritual laws were still observed, the religious life of the people was mechanical and formalistic. They went through the motions of serving God, but their hearts weren't in it. In addition, the worship of other gods was common. Economically it was a good time. Religiously it was a disaster—a disaster that ultimately led to the destruction of the kingdom.

The basic message of Hosea is that God continues to love his people in spite of their faithlessness. Like a husband who lovingly takes back his unfaithful wife, God would continue to love and care for Israel, if only she would come back to him in faithfulness. But the people continued to walk in their own self-seeking and idolatrous ways. At the end, no choice was left to God except punishment.

The reading chosen for this Sunday is in two parts. In the first part we hear the voice of the people, expressing a superficial and shallow repentance, looking for God's continued care and mercy, presuming that God would care for them and continue to send them blessings as certainly as the dawn brings light and springtime brings the rain.

In the second part of the reading, God responds. "What am I to do with you, Northern Kingdom. For that matter, what am I to do with my Southern Kingdom, Judah?" The people's devotion is as transitory as the morning dew. This is why God had found it necessary to rebuke them through the words of his prophets. At the end of the passage comes the general principle that God wants to teach his people: religious observance is only as good as the mind set it represents. Without love of God, without knowledge of God, sacrifice and ritual are meaningless.

The point that God is making is not that sacrifice and ritual are useless, but that they are useless if they are not informed by love and knowledge of God. Ritual acts are intended to externalize the interior spirit of love and adoration. Without these interior attitudes, all the external observances are a sham.

This reading from Hosea was appointed to be read on this Sunday because it is quoted in the Gospel (Matthew 9:9–13). To those who object to his contact with ritually unclean people (like Matthew), Jesus replies in the words that Hosea had put into the mouth of God: "I desire mercy, not sacrifice." (This must have been a specially dear Scripture quote for Jesus, since he cites it again in Matthew 12:7 when his apostles are being blamed for not observing the fine points of the law.)

But Jesus' use of the quotation adds something to the original text of Hosea. As the Old Testament text is presented to us in the lectionary, it has to do with the Israelites' relationship with God. The love that is called for is love for God. As Jesus uses the text in this Sunday's Gospel (and later in chapter 12), it is concerned not with the people's love for God, but with concern for our neighbor in his need, i.e., with mercy. Jesus has taken Hosea's words, modified them slightly, and applied them to our relationship with our neighbor instead of to our relationship with God. The kind of attention that Hosea called to be given to God is directed by Jesus to our neighbor.

There are many implications to this switch of direction. It seems to suggest that we can only offer authentic love to God when we are offering care and mercy to our neighbor in need. Jesus means to teach us that religious observance of any kind is not pleasing to God unless it is accompanied by concern for our neighbor. He also warns us that attention to religious ritual can lead us into a kind of unhealthy observance in which what is really important takes second place to superficial formalities.

Both Hosea and Jesus are talking about priorities. Neither discourages religious observance. But both remind us that sincerity of heart is more important than ritual exactness.

FOR REFLECTION AND DISCUSSION

How much of my religious life consists in observance of formalities?
What role does concern for my neighbor play in my faith life?

Tenth Sunday in Ordinary Time (B)

Genesis 3:9–15

This reading is from the third chapter of the book of Genesis. That chapter follows the second account of the creation. God has made man and put him in charge of all creation. God has also made woman to be a suitable partner for the man. They were in complete harmony with creation and with each other. They were naked without shame, since nobody had anything to hide, no energies or inclinations that were not in full accord with what God had made them to be.

At the beginning of chapter three, things change. The serpent induces the woman to induce the man to disobey the command that God had given them. They wanted to be in charge. Their eating of the forbidden fruit constituted a revolution against the love that God had shown them.

This is where our reading begins. God is still close to his human creatures, and presents himself to them on his evening stroll. But things have somehow changed. Adam and Eve hide from God because they are now ashamed. They no longer are what they had been. God tries to elicit from them an acknowledgment of their guilt, but the man blames the woman, and the woman blames the serpent.

Now God levies punishment on all three of these personages, beginning with the serpent. The serpent will now be different from the other animals, condemned to crawl on its belly and eat the dust of the earth. In addition to that, the serpent's evil-dealing plans will not be victorious in the story of God's creation. The offspring of the woman will crush the serpent's head, despite the serpent's ongoing attempts to destroy humanity. (This is where our reading ends. The part of Genesis 3 concerned with the punishment of the woman and the man are not read on this Sunday.)

The serpent is the image that the sacred writer chose for a being or a power that is hostile to God and an enemy to humankind. It is emblematic of the evil with which humanity would have to struggle. Later biblical texts (e.g. Wisdom 2:24 and Revelation 12:9) would make explicit the intent behind the imagery. God's curse on the serpent was intended to teach his people why the serpent seemed so repulsive (it didn't walk and eat like other animals) and also why they were continually beset with evil. There had been a primeval catastrophe which involved wrong decisions on the part of humanity, but which was also due to forces that were not clear at that time and which are still at work now.

Yet the serpent will not win in the end. The offspring of the woman will triumph over the evil represented by the serpent. The Christian faith has seen in this promise on God's part the first assurance of redemption. Consequently this passage is known as the "proto-evangel," i.e., the original proclamation of the good news, the first Gospel.

The second half of our reading—the part about the punishment of the serpent—provides the link with the gospel (Mark 3:20–25) where Jesus speaks about his overpowering of Satan. Jesus is quietly asserting that he is the fulfillment of the promise of victory over evil that God had made to Adam and Eve.

There are several elements in this reading from Genesis that are important for us to be attentive to. The first is the reality of evil. There is evil in the world, suffering that shouldn't happen, decisions and choices that are destructive, whole mind sets that are contrary to the will of the Creator. To try to pretend that everything is just fine and that there is nothing for us to be afraid of or be opposed to is simply not in accord with the way things are. To deny the presence of evil in our world may be one of the most evil actions of all.

The second thing that calls for our attention in the reading is that some of the evil comes from human beings. It's not all the result of mysterious forces whose origin and nature we don't fully understand. Human decisions are responsible for the unjust deaths of millions of other human beings. Human choices have resulted in worldwide destruction and sorrow. And the evil that results from human beings is not all due to world leaders guilty of cosmic wrongdoing. Some of it is our fault.

Finally, the proto-evangel assures us that sinfulness and wrongdoing will not be the last word. Thanks to the self-gift of Jesus, thanks to the Lord's unwavering obedience, the last word will be redemption, salvation and eternal happiness for all those who are willing to accept it.

FOR REFLECTION AND DISCUSSION

How do I experience evil in my life?
Where do I see the power of Christ overcoming evil?

Tenth Sunday in Ordinary Time (C)

1 Kings 17:17–24

This Sunday's overture reading is concerned with Elijah, the great spokesman for God in the ninth century B.C. in the Northern Kingdom of Israel.

The king of Israel at this time is Ahab, one of the unholiest men who ever ruled in Israel. As a punishment for Ahab's faithlessness, God has sent a drought on the land. With the drought comes hunger. Elijah, as God's spokesman, has informed Ahab that he is the cause of his people's misery. In order to escape the anger of the king Elijah flees to Zarephath, a village north of the northern boundary of Israel and thus beyond the reach of Ahab, though not beyond the sphere of the power of the Lord. While Elijah is there, he is cared for by a widow who provides not only food for him but lodging as well.

As our Sunday reading begins, things are not going well. The widow's son has fallen ill and died. The presence of a holy man like Elijah should have brought blessings on the household, but now there is only trouble. The widow is afraid that, thanks to Elijah's presence, some long forgotten sin of hers has been brought back to light and she is being punished by the illness and death of her son.

Elijah takes the young man's body up to the room where he was housed, prays to God, and stretches himself three times over the boy's body. The implication here is that the life force was so strong in the man of God that it would be able to communicate itself to the youth and bring him back to life. It does.

The prophet brings the now-living child back to his mother who acknowledges the power of the man of God and the vigor of God's word that comes through him.

The purpose of this narrative is to highlight the action and the presence of God in his prophets. In the face of powerful kings, in the context of universal deprivation, even in the face of death itself God can and will intervene through the agency of his prophets. God's power is not restricted by human limitations.

This Old Testament reading has been chosen for this Sunday to provide a background to the Gospel reading (Luke 7:11–17), the narrative of Jesus raising from the dead the son of another widow.

The people of Jesus' time would have been well acquainted with the Elijah stories, including the story of the widow of Zarephath. Jesus' miracle would have led them to a realization that Jesus was a representative of God in the tradition of Elijah. Here was someone who exercised the power of God even as Elijah had.

There are two differences between these two narratives that seem to call for comment.

First of all, Elijah's miracle was much more elaborate than Jesus'. Elijah carries the boy upstairs, puts him on the bed, stretches himself over him, prays for God's intervention. Only then does the boy return to life. Jesus, on the other hand, simply walks up to the funeral procession, touches the coffin, and tells the dead young man to arise. The simplicity of his actions and words are in contrast to the more complex actions of Elijah. It is not that Elijah needed to exercise some quasi-magical acts to elicit God's power, but that he needed to express somehow that God's power was something out of the ordinary, something that would come into action only after intense petition, even from one who was close to God. Jesus, on the other hand, exercises God's power with a simple gesture, a simple word. His relation to the power of God is different than Elijah's.

The second difference between the two narratives is that in the Gospel narrative there is nothing that corresponds to the Old Testament widow's suspicion that contact with the man of God brought trouble into her life. The widow was a pagan, and pagans had ideas about God that were not the same as the Israelites'. Pagans often looked on the power of God as dangerous, something that humans are better off not getting involved in. There is nothing like that in our Gospel. To be sure, "[f]ear seized them all," but it was a reverential fear, not fear that something bad was going to happen to them.

Sometimes a strain of paganism reasserts itself in the thinking of Christians. Sometimes people think that occurrences in their lives are punishments from a demanding God. While God may punish us sometimes, it is more often the case that God is preparing for us a blessing that we do not yet recognize.

FOR REFLECTION AND DISCUSSION

How have I experienced the life-giving power of God?
When have I judged as punishment something that was really God's gift?

Eleventh Sunday in Ordinary Time (A)

Exodus 19:2–6a

This Sunday's Old Testament reading provides the background for an important element of the Gospel. In the Gospel (Matthew 9:36—10:8) we see Jesus sending his apostles out to proclaim the kingdom. The primary audience for this proclamation was not to be the pagans nor the Samaritans, but the "lost sheep" of the house of Israel. The Jews were God's chosen people and they were to be the preferred addressees of God's ultimate saving intervention in Jesus. It was only after the Gospel had been offered to them that it was to be proclaimed to others.

Our Old Testament reading describes to us how God intended to deal with this people he was making his own.

The Israelites have been on the road for more than two months since their liberation from Egypt. They had now reached Mount Sinai where they would remain for nearly a year. Here God would manifest his will for them and teach them how they were to respond to his overtures. At this point, God had not yet given them the Ten Commandments. They had not yet fallen into idolatry. Their relationship with God was still unsullied and loving, one might almost say romantic.

Moses goes up the mountain to be with God. God shares with Moses his idea of what this people would be, how this people would relate to God. Moses is to bring all this to the people. In effect, God says, "You see how I have rescued you from the Egyptians and have brought you out here to the desert to be with me. In view of what I have done for you so far, I want you to know that if you are faithful to me, we will have a special relationship. You will be mine in a unique way, in a way that no other people on earth is mine, even though I have the right to choose any people I want to be mine. You will be a kingdom of priests, a holy nation."

In this passage God gives a description of what he intends his people to be. These verses have been called the introduction to the peak of the Pentateuch, a fundamental statement of theme for a series of chapters that would serve as the religious constitution of the Israelites for centuries to come. It's almost as if God is singing a love song to his people. God has eloped with Israel from Egypt and now God is wooing her, is sharing his plans with his beloved.

Israel remained God's beloved, and when the time came for God's definitive and final saving actions in Jesus, these saving actions took place first of all in the context of the house of Israel. They were still God's beloved. They were still God's "special possession." To them before any other people on earth the good news of Jesus would be addressed. Nobody was to have precedence over them in being presented with the Gospel. That's why Jesus gave his apostles the directions we heard in this Sunday's Gospel. Others would be addressed in due time, but only after the word had been given to the people that God had fallen in love with and run away with into the desert.

However, what is offered to the Israelites in this reading from Exodus will not be limited to them alone. In fact, the culminating gifts that God speaks of in this passage ("You shall be to me a kingdom of priests, a holy nation") are applied to the members of the church in the New Testament (cf. 1 Peter 2:9).

When God's word speaks of the Israelites and the church as a holy nation, it means that those people are different from the rest of the world, that they have a relationship with God that others do not share. This holiness, this relationship is not something that is earned or deserved, but an association with God that can only come by gift.

When God's word speaks of the Israelites and the church as a kingdom of priests, it doesn't mean that every member of the people exercises official, liturgical ministry. Rather, it means that the people as a whole have responsibilities for acting as intermediary between God and the rest of the world. They (we!) are to extend to the other peoples of the world the holiness that God has given to the people he chose first. This is the priestly activity that every member of the people shares.

The Israelites at Mount Sinai, the Jews of Jesus' time, members of the Body of Christ today: All of us have been loved by God, all of us have been offered holiness by God, all of us have been called to partake in the priesthood of God's care for all his human creatures.

FOR REFLECTION AND DISCUSSION

How do I experience the church as holy?

How do I experience the church as a kingdom of priestly people?

Eleventh Sunday in Ordinary Time (B)

Ezekiel 17:22–24

This is the first time we hear from the prophet Ezekiel on the Sundays of year B, and our reading is not one that we hear frequently. Thanks to the special solemnities like Trinity Sunday and Corpus Christi, which preempt the liturgy for the Sundays in Ordinary Time, and thanks to the fact that sometimes one of the weeks of Ordinary Time drops out when there are only thirty-three weeks of Ordinary Time in a liturgical year, it can happen that a given Sunday is excluded for several three-year cycles in a row. In fact, this reading was last used in 1997 and will not be heard again until 2012. If it doesn't sound familiar, that may be why.

Ezekiel belonged to a priestly family in the sixth century B.C. Because of his prominent position among the people, he was deported to Babylon in 597 B.C., ten years before the final destruction of Jerusalem. In Babylon he is called by God to the ministry of prophet in 593 B.C. He was still in Babylon, faithfully proclaiming the message of God, when the Babylonians finally destroyed Jerusalem and the kingdom of Judah in 587 B.C. Overall, Ezekiel's message was a word of hope, an assurance that, even though the people were sinful people and deserved the trials that they were experiencing, God would nonetheless rescue them and bring them to a new life in a renewed homeland.

Chapters 13 to 24 of Ezekiel contain a series of prophetic expressions in various forms: speeches, disputations, fables, dirges, etc. Chapter seventeen consists of a complex fable about the political realities of the time.

The fable starts off with an eagle that takes the topmost branch out of a cedar tree and transplants it in a foreign land where not much growth could be expected. This represented how Nebuchadnezzar would take the ineffectual king of Judah and transplant him to captivity in Babylon. Further details of the fable describe the catastrophic errors of the puppet king that Nebuchadnezzar would leave behind, and how these errors merited God's rebuke.

Now our reading begins. When the time is ripe, God, too, will do what Nebuchadnezzar had done. God will take a shoot from the top of the cedar tree that represents his people. God will plant the shoot in an appropriate place and it will grow and flourish. It will become a majestic tree, capable of giving shade and shelter to all the birds of the earth. This tree would demonstrate the power of the Lord. God can do whatever he wants with the tree that images his people. It will flourish because that's what God wants and that's the way things will be.

The flourishing tree that grows out of the tender shoot planted by God represents the reconstituted people. There would be a new king and a vigorous new kingdom. The contemporary sad political circumstances would give way to a glorious new messianic restoration.

It is easy to see the fulfillment of Ezekiel's prophecy in the kingdom of God that Jesus preached. In the Gospel for this Sunday (Mark 4:26–34) we have two parables about the kingdom. We hear Jesus speaking about the seeds that grow to harvest without the farmer fully understanding what is going on. We hear about the mustard seed that is sown in the ground which grows so big that the birds of the sky can find shelter in its branches. (It is not inappropriate to wonder whether Jesus was thinking of our passage from Ezekiel when he spoke this parable.)

In both of our passages we have teachings about the growth and maturity of God's plans. Those who listened to Ezekiel and Jesus did not know how a tiny shoot from the top of a tree could grow into a mammoth cedar, or how a small plant could develop into a size that could welcome the birds of the air. We ourselves may have a better understanding of botany and plant husbandry, but there is still a dimension of mystery to the unfolding of life of any kind. None of us understands it all. In the same way, none of us fully understands how the kingdom of God grows and flourishes. It is God's doing. It is beyond our comprehension. But it is real, and it will continue to grow to full maturity simply because that's the way God wants it to be.

Both passages are also messages of hope. There are better times ahead, better times for the exiles in Babylon, better times for the first disciples of Jesus, better times for Jesus' followers of the twenty-first century. God offers us visions of a happy future. It's up to us to listen and to respond.

FOR REFLECTION AND DISCUSSION

What signs of the growth of Christ's kingdom am I aware of?
What role does hope play in my life as a Christian believer?

Eleventh Sunday in Ordinary Time (C)

2 Samuel 12:7–10, 13

Chapter eleven of the Second book of Samuel gives us the famous story of David and Bathsheba. King David is entranced by the beauty of Bathsheba, wife of Uriah, one of his generals. David has sexual relations with Bathsheba and she becomes pregnant. David attempts to cover up the situation by calling Uriah back from the theater of war allegedly on business, but in actuality so that Uriah would sleep with his wife while he is home and thus assume responsibility for the unborn child. But Uriah refuses to come near her while he is home because he was engaged in a Holy War and thus was expected to abstain from having relations with his wife. David then takes other means to get himself out of his difficult situation. He arranges for Uriah to be killed in battle. He is now free to marry Uriah's widow.

In chapter twelve, Nathan the prophet is sent by the Lord to call David to justice for his sin. He tells David a story about a rich man who takes away a young lamb from his poorer neighbor. What should be done? David answers that such a man merits death because of his lack of sensitivity. "But that's just what you did, taking Uriah's wife away from him," Nathan answers.

Here is where our Sunday Scripture passage begins. Through Nathan God issues a stinging rebuke to David. God reminds David of all that he had done for him. He had given him everything he could possibly desire, and was ready to give David still more if he asked. Now David has shown contempt for the Lord by killing Uriah and taking his wife. David is to be punished by ongoing conflict within his kingdom and his family. David acknowledges his sin. Nathan announces that God has forgiven David's sin, and that his life would be spared.

Scripture shows us David as an enthusiastic servant of the Lord, as a successful king and conqueror. He and his son Solomon would constitute the high points of the monarchy. Future generations would look back to David's reign as the good old days. But David was also a sinner. He was like a spoiled son for whom nothing was ever enough. God had taken him from shepherding a flock of sheep and made him king. Now David is guilty of adultery, murder and unfaithfulness to his role as king and servant for the Lord. His wickedness constitutes despising God, showing contempt for the holiness of the Lord whose representative he was called to be.

But this passage is not primarily about sin. It is about forgiveness. David is more than a disobedient servant. He is also one who loves God and who manifests this side of his character by straightforwardly acknowledging his sinfulness. In response to David's acknowledgment, God assures him that he has already been forgiven. The punishments that God had levied on him would stand, but David would continue as king and as God's friend.

In the Gospel (Luke 7:36–8:3) we have another story of forgiveness. Jesus announces that the sinful woman who was honoring him so extravagantly had had her sins forgiven, as was clear from the love she expressed.

A sinful man, a sinful woman, the forgiveness of God: That's what this Sunday's readings are about. Note that forgiveness means loving in spite of. When we say that God forgives ours sins, it does not mean that God pretends that nothing has happened or that no harm has been done or that there is no need for us to make amends. Evil is evil. Evil does harm. The harm that evil does often persists for a long time. We need to be clear about all that. But God loves us anyhow, in spite of what we have done, in spite of what we still have to make up for. God is a God of forgiveness because God is a God who loves—in spite of the sinfulness of his creatures.

But God calls these forgiven creatures to forgive each other. That's one of the basic ways in which we express our desire to be like God: by forgiving as God does. In the prayer that Jesus taught us, we ask for forgiveness, but only to the extent that we forgive others.

Most of us are not big-time sinners like David was. But we are sinners nonetheless. In various ways and in various contexts we have all demonstrated disregard and ungratefulness for the gifts that God has given us. We all stand in need of God's forgiveness, in need of God's love in spite of our wrongdoing.

And for that reason we are all called to love those who have done wrong to us. We can't expect to get forgiveness unless we are willing to give it.

FOR REFLECTION AND DISCUSSION

What part has being forgiven played in my life?

What part has forgiving played in my life?

Twelfth Sunday in Ordinary Time (A)

Jeremiah 20:10–13

This Sunday's Old Testament and Gospel readings are about tension, struggle and fear. In the Gospel (Matthew 10:26–33) we see Jesus sending the Twelve out on an initial missionary journey. Almost all of Matthew's tenth chapter consists of the instructions that Jesus gave them. In the verses that are read today, he assures them that, in spite of what they face, there will be no need for fear. Three times in these eight verses Jesus tells them not to be afraid.

This Sunday's Old Testament reading is from Jeremiah, the most persecuted of the prophets. Our reading is a poetic reflection by Jeremiah that comes just after the narrative of how the prophet had been scourged and put in the stocks for proclaiming the destruction and exile that lay ahead of the Israelites at the hand of the Babylonians. Those events seem to have taken place some eighteen or twenty years before the final destruction of Jerusalem in 587 B.C. Now the prophet reflects with God about his situation.

The reading is in three parts. In the first part (verse 10) the prophet enunciates his situation. One of the phrases that Jeremiah often used to describe the condition of the people, "Terror on every side," has now become a kind of mocking nickname for the prophet himself. "They're all making fun of me," he says. "They're saying, 'Let's keep our eyes on him. Maybe he will make some mistake that we can use to destroy him and get back at him for all the discomfort that he has caused us.'"

In response to this Jeremiah expresses his confidence in God (verses 11–12). His persecutors will not triumph. God will see to it that they get what is coming to them. It is they who will stumble and fall.

Finally, in verse 13, we have a short hymn of praise. We are called to acknowledge the goodness of the Lord who defends those who rely on him, who rescues the weak from the hands of the wicked.

The verses that constitute this Sunday's readings are the most hopeful part of a much longer poem of lament in which Jeremiah gives fuller expression to profound distress and anxiety. "The word of the Lord has become for me a reproach and derision.... Cursed be the day on which I was born." He would like to stop proclaiming the Lord's message, but he cannot endure the pain of keeping silent.

There is no doubt about the threats that Jeremiah was facing, no doubt about his fear. But there is also no doubt about his confidence in the Lord. Eventually the apostles of Jesus would face persecution, too, but they, also, would have learned by then that the power of the Lord was at hand to deliver them from the threats that faced them.

Not many of us are called to be special agents of God to proclaim future catastrophe as Jeremiah was. Not many are called to give their entire attention and energy to announcing the Gospel as the apostles were. But all of us are called to give witness to the Lord Jesus. We are all called to let people know that in the Lord we find purpose and meaning in our lives. We are called to witness to our respect for all human life, from conception to natural death. We are called to show our respect for marriage and human sexuality. We are called to be men and women of prayer, willing to be seen and known as such.

And all this will not necessarily make us popular or admired. People will disagree with our beliefs. They will make fun of our convictions. They will suggest that it's all a pretext, that what we present as faith is nothing other than hypocrisy. Or we will simply be disregarded, looked at as women and men who really aren't in tune with the times, who are out of touch with the way things really are. We may not suffer outright persecution as Jeremiah and the apostles did, but we may find ourselves excluded from the inner circles at work or at school or in our community. We may find that we are subject to greater scrutiny than others because of what we profess.

To bear the word of God means to make oneself vulnerable to suffering, liable to be derided and misunderstood. God's word inevitably encounters hostility and rejection, and those who present it often get hurt. It's not unreasonable to be afraid of what might happen to us if we are serious about bearing witness to our faith. But it's also not unreasonable to share Jeremiah's confidence in the Lord and to take heart from Jesus' instruction to his apostles: "Do not be afraid."

FOR REFLECTION AND DISCUSSION
What do I fear?
What valid reason can a Christian ever have for being afraid?

Twelfth Sunday in Ordinary Time (B)

Job 38:1, 8–11

By the time the reader of the book of Job gets to chapter thirty-eight he or she has heard about a dozen speeches. In some of them Job's interlocutors (one hesitates to call them friends) have tried to explain Job's sufferings by insisting that he must have sinned, otherwise he wouldn't be punished like this. In other speeches, Job defends himself vigorously against such allegations.

He has not done wrong, he says. If his suffering is a punishment for sin, then he is being made to suffer unjustly.

Now God enters the conversation. God does not provide a ready explanation of what is happening to Job. Instead God speaks in awesomely poetic ways of his own works. The creation, the management of the universe, dominion over the great wild beasts: these are what God busies himself with. Can Job second-guess the Lord of such variety and power? Can Job demand that God explain himself to a mere creature, guiltless though he may be?

God does not ever really answer Job. Instead God gives Job to understand that the rationale for his actions cannot be comprehended by human beings. To understand why God acts as he does would require divine knowledge on the part of human beings, a knowledge that is beyond humans' capacity to provide for themselves, beyond human capacity even to receive as a gift of God. The only answer that can be provided to certain human situations is to acknowledge that God is God and that God's ways surpass even the deepest levels of human understanding.

The reading that the lectionary provides for this Sunday is from the beginning of this final section of Job. God now addresses Job "out of the storm." In the Old Testament the power of God is frequently expressed by God's association with storms. (See, for example Psalm 18:10 [NAB]: God "parted the heavens and came down, / a dark cloud under his feet.")

What follows is God's description of his control over one of the mightiest forces of nature: the sea. From the moment the sea was born, God had it under control. God put the sea where he wanted it to be. He determined how the sea was to be clothed: in clouds and darkness. He set the limits beyond which the power of the sea could not pass. He tamed its proud waves.

Often in antiquity the sea is presented as an untamable monster, an unbridled force, a source of fear. That's not how Job's God looks on the sea. God has absolute control over the sea from the very beginning. He deals with it as a stern parent deals with a child. That's how powerful God is! How can people like Job even think of demanding that God be accountable to them?

Obviously these verses were chosen to set the scene for this Sunday's Gospel (Mark 4:35–41). There we see Jesus quietly asleep in the boat's stern while a storm begins to arise from the sea around them. There is no need for him to be concerned. He knows how to deal with the sea. The apostles are not so confident. "Jesus, do something!" So Jesus gets up from his nap and with a few words quiets everything down. It's like God saying in Job, "here shall your proud waves be stilled."

It is clear that Jesus is here exercising the might of God. Effortlessly he stills the storm. His disciples are awestricken. "Who is this that even the wind and sea obey?"

God is powerful. God's works are beyond human understanding. And Jesus is God. That's what our readings teach us on this Sunday.

We are often tempted to overlook the incomprehensible power of God. Because we understand more about nature and its workings than the ancients did, we tend to think that we understand everything about everything. While we cannot calm the storms, we can predict them and take precautions to stay out of their path. We can deal with some kinds of human storms, too, by means of counseling and medication. We are highly skilled in turning to our own purposes the powers that God has hidden in his creation. We can rein in rivers to make electricity for us. We can use the tiniest components of creation to make explosive devices powerful enough to destroy the world itself. The most fundamental threats to our human life, hunger and disease, are increasingly coming under our control.

Yet we do not have all the answers. We cannot control everything. There are aspects of creation that seem to be far beyond our understanding, far beyond our power to regulate. There are aspects of our own selves that are beyond our grasp. We dare not pretend to give directions to God. We dare not underestimate the powers that only God can know and direct.

FOR REFLECTION AND DISCUSSION

What storms has God stilled in my life?

What storms is the world experiencing presently?

Twelfth Sunday in Ordinary Time (C)

Zechariah 12:10–11; 13:1

The Gospel for this Sunday in Ordinary Time continues the year's proclamation of the Gospel according to Luke. In the portion set out for this Sunday (Luke 9:18–24) we see Peter bearing witness to Jesus as Messiah, "[t]he Christ of God." Then, in the second half of the reading, Jesus foretells his suffering, death and resurrection, and teaches his followers that it is only by giving away their lives for his sake that they will make anything of themselves.

The Old Testament reading for this Sunday, like all First Readings for the Sundays in Ordinary Time, is chosen to highlight the Gospel. The choice for this Sunday seems to be directed principally to the second half of the Gospel, the part about suffering and sacrifice.

The reading comes from the second part of the prophecy of Zechariah. While the first part of Zechariah's book can be dated to about the year 520 (after the return of the exiles and before the rededication of the temple), the second part seems to date from the end of the fourth century B.C., almost two hundred years later than the original prophecy of Zechariah. Its author is not identified.

Chapter twelve, from which this Sunday's reading is taken, is concerned with the salvation and triumph of Jerusalem. Her enemies will not prevail.

Now comes our reading, in three parts. First of all, the Lord promises to pour out on Jerusalem and its people a new spiritual blessing, a spirit of kindness and of prayer.

Next the word of the Lord indicates that this blessing will be conferred on his people through the intervention of an unnamed sufferer, the one "whom they have pierced." The author does not make clear who this person is, whether he is an unidentified martyred prophet or whether he is a manifestation of the suffering servant that we find in Isaiah, chapters 52 and 53. Whoever he is, the citizens of Jerusalem will find safety only in their association with him, in the sorrow they express for him like the sorrow that family members experience at the death of a first-born, an only son. If Jerusalem is to be saved, it will be through mourning this unknown sufferer as people sorrow over "Hadadrimmon in the plain of Megiddo." (Scholars do not speak with certainty about this phrase. It seems to refer to the pagan ritual of sorrow that was part of the cult of fertility gods in the spring and the autumn, and to the place where one of the most devout of the kings of Judah, Josiah, had been killed in battle several centuries earlier. The phrase suggests that only deep, cosmic sorrow is appropriate to respond to the sufferings of the one "they had pierced.")

Third, the text returns to the gifts of God to his Jerusalem people. Forgiveness and purity would spring up for them through the suffering of the pierced one, as abundant as water gushing out of a fountain.

The theme of these verses in their original context is that victory and redemption will come to God's people only after suffering. Conversion/salvation is not just a gift of God. It is related to the mysterious mediation of a victim. The restoration of the people to God's grace depends on the suffering of the sacrificial servant.

The final chapters of the prophecy of Zechariah found deep resonance in the New Testament. They are quoted several dozen times by Jesus and by the apostolic writers. They seemed to strike a chord in the life and mission of Jesus, a chord that is as important as what Isaiah had to say about the messianic suffering servant.

God's word places great importance on suffering as a means of salvation and redemption. God does not take pleasure in human pain in itself, but faithfulness and dedication to the Lord are costly commitments. Such constancy in dedication to God often results in pain and sorrow and suffering. It is not the pain and sorrow and suffering that are pleasing to God, but the faithfulness that underlies them.

Jesus knew that his life of faithfulness would lead to suffering and death. He knew that being his follower would be like carrying a cross, like giving away your life. They all knew, sooner or later, that God had foreseen and foretold through his prophets the part that suffering would play in redemption and in discipleship.

FOR REFLECTION AND DISCUSSION

What part has suffering played in my life?
How does suffering affect the life of the church?

Thirteenth Sunday in Ordinary Time (A)

2 Kings 4:8–11, 14–16a

The Gospel for this Sunday (Matthew 10:37–42) is the conclusion of the second great discourse of Jesus in Matthew's Gospel, that part of the Gospel that scholars refer to as the missionary discourse. This discourse deals primarily with the work that Jesus would now be entrusting to his twelve apostles, but it also addresses the missionary activity of those who would come after them, indeed, the missionary activity of the whole church from after the Resurrection until the Second Coming of Jesus.

At the end of this speech (and of this Sunday's Gospel) Jesus promises rewards to those who welcome the spokesmen of God, the prophets. He repeats this promise twice more, substituting the terms "righteous person" and "little ones" for "prophet." It is this part of the Sunday Gospel that relates to the Old Testament reading.

In this Sunday's Old Testament reading we see a prophet being welcomed, and we see those who provide the welcome being rewarded.

Elisha is one of the greatest of the early prophets. He and his mentor Elijah did not leave behind written teaching as many of the later prophets did, but the collections of their exploits during their prophetic careers remain a very instructive—and important—part of God's word.

297

It is the ninth century B.C. Elisha has succeeded Elijah in prophetic leadership and moves about the northern Kingdom of Israel speaking and acting for the Lord. Shunem was a village northeast of the city of Samaria, about fifteen miles away from Mount Carmel. Mount Carmel was a holy mountain where the prophets used to go to be more intensely in touch with the Lord. Elisha had made friends with a family in Shunem and used to stop there for rest and refreshment on his way to and from Mount Carmel. Such personal contacts were important in an age before hotels. Finally the wife arranges for a guest room to be built for Elisha so that he could make his visits a little longer.

In verses omitted in the reading, Elisha asks the woman whether there is some favor he can do for her. Can he put in a good word for her family with the king? She courteously rejects his offer. Then, in the second half of our reading, Elisha's servant reminds his master that the woman had no son. Elisha sends for her and promises that, despite her age, she would have a son within the year. A great reward for her consistent hospitality! (Later Elisha would bring this boy back to life when he had died.)

There are a number of lessons inherent in this Old Testament reading. One is that those who represent God, i.e., the prophets, somehow share God's power over life and death. Another is that the prophets represent God's beneficent presence in the midst of his people.

But, given the Gospel to which this reading was chosen to relate, the church seems to be calling our special attention to our responsibility to receive the agents of God's word and the message that they bear. The point is not that we are called to make the preachers of God's word physically cozy and comfortable, but that we are to open ourselves to them and to the message that they bear. If the preachers have a responsibility to preach, those to whom the preachers are sent have a responsibility to listen. It is this receptivity that will bring us the reward that Jesus speaks of in the Gospel.

One might say that we are being called to spiritual hospitality, to warm openness to what the Lord wants to offer us, to offering hospitality to God's word. This will include common courtesy and kindness to the men and women who bring the Lord's message to us, but, even more, it will include a willingness to make our own the message, the teaching that God brings to us through his agents.

We twenty-first century Americans tend to be individualistic. We decide whom we will listen to. We decide how much of the message we will accept and respond to. We tend to form our own version of God's word, a version based on our preferences, on our likes and dislikes. We decide to whom and to what we will offer hospitality. But the real issue is not our preferences. The real issue is God's love, God's word, God's means of communication. If we want to be included among those that Jesus talks about—those that welcome a prophet because he is a prophet—then we cannot pick and choose among the prophets or among their messages. Every real prophet, every message from God calls for reception and hospitality.

FOR REFLECTION AND DISCUSSION

How can I offer hospitality to God's agents?
Who are the agents of God's word today?

Thirteenth Sunday in Ordinary Time (B)

Wisdom 1:13–15; 2:23–24

The book of Wisdom is a theologically sophisticated work that seems to have been written in Greek in Alexandria, Egypt about a hundred years before Christ. It was written to encourage the author's co-religionists to be faithful to their religious heritage in the context of pagan secularism.

Wisdom opens with an exhortation to righteousness, a righteousness that brings immortality. In speaking about death, the author seems to envision it more as a separation from God than as a mere biological fact, as a spiritual reality rather than an exclusively physical one. Biological death, the death of the body, is presented as a sign of human alienation from God.

This Sunday's reading is from these opening chapters of Wisdom. The lectionary presents us with two small selections of verses. The first selection is about the relationship of death and creation. The second is about the relationship of death and humanity.

God's creation is good. Death was not intended to be part of it. God made things to be. He didn't make them for death. Moreover, no part of the world was created to be harmful to any other part. It was all meant to exist together in harmony. "[T]he netherworld," i.e., the dominion of death, has no natural place in the world. The world was made to be like God, and godliness is undying.

Man was made in the image of God and therefore was made to be imperishable. If death is in the world, it is "by the envy of the devil." Those who belong to the company of the evil one experience the final, ultimate death of the spirit.

There are two principles inherent in these verses. The first is that God's creation is a good creation, made to be one harmonious whole in which no one part would be harmful or deadly to any other. The second principle is that the real evil and death that we experience in the world is not God's doing but is the result of the incursion of malice into the context of God's good creation, an incursion that has been welcomed and accepted by human beings. Human beings may not be the immediate cause of all that is destructive and inharmonious in the world, but human beings are responsible for allowing the forces of evil to gain a toehold in God's good creation.

These verses also suggest that bodily death may not be the last word. If the world reflects the goodness of God, if God formed humanity to be imperishable, if God made human beings in the image of his own nature, and if justice (i.e., godliness) is undying, then it seems reasonable to conclude that evil will not triumph in the end. The revelation of personal immortality after physical death is a truth that God gave us only gradually. But it seems that by the first century B.C. the idea was becoming more clear and was widely accepted, thanks to texts like this Sunday's reading.

This reading is obviously meant to prepare us for the Gospel (Mark 5:21–43) where we see Jesus raising the daughter of Jairus from the dead. Again there seem to be at least two lessons for us here. The first is that there is something above and beyond physical death. There is a realm from which this young girl could be recalled. The second lesson is that Jesus has power over death. He shares the creative might of the Father to restore creatures to the state that God meant for them from the beginning.

Death impinges on our life from every side. Our misuse of the good things of creation can harm and even destroy us. Our willingness to do violence to what we do not understand or appreciate can turn our world away from wholesomeness and harmony to a state of ongoing hostility. Our openness to selfishness and arrogance can lead us into a state of self-destruction that will render us simply incapable of sharing in the joy and harmony of the life of God. None of this is God's will for us. It's all the result of our acceptance of the powers of evil that are alien to what God had in mind for us from the beginning. It's all death in various guises.

Into this context comes Jesus, restorer of harmony, liberator of sinners, bringer of life, dominator of death. God hasn't abandoned his good world. He restores it in Jesus and offers life in Jesus to all who are willing to accept it.

FOR REFLECTION AND DISCUSSION
How/when/where have I experienced death?
In what ways does our world espouse a culture of death?

Thirteenth Sunday in Ordinary Time (C)

1 Kings 19:16b, 19–21

Almost without exception the Old Testament First Readings in Ordinary Time have been chosen because of their relationship to the Gospels. But the relationship varies from Sunday to Sunday. Sometimes the relationship is one of similarity of themes, as was the case last Sunday when both the Old Testament and the Gospel readings were about the suffering of the Messiah. Sometimes, however, the two readings are in a relationship of contrast. That's the case on this thirteenth Sunday in year C.

The second part of the Gospel (Luke 9:51–62) is what the

Old Testament reading relates to. In the Gospel we hear Jesus setting forth the demands he makes on those who claimed they wanted to be his followers: you won't have very good lodgings, you will have to forget about your relationships with your family, second thoughts will not be tolerated. Following Jesus calls for an immediate and unconditioned response.

The First Reading is about a call, too, the call of Elisha to succeed to the prophetic ministry of Elijah.

The beginning of the reading gives us the ending of Elijah's encounter with God on Mount Horeb. Elijah was disappointed and discouraged. He felt that his mission had been a failure. But then God came to him in a tiny, whispering sound and reassured him. His work would influence the life of Israel for decades to come. He would be instrumental in the anointing of two new kings, who would carry out God's will. And there would be another prophet to succeed him, Elisha son of Shaphat. This last promise on God's part is the first sentence of our Sunday reading. Our text then omits two verses of further encouragement from God and brings us to the call of Elisha.

Elisha is presented as a rich man. Twelve yoke of oxen was not petty cash! Elijah's gesture of throwing his cloak over Elisha expressed God's call for Elisha to share Elijah's mission, to begin to walk in his clothes, as it were. Seemingly the senior prophet kept on walking. Elisha ran after him, aware that he was being called to follow Elijah but not anxious to do so quite yet. He wanted to wrap things up at home first. Elijah's response is somewhat enigmatic. He seems to be telling Elisha to return to what he was doing as if the call had not occurred. Yet when Elisha does go home, he slaughters his oxen, uses his wooden plow for fuel, cooks a solemn final meal for his farm hands, and goes off to become Elijah's apprentice. Thus after some initial hesitation, Elisha makes an irrevocable decision and responds to the symbolic invitation he had received. He will develop into a prophet as great as his mentor, Elijah.

Both readings are about answering a call to discipleship. Elisha's response to Elijah's invitation is not unreasonable. He had responsibilities that he had to take care of first. He carries them out and follows his master as soon as he can.

This would not be good enough for Jesus. In Jesus' calls there was an urgency that would brook no delay. What Elisha did is precisely what Jesus would not allow: saying good-bye to the folks at home. Getting your affairs in order first was of no consequence as far as Jesus was concerned. If you wanted to follow him you had to forget everything else and come immediately. The kingdom to which Jesus called his followers was more important than anything else whatsoever. One wonders whether Jesus was thinking of Elisha when he laid down the requirements we find in this Gospel.

Each one of us has been called by God, more than once. We are called to our human existence, to our Catholic faith, to the circumstances of our life such as work, marriage, parish, personal interests. Some are called to public or church service. Some are called to carry the cross of ill health. All of this involves God's doing. All of this constitutes God's approach to us, God's invitation to become part of the kingdom. Priests are not the only ones to have a vocation! We all have a whole spectrum of vocations from God.

Each of us responds differently to God's calls because each of us is different. Sometimes it takes people a long time to respond to God's invitation, say, to faith. Sometimes it takes a while even to understand what God wants of us. On the other hand, sometimes God approaches us so clearly and forcefully that the only response that makes any sense is an immediate and unequivocal yes. The important thing is that we be attentive to the possibility of God's reaching out to us and that we answer as obediently as we can.

FOR REFLECTION AND DISCUSSION

How readily have I responded to God's calls in my life?
What demands have God's calls placed on me?

Fourteenth Sunday in Ordinary Time (A)

Zechariah 9:9–10

This Sunday's First Reading relates to the last paragraph of the Gospel. The two are linked especially by the word "meek." Jesus describes himself as meek, and Zechariah has God describing the Messiah who was to come with the same adjective.

The book of Zechariah seems to be divided into at least two sections. The earlier section (chapters 1–8) is from about 520 B.C., soon after the return of the exiles, when the temple was being rebuilt. The later section (chapters 9 ff.) seems to have been proclaimed some two hundred years later, during the last decades of the fourth century. It deals with the coming of the Messiah and with final judgment. Our brief Sunday reading is from this latter part of the prophetic book.

These two verses describe the coming of the kingly Messiah. His arrival would be an occasion of joy for God's people. He will not come like a victorious warlord, but as a bringer of peace. He will expel the instruments of war from Jerusalem. No more chariots and horses and bows and arrows! He himself will ride on a donkey, the animal used by noble personages in the golden ages of the past, a vehicle of peace rather than belligerence. He will not be arrogant and demanding. He will be a meek king, a bringer of justice, not of compulsion. And his domain will include all the known world, from the Mediterranean to the Persian Gulf, from the Euphrates to Cyprus and Crete, from north to south, from east to west.

This is a strong and clear messianic pronouncement, one that found resonance and fulfillment in the life and teaching of Jesus.

There is, most memorable of all, Jesus' triumphal entry into Jerusalem toward the end of his public ministry. All four evangelists take pains to point out that Jesus insisted that a donkey be provided for his use on that occasion. It was as if he wanted everybody to be clear about what was happening here: The prophecy of Zechariah was being fulfilled, the king of peace was taking possession of his realm.

Then there is the word used in Zechariah to describe the messianic ruler, the same word that Jesus uses to describe himself in Matthew's Gospel: meek. The dictionary defines *meek* as "enduring injury with patience and without resentment, not violent." Meekness is the opposite of arrogance. Zechariah's Messiah would be meek. So would Jesus.

Zechariah was contrasting his vision of the Messiah with the conquering kings of his time, fierce fighters who would lay siege to a city, capture it, carry off all its valuables, and force its inhabitants into slavery. Power and compulsion were their most prominent characteristics. They could make people do their will whether people liked it or not.

Jesus, in our Gospel, seems to be contrasting himself with the religious leaders of his time whose interpretation of God's will involved heavy burdens, ruthlessly imposed and harshly interpreted. These teachers were proud and arrogant in what they asked of those they taught. Jesus didn't want to be like them. He was "meek and humble of heart," offering his followers peace.

In our culture, we do not think highly of meekness. It is redolent of weakness. It suggests that we are not able to take care of ourselves. Meek people are those that everybody takes advantage of. We tend rather to respect power and self-assertion. We want to be able to look out for ourselves, and even though we may not be interested in grinding people under our heel, we certainly don't intend to allow ourselves to be pushed around.

All this was not of any particular interest to the Messiah that Zechariah spoke about, i.e., Jesus. Power and control and self-assertion were not of consequence to him. He didn't need them. They were not part of his equipment. Jesus was involved in proclaiming the love of the Father for his human creatures, a love that was and is strong enough to include mercy and patience. In return, Jesus looks for self-gift and generosity from his followers. He doesn't force anybody to follow him. He doesn't enslave anybody. He is strong enough to be able to invite us to share God's love and then to wait for our freely given response. He waits for us patiently, humbly, meekly.

We tend to like power because power works quickly and efficiently. You get things done if you are powerful. Results come more quickly if you can make people do what you want them to do. But Jesus is not interested in immediate results. Jesus is interested in the gift of our hearts to him and to his Father. So he approaches us meekly and with a humble heart.

FOR REFLECTION AND DISCUSSION

What part does meekness play in my life?

Does power have any role to play in Jesus' plan of salvation?

Fourteenth Sunday in Ordinary Time (B)

Ezekiel 2:2–5

Ezekiel was carried off to Babylon in the deportation that took place in 597 B.C. The destruction of Jerusalem and the definitive deportation of the Jews would occur in 587 B.C. In between these two dates, around about 593 B.C., Ezekiel received his call to be a prophet.

This call came in the context of a vision of God's majesty that is recounted in the first chapter of Ezekiel's book. In the second chapter (from which this Sunday's reading is taken) God's attention is focused on Ezekiel. God's words and actions spell out various elements that are involved in the prophetic vocation. God also tells the prophet to what kind of people he is being sent.

The reading begins with Ezekiel receiving God's spirit, i.e., power that would enable the prophet to hear God's word. Next God sets him on his feet, i.e., puts him in a posture of leadership. God informs Ezekiel that he is being sent to the Israelites to speak God's word to them. To be imbued with God's spirit, to have a certain prominence, to be sent, to speak God's word: all that is involved in being a spokesman for God, in being a prophet among God's people.

But our reading also describes the public to which the prophet is being sent. They are rebellious even as their ancestors were. They are hard-hearted and obstinate. They may or may not heed what God says to them through his prophet. God does not send prophets because the people are submissive and obedient. God sends prophets to rescue his people from their self-destructive sinfulness.

This Old Testament reading is linked to the Sunday Gospel (Mark 6:1–6) by two themes. The first is the theme of prophecy.

The second is the theme of disbelief and rejection.

Like Ezekiel, Jesus was a prophet and was fully aware of his prophetic calling. In the Gospel, it is Jesus who applies the term "prophet" to himself. This meant that Jesus was in touch with the Spirit of the Father. He had been given a position of prominence in the religious life of his time. He had been sent to God's people, sent to speak to them in God's own name. All the qualities that defined Ezekiel's vocation were also part of Jesus' mission. Jesus was a prophet like Ezekiel. His mission of prophecy was one that fit in clearly with the whole prophetic tradition of the Israelites, beginning with Moses. Jesus was sent to speak to the people with the voice of God. He was a prophet.

But, like the other prophets, Jesus was not received with openness and joy. God had warned Ezekiel that he was being sent to a people that had rejected God, a rejection that had brought them into exile in Babylon. The people to whom Jesus was sent were not particularly receptive of him. In this Sunday's gospel Jesus' own relatives and neighbors sneer at his prophetic claims. "He can't be special," they said, "he's just like us." "And they took offense at him." This offense that we see at work in Jesus' home town would eventually constitute the general response to his whole mission. By the end of Jesus' life, his prophetic mission, his proclamation of God's word, would win him a level of hostility that would lead him to the death of a criminal.

Being a prophet can be dangerous. The prophet finds himself in the middle between the demands of God and the reactions of the people to whom he is sent to speak. Almost by definition a prophet is unpopular. After all, if everybody were already in agreement with what the prophet was sent to proclaim, there would be no need of the prophet. The fact that a prophet is in their midst is a sign that the people are in need of teaching and exhortation that may not necessarily be comforting or welcome to them.

In our time the church carries forward the prophetic mission of Ezekiel and Jesus. The church has been constituted, called and sent by God to speak God's word to the world. And God's word is not always easily understood. God's word is not always easily accepted.

We shouldn't be surprised if not everybody accepts the dogmas of the church. We shouldn't be surprised if we ourselves find certain aspects of church teaching to be difficult to receive. God's word is always demanding, challenging, even threatening. And the human creatures to whom that teaching is addressed have always been selfish, defensive, sinful.

Prophets and prophetic proclamation are generally not popular. But they are very important if we are to remain in touch with God, and God with us.

FOR REFLECTION AND DISCUSSION

Is being a prophet something to be desired? Why or why not?
To what extent are God's people of today obedient? Rebellious?

Fourteenth Sunday in Ordinary Time (C)

Isaiah 66:10–14c

We have seen that, although the First Readings for the Sundays in Ordinary Time are chosen for their relationship with the Gospel, the nature of that relationship varies from Sunday to Sunday. Sometimes the relationship is one of similarity, when the Old Testament reading says much the same thing as the Gospel.

Sometimes the two readings are in contrast, as was the case last week when Elisha's response to his call by Elijah was different from the call that Jesus expected from those who would follow him. Sometimes one of the readings serves to illustrate the other, to enrich the outline or fill in the colors, as it were. That's what we have on this fourteenth Sunday of Ordinary Time for year C.

The Gospel (Luke 10:1–12, 17–20) is about the proclamation of the kingdom on the part of Jesus' disciples. Jesus tells them how to go about their task, and, at the end of the passage, they tell Jesus how they have fared. The basic message that they are to proclaim is that the kingdom of God is at hand, a message that occurs twice in our Gospel passage. But Jesus does not go into any detail about the nature of the kingdom: what it is or what it would be. It's up to the First Reading to give us some idea of that.

The First Reading comes from the last portion of the book of the prophet Isaiah, the very last chapter, in fact. This portion of Isaiah was written after the return from exile, a portion of the book that is both somber and optimistic. This is one of the more positive passages and it describes what God would do for his people when his plans finally came to fulfillment.

In the verses that precede our reading, the prophet says that Jerusalem, God's holy city, would bring forth a new people miraculously, abruptly, without effort, like a mother giving birth to a child without labor pains.

Now our reading begins. God calls on all those who love Jerusalem, all those who had been sorrowful because of her misfortunes, to rejoice in the new birth, to find abundant nourishment and security in her. Then the message is repeated. Jerusalem will comfort all those who love her, comfort them as a mother comforts her child. She will carry them and hug them and share with them the abundance of her riches. All will rejoice in what has come upon Jerusalem. And now the words that illuminate everything else: "the LORD's power shall be known to his servants."

It may be that the author of our passage was looking forward to a time of political security and economic prosperity. But in describing what was to come, the author's text is also describing in its highly poetic language the final kingdom of God, the messianic kingdom, the same kingdom that the disciples of Jesus were sent to proclaim.

Jesus' directions to his disciples do not go into detail about the kingdom that they are to proclaim. The reading from Isaiah does. When God finally and definitively takes over, "when the Lord's power shall be known to his servants," it will be a time of renewed affection between God and the world, a time when God will embrace the world as a mother embraces her baby. All needs will be satisfied and all danger eliminated. Everything good will be provided in abundance to the citizens of the kingdom. All creation will rejoice forever.

The author of this chapter of Isaiah seems to be saying more than he was conscious of. What may have been meant as a prophecy of material well-being was actually the proclamation of a final future that would surpass even the most optimistic expectations of the people of post-exilic Jerusalem.

The messianic kingdom was on the way when our passage of Isaiah was written. It was still on the way when Jesus sent his disciples out to preach. We cannot yet fully describe it and the words we use to try to describe it are, by definition, inadequate. We speak of final fulfillment, sharing the life of the risen Christ, a heavenly eternity. And it is all that. But somehow the poetic images of Isaiah provide other dimensions to our understanding of what God has in mind for us, ideas that are less abstract, sentiments that are warmer and more comforting.

The kingdom that the earliest disciples of Jesus preached is still being preached by their successors. It has already begun to arrive in and through the church. But its coming is not yet complete. What Jesus promised and Isaiah tried to describe, when "the LORD's power shall be known to his servants," is still to come. But God's word gives us at least some idea of what to expect.

FOR REFLECTION AND DISCUSSION

What does the kingdom of God mean to me?

What signs of the presence and future fulfillment of the kingdom have I perceived?

Fifteenth Sunday in Ordinary Time (A)

Isaiah 55:10–11

This Sunday's short Old Testament reading is from the last chapter of the second main part of Isaiah, the part called the Book of Consolation. These chapters of Isaiah (chapters 40 to 55) were proclaimed by a member of the "school" of Isaiah to the exiles in Babylon to offer them hope and encouragement in their time of trial.

This particular chapter is highly lyrical and seems to be a favorite for the church's liturgy. Portions of its first eleven verses are used no fewer than ten times in the three-year cycle of Mass readings for the liturgical year.

The two verses that constitute this Sunday's overture reading are about the word of God. Just as the rain and snow always and unerringly do their task of making the earth productive, so also God's word always achieves the purpose for which it was sent.

There are several important lessons about God's word in these short verses.

The first is that God's word it not merely content. It doesn't just say something. God's word is also event. It does something. God's word is always effective, bringing about a result. Those who heard these words proclaimed by their author would no doubt recall that all of creation is the result of God's word: "In the beginning...God said..." (NRSV).

Second, just as human beings do not cause rain and snow and their outcomes to happen, so also human beings are not the cause either of God's word or of the effect that God's word produces. God is the primary agent of the productivity and fertility of the earth. God is also the primary agent of all the blessings that result from his word. It all happens—the rains that produce food and the blessings that produce human well-being—through God's will, not through human effort.

Third, although God's word is effective and comes through God's initiative, it nonetheless involves some degree of human effort to produce the fullness of its results. The rain waters the earth and makes it fruitful and helps it to produce seed, but the farmer still needs to plant the seed in order to have the grain to make his bread. Similarly, God's word requires some degree of human collaborative effort if it is to bring the fullness of what God intends.

Finally, these words from Isaiah suggest that there is a cycle of generosity in the operation of God's word. It comes forth from the mouth of God. It reaches its goal. Then, having achieved its purpose, it somehow returns to God, presumably to return again to carry forward the next stages of God's providence for us. God's word is not a once-in-a-lifetime contact, but an ongoing process.

This reading was chosen to serve as an introduction to the

Gospel. The Gospel is the parable of the sower and the seed. This parable seems to have been important in the early church because it (and its explanation by Jesus) is preserved in each of the first three Gospels. It spoke to a question that must have been in the heart of many members of the early church: If what we believe is God's word, how is it that the results seem so sparse?

The parable indicates that there is nothing wrong with the seed, that God's word is not without power. If the results are not what we might expect, the fault is not the lifelessness of the seed, but the inhospitable earth into which it falls. When the seed, God's word, does fall on receptive ground, the results are nothing less than miraculous.

The Gospel parable offers us the same teaching as the reading from Isaiah. God's word is powerful. It is offered through God's initiative. It requires appropriate response from us. It involves an ongoing cycle of growth and fruitfulness.

Like the book of Isaiah and the teaching of Jesus, the church also offers us God's word. It has preserved for us the Sacred Scriptures. It expresses the work and will of God in the sacraments. It continues the teaching mission that Jesus fulfilled in his preaching and his parables. The church's action and teaching comes with the power of God. What the church offers is true and wholesome and holy. But it can be resisted. People cannot be forced against their will to pay any attention to what the church says. They cannot be compelled to accept what the church offers. But that doesn't make the church's proclamation any less true or any less the word of God.

FOR REFLECTION AND DISCUSSION

How have I experienced the power of God's word?

Where do I perceive resistance to God's word?

Fifteenth Sunday in Ordinary Time (B)

Amos 7:12–15

Amos was the earliest of the prophets to have his words and works preserved in writing. He was born in the Southern Kingdom of Judah. He made his living tending sheep and caring for sycamore trees. About 750 B.C. Amos was sent by God into the Northern Kingdom to speak the Lord's word to the people during the prosperous reign of King Jeroboam II.

In the reading from Amos provided for this Sunday, we see Amos in controversy. Bethel was one of the major shrines in the Northern Kingdom. It had special connections with the king. The priest in charge of this important shrine was one Amaziah. Amos had come up from the south and had been preaching against the king and the practices of the kingdom right there in the precincts of the king's shrine. It was clear to Amaziah that this could not be allowed to continue. After all, the king would expect the high priest of his very own shrine to see to it that nobody preached against the king there.

As our reading opens we hear Amaziah trying to get rid of Amos. Amaziah does not make any judgment about the truthfulness of the prophet or about the validity of his message. He just wants him to be gone, to go back home and stop embarrassing the king and the people in Bethel. "Go earn your living somewhere else," he says.

Amos replies that he is not there to earn a living. He is not one of the religious "professionals" who were seemingly paid by the king or perhaps by temple authorities to make pious pronouncements on public occasions. These religious types may have been on the ecclesiastical payroll, but Amos makes it clear that he was not. In fact, he was a country boy, "a shepherd and a dresser of sycamores." He had taken up prophecy at the command of God. He was not in Bethel to make a living. He was there because God had sent him there.

Apparently in certain Old Testament times the exercise of prophecy was not limited to people who had been called by God. Some people set themselves up as spokesmen for God because they discovered they could earn a livelihood that way. They were not necessarily false prophets, but they were not necessarily true and valid prophets, either. They were simply ready to take advantage of the pious generosity of the people of their time, people who were anxious to get reassurance from someone claiming to speak for God. Just as one could hire a poet or a musician to bring a little extra sophistication to a family event, so one could hire a prophet or two to provide a religious dimension. Being a professional prophet may have been a reasonably harmless way to earn one's livelihood, but it wasn't the same thing as being a real, true prophet, a speaker whose word came with a guarantee from God.

There are two tie-ins between the reading from Amos and this Sunday's Gospel (Mark 6:7–13). The first is that both Amos and the Twelve were sent out at the behest of the Lord. It wasn't their idea to go around speaking God's message. The second tie-in is what one might call pastoral economics. Just as Amos contends that he is not in the prophecy business for what he can get out of it, so also Jesus warns his advance agents not to be worried about their personal comfort as they went forth to preach repentance.

There is always some degree of tension between the fundamental prophetic vocation, being called by God to proclaim God's word, and the human needs of the prophet. A prophet needs food, clothing and shelter just as other people do. But a prophet also needs to be faithful to his calling. Speaking out God's message fully and faithfully is more important than having a decent place to stay and good food to eat. If a prophet shows too much interest in the fringe benefits of his vocation, he runs the risk of seeming to make the fringes into the center. He begins to look like other professionals for whom payment is primary and truth a by-product. At the same time, the prophet cannot deliver God's message if his basic human needs are not met.

It is in this context that Christians need to be attentive to the virtue of poverty. Poverty doesn't mean just being without things. Poverty means using the goods of the world only to the extent that we need them in order to carry out the central demands of our calling as Christian believers. We can't carry out our call to give witness to Christ if our main interest is getting as much as we can of the world's goods.

The trouble is that we live in a culture that stresses the importance of possessions. Getting by with a little for the sake of God's kingdom doesn't make much sense for most people.

FOR REFLECTION AND DISCUSSION

Who has been sent to proclaim God's word in our world?
How could one be a "professional" prophet today?

Fifteenth Sunday in Ordinary Time (C)

Deuteronomy 30:10–14

Sometimes the First Reading in Ordinary Time helps us understand how we are to read the Gospel. The First Reading serves to complement the Gospel, to lead us to understand it in the proper tonality. That's the case for this fifteenth Sunday of Ordinary Time.

This Sunday's Gospel (Luke 10:25–37) is in two parts. The first part is Jesus' response to the question from the scholar of the law who wants to know what he needs to do to inherit eternal life. Jesus, skillful teacher that he is, gets the scholar to answer his own question. The law says that we are to love the Lord our God with all our energy and love our neighbor as ourselves. (This answer is a combination of Leviticus 19:18 and Deuteronomy 6:5.) So the next question is, "And who is my neighbor?" Jesus answers with the second part of this day's Gospel, the parable of the good Samaritan.

The First Reading relates to the first part of the Gospel and tells us how we are to understand the command to love God with everything we've got and to love our neighbor as ourselves. It is a reading from Deuteronomy.

The book of Deuteronomy is one of the most frequently used books of the Old Testament for our Sunday First Readings. It is a collection of religious directives first gathered together from prior sources in the seventh century B.C., toward the end of Israel's life as an independent kingdom. It received its final form after the exile. Its purpose is to teach people how to live in the Promised Land. It is cast in the form of a series of sermons put into the mouth of Moses, imagined as addressing the children of Israel at the end of his life. The reading for this Sunday comes near the end of Deuteronomy.

The first paragraph of our reading requires some grammatical explanation. Moses' words to the people do not constitute a complete sentence. It may be that those who prepared the lectionary meant us to remember the words that precede our reading in the full text, something like, "God will bless you, if only you..." It is also possible that we are meant to take these clauses as an exclamation expressing a wish, as when we say, "If only it would rain!"

In either case, it is clear that the readers are being invited to repent of their sins and to observe the laws that are set down "in this book of the law."

Next we hear something more about the law. The author assures us that the law is not something "too mysterious and remote for you." We then have two illustrations of what is meant. The law is not something way up in the sky that we need to send astronauts to bring back, nor something way at the ends of the earth that we have to send explorers in ships to get for us. Now the author repeats what he said before: The law is not foreign and strange. It's right here. It's already in your mouth so you can talk about it. It's already in your hearts so that you can remember it without effort. All you have to do is carry it out!

This Old Testament passage tells us how we are to interpret what the scribe says and what Jesus agrees with in the Gospel. The directions that God gives us for our lives, whether in the Old Testament or the New, are not threats or burdens or esoteric directions that we can't really understand. God's law is the enunciation of the needs and demands of our own nature. God's law teaches us how we can most productively and most happily be and become everything that God meant us to be. The God of the law is not an authoritarian emperor who transmits to us his ineffable will and demands that we observe it whether we like it or not. The God of the law is a loving father who knows his children and who is anxious for his children to understand and carry out the directions that will make them most happy and most fulfilled.

At some time or another, all of us respond immaturely to

God's directions to us. We find ourselves thinking that God's law is restrictive, that it hasn't been properly presented to us, that we need to interpret it very carefully so that we don't end up doing more than God really demands of us. We tend to overlook that God's law is a gift given to us by a loving father for the sake of our own well-being.

Jesus and the scholar of the law were not engaged in a discussion about plea bargaining. They were two lovers of their heavenly Father who shared enthusiasm and gratitude for his loving guidance for his human creatures. Both of them would have said "Thanks be to God," in response to our verses from Deuteronomy.

FOR REFLECTION AND DISCUSSION

Where do I encounter God's law?

Am I more inclined to look on God's law as burden or as gift? Why?

Sixteenth Sunday in Ordinary Time (A)

Wisdom 12:13, 16–19

This Sunday's First Reading is from the youngest book in the Old Testament, the book of Wisdom. This book seems to have been written in Alexandria, Egypt, about fifty or a hundred years before the birth of Jesus. It was written to offer guidance and encouragement to the Jews who lived in the aggressively pagan atmosphere of hellenistic Egypt, for whom maintaining their Jewish religious identity was an ongoing challenge.

Our reading is from chapter twelve which is concerned with God's mercy. More specifically, it deals with the relationship between God's power and God's patience with sinners.

The author is addressing God. The reading starts off (in verse 13) by reflecting with God (and pointing out to the reader) that God is not answerable to anybody for his judgments. There is no god more powerful to whom the God of Israel must render an accounting either for his severity or for his forbearance. God is in charge of everything, and does not need to prove that he is just.

In the following verses of our reading (16–19) the text expands on how God's power relates to his justice and mercy. Precisely because God is all powerful he can afford to be lenient. God doesn't need to be afraid of anybody, especially sinners! Those who choose to be defiant of God's law will indeed experience his punishment. But God also lets us see his power by his refusal to be threatened by the more ordinary offenses of more ordinary people. God can act with leniency precisely because he is powerful. That's why he gives his children a chance to repent when they have sinned. In acting in this way, God also instructs us that those who are just must be kind.

In brief, these verses teach us that God's mercy is not a sign of weakness but of strength.

This reading seems to have been chosen to lead in to the first parable that we hear in this Sunday's Gospel: the weeds and the wheat. This parable is set out by Jesus in the first seven verses of the reading from Matthew and is then explained by him in the last eight verses. (Note that the optional shorter version of the Gospel that the lectionary provides consists only of the parable of the weeds and the wheat. This suggests that, in the minds of those who prepared the lectionary, this was the part of the Gospel that is most important.)

Why is evil allowed to continue? Why doesn't God root it out and get rid of it here and now? In the parable, Jesus suggests that rooting out the evil could also bring harm to the good. In his explanation of the parable, Jesus tells his disciples that the time will come when the weeds will indeed be rooted out and destroyed, but it's not up to us to worry about that at present.

If the author of Wisdom were explaining the parable, he might say that, in letting the weeds grow, God is demonstrating his power. God doesn't need to worry about whether the weeds will harm the harvest. It's God's harvest and God will see to it that the harvest is good.

Most of us, at some time or another, have wondered about the prosperity of evil. Why should bad people be successful? Why don't sinners get what is coming to them right away? Why does God wait so long to set things right? It's not because God is unable to do any differently. It's not because evil is more powerful than good. It's because God is God, a Lord whose power is demonstrated by his leniency toward those who have done wrong, a loving Lord who is generous to his children even when the children misbehave.

When we are disturbed by the seemingly untrammeled success of evil, it is often because we ourselves are not really convinced about the value of the good. Here we are, striving to do the right thing, keeping the rules, acting obediently even when it's hard, and over there are the bad people. Everything seems to be going all right for them. How come they're not being punished? Isn't God in charge here? Why should I keep trying to be good when there doesn't seem to be any payoff for it?

If what we are really interested in is the immediate payoff, if following the directions of the Lord is a kind of job for us, a series of chores that we neither understand nor appreciate, then we may not really be doing good at all. We may be working merely out of a sense of self-interest.

Or again, if God's mercy exercised toward others is a source of dismay for us, maybe that means that we, too, are in need of God's mercy.

FOR REFLECTION AND DISCUSSION

Where do I see God's forbearance being exercised in the church and the world?

How have I experienced God's patience and mercy?

Sixteenth Sunday in Ordinary Time (B)

Jeremiah 23:1–6

Only three books of the Old Testament are used more often than Jeremiah in the three-year cycle of Sunday readings: Isaiah, Genesis and Exodus. The figure of the prophet Jeremiah is often seen as a preview of Christ.

Jeremiah's career took place at the end of the life of the Southern Kingdom, before and after the conquest and destruction of Jerusalem by the Babylonians. The first twenty-five chapters of Jeremiah are prophecies of woe against the city of Jerusalem and the kingdom of Judah, against the religious and political leaders who led God's people to their doom.

This Sunday's reading seems to have been proclaimed just before Jerusalem fell to the Babylonians in 587 B.C., during the reign of the ineffectual King Zedekiah (whose name means "the Lord is my justice"). Jeremiah is referring to the last kings of Judah who have misguided the people. He speaks of the people and the leaders in terms of shepherds and flock.

In the first half of the reading, aimed at the kings of Judah, he berates the shepherds for their neglect of the flock. They have not protected the flock. They have allowed the sheep to go astray. But God will undo the harm they have done. God will gather the sheep again and bring them back to where they belong.

But there is more. In the second half of the reading God promises that there will be new shepherds for the flock, leaders who will deliver them from fear and bring them all back together.

Now the text abandons the image of flock and shepherd and speaks directly about a new king for the people, a king descended from David who will govern with wisdom and justice, who will bring Israel to live in security, whose name, in contrast to "the Lord is my justice," will be "the Lord is *our* justice." His interest will be the people, not the selfish demands of dynastic self-preservation.

The false shepherds will be replaced by a new shepherd, by a personage who would represent God's care for his people, by someone who would be everything a shepherd should be. Between shepherd and flock there should be trust and care. The flock would pasture with a sense of security, confident in the oversight of the shepherd. It will be the shepherd who provides direction for the flock. The flock over which the new shepherd watches will be the same scattered flock that existed before, only now it will be under new, God-given guidance.

What God promised through Jeremiah was fulfilled in the ministry of Jesus. That's the lesson the lectionary gives us by the juxtaposition of these verses from Jeremiah with this Sunday's Gospel (Mark 6:30–34). In the last verse of the Gospel we see the people of Jesus' time wandering astray like the people of Jeremiah's time. Their shepherds had not led them well. They were in need of a new shepherd. And Jesus presents himself as the shepherd promised by God. With his teaching he satisfies their spiritual hunger. He offers them direction. He loves them and is compassionate over them. He leads them in the direction that will insure their full well-being.

What we read about in this Sunday's Old Testament and Gospels is not merely the account of a pair of religious crises in times past. It's about more than the spiritual state of the Israelites just before the exile or the Jews at the time of Jesus. What we read about in these passages is about us.

We live in a time of great confusion and uncertainty. The principles of right conduct that everyone used to take for granted are now up for grabs. It is increasingly difficult to maintain a sense of purpose and direction in a world which stresses selfishness and comfort, self-determination and individual personal security. Each of us finds himself or herself called to wander afield by attractions that are not in harmony with our ultimate best interests. Trustworthy teachers are hard to identify in our culture of constant noise and constant distraction. There are plenty of voices to listen to, but it's hard to determine which of them are worth following, which of them are authentic guides and which are merely expressions of superficial self-interest— either on the part of the one who leads or the one who follows.

In this context God continues to fulfill the promise that was made to Jeremiah. He provides his people with a good shepherd who guides them and nourishes them. Jesus is moved with pity for those who seem to be wandering in aimlessness. Jesus shepherds us.

FOR REFLECTION AND DISCUSSION

How is Jesus shepherd and king of his people?

How do I experience Jesus as my shepherd?

Sixteenth Sunday in Ordinary Time (C)

Genesis 18:1–10a

The theme that ties the First Reading to the Gospel this Sunday is hospitality. In the Gospel (Luke 10:38–42) we see Jesus as the guest of Martha and Mary. Jesus gently rebukes Martha who seems to be more interested in the details of getting dinner on the table than she is in paying attention to her guest. "Mary has chosen the better part."

As a preview to this encounter, the lectionary gives us the narrative of Abraham offering hospitality to God.

At this point in the Genesis narrative, Abraham has been called by God to leave his homeland and head out to a country that God would show him. In chapter 15 God had promised him land and progeny and confirmed his promise with an oath, appearing in flames of fire. In chapter 17 God repeated his promises. Now, in chapter 18, we have still another encounter between God and Abraham.

Abraham was a nomadic chieftain, wandering slowly through the lands to which God had led him in order to provide pasture for his flocks, sometimes settling down for extended periods. Our narrative places him and his tents near Mamre and its landmark "turpentine tree." Abraham's was a hard life, but Abraham was rich and so enjoyed the benefits of prosperity. If nothing else, he didn't need to be out in the sun in the heat of the day.

Suddenly, three men were standing there. Conscious of the demands of nomadic hospitality, Abraham jumps us, greets them with the appropriate bow, and offers them rest and refreshment. "Let me get you just a little something to eat," he says. They accept his offer. Abraham rushes into the tent and tells his wife (and presumably her servants) to prepare what amounts to a banquet. Abraham was not one to stint when it came to hospitality! A half a bushel of flour made into bread, every cut of veal they could imagine, homemade yogurt—not bad for unexpected guests on the edge of the desert. Abraham stands courteously and attentively nearby to see that their every need is responded to.

Then one of them asks about Abraham's wife and promises that, despite her advanced age, she will bear him a child within a year. It was the promise that Abraham had heard before, God's promise, now repeated still again. And the one making the promise must be none other than the Lord himself, sitting at his table, as his guest.

In the eighteenth chapter of Genesis the narrative continues with an after-dinner stroll during which a discussion arises about God's exercise of justice and mercy. (This discussion is presented in next Sunday's First Reading.) But this Sunday's reading stops before that. It's as if the editors of the lectionary want us to focus our attention on this one fact, that God had been a guest in Abraham's tent and had been entertained at his table.

The text is rather ambiguous about the appearance and the presence of God. Three men appear. Abraham addresses one of them. They all express their acceptance of his invitation to dinner. Later one of them speaks of the son that will be born. Were they a group of equals? Was one of them clearly the leader? It may be that the text wants to suggest the mysteriousness and incomprehensibility of God. The Lord does not present himself in simple human terms, but in ways that require particular attention and openness on the part of the one being visited. Yet, before they parted company, Abraham knew for certain that God had been his guest.

One of the lessons that the lectionary seems to want us to

draw from this reading (joined with the Gospel) is that God sometimes enjoys socializing with his human friends. Abraham and Sarah, Martha and Mary: The Lord had a special concern for these people, a particular relationship with them. The Lord loved them and wanted to be with them and wanted them to be with him. The Lord walks and talks and dines with those he loves. It is up to them to respond to the Lord's presence in a way that is in keeping with who and what he is, as Abraham did when he respectfully offered every detail of courtesy and care to his guests, as Mary did when she sat listening attentively to Jesus as he spoke.

Human beings sometimes offer hospitality to God. But God offers hospitality to us as well. These two readings about human hospitality to God are meant to be proclaimed at the celebration of the Eucharist. The Eucharist is nothing less than God offering hospitality to us, having us to dinner, calling us to enjoy his company, giving us a preview of what is in store for us when we enjoy the eternal hospitality of heaven.

FOR REFLECTION AND DISCUSSION

Have I ever offered hospitality to God?

How do I enjoy God's company?

Seventeenth Sunday in Ordinary Time (A)

1 Kings 3:5, 7–12

The two books of Samuel in the Old Testament recount the history of God's people in the Promised Land from the period of the last "judges" (Israelite warlords who would be called by God to defend the people as needed) through the reign of Saul, the first king, to the end of the reign of King David. (David's reign began about 1000 B.C.) The two books of Kings recount the people's history from the time of King Solomon to the destruction of Jerusalem in 587 B.C.

This Sunday's Old Testament reading is from near the beginning of the first book of Kings. King David had grown old and feeble. He had survived the attempted revolution of his son Absolom. As he came closer to death, another son, Adonijah attempted to get himself named king to succeed his father, David. At this time, kingship was not passed automatically to the eldest son, but to the son chosen by the father. Some time previously, David had promised to confer the throne on Solomon, the son of himself and Bathsheba. As Adonijah was organizing his supporters, Bathsheba and others came to David to remind him of his promise. David then had Solomon anointed king to succeed him and died soon thereafter. Solomon's reign would be long and, in many ways glorious, though disappointing in the end. Our reading shows us the young king praying in the presence of God, the God who had so loved and supported Solomon's father, David.

God tells Solomon to ask for whatever he wants. Solomon responds in humble submission that he is still unskilled and that he recognizes that his responsibilities are great. He asks for the gift to govern well for the good of the people. That would be more important than anything else. God is pleased with Solomon's request, and gives him what he had asked for: an understanding and wise heart, a heart so wise and understanding "that there has never been anyone like you up to now, and after you there will come no one to equal you." In the verses that come immediately after our reading, God also promises to give Solomon gifts that he had not asked for: riches, glory and a long life.

Solomon—at least at this early time in his long life and reign—knew that the most important thing he had to do was to rule well and wisely over God's people. This was more important than any personal gifts he might have desired. And he asks God for the ability to do that. God is pleased because Solomon's priorities and God's priorities are the same: the well-being of the people.

This reading seems to have been chosen to correspond to the first two parables that the church offers us in the Gospel (Matthew 13:44–52): the parable of the treasure in the field and the parable of the merchant in search of fine pearls. Here, too, we have a question of priorities. Everything is secondary to the treasure in the field. Nothing is more important than the pearl of great price.

We all have priorities in our lives, whether we are aware of them or not. Some people's lives, consciously or unconsciously, are directed by the pursuit of wealth or comfort or security. Some people's lives are directed by the love of God and neighbor. Our priorities, whatever they may be, are what determine what kind of a life we have, and whether it is a self-serving life or a godly life.

Jesus' parables remind us that it is reasonable, even necessary to have priorities, to be aware that some things are more important than others, that no sacrifice is too great to acquire what is really important. And our Old Testament reading teaches us that one of the most basic priorities for a person of faith is the determination to do that which God wants done. In Solomon's case it was the care of God's people. In our case, it is love and concern for our neighbor in accord with what God wants for that neighbor.

Having the right priorities, having priorities that are in harmony with the priorities of God, is what constitutes wisdom. And that's what God confers on Solomon. That's what God invites us to pursue in our relationship with him. Wisdom does not mean the ability to work out esoteric problems that ordinary people can't handle. Wisdom means having the right priorities and knowing how to apply those priorities to the nuts and bolts of our ordinary life. Wisdom is not just for kings. Wisdom is something that God offers to every believer. It is something that every believer needs.

FOR DISCUSSION AND REFLECTION

What/Who is really important in my life?
How does my life involve wisdom?

Seventeenth Sunday in Ordinary Time (B)

2 Kings 4:42–44

The ministry of the prophet Elisha took place toward the end of the ninth century and the beginning of the eighth century B.C. He was the chosen successor of another mighty spokesman of God, the prophet Elijah. The Elisha narratives in 2 Kings show us this prophet involved with the great political figures of his day (the kings of Israel and Judah and Edom), but we also see him alleviating human distress. Sometimes these accounts of Elisha helping others deal with assistance given to individuals, sometimes with Elisha's interventions to take care of the guild or community of prophets that had arisen around him. Both kinds of stories are intended to illustrate the ongoing care of God for his chosen people.

This Sunday's First Reading is one of the stories that has to do with Elisha's instrumentality in looking out for his followers.

Chapter 4, verse 38 tells us that there was famine in the land and the one hundred members of Elisha's prophetic guild were reduced to eating whatever they could put their hands on. Just before our reading begins, we hear how they almost died from eating poisoned vegetation, but were saved by Elisha.

Now someone appears with a gift of twenty barley loaves and some unthreshed grain. Elisha orders the food to be distributed among his followers. "This will never feed a hundred men," his servant objects. But Elisha knows the Lord and has confidence in him. "The Lord says there will be more than enough," he says. And sure enough, the hundred guild members eat their fill, and there is even some left over, just as the Lord had promised.

This narrative was clearly chosen to harmonize with the Gospel. Notice, however, that the Gospel for this Sunday and for the following four Sundays are not from the Gospel according to Mark but from the sixth chapter of the gospel according to John. Apparently the experts who prepared the lectionary felt that there had to be some place in the Sunday cycle for John's account of Jesus' teaching about the bread of life. Since the Gospel of Mark is shorter than Matthew and Luke, it seemed appropriate to substitute John's narrative about the feeding of the five thousand for Mark's account (6:35–44) which should come at this point. This narrative will be followed by the rest of John's sixth chapter in which Jesus speaks in greater detail about the meaning of the bread that the people had just eaten. The semi-continuous readings from Mark resume with chapter seven on the twenty-second Sunday of this year's Ordinary Time.

There are several elements that are common both to the Elisha narrative and the Gospel narrative. First of all, both stories involve prophets, persons sent by God to bring his word to his people and to reassure them of God's continued interest in their well-being. John implies that Jesus is the successor of the great Elisha. He is the culminating figure in the long prophetic tradition of God's chosen people.

Next, both events take place in a context of need. The colleagues of Elisha, with their leader, are in a time of famine. The crowds in John need to be fed and there is no place for them to get food.

Third, both accounts show great results coming from very limited initial resources. In 2 Kings we see twenty loaves and a little grain feeding the hundred famished members of Elisha's prophetic association. In John we see five loaves and two fish feeding five thousand hungry men. Clearly Jesus' miracle was the greater because he does more with less.

In both stories there is skepticism. In the Elisha story, the prophet's servant doesn't see how he could possibly set that little bit of food in front of a hundred men. In John's narrative, the practical Philip has already figured out how much it would cost to feed the hungry crowd, and makes it clear to Jesus that they don't have resources like that. But in both cases, the Lord acts and the needs of the people are taken care of. The power of the Lord easily sweeps aside the concerns of practicality.

Finally, both stories are about abundance. When God takes care of his people, he doesn't skimp. There was "some" left over after Elisha and his followers had eaten. In the Gospel narrative, we have twelve wicker baskets of fragments after everybody had eaten as much as they wanted.

God takes care of his hungry people. God's agents use clearly inadequate human resources to carry out his will. And the results are more than anybody expected, more than enough for everyone.

It's the same God who takes care of us now.

FOR REFLECTION AND DISCUSSION

How does God care for his people today?

How have I experienced abundance in God's care for me?

Seventeenth Sunday in Ordinary Time (C)

Genesis 18:20–32

This Sunday's Old Testament reading is somewhat unusual. First of all, it comes from the same chapter of Genesis as last week's reading. The two readings constitute a brief semi-continuous series, which is not a normal arrangement of these First Readings in Ordinary Time.

The second unusual feature of this reading is its length. Most of the lectionary's Old Testament readings are relatively brief. This one runs for thirteen verses, which makes it the second longest Sunday Old Testament reading in the lectionary (not counting the readings for the Easter Vigil).

It's not a typical First Reading, therefore, and that suggests that it must be of particular importance, a reading that the church wanted us to hear even if it doesn't conform to the usual criteria.

Like last Sunday's reading, this one is about Abraham's intimacy with God. It begins after the meal that we read about last week. Abraham accompanies his three guests as they continue on their way. One of the three—the Lord!—reveals to Abraham the purpose for their visit. Sodom and Gomorrah have the reputation of being sinful cities and God has come down to see whether what he has heard is correct.

The two other men (who would be identified as angels later on) went ahead while God and Abraham stayed behind. Abraham now respectfully initiates a dialogue with the Lord. What is the Lord's intent? Is the Lord planning to destroy everybody in the city, even if, say, fifty people were innocent of the sins of the others? It doesn't seem fair. It doesn't seem to be in accord with what one expects of the justice of God. The Lord says that he would indeed spare the city for the sake of fifty just persons. Abraham continues to pursue his train of inquiry, always with submissiveness and reverence. What if there are forty-five, forty, thirty, twenty, ten? God continues to promise deliverance for the ever decreasing numbers in Abraham's hypotheses. After ten, the dialogue stops. (Breaking off at this point seems to indicate that both God and Abraham knew that there weren't even ten innocent people in the city. In any case, God's companions who had gone on ahead would see to it that Abraham's virtuous nephew, Lot, and Lot's wife and two daughters would not be included in the destruction of the city. The just were saved, though the city was destroyed.)

There are several elements that call for notice in this reading. The first is the closeness between God and Abraham. Obviously they are not equals. Yet they engage in a conversation, in an extended exchange of questions, answers, ideas, concerns. They are friends and they speak as friends speak.

Second, it is important to recognize what Abraham is doing here. He is not haggling with God to get God to go easy on Sodom. He is trying to understand how God thinks, how God decides what to do. Implicit in Abraham's questions is the desire to get a better grasp on the mind of God, to get to know God better and understand his work in greater depth. The issue that Abraham was addressing, the issue of the position of the innocent in a context of collective guilt, would continue to be asked over the centuries. Are the innocent important enough to postpone or prevent the punishment of the wicked? The dialogue between God and Abraham reveals God's patience and God's willingness to set aside the punishment of sinners for the sake of the innocent few. God's just anger is tempered by a readiness to save.

Finally, this passage teaches us that God listens to prayer. Abraham was asking for insight into God's way of thinking, and God gave him that insight. But the prayer was persistent and persevering. It wasn't a casual inquiry or request that Abraham addressed to God. He kept at it, almost to the point of pestering God. This aspect of the dialogue suggests not that our needs have to be repeated so God will understand, but that we need to keep praying so that we will appreciate the answer that God gives us.

Perseverance in prayer is what links our Old Testament reading to the Gospel (Luke 11:1–13). In that rather long reading from Luke, Jesus not only teaches his followers the Lord's Prayer, but also teaches us that we have to keep after God in our prayer, that we have to pester God like a man pestering his uncooperative neighbor. We are to keep asking, keep seeking, keep knocking, not so that God will understand what we want but so that we will recognize God's answer when it comes.

Jesus teaches us that perseverance in prayer is important. Abraham teaches us that it always has been.

FOR REFLECTION AND DISCUSSION

How is perseverance manifested in my prayer life?
What have I learned through prayer?

Eighteenth Sunday in Ordinary Time (A)

Isaiah 55:1–3

This Sunday we have a reading from Isaiah 55, the last chapter of the second part of the book of the prophet Isaiah which was addressed to the exiles in Babylon toward the end of their time of trial.

Just three weeks ago the lectionary gave us another reading from this same chapter. That reading was about the power and productivity of the word of God. This Sunday's reading, from the very beginning of the chapter, is about God's banquet.

The text seems to be divided into two parts. The first part is a call to come to and be nourished by God. God offers water, the basic necessity. God offers grain, the basic source of nourishment. God offers wine and milk, symbols of richness. And all of this is free! You don't have to have resources! All are included in the invitation apart from their social standing or means. Money is not important here.

In the second part of our text we learn what is required for access to the Lord's table: you have to listen. If you listen to God you will eat well, and you will have life, the most precious gift of all. Then, in a leap into a whole new dimension, God promises his people that the life he will give them will include the gifts that had been offered to David five hundred years before: that David and his people would dwell in peace, that his kingdom would last forever, that God's favor would be with David's family always (cf. 2 Samuel 7:8–16 and Psalm 89).

There are several things to notice in this reading. First of all is the urgency of God's invitation. "Come...come...come... Heed me...come": this string of imperatives suggests that God is like an importunate host who simply can't do enough for those he is inviting to his party. "Dig in and enjoy! Have a good time! I don't want you to be without anything!" All God asks is that his people answer the invitation.

Next, it's worth noting that what God offers is not being offered to a small, exclusive group. The food and drink, the sharing in David's promises are promised to all who want them, to all who thirst. And these blessings are offered "without paying and without cost" to all.

What God is saying here is that the messianic blessings that are imaged in the food and drink and the promises made to David have not been invalidated by Israel's defeat and exile. They are still available. They will be renewed for God's whole people, indeed, for all peoples.

It is clear that those who prepared the lectionary saw a fulfillment of these promises of Isaiah 55 in the feeding of the five thousand men in this Sunday's Gospel (Matthew 14:13–21). God's promise was now being fulfilled. The messianic banquet had begun.

These two readings about the messianic banquet are rich in meaning. For one thing, they speak of God's goodness to his people. Be they a band of exiles whose spirit had been broken by defeat or a formless crowd of people in need, God will take care of them and give them what they need.

Another dimension that these readings suggest is God's generosity. In the First Reading God urges his people to take advantage of what's being offered. It doesn't matter if you can't pay. Just come and enjoy and you will have life and share in the covenant made to David. In the Gospel we see Jesus recklessly inviting five thousand men to dinner, plus their wives and children, feeding them effortlessly, and having great quantities left over after the meal. Generosity indeed!

We should understand both of these readings as directing our attention to the Eucharist. In this sacred meal we receive the Body and Blood, soul and divinity of the risen Lord. It provides us all the spiritual energy and nourishment we need. It is freely given by God. We can't earn it or deserve it. Our participation in the Eucharist strengthens our ties to God's people, to the final state of fulfillment of the promises that God made to David. And it is all brought about by the same Lord Jesus who was moved with compassion for the hungry of his time and fed them abundantly.

It seems that God can't do enough for us. His goodness is generously bestowed to call us into association with his messianic people. He urges us to take part in the banquet which, in its final form, is nothing less than a sharing in his own life.

FOR REFLECTION AND DISCUSSION

How have I experienced God's generosity?

How do I respond to God's generosity?

Eighteenth Sunday in Ordinary Time (B)

Exodus 16:2–4, 12–15

The exodus from Egypt wasn't easy for anybody, not for the people who found the hardships of nomadic desert life more than they had bargained for, not for Moses and Aaron who were constantly being called upon to take care of the people's needs, not for Pharaoh who lost all his chariots and charioteers. Given the ongoing complaints of the people and their lack of understanding about what was going on, one might venture that the exodus experience wasn't even easy for God!

The Old Testament reading for this Sunday is from the beginning of the Israelites' desert experience. They had escaped from Egypt and slavery only a month before. Already they had grumbled against Moses because he had not provided good water for them to drink. God then gave them what they needed.

Now, as our reading begins, they are grumbling again against Moses and Aaron: "We don't have enough to eat. We were better off in Egypt. It's all your fault." Then God reassures Moses: "I will provide bread and meat for the people, as much as they can eat. Once more I will show them that I am their Lord and God." (The text as edited for the lectionary mentions the instructions that God would give the people about gathering up the manna each day. The details of these instructions have been omitted in our reading. They have to do with not gathering the miracle bread on the Sabbath.)

Then God fulfills his promise. Flights of quail covered the camp in the evening, providing them with meat. In the morning, the Israelites found flakes of a kind of bread on the ground which they called "manna," i.e. "What's this?" It was the Lord's gift to them.

There seem to be two important themes for us in this reading. The first is what we might call the grumbling theme. The Israelites seemed to be world class grumblers. God had brought them out of Egypt by means of a whole series of plagues inflicted on the Egyptians. God had gotten them through the Red Sea dry shod. God had destroyed their pursuers. But they still grumbled about the short supply of water and food, about Moses and Aaron's seeming inability to take care of them as they thought they deserved, about the lack of the comfort and security they had experienced in Egypt even though they were slaves there. It's important to note that the grumbling of the

Israelites was not just complaining about material needs. It also constituted a crisis of faith. Would God take care of them as he had promised?

The second important theme is the theme of God's generosity and patience with his people in spite of their defective faith. After all God had done for them one is inclined to think that God could do better simply destroying this thankless lot and starting over again with people who were more responsive to his goodness. In fact, this is what God offers to do in Exodus 32:10, but Moses dissuades him. The fact remains that God was consistently patient and generous with his people, not because they deserved it but simply because God had chosen to love them.

In the Gospel (John 6:24–35) to which our First Reading refers we see that the Israelites of Jesus' time had preserved some of the spiritual characteristics of their ancestors in the desert.

Jesus was trying to lead them to a deeper understanding of who he was and what he intended to do for them, but they are more interested in physical food. Just a day or so earlier Jesus had miraculously fed a crowd of five thousand. Now they want to know what kind of a sign Jesus will work so that they will be persuaded to believe in him. "Perhaps," they coyly say, "you could provide us with bread as Moses provided our ancestors with manna in the desert." Jesus replies that, first of all, it was not Moses that took care of them in the desert, but God. Next Jesus tells them that the kind of bread they ought to be looking for is not mere earthly food but the bread of heaven. "We'll take it!" they say. Jesus' response must have taken their breath away: "I myself am the bread of life. Whoever comes to me will never hunger."

We tend to think we know what we need. We turn to God in our necessity, often with detailed instructions about what we expect him to do for us. Often we not only give God an agenda, but try to put him on a timetable as well. But God is as patient and generous with us as he was to the Israelites of Moses' and Jesus' time. God does give us what we need, but not necessarily what we think we need. And God's gifts are often far different from and far better than what any of us would have dared to ask for.

FOR REFLECTION AND DISCUSSION

When/why have I grumbled against God?
How has God provided for me?

Eighteenth Sunday in Ordinary Time (C)

Ecclesiastes 1:2; 2:21–23

This is the only Sunday of the year when we hear the words of Qoheleth. Actually, Qoheleth is not a person's name but a title that seems to mean "one who convenes an assembly," perhaps in order to impart learning. The Greek translation of the word is "Ecclesiastes," which is the name by which this book of the Bible is generally known. The first verse of the book, just before our reading begins, says that Qoheleth was David's son and that he ruled in Jerusalem. This doesn't seem likely since there is no record of a son of King David by that name and since the kind of Hebrew the author uses seems to come from the third century B.C. What we have here is a literary convention in which the author is trying to claim the authority of David's son, Solomon, for his teaching.

The opening sentence of our Sunday reading offers us an overview of the whole book, of all of Qoheleth's philosophy.

"Vanity of vanities," is a Hebrew superlative like "king of kings" or "song of songs." Everything is filled with futility and emptiness. Nothing has any final worth or meaning.

The rest of our reading (from chapter 2) is one example of the kind of teaching that the author offers throughout the rest of the book. What's the point of thinking and planning and working hard? What's the point of worrying and sorrowing and losing sleep? At the end you have to leave behind everything you have gained, perhaps to an heir who has never lifted a finger. It doesn't make much sense. It's all vanity.

When Qoheleth wrote, the idea of an afterlife in which all wrongs would be set right and all deficiencies would be addressed was not yet part of Jewish belief. There were some initial intimations of more to come after death, and this conviction would grow in certain religious groups until survival after death was a widely accepted belief by the time of Jesus. But that was still in the future in Qoheleth's time. He addressed a public that was convinced that wealth and comfort here and now were the only really worthwhile things that human beings could hope for. And Qoheleth tells them that that isn't much to look forward to. It's all temporary. It's all relative. It's all vanity.

It may be that, in the providence of God, Qoheleth's teaching was intended to tease people into looking for something more, to stimulate their consciousness to see that merely earthly well-being really isn't enough.

In any case, the Lord Jesus seems to have accepted Qoheleth's basic lesson: that merely earthly success doesn't amount to much. That's what he tells us in this Sunday's Gospel (Luke 12:13–21) At the beginning of the reading, Jesus issues a warning against greed. Then comes a parable that Qoheleth would have appreciated. Here is a wildly successful man who has more goods of this world than he knows what to do with. He has to build bigger barns to hold it all. He looks forward to an easy future, effortless and comfortable. Then death steps in and God evaluates the man's life: "You fool!"

The point of the story is not that the man was evil and was now going to be punished. The point is rather that he had given all his attention to something that he himself would never get to enjoy, riches that would pass on to somebody else. All his effort was for nothing. It was all vanity. He should have read Qoheleth. (One wonders whether Jesus had Qoheleth in mind when he told his story.)

The world in which we live shares many of the same values that the people of Qoheleth's time seem to have held, values shared by people of Jesus' time as well. Our culture treasures wealth, security, comfort, power, control, autonomy. We want to be in charge of our own destiny. We want to be able to respond to any threat, inside or outside of ourselves. We don't like to think about death or deal with death (or even say "death") because it doesn't fit in with our presumptions and our plans. But if all we have to rely on is what we have here and now, then it's all vanity. If the kind of success we pursue is the same as that of the rich man in the Gospel, then we can look for the same evaluation from God: "You fool."

Both the Old Testament reading and the Gospel offer us the very same lesson this Sunday. Perhaps it is because we need it so desperately.

FOR REFLECTION AND DISCUSSION

How important to me are wealth and success?

Do I fear death? Why? Why not?

Nineteenth Sunday in Ordinary Time (A)

1 Kings 19:9a, 11–13

It is only two weeks since we have had a reading from the first book of Kings. That reading, for the seventeenth Sunday in Ordinary Time, showed us God bestowing wisdom on King Solomon. This Sunday's reading is from later in 1 Kings and describes an encounter between the prophet Elijah and the Lord.

Things have not gone well with God's people since Solomon ruled. The kingdom has been divided in two. The prophet Elijah has been proclaiming the Lord's word to the Northern Kingdom of Israel. He has just confronted the idolatrous priests of Baal and had them killed by the faithful followers of the Lord. Now he is on the run from King Ahab and his foreign wife Jezebel. He has fled from Israel toward Mount Horeb, also known as Mount Sinai, where God had given his covenant to Moses and the people. God had provided food and drink for him, and now he has arrived at Horeb, still discouraged, still frightened by the threats of his enemies. He has hidden himself in a cave on the side of the mountain. He complains to the Lord that he is the only one left to do God's work and his mission seems doomed to failure. This is where this Sunday's reading begins.

The Lord tells Elijah to go outside and wait for an encounter with the Lord. A series of awesome and frightening natural events follows: a tornado-like wind, an earthquake, a fire. These would have been the contexts in which Elijah's contemporaries would have expected the storm god Baal to express himself. But, although the Lord had used these vehicles to express himself to Moses in giving the covenant some four hundred years earlier, the Lord now comes in "a tiny whispering sound," the vehicle of intimate conversation, the way friends communicate with each other. This is where this Sunday's First Reading ends.

In the biblical text that follows this reading, God assures Elijah that his mission is not yet over, that the Lord would continue to be with him, that there were still people who were faithful, that a successor had been found to carry on Elijah's prophetic mission. We hear this portion of 1 Kings on the thirteenth Sunday of Ordinary Time in year C.

The point of the reading as provided for our present Sunday is that the manner of God's presence need not conform to our expectations. God doesn't always come to us as we think he should. It is true that God is Lord of wind and fire and power, but God is also the Lord of the fearful, the discouraged, the threatened, and extends himself to them in ways that are appropriate to their fragility and vulnerability.

We see God extending himself to the fragile and the vulnerable in the Gospel. We see the apostles in the midst of a storm. They are terrified by the unexpected appearance of Jesus. They cry out in fear. Peter asks to be allowed to approach Jesus, but becomes frightened as he walks ever so tentatively on the stormy water. As he begins to sink Jesus saves him and chides him for the weakness of his faith. As they get back in to the boat, the wind dies down and those in the boat express their faith in Jesus: "Truly, you are the Son of God."

In each of these two readings we find an encounter with God that takes place after the stilling of a storm. The Lord does not need to use the mighty forces of nature to communicate with his loved ones. He controls these forces, to be sure, and can use them to teach his own lessons, but he seems to prefer more quiet, one might almost say more respectful communication: "a tiny whispering sound" for Elijah, the quiet after the sea storm for the disciples to express their faith. Friends don't shout at each other. They communicate in softer tones.

The place to encounter God is not only in the awesome events of nature, but also in the quiet word of the Lord's love, in the Lord's quiet acceptance of our commitment of faith.

I suppose all of us at some time or other have experienced the presence of God in the power of nature. But the Lord's presence is more often offered to us in quieter ways: in the love that we share with other believers, in the calm expression of the Lord's teaching by the church, in the celebration of the sacraments, in the silence of prayer. We do ourselves a disservice if we only look for the Lord in earthquakes and lightning bolts. The Lord is more subtle than that. Sometimes he sneaks up on us in ways that we never would have expected.

FOR REFLECTION AND DISCUSSION

How have I experienced the presence of the Lord?

Have I ever been surprised by the presence of the Lord?

Nineteenth Sunday in Ordinary Time (B)

1 Kings 19:4–8

In this reading we have yet another narrative of God's care for those he loves. Elijah has just had a triumphal encounter with the prophets of Baal and Asherah. God had made himself known by accepting the sacrifice of Elijah after Baal and Asherah had been shown to be mere figments of their followers' imaginations. After God's miraculous intervention the Israelites killed all the prophets of Baal. In addition, God was now sending rain to bring a long drought to an end. Elijah should have been elated.

Instead, he is on the run, a fugitive once more, thanks to the implacable anger of Queen Jezebel. It seemed that he was to have no peace.

As our reading begins, we see Elijah heading south into the desert. He is tired and discouraged. He asks God to let him die. He feels that he is as good as dead already. "I am no better than my fathers." Exhausted, he lies down under a broom tree and falls asleep. He is awakened by an angel who has provided bread and water for him, a welcome provision after the long months of famine. He eats and drinks and falls asleep again. A second time the angel comes with bread and water. This time God's messenger tells him that this food is to serve as his nourishment for a long journey that lay ahead of him. Elijah eats and drinks again and sets off on the forty day journey to Mount Horeb.

The lectionary reading does not give us the end of this story. Elijah is heading toward an encounter with God, an encounter that would parallel that of the Israelites several centuries before. The Israelites had met God on Mount Sinai which was also known as Mount Horeb. The Israelites would wander for forty years in the desert, Elijah would take forty days to get to his meeting with God. Both were fed by God in the course of their journey.

In Elijah's contact with God, he would learn that God can be present without the wind and earthquake and fire that the Israelites had experienced at Mount Sinai. God can be present and active in the tiniest whisper. Elijah would also learn that there were still faithful people in Israel and that God had further important things for him to be involved in. Elijah's discouragement was not really appropriate.

The church intends this part of Elijah's story to be read and interpreted in the context of Jesus' bread of life teaching in the sixth chapter of the Gospel according to John. We have been hearing from this chapter in the Gospel passages for the last two Sundays, and we will continue to hear from it for two weeks after this Sunday.

In the Elijah story we see God providing energy and direction for this weakened and discouraged man, even as God had provided energy and direction to the Israelites during their years of wandering. Likewise, through the Eucharist Jesus provides vitality and meaning to us weak and frightened members of his flock. Care for his loved ones is one of God's principal characteristics.

The Elijah story also reminds us that God's care for us always involves self-revelation on God's part. By caring for the Israelites in the desert, God taught them something about himself. By providing nourishment for Elijah and by bringing him into contact with himself, God helps the prophet to know him more intimately and deeply. In this Sunday's Gospel (John 6:41–51) we see Jesus telling the people once more that he himself is the bread of life and that all those who accept this bread would be brought to know the Father in a new way. "They shall all be taught by God," and, through Jesus, will be brought into an eternity of togetherness with the Father.

Just about everybody experiences discouragement. Sometimes the demands that are made on us are greater than we seem able to bear. Sometimes our most carefully prepared undertakings fail and, instead of our being able to do something significant for God, we seem to end up with things in a worse state than they were before. Sometimes people we love and respect do not reciprocate. Sometimes poor physical or mental health make it impossible for us to do what we are expected to do. Sometimes it seems we can't do anything right. Sometimes it seems that nothing matters anyway.

We have all sat with Elijah under the broom tree thinking or saying, "This is enough, O Lord!" But the same Lord who took care of Elijah and brought him to a deeper level of knowledge of God also takes care of us and leads us into a closer contact with his goodness, a deeper knowledge of his love.

FOR REFLECTION AND DISCUSSION

How has God dealt with discouragement in my life?
What have I learned from God's care for me?

Nineteenth Sunday in Ordinary Time (C)

Wisdom 18:6–9

The Gospel for this Sunday (Luke 12:32–48) offers at least three themes. At the beginning of the passage Jesus encourages his followers to put their trust in the kingdom without fear. Then comes an extended passage about looking forward to the kingdom. We hear words like "await, ready, vigilant, prepared." Finally, in response to Peter's question, Jesus says that, during this interim time, we must busy ourselves doing the will of our master. Trusting in the kingdom, getting ready for the kingdom, working for the kingdom: That's what Jesus calls his followers to in this Gospel.

The introductory Old Testament reading is from the book of Wisdom. Wisdom is a unique part of the Old Testament in several ways. First of all, it was apparently written originally not in Hebrew but in Greek. We don't know anything about its author, except that he seems to be writing in Alexandria, Egypt. Wisdom is apparently the youngest book of the Old Testament, written less than a hundred years before the birth of Jesus. Finally, it appears no less than eight times in the Sunday lectionary, more frequently than any of the other books of wisdom literature.

Wisdom seems to have been written to offer instruction and encouragement to the author's fellow Jews at a time when their Jewish identity and culture were in serious danger. The danger may have come from an excessive receptivity to pagan Greek culture on the part of some Alexandrian Jews. The brightness and energy of the secular world was drawing many away from dedication to God, a situation not unlike our own!

This Sunday's First Reading comes from an extended section at the end of Wisdom in which the author is offering a reflection on the meaning of the exodus, Israel's delivery from Egypt. He highlights the providential aspects of the plagues with which God afflicted the Egyptians, explaining how these occurrences carried out the word and the will of God. Our reading is part of a commentary on the tenth plague, the death of all the firstborn males of Egypt. The Egyptians were destroyed while the Israelites were set free!

This passage begins with a reminder that "our fathers" knew beforehand what was going to happen. This enabled them to have courage and to trust in the oaths they had been given by God. The fathers mentioned here are probably the ancient patriarchs to whom God had promised liberation from Egypt when the need would arise. (See Genesis 15:13 ff. for such a promise made to Abraham and Genesis 46:3–4 for a similar promise to Jacob.) Hundreds of years before the exodus, God had made his plans known to the leaders of his people.

Next the author speaks of the Israelites who experienced this intervention of God. They were secretly carrying out God's commands about the ritual observance of the Passover as God destroyed the Egyptian firstborn, making possible the Israelites' escape from Egypt and constituting them as his people.

This passage of Wisdom deals with the same themes as the Gospel: confidence, openness to God's plans, diligence in carrying out God's commands. Together these two passages of Sacred Scripture remind us that God has plans, that these plans can be known beforehand, that they should be a source of confidence, and that we have a part to play in bringing God's plans to completion. From the time of the patriarchs, through the experience of the exodus, in later Jewish theological reflection, in the teaching of the Lord Jesus God keeps reminding us that there are plans, that things do not happen without goal or purpose, that God's plans promise blessings to us and that we are called to cooperate with God's execution of what he has in mind.

These are important lessons for us to keep in mind as we pass our lives in an increasingly secular, godless world. The culture around us encourages us to think either that everything happens without rhyme or reason or that everything is the result of human ingenuity. Neither of these things is true. The world has a purpose, a path, a goal established by God. We ourselves are neither helpless victims of mindless processes nor supreme arbiters of the course of the world. We are children of a loving Father who encourages us to take courage in what he has in mind for his good creation and to carry out what he asks from us in bringing his plans to completion.

FOR REFLECTION AND DISCUSSION

How do I identify God's plans in my life?
How do I respond to them?

Twentieth Sunday in Ordinary Time (A)

Isaiah 56:1, 6–7

This Sunday's First Reading is from the beginning of Trito-Isaiah. This is the last eleven chapters of the book of Isaiah as it is presented in our Bibles. These chapters were written by a member of the prophetic school of the eighth century B.C. prophet Isaiah after the exiles had begun to return from the Babylonian exile. This disciple's mission was to apply the basic teachings of the original prophet Isaiah to a new situation, a situation experienced by those who had been in exile and who had now returned to the hardships of the ancient fatherland. The author's mission is to try to apply to this new set of circumstances what the people had learned during its fifty or so years of exile in Babylon.

The year is about 520 B.C. The temple has not yet been rebuilt. The author of these chapters begins his proclamation (and our Sunday reading) with an announcement about what lies in store for the people: "[F]or my salvation is about to come, / my justice about to be revealed." The verses omitted in our reading assure the children of Israel that God's acceptance will be extended to all those who observe the Sabbath and keep their hands from evildoing, even to those whom one might expect God to exclude.

This last element is expanded in the two verses that constitute the rest of our Sunday reading. Foreigners will be welcome to worship the Lord if only they worship him by observing the Sabbath and by respecting the provisions of the covenant. Everybody will be welcome to worship in the temple of the Lord. The temple will be a house of prayer not just for the children of Israel, but "for all peoples."

What is at issue here is universalism as opposed to particularism. At the beginning God chose one people for himself. He protected them and guided them and taught them. God gave them laws and rules to help them preserve their religious identity as his particular people. But this was not to be the final and conclusive arrangement. Those who were outside the chosen people were also to have access to God. At a certain point in time, they, the foreigners, were to be invited to become God's people, too, to worship God in the same way that God's own people reverenced him. "[T]heir burnt offerings and sacrifices / will be acceptable on my altar."

Making membership in God's people open to outsiders did not come about easily. At about the same time that the author of this third section of Isaiah was offering fellowship in God's people to outsiders, others would have been remembering that Ezekiel (in chapter 44) had said that foreigners and the uncircumcised should not be admitted to temple worship. A century later Ezra, the scribe, would be fulminating against inappropriate relationships with foreigners. What we are dealing with here is a tension of values, a tension between clear and exclusive religious identity on one hand, and the extension of God's care to all his human creatures on the other. Both are important. Both are to be preserved. Yet how they are to come together is not always clear.

We see this same tension in this Sunday's Gospel. Jesus resists curing the daughter of the Canaanite women. She was a foreigner and it wasn't yet their turn to be included in the salvation that Jesus had come to bring. The mission to the Gentiles was to be the work of the missionary church, a work that would begin only after the death and resurrection of Jesus. Jesus' task was to preach only to his own people. But the woman's faith was strong enough to break through this temporary barrier.

God's Christian people, with the help of the Holy Spirit, has resolved the tension between particularity and universality. The Christian faith is catholic, that is, universal, addressed to all human beings throughout the world. But that is not to say that anything goes, that there are no demands that accompany faith. We are all called to salvation, to life in the risen Christ, but we are also all called to respond to the demands that accompany life in Christ: self-giving to Christ in faith, dedication to the needs of our brothers and sisters in faith throughout the world, worship of God through the sacraments, acceptance of the teaching of the Christian community, participation in the nuts and bolts of the church community. Membership in God's people is addressed to all. But it is not a gift without demands.

Each of us is called to participate in the community of faith. Each of us is to be brother and sister to all the other members. Each of us is charged with extending the boundaries of the church. It's a glorious calling. But it's not necessarily easy, not necessarily without tension.

FOR REFLECTION AND DISCUSSION

How have I experienced the universality of the church?
How do I participate in proclaiming the gospel to all the world?

Twentieth Sunday in Ordinary Time (B)

Proverbs 9:1–6

The book of Proverbs is not one of the Old Testament books that we hear from often in the Sunday liturgy. In fact, there are only three readings from Proverbs over the whole three-year cycle, one in each year.

The book of Proverbs seems to be an anthology made up of several collections of maxims or aphorisms. Some parts of it may go back to the time of Solomon in the tenth century B.C. Other parts are more recent. The whole collection seems to have been put together in the fifth century B.C., after the Jews had returned from their exile in Babylon.

The purpose of this book of the Bible is to inculcate wisdom, to provide a guide to successful living. In its biblical sense, wisdom consists in knowing and acting on the way things really are, the way God made them to be. Wisdom involves knowing the truth and doing what is proper in the context of human society, of nature, of the whole cosmos. Wise persons are those who are open to accepting the directives of God's will and learning from the experience of wise human beings over the centuries.

The reading for this Sunday is part of a longer poem that offers a contrast between wisdom and foolishness. Each is presented as a woman, presumably to suggest attractiveness: authentic beauty in the case of Lady Wisdom, false and superficial charm in the case of Dame Folly. Our reading consists of verses from the first part of the poem, the part that deals with wisdom.

Here we see Lady Wisdom surrounded by elegance and anxious to bring the hungry to share in a banquet that she has prepared. Her house is a place of architectural perfection. (This seems to be the significance of the seven pillars.) She has prepared an elaborate meal, including wine mixed with spices. She has sent out messengers (her maidens) to announce her hospitality to those who could benefit from it. She is offering the food and drink of divine teaching and virtue not so much to those who deserve it as to those who need it, to those without understanding, to those who have up to now known only foolishness. What Wisdom offers is life for all those who will accept it.

This reading is intended to lead us into the Gospel, still from the sixth chapter of John. As Jesus has presented his bread of life discourse over the last Sundays, he has moved from speaking of the bread of life as a figure for God's revelation in him (verses 35–50) to speaking of it as the Eucharist, his very own Body and Blood that is being offered to bring life to the world. This part of Jesus' discourse is in verses 51 to 58, the verses that constitute the Gospel for our present Sunday.

The Proverbs reading, therefore, is to be read in the light of what Jesus says about himself and the Eucharist in the Gospel. On the other hand, one might also venture that what Jesus says about the Eucharist in John 6 can be illustrated and interpreted in the light of the Proverbs passage.

Both passages are about life. Lady Wisdom encourages her potential guests to forsake foolishness that they might live. The wisdom that is offered them is a source of life. So is the Body and Blood of Jesus. Eating his flesh and drinking his blood brings eternal life. Indeed, Jesus tells us that unless we eat his flesh and drink his blood, we will not have life in us at all. Taking part in the life of Christ through the Eucharist constitutes life, even as wisdom constitutes life. Eucharist, wisdom, the life of Jesus, eternal life for each of us: they all overlap.

The Proverbs reading speaks of the acquisition of wisdom as a banquet. We Christian believers speak of the Eucharist as a banquet. The image of a solemn meal, of a banquet, is an image that teaches us something about wisdom but also something about the Body and Blood of the Lord presented to us in Holy

Communion. A banquet involves community, the togetherness of the host with his guests. One may eat alone, but one can hardly banquet alone. A banquet also involves richness, elegance, abundance. A ham sandwich is not a banquet. Finally, and obviously, a banquet involves nourishment, the sustaining and strengthening of life. Community with the Lord and ongoing abundance of life: That's what both wisdom and the Eucharist are about.

In these readings God's word teaches us once more about God's love and care for us. As wisdom and as Eucharist the Lord leads us away from foolishness and superficiality to an ongoing participation in his life, a participation that will culminate in the eternal banquet of heaven.

FOR REFLECTION AND DISCUSSION

How does God call people to wisdom today?
How have I grown in wisdom?

Twentieth Sunday in Ordinary Time (C)

Jeremiah 38:4–6, 8–10

We know more about the life of Jeremiah than we do about any other of the prophets from the biographical sections of what has come down to us as the book of Jeremiah. These sections were not written by Jeremiah but about him by one or more of his disciples.

This Sunday's reading gives us one of the more memorable events of Jeremiah's prophetic career.

The year is 587 B.C. The king of Judah is Zedekiah who had been made king—a puppet king—by the Babylonians some ten years before. He is a weak king, unable to deal effectively with the nobles who surround him. Now, at the urging of these nobles, Zedekiah has revolted from the Babylonians. The Babylonians have conquered all of Judah except Jerusalem, and Jerusalem is under siege.

Meanwhile, Jeremiah has been urging surrender. Just before our passage begins we hear him saying, "Thus says the Lord: those who stay in this city shall die by the sword, by famine, and by pestilence; but those who go out to the Chaldeans (i.e. the Babylonians) shall live.... This city shall surely be handed over to the army of the king of Babylon" (NRSV).

This is where our reading begins. The nobles come to the king and demand that Jeremiah be put to death. He is a traitor! He is demoralizing the people! Zedekiah felt he was unable to resist his nobles and tells them to do what they want with Jeremiah. They put him into a partially dried up well with mud at the bottom. He would certainly die there of hunger or thirst or suffocation, and they would not, strictly speaking, be guilty of shedding his blood. Jeremiah sank into the mud.

In a verse that has for some reason been omitted in the lectionary reading, we learn that Zedekiah was at the Gate of Benjamin and that Ebed-melech, an Ethiopian palace official and a friend of Jeremiah, went to the king "there."

Ebed-Melech pleads for Jeremiah, pointing out that he will certainly die in the well. Now Zedekiah is swayed again, this time in Jeremiah's favor. He orders Jeremiah to be taken out of the well before he could die.

In what follows in the full text of Jeremiah, we learn that Jeremiah remained under arrest, that Zedekiah came secretly to him for advice, which he then rejected, that the Babylonians finally captured the city, that Zedekiah tried to run away but was captured, and that, after his children had been killed in his presence, he himself was blinded and led off in chains to Babylon. Jeremiah was left behind in Jerusalem.

This reading teaches us that the truth can be dangerous. Jeremiah speaks out as God had inspired him and only just escapes being put to death for it. The truth that comes from God is not always comforting. It can be demanding and divisive.

This is the lesson that we also hear in the Gospel (Luke 12:49–53). Jesus has not come to make everybody cozy and comfortable. His teaching will bring fire and every kind of division.

And if the truth itself can be dangerous, so can the telling of it. People don't like to hear hard truths and those who bring such truths often find themselves rejected and attacked. If Jeremiah had only kept quiet, he wouldn't have been thrown in the well. But he wouldn't have been faithful to his calling, either. If Jesus had been less outspoken about the demands of salvation, he wouldn't have ended up on the cross. But he wouldn't have been our Savior, either.

Telling the truth can be costly. But not telling it can be more costly still.

There are plenty of situations in which telling God's truth can be costly for us. The world around us does not share many of our basic values: the meaning of human existence, the worth of human life, the purpose of human sexuality, the dignity of the poor, our need for salvation, our need for the church and the sacraments. Speaking up on such matters, even speaking carefully and gently, can quickly make us unpopular. Suddenly we will be outsiders.

Christian thinkers have seen lots of parallels between Jeremiah and Jesus. One parallel is that they were both troublemakers because of the truth they told. We may not like the idea of being troublemakers ourselves, but our calling as disciples of the Lord will not permit us to run from telling the truth.

FOR REFLECTION AND DISCUSSION

Has my faith ever caused me to be a source of division?
Have I ever suffered for telling the truth?

Twenty-first Sunday in Ordinary Time (A)

Isaiah 22:19–23

This Sunday's First Reading relates to the Gospel via the image of a key. Eliakim is promised the key of the House of David to carry on his shoulder. (Keys were bigger then than they are now and may have been carried around visibly by an office holder as a sign of his authority.) In the Gospel we see Jesus promising the keys of the kingdom of heaven to Peter. But there is a deeper parallel between these two readings than the use of a symbol, as we will see.

First of all, however, it's important to say a bit about the characters in our reading. Shebna is presented here as the master of the palace, that is as prime minister to the king. In the verses that precede this reading we learn that Shebna is a self-seeking and ambitious person. He takes pleasure in elegant chariots and has carved out for himself a tomb of royal proportions. This is not what God expects of a royal servant.

As our reading begins we hear that God will take away Shebna's lofty position and give it to Eliakim, son of Hilkiah. Eliakim would wear the robe and sash of office and exercise the authority that Shebna now wields. In this capacity, he would be a father to God's people. Eliakim would carry the key that opened and closed all the doors of the palace and that symbolized his control over the affairs of state. Eliakim would be a source of security for the kingdom and would bring honor to his family. (We see Shebna and Eliakim again in chapter 36 of Isaiah negotiating in the king's name with the Assyrian invaders that were threatening Jerusalem in 701 B.C. Here Eliakim is referred to as master of the palace and Shebna as "the scribe." It seems that the cabinet shakeup that Isaiah had threatened had now taken place and that, in accord with what the prophet had foretold, Eliakim and been promoted and Shebna demoted.)

The lectionary does not give us this reading just to instruct us on a minute point in the history of the Near East in the late eighth century B.C., nor to make us aware that the image of the keys that Jesus uses in speaking with Peter has Old Testament antecedents. The reading also says something about how God deals with his people: He uses human agents to carry out his will.

Because we are used to dealing with human church ministers, with priests and bishops, because the pope is an important element in our faith life, we tend to take for granted God's use of human beings as his agents. But it doesn't really have to be that way. God could deal with each of us and with his community directly if he so chose. He could put his teachings into our hearts through immediate inspiration and give us directions about how to live and serve by means of ideas that came directly from him, without intermediary. But God generally doesn't work that way. Generally God chooses to provide teaching and direction through other human beings: through authorized teachers in the church, through human beings (ordained and lay) in the celebration of the sacraments, through specified office holders in providing for the good order of the community. God lets certain of his creatures wield the keys of the kingdom. Eliakim wielded the keys of the Kingdom of Judah in the time of Hezekiah, and Peter (and his successors) wields the keys of the kingdom of the faith.

But our reading teaches us something more than God's use of human creatures to carry out his will. These human agents of the Lord are expected to maintain a certain level of good character. These leaders are supposed to be indicators of what God wants from all his people. Of course God can use bad people as well as good for his purposes, but good leaders bring a dimension of credibility that bad leaders do not.

This is not to say that all leaders of God's people, whether in the Old Testament or in the kingdom of Christ, were and are to be the same. We have all experienced differences of personality in the persons who have exercised leadership in the church community. Different kinds of people bring different gifts to their responsibilities. But, if they are to be effective representatives of God's love for his people, they have to be in touch with the Lord. God's representatives are most convincing when it is clear that they are familiar with the God that they represent.

FOR REFLECTION AND DISCUSSION

How do I relate to authority in the church?

What kinds of people have I met in positions of responsibility in the church?

Twenty-first Sunday in Ordinary Time (B)

Joshua 24:1–2a, 15–17, 18b

The lectionary gives us readings from the book of Joshua only twice in the three-year Sunday cycle. We hear from one of

Joshua's early chapters on the fourth Sunday of Lent in year C as part of that year's lenten survey course in Old Testament salvation history.

Our present Sunday's reading is from the last chapter and was chosen to harmonize with and illuminate the Gospel. The book of Joshua has been recounting how Joshua, son of Nun, had been chosen by God to become the leader of the people after the death of Moses. The children of Israel had then crossed over the Jordan and taken possession of the lands that the Lord had set aside for them. Each of the tribes had been assigned its portion.

Now, in chapter 24, Joshua is an old man. He knows that his days are numbered and he calls a general assembly of all the tribes at Schechem. Schechem was a centrally located town, suitable for a gathering place. Scholars think that the dialogue that is recorded in this reading was not a onetime occurrence, but may reflect some sort of recurrent covenant renewal ceremony that was celebrated in later times.

Joshua asks the people which gods they intend to serve, the false gods that Abraham's ancestors had served back in Mesopotamia or the local gods of the pagans among whom they now lived. Joshua proclaims that he and his family will serve the Lord God. The people recall that it was the Lord God who had freed them from slavery in Egypt, that it was the Lord God who had protected and guided them through the years of their wandering in the desert. They too, therefore, also dedicated themselves to serving the God of Joshua, the God of their fathers.

This reading and the Gospel (John 6:60–69) are both about decisions. Joshua calls on the people to reaffirm the decisions they had already made. Jesus asks his apostles to decide whether they will continue to follow him or whether they, too, would walk away like some of his other disciples were doing, repelled and confused by what Jesus had been saying in the bread of life discourse. Peter, in the name of all of them, replies "Lord, to whom shall we go? You have the words of everlasting life. You are the Holy One of God, and we will stay with You."

Every human being has to make decisions, dozens of decisions every day, some small ones, some big ones. We make decisions about career and business and family and marriage and friendships. As Christian believers we have also made decisions about faith. Like the Israelites under Joshua, like the Twelve after Jesus' Eucharistic discourse, we have decided to give our lives to the Lord and to be responsive to God's will and God's direction in our lives. We have dedicated ourselves to the Lord.

Decisions once made do not always persist with the same intensity they had at the beginning. Both the ancient Israelites and the apostles experienced this. It's easy to make decisions and then take them for granted or put them on the back burner so we can give attention to more immediate matters, or even back away from them in times of trial. It's easy to lose sight of what we are doing as we go about the doing of it. That's why we need to renew and enliven our decision every so often. It's not so much that we want to reconsider the commitments we have made with an eye to changing our decisions or reorienting our dedication. It's rather a matter of bringing our decisions back to their original intensity so that they can exercise a deeper and more explicit influence on all the subsequent, smaller decisions that are part of our ordinary life.

Every Eucharist celebrates decision: the decision of God's Son to become a human being, the determination of Jesus to give his life in love for our salvation. Every Eucharist invites us to decision, too. Every Eucharist calls us to associate ourselves with

Christ's gift of himself, to renew our basic decision of faith. Over and over again as we move forward toward the heavenly Promised Land toward which God is leading us, the Lord says to us as Joshua said to the Israelites: "Decide whom you will serve and how." Over and over again Jesus invites us to make Peter's words our own: "Lord, to whom shall we go? You alone have the words of everlasting life."

FOR REFLECTION AND DISCUSSION

How and why am I dedicated to God?
What difference would it make if I were not?

Twenty-first Sunday in Ordinary Time (C)

Isaiah 66:18–21

This reading comes from the very last chapter of the book of Isaiah, that vast river of prophetic proclamation whose composition stretched over several centuries. This last part of Isaiah was written after the return of the exiles in the sixth century B.C. It was a time of disappointment and disillusionment. Coming back home was not as triumphant an experience as the exiles had expected. Times were hard and they wondered whether all the effort was worthwhile.

In this context, almost as a last word, the author assures his hearers that there was still more to come, that God's sovereignty would be acknowledged not only in the tiny country of Judah, but throughout the world.

Our reading begins with God's promise that neighboring nations would be brought to worship in the Jerusalem temple. They would see God's glory there. But that's only the beginning.

Members of these neighboring nations, the survivors of those who had been led to Jerusalem by God, would become missionaries. These non-Jewish messengers would go out to the limits of the world: to Spain, to Africa, to the Black Sea, to the Greek-speaking cities of Asia Minor, to the farthest places one could imagine. They would proclaim the glory of God among the nations, to peoples who had never before heard of the glorious majesty of the God of the Israelites.

In addition to that, these Gentile missionaries would bring home the Jews still in dispersion. Wherever in the world these Jewish refugees might be, the new proclaimers of God's glory would bring them back to Jerusalem. They will come by every means of transport that one could imagine. They will come to Jerusalem as offerings pleasing to the Lord.

But there is still more. These foreign proclaimers of God's glory will themselves become priests and Levites in the temple, specially chosen ministers of the cult of the Lord.

Here we have God's promise, God's plan for worldwide salvation. Jews and Gentiles will come together to become one new people and to worship together in Jerusalem with no distinction based on birth or nation. It is to be a gathering of all humanity before God.

This is not the first mention in Scripture of God's universalist intentions. Already in Genesis 12:3 (NRSV) God had told Abraham, "In you all the families of the earth shall be blessed." In the first part of Isaiah (25:6, NRSV) the prophet proclaims that God would provide a feast of rich food and choice wines "for all peoples." Again in the second part of Isaiah (40:5, NRSV), at the beginning of what is called the Book of Consolation, the voice of the prophet proclaims, "The glory of the LORD shall be revealed, and all people shall see it together." And in the second servant song (Isaiah 49:6, NRSV), God says to his servant, "I will give you as a light to the nations, that my salvation may reach to the end of the earth."

God had always intended to enfold all of humanity in his love and concern. But he had to go about it a little at a time, first dealing only with one man, Abraham, then with one nation, the Jews, and only later proclaiming his plans throughout the world. The first recipients of God's overtures needed to be reminded that they were not the be-all and end-all of God's work. They would be God's instruments, but God's goals were much wider than one man or one family or one people.

This is the reminder that Jesus gives his hearers in this Sunday's Gospel (Luke 13:22–30, NRSV): "People will come from east and west, and from north and south and will eat in the kingdom of God." Jesus was not proclaiming some revolutionary new theological theory. He was merely repeating what God had already said, enunciating what he himself had come to fulfill.

We all need to hear Isaiah's message. We all need to hear Jesus' teaching. If we are not reminded regularly of God's intent, we run the risk of thinking of ourselves as the only ones that God cares about and so make God into a kind of family servant or personal valet. We need to recall that God's salvation is catholic, i.e., universal in intent, that God's love is catholic, i.e., universal, that God's church is catholic, i.e., directed to the whole world, to Tarshish and Tubal and Javan, to the distant coastlands, to the east and the west, the north and the south.

FOR REFLECTION AND DISCUSSION

What difference does being in the catholic (i.e. universal) church make to me?

What relationships do I have with the church in other parts of the world?

Twenty-second Sunday in Ordinary Time (A)

Jeremiah 20:7–9

Jeremiah's prophetic career was long but not happy. It was his calling to be God's spokesman when the kingdom of Judah was headed for ruin, a ruin that was finally brought about by the destruction of Jerusalem and the deportation of most of the Israelite leaders in 587 B.C. He was, literally, the prophet of doom.

The book of the prophet Jeremiah contains five passages in which the prophet voices his hurt, frustration, disappointment with the mission he has received and with the God who is the source of the mission. These passages are called the "confessions" of Jeremiah. These are intimate, sometimes heartrending conversations or prayerful arguments with God in which Jeremiah addresses God with questions like: Why do the wicked prosper? Why do I suffer for delivering God's word? Why are the threats I deliver not heeded? Why do my enemies continue to plot against me?

Our reading for this Sunday gives us a small portion from the beginning of the fifth of these confessions. (Just ten weeks ago, on the twelfth Sunday in Ordinary Time, we heard another selection from this same section of Jeremiah.)

Jeremiah says that he feels that he has been deceived by God, that God has forced him into an impossible situation. Nobody listens to him. He is a source of derision among the people. The only words he can say are words that speak of violence and destruction. He can't even keep silence! When he tries not to proclaim God's word, God's message becomes like a burning fire within him and he can't hold it in.

Jeremiah seems to have expected that his message from God would at least win a hearing from God's people. Instead of getting attention and response, all he gets is reproach and disdain. It seems that God has tricked him into a mission that he would not have chosen for himself, yet a mission that he is unable to walk away from. He finds no joy in his prophetic vocation, yet he cannot stop preaching. Jeremiah is face to face with the spiritual paradox that doing the will of a loving God can sometimes bring suffering.

Jeremiah wasn't the only one who seemed to find God's service disappointing. We all tend to expect that doing God's will is going to bring us happiness and contentment here and now. And we learn that things don't generally work that way.

Peter seems to have been of this same mind in this Sunday's Gospel (Matthew 16:21–27). Jesus tells his disciples that he is going to suffer and die at the hands of the Jewish religious leaders, but Peter will have none of it. "God forbid, Lord! No such thing will ever happen to you." Jesus turns on Peter and rejects that kind of thinking as human thinking, not God's.

Jesus then goes on to tell all his disciples that following him requires self-sacrifice even to the point of giving up one's life. Serving the Lord is not a source of immediate fulfillment.

Why is that? Why is serving the Lord so often difficult? To some degree, at least, it's because the Lord asks for so much from us. Our humanity has been weakened by sin. As a consequence, it is hard to do good. It requires effort and energy, sometimes more effort and energy than we think we have. It's painful to work that hard at doing the right thing. It sometimes seems that God is asking more of us than we have to give, but actually what God is asking for is more than we think we are capable of. Moral and spiritual exertion is often painful.

Of course, it is not the case that God derives pleasure from the painfulness of our effort. It doesn't make God happy to see us sweat and struggle as we try to carry out what he asks of us. God's demands are a gift, a gift that elicits more from us than we tend to think we are capable of. God is like a loving father who makes demands on his children in order to make them grow and help them to develop. Providing only ease and comfort for them would be a disservice.

Nor is it the case that there is never any joy in serving the Lord. Once we become accustomed to the nature of the Lord's demands and to his reason for asking so much of us, we begin to find joy even in effort.

Most of us don't have to bear Jeremiah's burdens. Most of us understand that Peter's protest was ill conceived. But we still have to remind ourselves occasionally that the Lord's love for us can be demanding to the point of pain.

FOR REFLECTION AND DISCUSSION

How have I suffered as a result of my calling from God?
How has my calling from God brought me joy?

Twenty-second Sunday in Ordinary Time (B)

Deuteronomy 4:1–2, 6–8

The word deuteronomy means "second law." This book of the Old Testament is intended to be a repetition or restatement of the law that God gave to Moses and the people of Israel on Mount Sinai after they had fled from Egypt. While Deuteronomy is based on the law that Moses taught, it seems to have arisen in the form we have it today somewhat later. Originally it may have come from the Northern Kingdom, but was then revised and put together more or less in its present form during the reign of King Josiah, a king of Judah who spearheaded a religious reform in the last quarter of the seventh century B.C. (after the Northern Kingdom had been destroyed).

In Deuteronomy Moses is presented as giving final instructions to the people before their entry into the Promised Land. At the beginning of the book, we have a kind of historical overview of the events that had brought the Israelites to their present position, ready to end their wandering and enter the land that God had promised them. This overview is followed by some twenty-six chapters in which Moses is presented as giving final instructions to the people. The last four chapters of Deuteronomy deal with the choice of a successor for Moses and with the death of Moses.

The text that constitutes our First Reading for this Sunday is from near the beginning of the book. It is a bridge passage between the historical overview and Moses' extended discourses about the details of the law. It speaks of the general blessings that are involved in God's gift of the law to his people.

First of all, Moses calls on the people to be faithful in their observance of the law. Full and exact obedience to the directions of the Lord would remain the basic condition of the people's continued possession of the land that they were about to take possession of.

In the second half of our reading, Moses offers some deeper motivation for their observance of the law. Their willingness to do what God commands would be a sign of their intelligence. It would demonstrate their wisdom, their ability to recognize the true values of their human existence. But even more significant than the content of God's law was the nearness of God that was implied in the law. By giving this body of directions to his people, God was entering into a unique level of intimacy with them. Israel would be unlike any other nation in its closeness to God. This was why the law would be so important, so central in their life as a nation.

In this reading, Scripture teaches us that the law of God, God's directions for living out the existence that he has bestowed on human beings, is not a series of restrictions and prohibitions, but a gift. In the moral and spiritual directions that God gave the Israelites—and us—we learn how we can best bring to fulfillment the potential that God has put into the life of each one of us.

Generally speaking, the ability and the determination to follow directions are indications of intelligence. This is even more the case when the directions are aimed at bringing meaning and fulfillment to our one human life. Still more is obedience to the law a sign of intelligence when the one giving the law and the directions is the Creator who knows his creation inside and out and who loves his creatures in ways that surpass all human understanding. It is a sign of wisdom to follow God's law. It is a sign of folly to neglect it.

This reading provides a focus for our understanding of the Gospel (Mark 7:1–8, 14–15, 21–23). (Note that we have now returned to the Gospel according to Mark.) Jesus is being accused of being soft on the law, of not insisting that his followers carry out all the Jewish ritual precepts with full rigor. Jesus replies to his objectors that they have twisted the purpose of the law. They have made human ritualistic traditions into God's will, while forgetting that what is important is not so much the exact fulfillment of traditional rubrical practices as dedication of the heart and mind to the goodness that the Lord offers us. Evil is less an exterior deficiency than an internal direction of the heart.

These two readings are about the perils and the rewards of God's law. If we respond to it appropriately, we grow ever closer to God, ever more into what God intended us to be, ever nearer to the Lord. If we make the law into a complex of merely superficial observances, we twist it into a kind of self-help mechanism that can only lead us astray.

FOR REFLECTION AND DISCUSSION

Do I look on God's law as gift or as restriction? Why?
How do I experience the nearness of God?

Twenty-second Sunday in Ordinary Time (C)

Sirach 3:17–18, 20, 28–29

The earliest title of the book from which this Sunday's reading is taken seems to have been The Wisdom of the Son of Sirach. The book seems to have been written in Hebrew between 200 and 175 B.C. It was translated into Greek about 132 B.C. by the author's grandson. Somehow the Hebrew original was lost, and only the Greek version was known. For this reason, the book of Sirach (like the book of Wisdom) was not accepted as an inspired book by the Hebrew scholars who drew up the definitive list of inspired books nor by the Protestants who accepted as inspired books of the Old Testament only those books that were written in Hebrew. The book of Sirach has always been accepted by Catholics as inspired and therefore as one of the official books of the Old Testament. At the end of the nineteenth century (and since) manuscripts of this book in Hebrew were discovered, at least one of which dates from before the time of Christ.

The church made extensive use of this book of Sacred

Scripture in presenting its moral teaching both to catechumens and to the Christian faithful. For that reason, it came to be known as *liber ecclesiasticus*, the church book. As a result it is often referred to as Ecclesiasticus. (Careful readers will distinguish between Ecclesiastes, the book of Qoheleth from which we read several weeks ago and the book of Sirach, Ecclesiasticus.)

Like much of biblical wisdom literature, Sirach is composed of short sayings or maxims. It is a collection of proverbs, little pieces of wisdom that were intended to enable the reader to live his or her life according to God's will. Sometimes we have a whole series of sayings on one subject. At other times, there does not seem to be much connection between the verses.

The reading that the lectionary gives us for this Sunday seems to be a collection of pronouncements on several different subjects.

The last sentence of the reading is a general statement about the effects of generosity. The sentence before that is a general comment about the attentiveness and respect that wise people give to the wisdom of their elders.

The first part of the reading is about humility. The son of Sirach tells his listeners that humility elicits respect and affection from those with whom the humble person conducts his or her affairs. Humility, especially in persons who enjoy some prestige, finds favor with God. Then, in a more negative way, the author points out that we should not try to grasp what is beyond our capabilities nor involve ourselves with matters that are beyond our strength.

It is this little essay on humility that connects our introductory reading to the Gospel (Luke 14:1, 7–14). At the beginning and at the end of the Gospel, we hear Jesus offering direction about getting along with others. Don't try to make an issue of your own worth, because you may end up being embarrassed. Don't extend yourself to other people for what you can get from them but for what you can give them. Between these two pronouncements comes a wisdom saying that the son of Sirach would have understood and appreciated: "For all who exalt themselves will be humbled and those who humble themselves will be exalted" (NRSV).

Humility does not call for us to make a big production of our own unworthiness. It doesn't call for us to crawl on our bellies and ask people to acknowledge that we are little better than dirt. Rather, humility calls for us to be realistic. We are not vermin, but we are not the be-all and the end-all of creation, either. We are limited, sinful people to whom God has been generous. We are the recipients of God's gifts. We must not deny the gifts. But neither must we pretend that they are our own achievements. They are God's doing and to claim in any way that they are our own is simply not being realistic.

We must be ready to acknowledge all the fascinating elements that contribute to making us what we are. But we have to be honest about where they all come from. It is wrong and unrealistic to claim that we have no good qualities, no resources for doing good. But it is equally wrong to suggest that all these good qualities are the result of our own effort.

In the last analysis, humility is not about our own worthlessness nor about our own accomplishments. It's about God's generosity. Humility is the realistic acknowledgment of our indebtedness to the Lord.

FOR REFLECTION AND DISCUSSION

Who is the most humble person I know? On what grounds do I make that estimation?

How do I practice humility?

Twenty-third Sunday in Ordinary Time (A)

Ezekiel 33:7–9

The prophet Ezekiel seems to have spent his whole prophetic career among the exiles in Babylon between 593 and 571 B.C. He was a member of a priestly family, apparently of some prominence. This may explain why he was carried into exile when Jerusalem fell to the Babylonians for the first time in 597 B.C. His prophetic calling came soon after that. He would learn from afar of the final destruction of Jerusalem in 587 B.C. and would help his countrymen in exile understand what it meant to be God's people now that the homeland seemed to be definitively destroyed.

This Sunday's reading is from a section of Ezekiel which is intended to offer hope and encouragement to the exiles, to help them from falling into desperation. It is designed to lead the Israelites to a knowledge of God's readiness to forgive them and, eventually, to bring them back to a new kind of life.

Our reading begins with God addressing the prophet: "You, son of man..." In the *New American Bible*, this phrase seems to be God's preferred way of addressing Ezekiel. It occurs some ninety-six times in this book of the Bible. It is God's term for "human being" and seems to indicate a creature fully absorbed by its humanity while being totally separated from the divine. One is inclined to suggest that it stands for something like "tiny product of my omnipotence." God loves human beings, but God is no less infinitely distant from them for that reason. ("Son of man" would be Jesus' preferred way of referring to himself. The phrase occurs in his mouth seventy-eight times in the Gospels. Scholars have speculated about the theological significance of the phrase, but the only thing they can agree on seems to be that, at the very

378

least, the phrase stands for the first person pronoun "I" or "me.")

Our Ezekiel passage goes on to describe this son of man's prophetic responsibility: He is a watchman, deputed to look after the safety and well-being of his countrymen, to warn them of impending danger. He is charged with forwarding God's message to those to whom it is addressed. If God wants to warn a sinner to change his ways, the prophetic watchman is charged with delivering the message. If he does not deliver the message and the sinner dies in his sins, the prophet will share the responsibility for the sinner's destruction. If, on the other hand, he does deliver the message, but the sinner rejects it, the sinner alone will be responsible for his fate.

This reading has been chosen to harmonize with the first part of this Sunday's Gospel (Matthew 18:15–20). Both are concerned with fraternal correction, with dealing with the sinfulness of the brothers and sisters who surround us.

The first thing that these two readings teach us is that human beings have responsibility for each other's well-being. In the case of Ezekiel, it seems that only some are chosen to exercise the mission of looking out for the sinner's well-being. Not everybody is a watchman. In the Gospel, on the other hand, it seems that our brothers (or sisters) have a claim on our concern for their sinfulness simply because they are brothers or sisters. Moreover, this concern is not just between two individuals. It includes other "witnesses" and then the whole assembly of the faithful. We all share responsibility for dealing with the sins of those around us.

But we need to be clear about what fraternal correction entails. It is not a matter of vindictiveness, of getting even with the sinner for what he or she may have done to us or to others. It is not a matter of exercising moral superiority, of looking down on our brother or sister from the mountaintop of our own righteousness. Fraternal correction is rather a matter of sharing the goodness of God, of extending God's love to those who have allowed themselves to wander from his care.

These two readings teach us that we have interlocking responsibilities for one another, that we are all watchmen, that we are all agents of God's care for his human creatures, and that, in helping our brothers and sisters address their sinfulness, we are sharing God's love for them.

Some people seem to enjoy correcting others. Most of us find it a task that we would sooner avoid. The reason is that being a watchman is not pleasant when what we have to announce is painful. But sometimes painful news can prove to be saving news.

FOR REFLECTION AND DISCUSSION

Have I ever tried to dissuade someone from wrongdoing?
Has anyone ever tried to dissuade me from wrongdoing?

Twenty-third Sunday in Ordinary Time (B)

Isaiah 35:4–7a

This Sunday's reading is from the first part of the book of the prophet Isaiah. Most of the material in these early chapters of the book date back to the time of Isaiah of Jerusalem, i.e., to the last part of the eighth century and the first part of the seventh century B.C. However, some of the material seems to be from a later time. This Sunday's reading is a case in point. It seems to date from the time of the exile, i.e., from the sixth century B.C.

These verses are part of a rather long poem about Israel's deliverance from its captivity in Babylon. It is a lyrical description of the joy that will accompany the people as they return to their homeland.

Our reading opens with a proclamation of general reassurance. "Don't be afraid. God is coming to rescue you." Next the prophet speaks of deliverance in terms of physical disabilities. "The blind will see. The deaf will hear. The lame will dance. The mute will sing." Finally the prophet expresses God's care for his people in terms of one of the most basic needs of the arid Middle-Eastern landscape, the need for water. In every imaginable way, in every imaginable place there would be life giving water: streams, rivers, pools, springs. They would not be thirsty on their way home!

In this passage God gives his people a message of comfort and hope. He consoles and encourages them as they look forward to their return home. In three different sets of images (i.e., in general promises addressed to the people's fear, in promises about their physical deficiencies, in promises about abundant water in a context in which the dryness of the desert was a basic reality) God tells his people that he will take care of them. He will see that they get to where he wants them to be no matter how great the obstacles may seem. God is concerned with their final well-being and will do whatever it takes to see that they reach the goal that his loving care has set for them.

The basic message is enunciated in the first section of our reading: "Fear not. God is coming to save you." Scholars have observed that the pervasive message of the Old Testament, its basic teaching, its gospel, so to speak, is God's determination to save his people. He strives to save them from present oppression. But God also plans to lead them into a new, transformed, unending era of peace and well-being. It is not just a material or physical salvation to which God leads them.

In the Gospel (Mark 7:31–37) we see Jesus bringing to fulfillment the promises that God had made in the prophecy of Isaiah. The poetic prediction that God had addressed to the exiles was now being carried out. Jesus brings hearing and speech to the afflicted man. The central significance of Jesus' action is not just the restoration of the man's senses. The central significance of what Jesus did was its implicit proclamation of the arrival of the kingdom of God. Those in need were being relieved of their burdens and thus were being brought to the final state of well-being that God had planned for them.

Jesus ran a risk when he cured people. The risk was that those who witnessed his miracles would begin to look on Jesus merely as some sort of physician who could do things that other doctors couldn't do. Jesus was not a physician. Jesus was the Son of God who worked miracles to teach people that their Lord was in their midst and that the promises God had made to his people long ago were not only still valid but were now in the process of final fulfillment.

God looks after the weak and the frightened, those who are handicapped in any way, those suffering from fatigue and thirst. God looked after his people during their exile in Babylon and kept them conscious of his care for them in the words of his prophets. God offered his people new evidence of his care and concern for them in the teaching and the miracles of Jesus.

God looks after us, too. God promises us deliverance from the various limitations and weaknesses we endure in our time of exile here on this earth. God leads us to confidence through the words and works that the Lord Jesus carries out in our lives. These two passages from Isaiah and Mark are not just about a political event in the sixth century B.C., not just about a deaf-mute who was cured in the first century of the Christian era. The central teaching of these readings is also about us, about the Lord's involvement in our present and in our future. "Fear not. God comes to save you!"

FOR REFLECTION AND DISCUSSION
How has God cared for my needs and deficiencies?
How is God leading us to his kingdom now?

Twenty-third Sunday in Ordinary Time (C)

Wisdom 9:13–18b

This Sunday brings us another reading from the book of Wisdom, that youngest book of the Old Testament. It has only been four weeks since we heard from Wisdom, a book written to speak to Jews living in the highly sophisticated pagan world of Alexandria. This is one of those books of the Bible called "deutero-canonical" (i.e., belonging to a second canon or list of sacred books) because they were handed down in Greek rather than in Hebrew or Aramaic. Another way to deal with this distinction is to call one collection of sacred books the Palestinian canon (or collection) and the other the Alexandrian canon. The former was basically a Hebrew Bible. The other was the Old Testament in Greek. This Greek Old Testament contained seven books that were not in the Hebrew collection (e.g., Sirach and Wisdom). It was the Greek Old Testament that was most widely used among the Jews living outside Palestine and among the early Christians. Catholics believe that the Greek Old Testament is as much the inspired word of God as is the Hebrew version.

The reading for this Sunday is from the middle section of the book of Wisdom in which the author presents an extended reflection about wisdom. The author attributes this section to King Solomon, famous for his wisdom. Our reading comes from near the end of Solomon's prayer and is divided into two parts of unequal length.

The first part speaks of the limitations of human understanding. We humans cannot grasp the intentions of the Lord. We are limited, vulnerable, weighed down with our humanity. We can scarcely understand the things of earth. How can we expect to deal with the things of heaven?

In the shorter second part of the reading the author, though addressing himself to God, tells his readers that the only way to understand the ways of God is through the gift of God's wisdom, the gift of God's Spirit. From this source alone we have a sense of direction, an awareness of how things are supposed to be.

This passage contrasts the limitations of human weakness with the endless possibilities opened up to us by God's gift of his wisdom. Human striving cannot bring us to share in the wisdom of God. Only God's gift of his wisdom can lead us to an understanding and appreciation of our existence.

This Old Testament passage provides the background for what Jesus teaches us in the Gospel (Luke 14:25–33). At the beginning of the Gospel passage Jesus tells his listeners that everything in their lives must be secondary to their dedication to him. Being his follower is costly. Then come two little parables about being aware of the cost of discipleship. The man building a tower and the king going to war must calculate whether they have the resources to carry out what they have in mind. It doesn't make much sense to begin a project if you don't have the wherewithal to bring it to conclusion. Then Jesus repeats what he had said at the beginning: "You can't be my disciple unless you are willing to give up everything you have for me."

The Old Testament reading and the Gospel both have to do with the limitations of human resources. We can't have access to God's wisdom until we recognize that it can only come to us as God's gift. We can't be disciples of Jesus until we are willing to give up whatever we have for him.

These are hard lessons for twenty-first century Americans. We are proud of our self-reliance. We think that if we are good enough and dedicated enough, if we try hard enough God will somehow be compelled to pay attention to us and take us into his confidence. The fact of the matter, however, is that as long as we keep striving to make God responsive to us through the efforts that we exert, we will only gain frustration. Our relationship to God does not depend on what we do for God or what we give to God, but on what we allow God to do for us and give to us.

That's why making everything else secondary to our relationship to God is so important. We have to put ourselves into a posture in which the only source of worth and wisdom is the generosity of the Lord. We have to give away everything in order to receive everything. Wisdom, understanding, a sense of direction, a relationship with the Lord, a healthy sense of where our worth lies, all that comes only from giving ourselves away and letting the Lord take charge. God calls us to renounce our own resources, not in order to keep us poor but in order to make us wise and rich.

FOR REFLECTION AND DISCUSSION

How has my faith been costly to me?

Where do I look to discover the Lord's wisdom and will?

Twenty-fourth Sunday in Ordinary Time (A)

Sirach 27:30—28:9

The book of Sirach dates from the second century B.C. It is a sort of handbook of practical ethics and consists of short collections of maxims or proverbs concerned with various aspects of human behavior. Until the late nineteenth century, only the Greek text of this book was known, and so it was not accepted as being inspired in the Hebrew or Protestant Bible.

Sirach was written to counteract the effects of the pagan hellenistic culture that was making its influence felt in second century B.C. Palestine. It was also much used as a guide for moral education in the early Christian church, to the extent that it became known by another title among Christians: Ecclesiasticus or "the church book." Even today, Sirach or Ecclesiasticus is the Old Testament book that is most frequently quoted in the Christian liturgy, second only to the psalms.

This Sunday's reading from Sirach was chosen to serve as a commentary on Jesus' teaching about forgiveness that we hear in the Gospel parable of the unmerciful servant (Matthew 18:21–35). The First Reading consists of a series of aphorisms that deal with the contrast between vengeance, anger and hatred on one hand and forgiveness, pardon and mercy on the other. In several different ways the author teaches that hostility toward our neighbor is destructive and that forgiveness brings blessing.

The first sentence of the reading is a kind of general introduction: Vengeance and anger are things that sinners like to hang on to.

Next come two verses about outcomes: If you are vengeful you will experience the Lord's vengeance; if you forgive you will be forgiven.

Now come three questions, each making more or less the same point: How can you expect God to forgive you if you refuse mercy and harbor anger toward another?

Finally two verses about remembering: Remember the judgment that lies ahead of you; remember God's commands and forgive.

In all these different ways God's word tells us the same thing here: God expects us to be merciful, to forgive whatever wrong our neighbor may have done to us. This is the same lesson Jesus teaches Peter ("not seven times but seventy-seven times") and then illustrates with the parable of the unforgiving servant. Jesus also gives us this teaching in the prayer he taught us to pray: "Forgive us our trespasses as we forgive those who trespass against us." If we expect to be forgiven, we must forgive. There are several important elements in all this.

First of all, we all need forgiveness. There is not one of us who can say that we have carried out to the letter all the directions that God has given us. Not one of us can say that we deserve God's love because of our own virtue and goodness. No, we are all sinners, and we all need to be forgiven.

But why do we have to forgive our neighbor? Couldn't we just deal with God on our own and leave our neighbor out of it? That's not the way God intended things to work. God wants us to be holy, and being holy means being like God, and God's nature is a forgiving nature. So if we are going to be what God wants us to be we have to be like God, merciful and forgiving.

There are two more fundamental elements that we need to be aware of in this context of forgiving our neighbor. The first is that forgiveness does not mean pretending that nothing happened, that there are no wounds that need to heal, no reparation to be made by the person who has offended us.

Forgiveness doesn't mean simply forgetting about the offense. Rather, forgiveness means loving the person in spite of the offense that was done to us. It means acknowledging that the offender is precious to the Lord, and for that reason has to be precious to us. Forgiveness means wanting and doing good to the person who may have done bad to us.

The other fundamental element in forgiveness is that God does not forgive because the sinner deserves forgiveness. God forgives simply because God is a forgiving God. It must be the same with us. We are not called to forgive (to love "in spite of") because the offender deserves forgiveness, but because God calls us to forgive, to express his love even to those who may not deserve that love.

Forgiving is not particularly easy. But it is always important for those who want to be like God.

FOR REFLECTION AND DISCUSSION

Do I find it easy to forgive?

How and when have I been forgiven?

Twenty-fourth Sunday in Ordinary Time (B)

Isaiah 50:5–9a

In the second main section of the book of the prophet Isaiah, the section that dates from the Israelites' time of exile, there are four poems that are known as the "servant songs." These oracles describe the ideal servant of God and the servant's struggles and accomplishments. Isaiah 50:4–9 (or 4–11 according to some scholars) is the third of these songs and deals with the sufferings

of the servant. Most of the verses of this song are proclaimed
each year on Palm Sunday and again on Wednesday of Holy
Week. An abridged form of the poem also serves as the First
Reading on this twenty-fourth Sunday in Ordinary Time,
making it one of the most frequently read portions of the Old
Testament in the church's liturgy.

As the text is presented to us on this Sunday, it falls into two
main parts. In the first part, the servant expresses his dedication to
the service of God in spite of the insult and degradation that
such dedication entails. No matter how misused the servant may
be, no matter how brutally he is treated, he does not abandon his
dedication to the service of God. He receives his directions from
the Lord and follows them and readily submits to whatever
sufferings arise from his obedience to his calling. He makes no
effort to escape.

In the second portion of our reading the servant expresses his
confidence in God's support. He knows that he does not need to
be afraid of anything that human opposition can bring against
him. The Lord is on his side. Disgrace and oppression will not
have the last word.

It is not totally clear whom or what the prophet is talking
about in this poem. He may be describing the fate of anyone
who is called to be God's spokesman. Suffering is part of the
prophetic calling. It is also possible that the author is describing
the mission of the whole people. The people suffers insult and
adversity in defeat and exile, yet it maintains its loyalty to the
Lord God, a loyalty that is eventually vindicated by the people's
return to its homeland.

The reason for this text's presentation here is clear enough.
In the Gospel (Mark 8:27–35) Jesus speaks to his disciples for the
first time about his suffering and death. Peter is unwilling to

accept such a possibility. Jesus rejects Peter's objections and tells his disciples and the crowds that, not only would he himself suffer, but so would anyone who wanted to be his follower. Jesus knew what lay ahead of him. He knew what God's servants would have to endure.

Why do those who are devoted to God—the servant in Isaiah, Jesus, the followers of Jesus—have to suffer? It is not that God takes pleasure in human suffering and likes to see his loved ones in pain. Suffering in and of itself is always a negative thing. It is not something that God promotes, not something that pleases him. Yet God's servants do suffer.

One reason why they suffer is because they carry out their life and their work in a context of sinfulness. The world in which we live, the world in which Jesus lived, the world in which the suffering servant in Isaiah lived is and was a world filled with sinfulness. God's directions for a virtuous life run counter to what most people find appealing. Generosity, self-sacrifice, humility, obedience to God—these are not habits that most people in the world find attractive. They are not virtues that most people practice. Moreover, people who do preach and practice such things are often looked upon as a threat and an accusation to the rest of humankind. Good people make bad people or even indifferent people uncomfortable. The reaction is rejection, rejection of what the followers of the Lord stand for, rejection of the followers of the Lord themselves. The world inflicts pain and suffering on what it does not like.

Another source of suffering for the servant of the Lord is the sheer effort of discipleship. God is a demanding master who doesn't always shield his servants from harm. God doesn't always give them clear and detailed information about what to expect. God doesn't always give immediate responses to their pleas for help. It is hard to be a servant of the Lord, hard to the point of being painful.

We cannot explain every suffering. Sometimes there doesn't seem to be any reason why good people suffer. Yet God's word and the example of Jesus reassure us that no suffering is ultimately meaningless.

FOR REFLECTION AND DISCUSSION

What sufferings have I seen God's servants endure?
How have I suffered in my service of the Lord?

Twenty-fourth Sunday in Ordinary Time (C)

Exodus 32:7–11, 13–14

The book of Exodus teaches us about Israel's roots, about the transformation of a loose confederation of clans into one people. The book is the product of several different authors over a somewhat extended period of time. It is a compilation of corporate memories rather than a carefully researched work by a single historian.

This Sunday's reading describes a memorable incident during the Israelites' wandering in the desert, sometime about 1275 B.C. Moses has received the Ten Commandments from God on Mount Sinai, together with another corpus of laws that would govern the community life of the people. The people agree to do what God had commanded (cf. Exodus 24:3). Moses erects and consecrates an altar on which the covenant with God is ratified. Moses then goes back up the mountain to be with God and to receive God's instructions about how God was to be worshiped. He remained there for a long time ("forty days and forty nights"), and the people were perplexed at his absence. So they asked Moses' second in command, his brother Aaron, to provide them with a different kind of attachment to God. Aaron had them make a golden bull or calf. It seems that this was not so much an image of a new and different god but a representation of the strength and power of the one God who had brought them out of Egypt. God had already commanded them not to try to worship him under visible forms, but they preferred to worship God on their own terms.

This is where our reading begins. It consists of an exchange of discourse between God and Moses, followed by God's decision. First God tells Moses what has happened down below. God says, in effect, "*Your* people whom *you* brought out of Egypt have become unfaithful. I don't want to have anything more to do with them. They have made a false image of me. I'm going to destroy them. We'll start over again and you will be the new Abraham, the father of a new people."

Moses won't allow God to talk that way. "They're *your* people and *you* brought them out of Egypt. Do you want everything you have done for them to be wasted? Besides, you made commitments to Abraham and Isaac and Jacob and you ought not be unfaithful to them."

So the Lord agreed to relent. In response to the intercession of Moses, God forgives the sin of his people.

Forgiveness is the theme that unites this Old Testament reading with the Gospel (Luke 15:1–32). In the reading from Luke we have three parables: the lost sheep, the lost coin, the lost son. Jesus teaches us that God is gladdened by recovering that which was lost. In the story of the lost son, recovering that which was lost takes the form of forgiveness.

Both of these readings teach us that God does not take pleasure in punishing those who have done wrong, whether it be his whole people or a solitary sinner. God loves and cares for the sinner, for all sinners in spite of what they have done. That's not to say that their sinfulness was not real. It's not to say that they have done no harm to themselves or to others. It's not to say that there are no continuing results from their wrong-doing. God forgives them, and forgiveness means loving and seeing worth in sinners, a single sinner or a multitude, without denying that they have done wrong. God loves nonetheless. God's love is greater and more insistent than human error. That's what God's word tells us in this reading from Exodus. That's what Jesus teaches us in the parable from Luke.

If we are to benefit from God's forgiveness, however, we have to acknowledge that we have sinned. Without the acknowledgment of our wrong-doing, God's continued love has no significance. To take comfort from the fact that God loves us in spite of our sins is meaningless if we have no sins.

The sins that we hear about in this Sunday's readings are sins that we ourselves are familiar with. At some time or other, we have all been idolaters, we have put our trust in powers other than the Lord God, powers like money or sex or comfort or personal achievement. At some time or other we have all strayed like the prodigal son, looking in vain for happiness in distant lands, far from home. We need to acknowledge our wandering so that we can become aware that God loves us anyhow, in spite of our sins.

God forgave the Israelites in the desert. The loving father forgave the prodigal son. God wants to forgive us, too.

FOR REFLECTION AND DISCUSSION

How have I experienced the forgiveness of God?
Is there anyone I need to forgive?

Twenty-fifth Sunday in Ordinary Time (A)

Isaiah 55:6–9

This Sunday's First Reading is from the fifty-fifth chapter of Isaiah. It is the closing chapter of the second part of Isaiah, the part known as the Book of Consolation. This section of Isaiah was written during the Babylonian exile to keep the Israelites in touch with God during the decades of separation from their homeland. This last chapter has been called "an invitation to grace" and it speaks about many expressions of the graciousness of God: the heavenly banquet to which all peoples are invited, a worldwide covenant, the breadth of God's forgiveness, the effectiveness of God's word, the joy the Israelites will experience as they return home.

Chapter fifty-five of Isaiah is used more than any other chapter. We hear from this "invitation to grace" six times in the three-year Sunday cycle. Already in year A we have had two readings from Isaiah 55, three if all the Old Testament readings were used at the Easter Vigil. This chapter seems to resonate more completely with the teachings of the Gospel of Jesus than any other extended portion of the Old Testament.

Our reading is from the middle of the chapter. It starts off by suggesting that God can be sometimes near to us and sometimes remote. That's why we have to reach out to God when he is near.

The text then encourages the sinner to turn to God for mercy, because God is "generous in forgiving." In fact, God is superabundantly generous in forgiving. God's way of dealing with forgiveness is far different from ours, as different as the heavens are distant from the earth. God doesn't deal with forgiveness as we do. God is merciful in ways that are far beyond anything we can imagine.

"Seek the LORD," our text says. God offers us an invitation to interior conversion. God is ready to forgive, ready in a way that far surpasses any human inclination to exercise mercy. This theme of God's readiness to forgive is one that arises over and over again in the Old Testament. It's almost as if God can't tell us often enough how urgently he wants to pardon our sins, how much he wants us to benefit from his mercy. God is a God of forgiveness, and the breadth and depth of his desire to forgive is as immense as God's own infinite being.

This reading seems to have been chosen to provide theological underpinning for the Gospel parable (Matthew 20:1–16), the story of the laborers in the vineyard, and the one word that ties both readings together is "generous." The landowner, at the end of the parable, tells the complaining worker that he should not be envious because the owner is generous. And in the Old Testament reading we heard that God is generous in forgiving.

Sometimes people have trouble with this parable. It just doesn't seem right that everybody gets the same payment, even those who have done hardly any work. But that's the way it is with God. God is not bound by human conventions. God is not an employer like human employers. For that matter, what we receive from God is not something that we can earn or deserve. Our life in the risen Lord is not a pay-off for work well done. It's a gift, pure and simple, and the kind of work and the extent of the work that we have done for God is secondary if not totally irrelevant. God is generous to us because God has chosen to be generous to us. There's no other explanation. It's just the way God is.

The Old Testament reading situates God's generosity in the context of mercy and forgiveness. God is "generous in forgiving."

This means that we don't have to earn or deserve God's forgiveness. We can't, even if we were to try. God's forgiveness is a gift, pure and simple. It's a gift that we receive just because God wants us to have it, a gift that is not bound by human criteria for kindness and mercy. "As the heavens are higher than the earth" (NRSV) are God's ways of forgiveness and God's criteria for mercy.

Neither reading draws the obvious conclusion about how we ourselves are to forgive, but it's easy to tease it out of our texts. If God is so generous in forgiving, and if we are invited to be like God and share God's life, then it seems clear that we must be merciful and forgiving, too. Jesus teaches us this in the prayer he taught us: "Forgive us our trespasses as we forgive those who trespass against us." The measure of our mercy toward one another must be the generosity of God.

FOR REFLECTION AND DISCUSSION

How do I experience the generosity of God's mercy?

How generous am I in forgiving?

Twenty-fifth Sunday in Ordinary Time (B)

Wisdom 2:12, 17–20

When the book of Wisdom was written in Alexandria, Egypt, in the first century B.C., the main issue facing the Jews was not liberation from slavery or the hostility of the Philistines or the burdens of Babylonian exile. It was the relationship between observant Jews who strove to follow the law of God and others who looked on such religious observance as ridiculously old fashioned and irrelevant. These others were not just pagan

Greeks, but also, perhaps mainly, hellenist Jews who had bought into the culture of their time and place. To such up-to-date persons, philosophically and socially sophisticated, their fellow Jews who held on to the old-time religion of their fathers were not only outdated but also embarrassing. The old timers, eccentric and set apart, claiming to be specially chosen by God, claiming to have access to the wisdom of God, were not people whom the sophisticates looked on with kindness or reverence. On the contrary, the apparently retrograde religion and philosophy of pious Jews constituted a challenge to the modern mind-set of those who had espoused the ideas and way of life of the Greeks. But what the faithfulness of the observant Jews offered was more than a challenge. It was also an accusation, an accusation of faithlessness.

In this Sunday's reading we see the reaction of the sophisticates to the challenge and the accusation offered by the dedication of the faithful Jews. We are in the second chapter of the book of Wisdom. The first chapter offers a description of authentic wisdom. Now, in chapter two, we see the reaction of those who do not accept such wisdom. Their approach is to deride and persecute the virtuous man to test the depth of his beliefs.

"Let's give him a hard time and see how he holds up. His posture of righteousness is an accusation to us, a reproach for our lack of observance of the teachings of Moses. If we make him suffer we will find out just how sincere he is. He claims that God will take care of him. Let's see if that is really so."

This reading offers an overture to the Gospel (Mark 9:30–37). There we see Jesus, for the second time, predicting the sufferings that he knew lay ahead of him. Jesus was the wise man, *par excellence*, the Servant of God foreseen by Isaiah. He knew what he could expect. He was not mistaken. What the book of Wisdom spoke of as the fate of the faithful servant of God would come to pass in the life, suffering and death of Jesus. In fact, the Gospel of Matthew (27:43) shows us the enemies of Jesus deriding him, in the words of this passage from Wisdom, as he hung on the cross: "He trusts in God; let God deliver him now, if he wants to."

The central feature of our redemption through the life, death and resurrection of Jesus is not the fact that he suffered so intensely. It is rather that Jesus was faithful. Because of Jesus' dedication to the Father, he roused the animosity of the religious leaders of his time. They saw his dedication to the will of the Father as somehow excessive, idiosyncratic, eccentric, dangerous. Jesus could have watered down his teachings. He could have proclaimed a heavenly Father who was less loving, less forgiving, less merciful, a Father more along the lines of what Jesus' contemporaries in religious leadership would have been more comfortable with. But Jesus didn't do that. He proclaimed and he exemplified what he knew to be true, and his enemies hated him for it. They saw him as a posturer, intent on making them look bad. So they took their cue from the book of Wisdom and "beset the just one.../ put the just one to the test.../ condemn him to a shameful death." If Jesus had not been consistent and faithful and dedicated to the will of his Father, he would not have had to undergo the shame and the sufferings foreseen for the just one in God's word.

We live in a world in which Catholic Christian values are not generally prized or respected. God's teaching about the meaning of our human existence, about marriage and sexuality, about the inviolability of human life, about justice, about our responsibility for the moral quality of our lives, God's teaching about all these matters and others is not accepted by most of the world around us. And those who espouse such teachings are not respected, either. We are looked upon as old fashioned, eccentric, out of touch. We may not be destined for "revilement and torture," but that doesn't mean that everybody looks on us kindly.

FOR REFLECTION AND DISCUSSION

How do virtuous people suffer persecution today?

In what ways and for what reasons have I suffered scorn and derision for my beliefs?

Twenty-fifth Sunday in Ordinary Time (C)

Amos 8:4–7

Today we hear from the prophet Amos. We will hear from him again next week. The only other time he appears in the Sunday lectionary is on the fifteenth Sunday of Ordinary Time in year B.

Amos was a native of the Southern Kingdom of Judah, but his prophetic activity unfolded at the temple of Bethel in the Northern Kingdom of Samaria. He spoke out for the Lord there about 760–750 B.C., at a time of great prosperity in the Northern Kingdom, but just a few decades before the kingdom's destruction at the hands of the Assyrians in 721 B.C.

Amos is the earliest prophet who has a book left behind in his name. There were spokesmen for the Lord before the time of Amos, but their words do not seem to have been written down as were the words of Amos and his successors in the prophetic mission.

Amos has been called the prophet of divine judgment and the prophet of God's justice. God sent him to the Northern

Kingdom to preach against the kingdom's hollow self-confidence and fragile economic and social well-being.

Our short passage from chapter eight is an oracle, a pronouncement against greed. Greed has been defined as reprehensible acquisitiveness, the unhealthy passion for more.

The greed of the wealthy Samaritans was leading them to increase their resources at the expense of the poor of the land. They trampled on the poor to the point of destroying them. These powerful rich people couldn't wait until the feast of the new moon was over, a religious observance that halted business. Then they could get back to their commercial dealings. No stratagem was too shameful when it came to making a profit. They would tamper with the grain measurements and with the coinage so that people had to pay more to get less. The scales that merchandise was weighed on would no longer be honest. Men and women would be sold into slavery. Even the most inferior product would become a source of profit. But the Lord will not stand by and watch such evil go on. God swears by the pride of Jacob (the people's arrogance that was so constant, so unalterable that it became a suitable basis for an oath) that he will never forget what this people has done.

This is a passage about social justice, that is, about how people are supposed to relate to one another in the context of the use of the world's goods. God is not content to let each of us strike the best deal we can get at the expense of the dignity and well-being of our brothers and sisters. The bottom line is not making a profit. The bottom line is treating other human beings like human beings.

This reading from Amos provides another aspect from which to view the subject that is treated in the Gospel for this Sunday (Luke 16:1–13). There we hear about the steward, the business manager who was found to be wasting his master's goods. When the steward realizes that the jig is up, he sets out to do the best he can with the resources at his disposal. He writes off the commissions that he had rightfully charged in conducting his master's affairs so that the master's creditors would treat him well once he had lost his position. What the master praises at the end of the parable is not the steward's bad administration, but his cleverness in using money to deal with the situation into which he had gotten himself.

Both Amos and the Gospel parable teach us that it's important to know how to use our material resources well. The Gospel parable puts it in more general terms. The oracle of Amos expresses it in more clearly theological terms. Money, wealth, riches are not morally neutral. It is not the case that, as long as we don't do out-and-out violence to others, any kind of practice is acceptable.

There are good ways and bad ways, right ways and wrong ways, intelligent ways and silly ways to use the resources that God has entrusted to us. The manager in the Gospel is praised for knowing how to make the most of what he has to bail himself out in a time of crisis. The rich Samaritans in Amos are rebuked for seeing their wealth only as a means for getting more.

Most of us may not find ourselves in the critical situation of the manager whose very survival depends on his financial adroitness. Most of us may never be in a position in which we can drive other people into ruin by our own personal financial sharpness. But that doesn't mean that the teachings of Amos and Jesus don't apply to us. Each of us has to decide carefully what's important as we use the resources that we have from the Lord.

FOR REFLECTION AND DISCUSSION

In what ways am I wealthy?

For what do I use my wealth?

Twenty-sixth Sunday in Ordinary Time (A)

Ezekiel 18:25–28

The exiles in Babylon after the destruction of Jerusalem seemed to have liked to invoke an old proverb: "Fathers have eaten green grapes and so their children's teeth are on edge." The people thus claimed that they were being punished for their ancestors' sins rather than their own. The only reason they were in exile was because of what their ancestors had done. Their present situation didn't seem right, but that was apparently the way justice worked in a world that was under divine governance. One result of this way of looking at things was that the people felt no need to look after their own relationship with God. After all, if God was going to keep punishing them for some sort of corporate guilt that they bore because of the misdeeds of their ancestors, what was the point of striving to be virtuous?

It is true that in the Decalogue God promised to inflict punishment on the children of sinful fathers "down to the third and fourth generation" (cf. Exodus 20:5, NAB). But as the religious sense of the Israelites matured, they saw that the punishment of the descendants was not due exclusively to the family connection, but also to the freely chosen perpetuation of the sinful conduct on the part of the later generations. The way the exiles in Babylon interpreted God's justice was therefore more than a little self-serving. By making God's way of treating them unjust, they freed themselves from any responsibility for the quality of their relationship with him.

Ezekiel takes them to task for this attitude in chapter 18. This Sunday's reading is a summary of what the prophet says there.

They shouldn't claim that the Lord's way of acting is unfair. If they do so, it is they themselves who are unfair. Each individual person, the prophet says, is responsible for the quality of his or her relationship with God. If a person was virtuous and turns to sinfulness, that person will be treated as a sinner by God. If a sinner reforms, the former sinner will be counted as virtuous. Sin brings death, i.e., ruptures the sinner's relationship with God. Virtue brings life, i.e., a loving oneness with the Lord.

Ezekiel's message here is that the standing of each individual in the sight of God is determined, not by the nation to which that person belongs, not by the person's ancestors, but by the individual person's behavior.

Ezekiel's teaching is echoed in the teaching of Jesus that we hear in the Gospel for this Sunday (Matthew 21:28–32). Through the parable of the two sons Jesus underlines the importance of individual, personal responsibility. The son who agreed to go work in the vineyard but did not do so seems to represent the chief priests and elders of the people who apparently thought that their standing exempted them from actually carrying out the will of God. The son who refused but later went represents the sinners who listened to Jesus and turned from their sinfulness. Whatever they might have been, they are now participants in the kingdom of God.

Our Catholic Christian religious culture has never been insistent on corporate guilt, that individuals would be punished for the sins of their ancestors. We have always given greater emphasis to individual responsibility. While God's favor to us is a free gift that we can do nothing to deserve, the personal behavior of each individual determines the quality of our response to God's gift. We are responsible for whether we are saints or sinners.

But there is a corporate dimension to our personal moral life. Each of us is a sharer in the life of the world around us. Each of us is touched and influenced by the values of our culture. Each of us finds comfort in belonging, in being part of the life that goes on around us. There is security in being part of the group. Being a loner is not necessarily something we treasure. Yet the world around us is in many ways not a Christian world, not even a humane world. It is a sinful world, a world that not only does evil but makes evil attractive. As individuals, we may not be guilty of the sins of the world. But as individuals we are in danger of buying into the world's sinfulness. The issue for us is not whether we are being punished for the sins of our fathers. The issue for us is whether we choose to buy into the sins of our brothers and sisters.

FOR REFLECTION AND DISCUSSION

Do I see myself as responsible for my personal spiritual situation? How am I affected by the sinfulness of the world around me?

Twenty-sixth Sunday in Ordinary Time (B)

Numbers 11:25–29

The book of Numbers is the fourth book of the Pentateuch. It is a combination of law and history. It gives the history of the Israelites' wanderings from the end of their encampment at

Mount Sinai to their arrival at the borders of the Promised Land. Interspersed with the historical material are sections of legal ordinances.

This Sunday's reading is from Numbers' historical material. The people have now gone a three-day journey from Mount Sinai and they are complaining—again! They want more meat. They remembered all the wonderful things they used to eat in Egypt, and now all they have is the tiresome manna that God sent them each day.

Now it is Moses' turn to complain. He goes into the presence of the Lord and laments the seemingly unending clamor of the people. "How can you expect me," he asks God, "to take care of a multitude like this? How can I provide what they claim they need? I can't stand this much longer." God responds, first of all, by assuring Moses that the people would soon have more meat than they could handle. The next day a flight of countless quail descended on the camp and the people had all they wanted and more. God also responded to Moses by promising him help in the person of elders and authorities among the people. They would share the burden of governance. Presumably these men would assist Moses in organizing the people, in pronouncing judgment in disputes, in offering advice.

As our reading begins, Moses has led the selected men outside the camp to stand around the tent that held the presence of the Lord. Now the Lord made the elders to be like Moses by giving them a share in the spirit that had been given to Moses. As they received their share of Moses' spirit, "they prophesied," that is they proclaimed the praises of God and began to interpret God's word.

But there was a snag. Two of the chosen men, Eldad and Medad, were supposed to be in the group of the elders, but for some reason had remained behind in the camp. Now they were discovered prophesying, too, just like the others! Joshua, Moses' right hand man, urges him to make them stop, because it looks like there are sources of the spirit that are not connected with Moses. But Moses is not disturbed. It's not his spirit that's being portioned out, but the Lord's, and if the Lord wants Eldad and Medad to be among those who prophesy, so much the better. Best of all would be if everybody shared in the spirit!

In the first part of the Gospel for this Sunday (Mark 9:38–41) we see an occurrence that is almost an exact parallel to the story about Eldad and Medad. Somebody who was not of Jesus' company was casting out demons in Jesus' name. The disciples want Jesus to make him stop. What right had this outsider to invoke the power of Jesus? But Jesus will have none of it. "Let him alone," Jesus says. "he's not doing any harm and he may win a bit of good will for us all."

What God's word teaches us in these two readings is a lesson that we might not advert to very often. The lesson is that the working of God's power is not confined exclusively to channels that God has already identified. God can and does work in ways that are different from and beyond the instrumentalities that he has informed us about. God's actions in the world are not limited to the means that have been revealed to us.

God reaches out to us through the sacraments. But that doesn't mean that God can't also reach out to people without the sacraments. God leads and guides us through the sacred Scriptures. But that doesn't mean that God can't also lead and guide people without the Scriptures. In the teaching of the church God brings us to the knowledge of the truth, to access to the life of the risen Christ, to guidance for upright living. But that doesn't mean that everybody who is not a card-carrying church member is therefore excluded from God's loving care.

The sacraments and the Scriptures and the church are the ordinary means of God's care for human beings, the means through which most people are brought to salvation. But God is bigger and more powerful than sacraments and Scripture and church. He is not obliged to limit his love and goodness to those particular means.

Even today there are Eldads and Medads.

FOR REFLECTION AND DISCUSSION

Where do I see God at work outside the structures of the church?
Do I find such action on God's part troubling or edifying?

Twenty-sixth Sunday in Ordinary Time (C)

Amos 6:1a, 4–7

Once more this Sunday we hear from Amos, the first prophet whose preaching is preserved in writing, a Judean country boy who was sent by God to preach conversion to the prosperous and sophisticated Northern Kingdom.

Last week we heard Amos inveighing against social injustice. This Sunday he deals with private luxury.

The moral issue that Amos addresses in this passage is not sinful behavior but complacency, overconfidence in one's personal security, satisfaction with oneself, with the way things are. This passage is part of the last of a series of "woe" pronouncements that occurs in chapters five and six of the book of Amos. "Woe" was the opening expression for funeral laments and it signifies pain and impending distress. "Woe to the complacent."

Amos goes on to describe the lifestyle of the complacent wealthy socialites. It is a thumbnail sketch of *la dolce vita* in eighth century B.C. Samaria: imported beds and comfortable couches to stretch out on for dining; tender meats from animals that were slaughtered before they reached the age of producing wool or milk; leisurely exercises in musical composition; wine in quantity and expensive perfume.

They don't seem upset at all that their country was wasting away in its own luxury. But once the party is finally over, these social leaders would lead the procession into exile.

The lesson that is expressed in this passage of Amos is the same as the message expressed by the parable of Lazarus and the rich man in the Gospel (Luke 16:19–31): it's dangerous to be rich. The high-living Samaritans weren't doing anything wrong. Neither was the rich man in the parable. But their high living was a distraction from more important matters, matters like the perilous state of the country or the needs of the poor man lying at the gate. Too much comfort brings selfishness, and selfishness keeps people from trying to come to grips with the needs of the society in which they live and with the condition of those who are lower down on the social and economic ladder. As a result, situations go from bad to worse until final destruction is inevitable. Too much comfort is destructive.

It would not be difficult to recast Amos's message into more contemporary terms. It would be easy to describe modern-day Samaritans with their expensive four-poster beds and their elegant dining rooms. They dine regularly on filet mignon or range-fed chickens. They hum along with the latest music brought to their ears by CD players that offer the highest quality of sound. There is plenty of high-priced wine and French perfume.

And all that is not to mention our ever-present air

conditioning, immediate access to clean, safe water, refrigeration to preserve our food, easy and cheap transportation ready to take us wherever we want to go, modes of entertainment like television and the movies that would have rendered an eighth-century B.C. Samaritan speechless with wonder. We have come to believe that any discomfort is an outrage, that every ache and pain should be immediately curable, that we have a right to all the conveniences that our world makes available.

Probably no society in the history of the world has provided more comfort to more people than we have in twenty-first century America. Kings and emperors of the past did not live as well as we do. There's nothing morally wrong with living the way we do, of course. But it's dangerous.

Comfort is dangerous because it is so addictive. When the refrigerator breaks down or the car doesn't start or the computer doesn't work, we find ourselves in a state of desperation. We don't know what to do—except to call somebody to see to it that comfort is restored as soon as possible so we will be at ease again.

But our modern comforts, like the comforts Amos spoke about, are also distracting. They make us turn our attention ever increasingly toward ourselves and help us to forget about our responsibilities for the society in which we live, our responsibilities for the people around us who are not as comfortable as we are—and are not likely to become so.

It has been said that the strength of a society is manifest by the concern with which it treats its most vulnerable members. That idea might very well make us uncomfortable. Sometimes it's important to be uncomfortable.

FOR REFLECTION AND DISCUSSION

How much comfort is there in my life?
How do I exercise care for those in need?

Twenty-seventh Sunday in Ordinary Time (A)

Isaiah 5:1–7

Scripture scholars tell us that this Sunday's reading is from the earliest part of Isaiah's prophetic ministry. It dates from about 742 to 735 B.C., before the destruction of the Northern Kingdom. It is a poetic parable that may have been first sung at a festival celebrating the grape harvest.

The parable is in three parts, the last of which constitutes a surprise ending.

First of all the prophet announced that he is going to sing a song about his friend's vineyard. It was a good vineyard and the prophet's friend took extraordinary care of it. He did everything imaginable to see that it produced good fruit. "[B]ut what it yielded was wild grapes," a totally useless harvest.

In the second part of the poem, the speaker is no longer the prophet but his friend, the owner of the vineyard. The friend calls on his hearers to join with him in deploring the disappointing outcome of all his work. The owner tells his hearers what he plans to do. He will take away the wall and the hedge that protect it from animals. He will not cultivate it any longer, but allow it to be taken over by wild growth. There will be no rain.

Now comes the third part of the poem, the surprise ending. So far Isaiah has not disclosed the identity of the characters in the parable. He has led the hearers ("inhabitants of Jerusalem and people of Judah") to condemn the vineyard's fruitlessness and ingratitude. Now comes the surprise: The master of the vineyard is the Lord and the vineyard is the people of Judah. They are guilty of producing the wrong kind of fruit. God expected faithful fulfillment of his will from the people, and instead they yielded social injustice. He expected righteous care for the poor and the yield was the cry of the oppressed. By the time the parable is finished, the prophet's lesson is clear: "It's about you that I am talking! God has given you everything and you have yielded nothing. You are a harvest of unfaithfulness."

It is obvious that this reading was chosen for this Sunday in view of the parable of the wicked tenants that the Gospel gives us (Matthew 21:33-43). In fact, it seems quite clear that Jesus himself was basing his parable on Isaiah's, and Jesus' hearers would have recognized the Isaian prototype as soon as Jesus began to tell his parable.

But there is a surprise here, too. Jesus changes Isaiah's parable so that it is no longer about the people at large, but about tenants brought in to tend the vineyard. These tenants (or share croppers) end up taking over for their own benefit what properly belonged to the owner of the vineyard. Here was a new kind of unfaithfulness, not of the people at large but of the religious leaders who misused the vineyard that is God's people.

The purpose of both parables is to underline unfaithfulness (of the people as a whole in Isaiah and of the people's leaders in Jesus' story) by contrasting it with the loving care of God and God's rightful expectation of an appropriate yield.

It is not hard to apply the general lesson of these parables (God's demand for faithfulness) to ourselves today. God has certainly taken pains to insure the fruitfulness of each of us. In baptism we are grafted onto the life of God, so that we live with God's energy. In the Eucharist we are further cultivated and enriched by the Lord. The other sacraments deal with various aspects of our lives, each sacrament expressing a particular aspect of the Lord's care for us. Then there is God's word in Scripture which gives us light and direction. Our brothers and sisters in the Lord also serve to improve the quality of our lives in the Lord, affording us example and encouragement. God has every right to ask us, "What more was there to do for my vineyard that I have not done?"

And how faithful have we been, how responsive to God's care for us—individually and as a community? Certainly none of us can say that we have responded fully to God's initiative and that we have brought forth everything that God could have expected from us. There is still pettiness in our hearts, still injustice in our world, still lukewarmness in the church. We tend to look out much more attentively for our own immediate well-being than for the productivity of God's planting. We are all sinners.

What Isaiah said to the people of Jerusalem in the eighth century B.C., God's word says to us today: "It's about you that I am talking!"

FOR REFLECTION AND DISCUSSION

How conscious am I of God's care for me?
Am I a fruitful vine in God's vineyard?

Twenty-seventh Sunday in Ordinary Time (B)

Genesis 2:18–24

Scripture scholars tell us that Genesis, while reflecting the basic and fundamental religious and theological revelation that constituted the foundations of the Hebrew people, is actually a compilation of several literary sources. These sources were created at different times, and finally melded together to give us the biblical texts that we now have.

This multisource origin for Genesis explains why there are two narratives of the creation. They come from different sources. The first creation narrative, which we hear at the Easter Vigil, runs from Genesis 1:1 to 2:4. The second creation narrative runs from 2:5 to 2:25. The second version of the creation story is generally considered to be much older than the first version. This Sunday's reading is from this second (more ancient) account of creation.

In the first creation narrative human beings are created last, the final product of God's plan of loving providence. The second narrative proceeds in the opposite direction. First God creates man, carefully molding him out of the clay of the earth (2:7). Then God creates the garden and puts man in charge of it.

This is where our Sunday reading begins. To grasp the meaning of what follows, it is important to remember that in the world in which these various accounts of creation were set down, women were generally regarded as inferior beings, a kind of lower creature, often looked on as property.

As our reading proceeds, we see that the man that God has created is not really complete when he is alone. He needs a partner. So God creates all kinds of living creatures and puts the man in charge of them, but it's not enough. No bird or wild animal was enough to make man complete.

Then God creates woman. First God puts Adam to sleep so that he will not witness the mysterious creative process that God engages in. God makes woman out of Adam's rib to demonstrate that she is of the same nature and dignity as he is, equal to man in the very basics of his humanity. In woman, man encounters another self, a self for whom future men would move away from the most basic familiar relationships—father and mother—and give themselves to something deeper and better, to a union in which the origin of woman from man's body is expressed again as the two of them become one flesh.

These verses of Genesis have been chosen for this Sunday's First Reading because their conclusion is quoted by Jesus in the Gospel (Mark 10:2–16) as he disputes with the Pharisees about the permissibility of divorce. Man and wife are not really two beings, Jesus says, but one.

Jesus' point is that allowing either man or woman to walk away from a marriage into which either has entered is simply wrong. Granted, there may be circumstances in which the two should not live together, but, because of the nature of man and woman, because of the nature of their marriage relationship, they cannot simply undo the relationship they have entered.

In Jesus' time, as well as in the time that the material that became Genesis was written, divorce was simple and easy. For practically any reason whatsoever, a man could dismiss his wife and marry another. She didn't count for very much. She was easily replaceable.

Both Genesis and Jesus teach that such an attitude is unacceptable to the Lord. Woman was not to be looked on as a throw-away product. She was of the same nature, the same dignity, the same worth as man. Once they joined in marriage they were indivisibly one.

Over the years, indeed, over the centuries, the dignity of woman has not always been appropriately recognized. For most of human history the teaching of these two readings has been quite countercultural, in disaccord with the standard practices of the world in which they were proclaimed.

Still today, in many parts of the world, women are looked upon as property, to be disposed of when they no longer seem useful. In the church, as well as in the society in which we live, women have not always been given the respect that the words of Scripture seem to demand for them. This suggests that the teaching of this Sunday's readings is not only relevant to our time and our culture, but is absolutely essential for it if we are going to live according to the will of God.

FOR REFLECTION AND DISCUSSION

How do I experience and respect the dignity of women?

In what way so I see today's teaching as countercultural?

Twenty-seventh Sunday in Ordinary Time (C),

Habakkuk 1:2–3; 2:2–4

This is the only Sunday in the three-year Sunday lectionary cycle that we hear from the prophet Habakkuk. Habakkuk's prophetic career seems to have unfolded from about 605 B.C. to about 597 B.C., that is, about ten or twenty years before the destruction of Jerusalem in 587 B.C. Habakkuk was therefore a contemporary of Jeremiah.

Habakkuk is one of the so-called minor prophets. The minor prophets were no less inspired than the major prophets. But their writings were relatively brief, with the result that the works of all twelve of them could be packed into a single scroll with a common title.

The book of Habakkuk is only three chapters long and the first part of it, from which our reading is taken, is a dialog between the prophet and the Lord.

The first half of our reading, i.e., the two verses from chapter one, give the prophet's complaint to God. The Babylonians were beginning to exert their power near the kingdom of Judah. They were a new threat on the horizon. Habakkuk complains that God doesn't seem to be listening. "We need help but You don't seem to be doing anything for us. Are you going to let us be destroyed?"

The second half of the reading, i.e., the three verses from chapter two, give God's response. "I've got a plan," God says, "a clear vision of the future. It's important enough to be written down in letters big enough for people to read without effort. It will be fulfilled in due time and if it seems to be taking too long, you'll just have to wait for it, because it will indeed come to pass."

Next comes a statement that sums up the relationships that are involved in God's visions and plans. "The rash one has no integrity." (The Hebrew text here seems to be somewhat unclear and apparently means something like, "The wicked man is puffed up with pride and has within him the seeds of his own destruction.") On the other hand, "[T]he just one, because of his faith, shall live." The evil man's reliance on himself will only bring him to ruin. The rescue that the prophet is looking for will come from confidence in God's vision.

The key teaching in this reading is at the very end: "[T]he just one, because of his faith, shall live." This connects our Habakkuk reading with the Gospel (Luke 17:5–10) whose first paragraph likewise has to do with faith. What Jesus called for from those who would follow him is also what God called for from the people of Habakkuk's time: faith.

In our text from Habakkuk, "faith" seems to mean a constant conviction about the goodness of God. It involves patience in awaiting the execution of God's goodness. That's what's going to enable God's people to survive the troubled times in which they find themselves. Faith as ongoing confidence seems also to be what Jesus had in mind in his encouragement to his followers. Even a little bit of unswerving confidence ("the size of a mustard seed") can work wonders.

But this last sentence of the Habakkuk reading was also important for Saint Paul who quotes it twice (Romans 1:17; Galatians 3:11) in the context of the salvation offered by Christ. For Saint Paul, faith is not so much holding on in the midst of adversity as it is an openness to receive the justifying action of Christ as a gift rather than as something we can earn.

These two different approaches to faith are not necessarily in opposition to one another. The faith that leads us to accept the gift of salvation from Christ also enables us to maintain our confidence in the face of adversity. We can stand up to our enemies thanks to the life of Christ that we share as members of Christ's body. Faith as acceptance is the foundation for faith as confidence.

People sometimes look on faith as intellectual assent to a body of truths ("the Christian faith"). It is that, of course, but that's only part of it. More fundamentally, faith is commitment, the gift of ourselves in response to God's invitation to share the life of Christ, a gift that brings security and courage when times are hard.

The righteous will live because of faith. The righteous one will live the life of Christ. The righteous one will escape destruction and harm. Faith is a complex theological concept. But God's care for his people is complex, too.

FOR REFLECTION AND DISCUSSION
How has my faith been a source of life for me?
How has my faith been tested?

Twenty-eighth Sunday in Ordinary Time (A)

Isaiah 25:6–10a

Scripture scholars tell us that, although chapters 24 to 27 are
found in the first part of Isaiah, they are not the work of the
eighth century B.C. Isaiah of Jerusalem. Rather, these chapters are
a collection of poems that date from after the destruction of
Jerusalem. They are on apocalyptic themes, that is, they are
concerned with the final stage of God's plans for the world when
all evil will be punished and all good will be definitively united
with God.

This Sunday's reading has to do with final universal salvation.
The first and the last verses speak of God's action "[o]n this
mountain," that is, on Mount Zion which is a symbol of the
heavenly Jerusalem, the final fulfillment of God's work of love for
creation. The reading itself is divided into four parts, each of
which alludes to the all inclusive nature of what God has been
busy with.

In the first section God promises a rich banquet, a joyful feast
of unimaginable proportions "for all peoples."

In the second section God promises that the oppression and
destruction, the veil of mourning that had covered all the peoples
of the earth at various times and in various ways would be
removed and that death itself would be destroyed.

The third section again speaks to the nations at large and
foretells the removal of all shame that might have come upon
them as a result of their weakness and defeat. "[T]he reproach of
his people" seems to refer to all the nations.

Finally all peoples and all nations cry out in praise to "our
God" for the salvation that has been bestowed on them "[o]n this
mountain."

The author of these inspired words is trying to bring home to his readers the exquisite joy of that final day when all peoples would be united with the Lord forever. He uses images of a sumptuous banquet, of protection from vulnerability, of a renewal of gladness after a time of tears. He implies that God's final plans for us cannot be simply described in ordinary words, and that no one image is adequate to suggest what God has in store for us.

This reading from Isaiah serves as a lead-in to the Gospel parable of the wedding feast (Matthew 22:1–14). It may well be that Jesus was thinking of this very passage as background for his more complicated story. Jesus starts with the idea of a feast, but then renders it more complex with the refusal of the invitation on the part of those who had been invited, with the inclusion of other guests, and with the inappropriate vesture of the one guest. Jesus' conclusion ("Many are invited, but few are chosen") seems to bring his story to a different conclusion than Isaiah's promise of universal inclusion.

What seems to be happening here is that Jesus and Isaiah are using the same image for different purposes. Isaiah wants his readers to be aware that God's providence is not limited to Israelites, while Jesus wants his hearers to recognize that being called to God's feast carries with it certain responsibilities.

If we focus our attention on the passage from Isaiah, we see two main themes: abundance and universality.

The banquet isn't a picnic lunch to get the guests through the afternoon until it's time to eat again. No, it is "a feast of rich food and choice wines, / juicy, rich food and pure, choice wines." It's the kind of meal you settle down to and consciously and deliberately enjoy. God does not deal in carefully weighed out portions nor in basic survival food. God's banquet is luxurious and abundant.

So are God's other gifts: the Scriptures, the sacraments, the church, the love that we share with our brothers and sisters in Christ, the individual providence that God exercises over each one of us. It's almost as if God can't do enough for us. "Here, have some more. Try this gift that you haven't experienced yet." God is a God of abundance.

And he is a God of universality. Women and men of every race and nation and time and place are called to share in the banquet and to enjoy God's protection. What began as a plan for a single people soon developed into a providential project for each and every human being, and that providential project is still being implemented today.

We do God no honor if we conceptualize his gifts or his intentions too narrowly.

FOR REFLECTION AND DISCUSSION

How have I experienced abundance from God?

How have I seen God's providence directed toward all peoples?

Twenty-eighth Sunday in Ordinary Time (B)

Wisdom 7:7–11

It has only been three weeks since we heard from the book of Wisdom. Readings from Wisdom occur eight times during the three-year Sunday cycle, all of them assigned for Sundays in Ordinary Time. During Ordinary Time we experience the annual retelling of the public life and ministry and teaching of Jesus, and the recurrence of readings from Wisdom may be meant to suggest that wisdom is a kind of basic theme that underlies all that Jesus said and did in his public ministry.

This Sunday's reading is from the second main section of the book. This section runs from the end of chapter six through chapter ten. It is a reflection on the nature and origin of wisdom that is put into the mouth of King Solomon, the wise man *par excellence.*

This Sunday's reading describes the value that Solomon puts on the wisdom that he has asked for and received from God. Wisdom is better than power and wealth, more attractive than things like precious stones and gold and silver. It is more lovable than health and beauty, more appealing even than basic necessities such as light. Everything that is good comes with wisdom, and to gain wisdom is to gain riches beyond counting.

What is this wisdom about which Solomon waxes so lyrical? Scholars tell us that wisdom, as presented in Sacred Scripture, is a many-faceted reality. It consists most basically in knowing how to conduct one's life so as to attain true happiness. The wise person is the person who knows how to make the most of his or her earthly existence, not in the sense of acquiring an abundance of the good things of this world, but in the sense of knowing what is really worth the effort of human pursuit. Wise people know what is really important, and they know how to go about getting it.

But wisdom is not just a human quality. God has wisdom, too. Indeed, God is the source of all wisdom. It is God who has created the world with all its blessings, God whose providence leads every creature toward the end that he has destined for it. One could say that wisdom is the mind of God which human beings have been invited to know and share, not because they have earned it or deserved it, but simply because God is generous.

This reading about the value of wisdom seems to have been chosen to illustrate the Gospel (Mark 10:17–27). There we see a man coming to Jesus to ask what he had to do to inherit eternal life. In effect, he was asking how he could acquire wisdom. Jesus answers by encouraging him to keep the commandments, and secondly to detach himself from earthly wealth. The man goes away sad, because, although he had kept the commandments from his youth, the lure of wealth seemed to pull him more forcefully than the call of the Lord. He did not prefer wisdom to gold and silver and priceless gems, as did the teacher of our First Reading. As a matter of fact, what God was offering him took second place to the security of possessions.

Some people (maybe all of us at one time or another) look on the commandments and on the teaching of Jesus as a complex of rules and regulations, which, if observed with exactitude, will earn them salvation. Because they are dealing with rules and regulations, these people tend to observe them the same way they observe the rules and regulations for their income tax: Do whatever you have to do to stay on the right side of the law, but nothing more. People like this do not gain true wisdom because they are not really seeking wisdom. They are seeking a kind of cut-rate spiritual security, to be bought from God as cheaply as possible.

What God offers us in his commandments, what Jesus offers us in his teaching, is the way to wisdom. If we observe what God asks of us, we will live as God intends us to live. We will be in harmony with what God planned his creation to be. We will be wise. We will find ourselves, in the end, in a situation of total peace and fulfillment, in eternal communion with the Lord.

The core of Jesus' preaching was the kingdom of God, that ultimate state of well-being in which God is fully in charge, in which God's creatures are responsive to God's providence, in which their lives are all that God intended them to be. The kingdom of God is another term for wisdom. This Sunday's readings remind us that there is nothing more precious, nothing more important.

FOR REFLECTION AND DISCUSSION

How have I experienced God's law as wisdom?
How has God's law enriched me?

Twenty-eighth Sunday in Ordinary Time (C)

2 Kings 5:14–17

The Old Testament reading for this Sunday consists of the ending of a long narrative from the first part of the second book of Kings. This first part of 2 Kings is devoted to the ministry and miracles of the prophet Elisha.

At the beginning of chapter five we learn about Naaman. He was a general in the army of the king of Aram. The Arameans were not particularly friendly to the Israelites. This Naaman was afflicted with some kind of disfiguring skin disease that the text refers to as leprosy. Naaman's wife had a slave girl who had been carried off from the land of Israel. This slave girl urged her mistress to get their master to go to Israel and be cured by Elisha, the famous man of God. Naaman gets the king of Aram to write to the king of Israel instructing him to see that Naaman gets cured. The king of Israel sees this action as a political provocation. But then Elisha instructs the king to send Naaman to him (Elisha). Naaman goes to Elisha, expecting that there would be great ceremony and complex ritual connected with the healing process. Instead, Elisha doesn't even come out of the house. He sends word to Naaman to go wash in the Jordan river seven times. Naaman is outraged. "The Jordan! We've got better rivers than that at home!" But then the members of his entourage convince Naaman to give it a try. This is where our Sunday reading begins.

Naaman washes in the Jordan as he had been instructed. He is cured. Now he returns to Elisha's house and proclaims that the God of Israel is the only real god there is. In gratitude he offers gifts to Elisha which the prophet refuses. (After all, it was the Lord, not Elisha, who did the curing.) Naaman, now devoted to the God of Israel alone, asks that he be allowed to take two mule-loads of earth home with him so that, from now on, he could worship God on God's own terrain.

The Gospel narrative for today (Luke 17:11–19) shows many features that are parallel to the Naaman narrative. Jesus is dealing with lepers (in greater numbers than Elisha was, to be sure). They are cleansed. There is some (admittedly inadequate) expression of gratitude. The gratitude is expressed by a Gentile, an outsider, a foreigner.

There are at least two elements in these narratives that call for our attention.

First of all, there is gratuity. Neither Elisha nor Jesus owes anything to those asking for a cure. Naaman was an enemy to Elisha's people. The ten lepers of the gospel were an anonymous band of social outcasts. Yet in each case the Lord God extends his merciful power to them and they are healed. God heals people not because they are deserving but because God is kind and merciful. And the people God heals are not members of a specially chosen group. Some are members of God's people, to be sure, but some are foreigners, outsiders, even enemies. God's generous care is not exclusive. His concern is for all those in need, Jews or Gentiles, home folk or strangers. God's will to save is universal.

Second, there is gratitude. Naaman and the cured Samaritan take pains to express their appreciation for what God had done for them. Nobody can make a fully appropriate response to an intervention from God. But we can express our obligation to God. We can acknowledge that God has gifted us in ways that we do not deserve, that we have been the objects of God's generosity. What God looks for is not payment but humble acceptance.

God continues to care for our sickness and weakness today. We may not be suffering from maladies that cause public disfigurement, but we are all sick and weak in one way or another. We are selfish. We are ignorant. We are afraid. We are lazy. We are constitutionally distracted from paying attention to God. And, apart from these chronic disabilities, we are also deliberate sinners. God extends his gratuitous, free attention to us in lots of different ways: in the cleansing waters of Baptism, in the strength and energy of the Eucharist; in the guidance that comes from the Sacred Scriptures; in the encouragement and direction that comes through prayer and reflection; in the encouragement that we receive from our brothers and sisters in the family of faith. Then, too, there is the sacrament of reconciliation, God's healing touch *par excellence*. For all this we owe God our gratitude.

From Elisha to Jesus, from Jesus to the church of today, God has been cleansing lepers for a long time. It's important to remember that God still cleanses lepers today, and that, in one way or another, we are they.

FOR REFLECTION AND DISCUSSION

How has God intervened in my life?

What part does gratitude play in my spirituality?

Twenty-ninth Sunday in Ordinary Time (A)

Isaiah 45:1, 4–6

Cyrus the Great (c. 585–c. 529 B.C.) was one of the most remarkable figures of all classical antiquity. Originally a tribal ruler in southwest Iran, he defeated his overlords, the Medes, and laid the foundations for what became the Persian Empire. Soon he conquered the rich kingdom of King Croesus of Lydia, and then, in 539, the vast empire of the Babylonians, thus becoming ruler of the greatest power in the civilized world of the time. Cyrus administered his empire with wisdom and tolerance. He respected the customs and religion of the nations he conquered. He allowed and encouraged captive peoples, including the Israelites, to return home. For centuries after his death, Cyrus was regarded by thoughtful people as the model of a wise and effective ruler.

Today's First Reading is about Cyrus. The author of the second part of Isaiah offers his readers God's reflections on this great conqueror who had now been victorious over the oppressors of the Israelites. At the end of the chapter that precedes our reading (45:28) God calls Cyrus his shepherd who would fulfill God's every wish and see to the rebuilding of Jerusalem and the temple.

As our reading begins, God refers to Cyrus as "his anointed," i.e., as God's messiah. This is a term that was usually reserved for Israelite kings and prophets, but here it is applied to Cyrus as God's agent. Cyrus (a pagan!) would be in a one-of-a-kind relationship with God.

The text then goes on to describe what God would do for Cyrus. God would be his friend and subdue kings before him and give him easy access to everything he wanted.

But in the next part of the reading, God makes it quite clear that it was he, God, who was in charge of what was going on and that Cyrus, for all his greatness, was a servant of God. Even though Cyrus may not have been aware of the influence of God in his life, it was nonetheless the Lord who was the ruler of all. Without Cyrus even being conscious of it, God would see to it that he would bring knowledge of God to the whole world.

Note the recurrent first-person pronoun in the second part of our reading: "I call you...I am the LORD...I arm you...I am the LORD and there is no other" (NRSV). Cyrus would be a unique instrument of God's providence for his people, but he would nonetheless remain the servant of the God of the Israelites.

This reading has to do with the relationship between civil society and the Lord, and it was chosen to provide background for the Gospel (Matthew 22:15–21) in which Jesus addresses this same issue with the Pharisees.

Jesus does not speak of Caesar in the same extravagant terms that God uses to describe Cyrus. The sociopolitical situation in which Jesus lived was different from that of the soon-to-be-repatriated exiles in Babylon. It wasn't quite clear what the relationship between the Jews and their Roman occupiers was supposed to be. But Jesus makes a point that applies to the relationship of God and Cyrus as well as to our situation today. That point is that both civil society and our relationship to God are important, and that each should receive proper attention.

Cyrus and Caesar and the government leaders of our own time are, in various ways, instruments of the Lord. God does not mean for his human creatures to live in anarchy. Some kind of secular government is necessary to enable us to live in peace with one another and to enjoy the gifts of creation that God intended us to have. God uses civil society to attain these ends.

At the same time, political power and secular government are only relatively important. In the final analysis, Cyrus and Caesar and contemporary leaders are all secondary and subordinate to the power and the will of the Lord. What God says to Cyrus in the second half of today's reading ("I am the LORD, and there is no other" [NRSV]) applies to every secular ruler of every age and place. When secular rulers forget that there is a higher power to which they are ultimately accountable, they lead their people into tyranny and oppression. Any power that does not acknowledge the ultimate power of God will sooner or later become an unjust power.

The agents of civil government—Cyrus and Caesar and contemporary elected officials—have a claim on our respect and obedience. Jesus tells us to give them their due. But God has a claim, too. God's claim may be expressed differently in different societies, but God is still the Lord and there is no other and we must render to God what is God's.

FOR REFLECTION AND DISCUSSION

Do I see any connection between my religious faith and political life? Where do I see God at work in contemporary events?

Twenty-ninth Sunday in Ordinary Time (B)

Isaiah 53:10–11

Five weeks ago, when the Gospel (Mark 8:27–35) gave us Jesus' first prediction of his Passion, the First Reading was from the third of the servant songs found in the second part of the book of Isaiah. Now, on this twenty-ninth Sunday in Ordinary Time, when Jesus instructs his disciples about the costs of discipleship, we hear from the last part of the fourth servant song.

These four pieces of fine poetry were composed during the Babylonian exile. They describe the ideal servant of God. Some look on this servant as an image of the people of Israel. Christian tradition has seen in the servant a foreshadowing of the life and ministry of Jesus.

The fourth servant song, in its entirety, runs from 52:13—53. It is concerned with the sufferings of the servant in the execution of his mission from God. The song is used in its entirety as the First Reading for the liturgy of Good Friday. This Sunday's reading is from the last part of the poem which deals with the results of the servant's suffering. It is a short reading, but it teaches us about some very important aspects of our salvation.

First we have a general statement: "Yet it was the will of the Lord to crush him with pain." The point here is not that God takes pleasure in the suffering of the servant, but rather that God was at work in this aspect of the servant's mission, that God accepted the servant's suffering (and death) as a gift proffered to the Lord by this special servant of his. It was in accord with what the Lord asked of him.

But there would be outcomes of this generosity and self-gift on the part of the servant. These outcomes are expressed in the three statements that follow the topic sentence, each pointing out a result of the servant's suffering. Because he gave his life as an offering for sin, the servant will be the father of a great family and will bring about the fulfillment of the Lord's will. Because of his affliction, the servant will be glorified ("he shall see the light"). Finally, through his suffering the servant will bear the guilt of "many" (i.e., all) and bring them to a state of justice, i.e., to redemption and salvation.

The point here is fundamental in the Christian teaching about our salvation: The sufferings of the righteous can make up for the sins of others. By voluntary suffering, the servant atones for the sins of all his people.

It is important to realize, however, that what is pleasing to God, what makes up for the sins of the whole people, is not the suffering of the servant in itself. God does not take pleasure in the pain of those he loves. What is important is the faithfulness of the servant, his dedication to God even when that dedication brings him to suffering and death. The faithfulness of the servant is not limited to the ordinary matters of ordinary life. It also extends to the deepest reaches of human endeavor. Nothing is too costly, nothing is too painful, even death itself, in the context of the servant's willingness to carry out the plans of God. It is this generosity, this willingness to give of himself, that makes the suffering significant. In itself, human hurting is not redemptive. It only becomes so when it is an expression of human dedication to the loving will of God.

The Christian theological tradition reads the fourth servant song as an interpretation of the life and death of Jesus. He is the servant whose suffering takes away the sins of the world. His faithfulness to the Father, both human and divine, won salvation for all of us, not because it caused Jesus suffering, but because it was a faithfulness of unique dimensions. Jesus' suffering and his terrible death on the cross were expressions of that faithfulness. It was the faithfulness that mattered most.

The choice of this Old Testament reading to introduce this Sunday's Gospel applies the fourth servant song to Jesus' disciples. He is very clear about the sons of Zebedee drinking the same cup that he himself is destined to drink. And what Jesus says to James and John also applies to us. We are all called to be followers of Jesus in his faithfulness to the Father, even when that faithfulness is painful and costly. It's not the suffering that counts most, but the faithfulness behind the suffering. The suffering is only the expression of our willingness to maintain our dedication to the Lord, come what may. But it is part of our vocation as disciples.

FOR REFLECTION AND DISCUSSION

What has suffering contributed to my life?

What has my response to suffering contributed to the lives of others?

Twenty-ninth Sunday in Ordinary Time (C)

Exodus 17:18–23

This Sunday brings us another reading from Exodus. Our last reading from this book of the Pentateuch (the first five books of the Old Testament) was only five weeks ago. Exodus is one of the most frequently presented books of the Hebrew Scriptures in the Sunday cycles. Only Isaiah and Genesis are used more.

This Sunday's reading shows us the children of Israel at the very beginning of their journey from Egypt to the land the Lord had promised them. They have been on the march for about two months. During these weeks there have been ongoing tensions between the people and Moses, between the hardship that the people's emigration involved and their duty to show gratitude to God for the great works he had already done for them.

As a result of, or as a response to their ongoing complaints against God and against Moses, God has provided them with quail and manna to eat and with good water to drink. Moses had been their intercessor with God. Moses had been God's agent in explaining to the people what God was doing and how they were to respond.

Now, as our Sunday reading begins, comes a new threat: the Amalekites. The Amalekites were an ancient, some say an aboriginal people who lived in the Sinai Peninsula. They would turn out to be more or less constant enemies of the children of Israel for many centuries in the future. Would God provide for his people in the face of their first non-Egyptian enemies as he had provided for them in the face of hunger and thirst? Yes, God would continue to care for his people and he would do it, once again, through the agency of Moses.

There are four personages involved in the narrative that this Sunday's reading presents. The first is Joshua, who is introduced here in the exodus narrative without any explanation. Of course, all the readers of Exodus would have known that Joshua was a warrior who would succeed Moses and leader of the people and bring them into the Promised Land. Then there is Aaron, Moses' brother, who had stood by him before Pharaoh and who would play a large part in the events that were still to come. Next there was Hur, about whom the Scriptural texts say very little. Hur seems to have been a well-known leadership figure in the exodus tradition, even though he is only mentioned once more in the narrative (cf. Exodus 24:14). And finally, Moses, the friend of God, the leader of God's people.

Moses sends Joshua out with select soldiers to face Amalek (the king of the Amalekites) in battle. Moses goes up a nearby hill with his staff in his hand, the same staff he had used to perform marvels before Pharaoh and to split the Red Sea in two (cf. Exodus 4:17 and 14:16). Aaron and Hur are with him. As long as Moses holds the staff up straight, the Israelites win the battle. But when Moses' arm gets tired, the Amalekites gain the initiative.

Finally Aaron and Hur sit Moses down on a stone and hold up his arms (presumably with the staff) until Joshua had mowed down the Amalekites. Moses brought victory to his people because "his hands remained steady."

The original point of this passage seems to have been to highlight the importance of Moses and his heroic powers. He who brought the plagues on the Egyptians and who split the Red Sea in two now delivers his people from their enemies.

But later tradition sees another dimension in this narrative. It is a narrative about persistence in prayer. As long as Moses held his hands up in prayer, the Israelites won. He was steady in his intercession for the people, and God was attentive to him.

The Gospel (Luke 18:1–8) is also about persistence in prayer. Jesus (half humorously, it seems) tells his hearers that they are supposed to pester God in their prayer just as the widow pesters the judge.

Put in more sober terms, what God seems to be teaching in both of these readings is that we need to be steady in our prayer, persevering in our address to the Lord. This is not because God needs to be informed about our needs, nor because God will answer us only when he can't stand our pestering any more. It's because *we ourselves* need to be aware of how much we are dependent on God. Persistent prayer doesn't change God; it changes us. It brings us to realize that God is not some kind of vending machine that responds to the first deposit that is made. The Lord God is personal and relates to us as persons ever more generously as we steadily come to realize how much we depend on our relationship with him.

FOR REFLECTION AND DISCUSSION

How persistent is my prayer?
How does prayer change me?

Thirtieth Sunday in Ordinary Time (A)

Exodus 22:20–26

This Sunday's Scripture passage is from the part of Exodus known as the Covenant Code. It is found in Exodus in chapters 21 to 23, immediately after God's proclamation of the Ten Commandments to Moses on Mount Sinai in chapter 20. Scripture scholars tell us that the Covenant Code, in the form in which we have it now, comes from a later time than the Ten Commandments, although its underpinnings are to be found in God's basic contact with Moses on Mount Sinai. The Ten Commandments give God's people the key demands of their relationship with him. They constitute a summary. The more detailed and specific legislation by which the people were to live when they had settled down in the land God gave them would develop gradually as the years went by, and would eventually be linked with the Ten Commandments when Exodus was composed.

The directives of the Covenant Code are civil and penal legislation, laying down directives about how the people were to live together and establishing penalties for noncompliance. Their basic teaching is that God's people were to strive to be like God.

The section of the Covenant Code that the lectionary gives us today deals with the treatment that was owed to the legally helpless, to the defenseless.

First we hear about aliens, the outsiders who did not enjoy the full spectrum of civil rights that full-fledged Israelites did. God says that these persons must be treated fairly. This fair treatment was to remind the Israelites of their own history, when they were aliens in Egypt.

Next God speaks about widows and orphans. (Note that in

the Bible, "orphans" generally means young persons who were without a father.) They were particularly vulnerable members of society because one's standing in society as well as one's economic resources depended on one's association with the male head of the family. If there was no husband or no father, the widow or the orphan was basically defenseless, at the mercy of those around them. God is stern in his directives about how widows and orphans were to be treated: They are not to be wronged, and if they are wronged and cry out to God, God will punish the wrongdoer by depriving the wrongdoer's wife and children of their husband and father. The way you treat others will be the way God treats you and yours.

Finally, we learn about the neighbor who is poor. The fact that the neighbor is poor and therefore not powerful does not mean we can treat the neighbor any way we please. It is wrong to impose harsh terms on the neighbor when the neighbor needs our help. Like the widows and the orphans, the poor neighbor can cry out to God, too, and God promises to hear him, "for I am compassionate."

This reading from Exodus fits in very nicely with the Gospel (Matthew 22:34–40). There Jesus gives the general rules of behavior for the law-abiding Israelite: Love God and love your neighbor. In the Old Testament reading we learn in greater detail what that involves. We learn that God has a soft spot in his heart for the defenseless, for those who have no potential of their own on which to rely. God wants his people to look out for those who are helpless because he, God, looks out for the helpless. Thus, those who would be godly must conduct themselves with care and compassion toward those in need.

There are countless lessons in these two readings. One is that we human beings do not need to rely only on ourselves for what we need in this world. God assures us that we can look to him for help, and to our brothers and sisters as well. Another lesson is that being poor and defenseless is not a sin. Poor people are not poor because they are bad. Another lesson is that the vulnerable—aliens, widows and orphans, the poor—have the right to cry out in their need. It's appropriate for them to make their needs known to God and to their fellow human beings. Still more: In these readings God teaches us that being holy, being godly, being religiously observant does not consist exclusively in carrying out religious practices like prayer and attendance at public worship. That's part of loving God, to be sure, but only a part. Godliness also involves defending the defenseless and providing for the helpless. That's how God treats his people, and that's how God expects us to treat his people.

In sum, the greatest commandments are to love God and love our neighbor. Loving God demands loving our neighbor. Loving our neighbor demands caring for those who cannot care adequately for themselves.

FOR REFLECTION AND DISCUSSION

How do these Exodus directives apply to us today?

How do the poor and the weak cry out in our society?

Thirtieth Sunday in Ordinary Time (B)

Jeremiah 31:7–9

The prophetic career of Jeremiah was a long one, extending from about 626 B.C. to about 580 B.C. The Northern Kingdom had fallen to the Assyrians about a hundred years before Jeremiah was called to be a spokesman for the Lord. The end of his ministry came after the destruction of the Southern Kingdom in 587 B.C.

Chapters thirty and thirty-one seem to be from the beginning of Jeremiah's prophetic activity. (Note that the material in the prophetic books of the Old Testament is not always presented in strict chronological order. Sometimes earlier proclamations come later in the book and vice versa.) The Assyrians had fallen into decline and hopes began to arise that the descendants of those who had been carried into exile in 721 B.C. might return to their homeland. These two chapters of Jeremiah originally sang of the return of these exiles. As the years passed, it became clearer that the ten tribes which formed the people of the former Northern Kingdom would not be returning, but that the Southern Kingdom might soon share their fate, this time at the hands of the Babylonians. These songs of return would also be applied to the not far distant Babylonian exile. Somehow God would bring his people home from wherever they had been carried off to.

This Sunday's reading, then, dealt originally with the return of the exiles of the Northern Kingdom. At the beginning the prophet speaks of Jacob, at the end of Ephraim. Both are synonyms for the Northern Kingdom.

At the beginning of our text comes the statement of the theme of this passage: the Lord delivers his people. Then we have a description of the returnees: They will be reassembled as a people by God who will bring them back from their exile in the distant north (Assyria). God will bring them home from the ends of the earth. The assembly will include even those for whom travel is difficult: the blind, the lame, the pregnant women— they'll all return. God will console them all, leading them along easy paths where fresh water runs. No one will find the journey too demanding. And why is the Lord doing all this? Simply because God loves his people.

Scholars point out that the theme of homecoming is one of the recurrent motifs of the Old Testament. God promises Abraham a home for himself and his family. God leads the Israelites out of Egypt to their traditional homeland. When God allows the people to be punished, the punishment consists of being deprived of their homeland. In the end, however, God always brings them home again, maybe not according to the timetable they would prefer, maybe not in the ways they might have imagined, maybe not to a homeland that immediately fulfills their every dream, but God does bring them home simply because he is God, simply because God loves his people.

This reading connects with the Gospel (Mark 10:46–52) in two ways. First of all, there is Bartimaeus the blind man. The Lord has pity on him just as the Lord had pity on the blind and the lame who would be returning from exile. But there is also the journey theme that is common to both readings. Jesus is journeying to Jerusalem and, at the end of the Gospel, Bartimaeus follows along with him. This journey of Jesus would end in the salvation of all humankind, just as the Old Testament journey would end in the restoration of the people.

God does whatever is necessary to guarantee the final well being of his people. He is determined to save them, to bring them to happiness and fulfillment. Toward that end he reverses their exile and brings them back to their homeland. For that purpose he gives sight to the blind and makes the lame able to walk. No handicap is too great to be overcome by God's care. No journey is too long, too demanding for God's plan of salvation.

We have already heard these themes in our Sunday readings. Just a few weeks ago, on the twenty-third Sunday in Ordinary

Time, we had a song of return from Isaiah (35:4–7a), a song that included the tongue of the mute made capable of song. In the Gospel for that Sunday (Mark 7:31–37) we saw Jesus giving speech to a man with a speech impediment. What Isaiah had promised, Jesus delivered. What Jeremiah looked forward to, Jesus fulfilled.

But all this is not just material from the past. God is still busy leading us home, healing our disabilities, bringing us out of exile. Why? Just because God loves us. Just because he is our Father.

FOR REFLECTION AND DISCUSSION

From what has God delivered me?

In what direction is God guiding me?

Thirtieth Sunday in Ordinary Time (C)

Sirach 35:12–14, 16–18

This week's First Reading and Gospel seem to have quite a bit in common with the readings of several weeks ago, those of the twenty-second Sunday of the year. For one thing, both Sundays have a First Reading from the book of Sirach, that late Old Testament wisdom book that the church made so much use of in the moral formation of its members. It is a book which groups together numbers of short detachable sayings into little essays about how to live in accord with God's providential plans for us.

Likewise, the Gospel for both these Sundays includes one of the most memorable of Jesus' sayings: "For all who exalt themselves will be humbled, but all who humble themselves will be exalted" (NRSV). In addition to being presented in our two

Sunday gospels (Luke 18:14 and Luke 14:11), we also find this pronouncement of the Lord in Matthew 23:12. It was obviously a teaching and a saying that found some resonance in the hearts of Luke and Matthew.

However, the lessons offered by these two similar sets of Sunday readings are not exactly the same. Both Sundays offer teachings about humility. On the twenty-second Sunday in Ordinary Time the lesson is about the general practice of humility in our relations with one another, exemplified by the guests at the banquet. This reading expresses the need for us to be realistic about ourselves and generous toward others. On the thirtieth Sunday, however, in the parable of the Pharisee and the tax collector in the temple, the teaching about humility is more narrowly focused and has to do with humility in prayer.

The reading from Sirach that is assigned for this Sunday makes that context quite clear. It comes from a section of Sirach that seems to be intended to discourage extortion and injustice toward the defenseless. In the full text, the author tries to discourage powerful people from thinking that what has been squeezed out of widows and orphans can be used to provide a sacrifice with which God will be pleased. As the edited text is presented in the lectionary, the teaching is considerably broader and applies more generally to everyone's relationship with God in prayer. It is in two parts.

The first part (verses 12 to 14) is about God. God cannot be bought. God is fair to everybody, weak and strong alike. But that means that he is attentive to the weak and defenseless even as he is to the powerful and important.

In the remaining verses of the reading, the author talks about the prayer of the poor. It pierces the clouds like a flaming arrow.

It reaches the very throne of God where it will not be put aside until God sends back an answer. The answer will be just and right, and it will come speedily.

This reading from Sirach, as well as the Gospel parable, teach us that God is even more attentive to the prayer of the oppressed and the lowly than he is to the powerful and prominent. Why is this? Sirach makes it quite clear that God does not play favorites. There must, therefore, be something special inherent in the prayer of the lowly that makes it more acceptable to God. That something special is the lowly person's awareness of need.

To know how vulnerable we are, how dependent we are on the freely given goodness of God is to give our prayer a special urgency. It is an urgency that is lacking in the prayer of the one who, consciously or unconsciously, thinks that he or she is somehow doing a favor to the Lord by spending time with him.

The proud, self-assured person is inclined to use God as a kind of mirror to reflect the personal excellence of the one doing the praying. "I'm glad I'm not like the others, Lord. I'm sure you are, too." The humble person, on the other hand, prays with an awareness that he or she doesn't have a leg to stand on, that the Lord is doing a favor simply by allowing this person to address him. One might suggest that the prayer of the person in need is louder in God's ears than the prayers of other people because it more accurately echoes the true relationship between God and God's human creatures. The humble person expresses more clearly who he is and who God is than the proud person does.

Probably nobody consciously addresses the Lord in the terms used by the Pharisee in this Sunday's Gospel. But it may well be that many of us are not particularly willing to cast our prayer in the terms that the tax collector uses. Why? Maybe because we are afraid that God will not bother with us if we do. Or maybe because we don't really believe that we are lowly, needy and truly sinful.

FOR REFLECTION AND DISCUSSION

In what ways do I consider myself lowly?

Do I trust that God will answer me when I pray? Why?

Thirty-first Sunday in Ordinary Time (A)

Malachi 1:14b–2:2b, 8–10

The First Reading and the Gospel for this Sunday are both concerned with religious leadership. Both readings are a call to consistency in those who spoke for God. In both the Old Testament and the New, religious leaders did not practice what they preached and, as a result, led the people astray.

The book of Malachi dates from about 450 B.C. The Israelites had returned from exile. The temple had been rebuilt some sixty-five years before. But both priests and people seemed to have lost interest. It was a time of religious superficiality and general spiritual drifting. The priests were self-serving. They were no longer careful to offer the kinds of sacrifices called for by the law and they seem to have abandoned their responsibilities of teaching and guidance. The ordinary people, on the other hand, were no longer willing to expend their energy in preserving their religious identity. There seems to have been a widespread practice of Israelite men divorcing the wives of their youth and marrying foreign, idolatrous women.

We don't know much about the author of Malachi. That probably wasn't his real name. It is Hebrew for "my messenger." We only hear from him one other time in the three-year Sunday cycle (i.e., on the thirty-third Sunday in Ordinary Time in year C).

Our reading from Malachi begins with a kind of trumpet flourish that calls for attention from all the prophet's hearers.

Then the text calls for attention and response from the priests. If they did not listen to the Lord, the Lord would undermine their service, and their ministry would become not only ineffective but downright destructive.

The following section of the reading deals with the instructional and directive responsibilities of the priests. They had been unfaithful to their calling and have lost their credibility in the eyes of the people.

The reading speaks of "the covenant of Levi." There does not seem to be any mention in the Pentateuch or in the historical books of a special contract or covenant between God and the priestly classes. However, in Deuteronomy 31:9–13 and 33:10 God entrusts the members of the tribe of Levi with the task of teaching the law to future generations of Israelites. Thus, they were not just to be agents of ritual, but also guardians and teachers of the traditions of the people.

The last verse of our reading ("Have we not all the one father…") really belongs to the next section of Malachi's prophecy, in which he will take out after the inappropriate marriage practices of the people. However, its inclusion here seems to indicate that those who chose the texts for the lectionary wanted to suggest that what is said about the priests and Levites also applies in some way to the people at large. The religious leaders are not detached and separated from the people. Because God is the father of all, all have some responsibility for right worship and for careful handing on of the religious tradition. Jesus seems to be making a similar point when he says that religious leadership should not be disjoined from the rest of the people as if they were some sort of elite class in a special relationship with God. "You have but one Father in heaven."

There may be different roles in the community, whether in the community of Malachi or the community of Jesus, but the basics are shared by everybody. We are all called to contribute to proper worship. We are all called to help hand on the laws and traditions of the Lord. Our common fatherhood in God calls us all to participate in what pertains to God.

Sometimes it seems easy to criticize our religious leaders. The pastor isn't doing what we would like. The liturgy isn't according to our taste. What's taught is not being taught effectively. "They," our bishops and priests and other church ministers, really aren't doing a very good job. That may indeed be the case. Certainly there is always room for improvement in the quality of our worship and in our catechetical efforts. But merely standing back to evaluate and offer judgment doesn't seem to be what the Lord is calling for in today's reading. If we are all children of our father, then the proper response to what our brothers and sisters do is not detached criticism but a willingness to help carry out our father's will. After all, faith is a family enterprise.

FOR REFLECTION AND DISCUSSION

How fervent is my religious practice?

What are my teaching responsibilities as a Christian believer?

Thirty-first Sunday in Ordinary Time (B)

Deuteronomy 6:2–6

The rationale for the lectionary's presenting this particular Old Testament reading on this particular Sunday is clear. Jesus quotes it in the Gospel (Mark 12:28b–34) in response to the question of the scribe about which of God's commandments is most important. Reading the original text from Deuteronomy provides us the context that Jesus was referring to.

In Deuteronomy, the Israelites are portrayed as ready to enter the Promised Land and Moses is giving them a series of final instructions. In chapter five, Moses has reviewed for them the Ten Commandments that they had received at Mount Sinai earlier on in their years of wandering. Our text, from chapter six, provides a summary of what had gone before. It is a kind of wrap-up of what God expects of his people, a summary of the whole law.

In the first two verses there is a kind of introductory statement. "Keep the laws that God has given you," Moses says. "If you observe what I have commanded, you will grow and prosper when you enter the land that I have promised you." Then comes the great commandment, "Only the Lord is God and you must love him with all your heart and soul. Pay attention to what God is saying!"

These last verses constitute the basic principle of the whole Mosaic law. They are the keynote of Deuteronomy and became the basic prayer of Judaism, a prayer that observant Jews recited three times each day. There are several absolutely basic truths here.

First of all, the prayer teaches us that God is one. The God of Israel was not to be fragmented into various functions as the pagan gods were: fertility, rain, sun, moon, warfare. God is one and there is no other.

And God's people are to respond to him with full commitment of heart and mind and strength. There is nobody else, nothing else that deserves our full energy and attention. Just as God is one, so also our response to God must be one, a single undivided heart. Nothing and nobody is more important than the Lord. Nothing and nobody has a deeper claim on us than the Lord. We are to love God with the totality of our being.

The response that God asks for from us is not just reverence and submission. God calls for love, for personal dedication of heart and mind. It is on our loving response to God that all righteousness depends.

Scripture scholars point out that, while the call to love God is implicit in many other places in the Old Testament, this is the only time that we have a deliberate, explicit commandment to love. Maybe that's why this passage became so central, so important to the religious life of God's people.

Finally, we need to be aware that this command is given in the second person singular. That is, it is directed not to the great collective of the people, but to each individual Israelite. What's called for is not some sort of corporate mind set, but personal response from every member.

When Jesus quotes this passage in the Gospel, he immediately adds a second commandment: "[L]ove your neighbor as yourself." This, too, is a quotation from the Old Testament (Leviticus 19:18). In its original context, "neighbor" seems to have meant "fellow countryman." Jesus would teach that "neighbor" embraces all other human beings, even our enemies. The point of Jesus' response to the scribe is that two loves are required from the person who wants to observe the law of the Lord: love for God and love for neighbor. Neither is sufficient in itself. Neither is authentic loving without the other. It is both together that make us eligible for God's kingdom.

But out of all this there arise questions. What does it mean to love God? How do we go about it? How are we to address ourselves to the Lord with all our heart and soul and strength? How are we to love our neighbor? What kind of love do we owe to the men and women around us, men and women we may not even know, men and women who may not be likely to love us in return? These are not easy questions to which there are simple and easy answers. Loving God and loving our neighbor can be very demanding and the results of them are not always immediately forthcoming. But if nothing else, we know the principles. God has given us the basics. How we implement the basics is what constitutes the story of our lives.

FOR REFLECTION AND DISCUSSION

How is my relationship with God most basically expressed?
What does the oneness of God mean to me?

Thirty-first Sunday in Ordinary Time (C)

Wisdom 11:22–12:2

This Sunday brings us another reading from the book of Wisdom, that youngest book of the Old Testament, written possibly only fifty or a hundred years before the birth of Jesus. In some ways, it is one of the most modern books of the Old Testament because it was written for a situation not unlike our own. There was a large Jewish community in Alexandria in Egypt. Alexandria was a cosmopolitan city where the secular pagan culture of the hellenistic (Greek-speaking) world flourished. The book of Wisdom seems to have been written to help these Jews maintain their religious and cultural identity in the context of a lively and appealing secular culture. Part of our own religious life today is the struggle to maintain our convictions about the relevance of God and church in the pagan, or at least secular, world that surrounds us.

The reading from Wisdom that is assigned for this Sunday is from the last section of the book. This section is an extended reflection (nine chapters long) about God's providence for his people during the exodus, their escape from Egyptian slavery, and their entrance into the Promised Land. It describes how God used his creatures, like water and insects, to punish and defeat the Egyptians and benefit the Israelites. In the course of this extended reflection, there are two digressions or subsections, one concerned with God's mercy, the other with the futility of idolatry. This Sunday's reading is from the subsection on mercy.

Before we turn to the text, it's important to be sure we know what mercy involves. The dictionary defines mercy as compassion or forbearance shown especially to an offender or to a subject. A judge can exercise mercy in giving a lighter sentence than the offender deserves. Mercy is compassionate treatment to those in distress. It is kindness to those in misery.

Our text explains *how* God can be merciful and *why* God is merciful. The question in the back of the author's mind seems to be, "Why didn't God just destroy the Egyptians at the time of the exodus?" Behind this question is still another: "Why doesn't God just destroy the secularistic pagans of the present?"

Our reading begins with a general statement about the power and greatness of God. From God's point of view, all creation is like a drop of dew or like a tiny grain of sand used for weighing on sensitive scales. Compared with God, everything created is infinitesimally small. Then the author begins to deal with God's mercy.

God is merciful, he overlooks people's sins because he is all-powerful and loves what he has created. Nothing in creation is foreign to God's care. It exists because God wanted it to begin with and it continues to be because God wants it to remain. He preserves everything from destruction because it is all his and he loves it. Because of God's power and love, he can be merciful to sinners. He can lead them away from their sins and gradually bring them back to himself.

Scholars have said that this passage is one of the high points of Old Testament literature and that nowhere else in the Old Testament is God's love for his creatures so clearly seen.

In these verses we hear about the gentleness and patience and generosity of the all-powerful God. God is merciful to sinners, not because sin is unimportant, not because God is weak, but because God is strong, because he is Lord of all creation, powerful enough to love and heal even those who reject him.

This text from Wisdom provides the theological underpinnings for the behavior of Jesus in the Gospel (Luke 19:1–10). Here was Zacchaeus, a tax collector, a professional extortionist, a collaborator with the detested Romans. Jesus responds to Zacchaeus's curiosity by inviting himself to this sinner's home. The sinner responds by committing himself to significant acts of repentance and generosity, but the fact remains that he was a public sinner as the bystanders were not slow to note. Why did Jesus bother with this person? How could Jesus lead him to repentance as he did? Because he is strong and loving and merciful.

The teaching of this passage of Wisdom and the words and actions of Jesus in the gospel answer a lot of questions. Why didn't God just destroy the Egyptians at the time of the exodus? Why didn't God destroy the pagans of first-century B.C. Alexandria? Why doesn't God destroy the sinful culture in which we live? For that matter, why does the Lord bother with us, selfish and sinful as we are? Because God is powerful. Because God is loving. Because God is merciful.

FOR REFLECTION AND DISCUSSION
Where/how do I experience God's power?
Where/how do I experience God's mercy?

Thirty-second Sunday in Ordinary Time (A)

Wisdom 6:12–16

There is a large section of the Old Testament that is known as wisdom literature. This section includes the books of Job, Psalms, Proverbs and Wisdom. The concept of wisdom underwent a long process of development over the centuries. Early on, wisdom was concerned with learning how to live in the court of the king. It was a kind of Dale Carnegie quality whose practice would guarantee success. As time passed, the idea of wisdom became more sophisticated. It became concerned with the pursuit of understanding that would bring rationality to human existence, while yet acknowledging that there are limits to what human understanding can grasp. As theological reflection deepened, wisdom appeared in our inspired texts personified as a beautiful woman who was God's companion in the creation of the world and who works with God in carrying out the goals of his providence. She is seen as the mediator between God and humanity. Many scholars see the gradual evolution of the idea of wisdom that we find in the Old Testament to be a preparation for the revelation of the Holy Spirit that we receive in the New Testament.

This Sunday's reading comes from the book of Wisdom, the youngest book of the Old Testament. Wisdom is concerned with staying in touch with God in a secular world. (It seems to have been written in the lively pagan city of Alexandria.) It gives us the final stages of the Old Testament evolution of the concept of wisdom.

The verses that the lectionary gives us here are part of a long exhortation to kings and magistrates to seek wisdom. This chapter then leads into an extended praise of wisdom (more than four chapters long) that the first-century B.C. author puts into the mouth of the wise King Solomon.

Our five verses are concerned with the accessibility of wisdom. One edition of the Bible entitles this section, "Wisdom sought is wisdom found." The message is simple and the passage is insistently repetitious in proclaiming it.

Wisdom is easy to see. She wants to make herself known and eagerly presents herself at the door of the one who seeks her. She responds quickly to those who watch for her. She seeks out those who seek for her and presents herself to them in kindness and solicitude.

All of this is a way of saying that God wants his love and his care and his providence to be known and accepted by those that God loves. God is a God of outreach. His knowledge and his intentions are not obscure or elusive. God loves his human creatures and wants to be known and appreciated by them. Our reading, therefore, is a poem of praise to the kindness of God and a song of encouragement leading God's people into a deeper relationship with their Lord. It calls its readers to be wise, that is, to accept the gift of understanding and appreciation of the Lord's works.

This reading is intended to describe what characterized the wise virgins of the Gospel (Matthew 25:1–13). They waited intently for the coming of the heavenly bridegroom. They were wise because they responded to God's offer of closeness to himself, because they remained ready to take the part that the bridegroom had assigned to them.

The wisdom of God is still accessible to us today, indeed more accessible than ever before. We have been given the life of God's own Son to live. Through his church the Lord has made known to us his plans for the world and for the community of faith. Each one of us has been touched by the hand of God in baptism and the other sacraments. Through the availability of the word of God in Scripture we are given the wherewithal to understand and appreciate the providence and the kindness of the Lord. In our weekly Sunday community gathering we learn to be attentive to God's word and to unite ourselves with Christ in praise and thanksgiving and self-gift to the Father. It all involves wisdom because it all involves God's outreach to those he loves and our response.

Wisdom is not some inert quality that we acquire once and for all. It is a habit of the mind, a way of seeing things that comes to us and grows in us a little at a time. One might say that the purpose of the Christian life is the pursuit of wisdom. Our reading assures us that wisdom does not play hard to get. Wisdom wants to be accessible to us. But we have to be willing to accept the gift when God offers it to us and as God offers it to us.

FOR REFLECTION AND DISCUSSION

Who is the wisest person I know? Why?

Have I grown in wisdom over the years?

Thirty-second Sunday in Ordinary Time (B)
1 Kings 17:10–16

Chapters seventeen and eighteen of the first book of Kings are concerned with the struggles of the prophet Elijah with King Ahab. Ahab ruled the Northern Kingdom in the ninth century B.C. In his twenty-two year reign, Ahab "did evil in the sight of the LORD more than all who were before him" (1 Kings 16:30, NRSV). His greatest iniquity was his devotion to Baal, the Canaanite god of fertility. Not only did Ahab and his family worship Baal, but he imposed the worship of Baal on the people at large.

In response to Ahab's wickedness, God sends Elijah the prophet to the king to tell him that there would be drought in the land until God decided otherwise. The fertility that Baal was supposed to provide would not be forthcoming.

As the drought begins to make itself felt, God provides ravens to bring food to Elijah and a stream to provide water for an initial period, but then the source of the water dries up and God sends Elijah north to Zarephath, near Sidon, where he would be taken care of.

This is where this Sunday's reading begins. Elijah finds the person whom God had designated to take care of him, a widow with a young son. When Elijah asks her for food and water, she lets him know that she is suffering from the drought like everybody else. She only has enough to survive on for a short time. Elijah tells her not to be afraid, but to do as he says. She does, and her meager supply of flour and oil proved to be enough to feed Elijah and the widow and her son for a whole year.

In this context of Elijah and the widow and her son, God does what Baal was supposed to do: provide for his people. He preserves his prophet from harm and includes the weak, poor, powerless widow and her son in his loving care.

In its original context, this brief story is a narrative of power and of faith. By the power of God's word through Elijah, the fertility of the earth dries up. In response to the faith and trust of Elijah, not only he but also those who care for him are taken care of. This whole section of the history of God's people is intended to lead the readers into deeper faith and confidence in God's power. The pagan gods will not prevail. The word of the Lord will both punish his enemies and protect his friends.

In the Gospel (Mark 12:38–44) we hear about another widow. This time it is a widow who puts two small coins into the temple treasury and who is praised by Jesus for her generosity. "She, out of her poverty has put in everything she had, all she had to live on."

The juxtaposition of these two readings seems to suggest that there are two themes that the lectionary intends to bring to our attention. The first is God's concern for the weak and the powerless. In the midst of the drought, God provides for the widow of Zarephath and her son. She is poor, unimportant, without resources. But she nonetheless attracts the care and the attention of God. So does the widow of the Gospel who wins the praise and the attention of the Lord himself. You don't have to be important in the world's categories to be important in the sight of God.

The second theme is the theme of generosity. Both widows were poor. Neither one had much to give. But they gave of what they had. The Old Testament widow shared her flour and oil with the prophet. The New Testament widow gave her all to help provide for the upkeep of God's house. The quantity of their giving was not its most significant element. What mattered was their reverence for God's prophet and God's house which they expressed by freely sharing the little bit that they had at their disposal.

Obviously these readings call on us to be generous. We are all called to look out for the prophets of the Lord. We are all called to help provide for the praise of God in his church. And what counts is not so much the quantity of what we give, but the portion of our own being that accompanies our gift. Generosity is not measured by the amount that we give, but by the amount that is left for ourselves after we have given.

And we are also called to be grateful for the care and attention that God lavishes on us. It is not for our personal importance that God pays attention to us, not because of our individual virtuousness. God pays attention to us because he loves us. In God's sight we are all poor, all dependent, all limited. But those are precisely the kind of people that God loves most.

FOR REFLECTION AND DISCUSSION

How have I been helped by someone apparently without resources? What resources do I have to offer to others?

Thirty-second Sunday in Ordinary Time (C)

2 Maccabees 7:1–2, 9–14

You won't find the two books of Maccabees in a Jewish or a Protestant Bible. The reason is that the earliest texts of neither of them is written in Hebrew. The first book of Maccabees seems to be a Greek translation of a Hebrew language original, and 2 Maccabees was originally written in Greek. When Jewish religious leaders were putting together the official list of the books of Sacred Scripture in the first century A.D., they excluded everything that was not in Hebrew. The Protestants adopted this criterion for the Old Testament books of the Bible when they began to publish the texts of Sacred Scripture in the sixteenth century.

The two books of Maccabees are both concerned with a revolt against the hellenistic kings who ruled what had been the kingdom of Judah from the fourth to the second centuries B.C. These kings were the successors of Alexander the Great's generals who took over various parts of his empire when he died in 323 B.C. Near the beginning of the second century B.C., a succession of these kings began to try to impose cultural uniformity throughout their realm, which included the Jews of Judah. The kings wanted everybody to live and speak and worship like the hellenists, Greek-speakers who predominated throughout most of the civilized world at that time. Consequently the Jews would have to give up their Scriptures, the practice of circumcision, and the observance of their dietary laws. In effect, they would have to stop being Jews. Ultimately the temple itself was defiled by the king. That's when the Jews revolted. Their leader was called Judas the Hammer (the Maccabee). They succeeded in expelling the hellenists from the country. The two books of Maccabees are an account of that rebellion. They seem to have been written for the edification of the Jews in Alexandria (which was the audience for which the book of Wisdom would be written some seventy-five years later).

The second book of Maccabees is not a sequel to 1 Maccabees, but rather a retelling of much of the same material.

This Sunday's reading (which is the only reading from either book in the Sunday reading cycle) is from 2 Maccabees. King Antiochus is trying to induce people through torture to apostatize from their Jewish faith by eating pork. Our reading is about a mother and her seven sons resisting the king's commands.

The account is rather gruesome in the full text and has been edited for the lectionary to remove some of its more lurid details.

The point of the reading as presented in the lectionary is not only to show the courage of the young men as they are being tortured for their faith, but also to show their conviction that the death of their bodies was not the end of everything. They were sure that "the King of the world" would raise them up to everlasting life, that any mutilation that they suffered in connection with their faith would be made good by God, that God had given them hope of resurrection.

For a long time, the Israelites did not have a clear conviction about life after death. They believed that there was a kind of shadow existence after death, but that was all. Gradually, during the second century B.C., we find an awakening awareness that the God who loves us in this life will continue to care for us after our death. This awareness is expressed in chapter twelve of the book of Daniel and in this passage of 2 Maccabees. It seems to have been sparked by the tribulations the people were suffering in this cruel persecution. God could not allow these terrible events to be the conclusion of the life he had conferred on the members of his people. There had to be something more still to come.

This development in Jewish religious faith was not without its questions. What about bad people? The last young man in the reading is clear that "for you, there will be no resurrection to life." Nor was belief in the resurrection of the dead accepted by all Jews. In this Sunday's Gospel (Luke 20:27–38) we hear Jesus dealing with some Sadducees, "those who deny that there is a resurrection." The case they put so silkily to Jesus seems to suggest that there are impossible consequences connected with belief in resurrection. Jesus responds that, in the realm of resurrection, things are not like they are here. He is very clear that the dead would rise.

The resurrection of the dead was not part of God's original revelation to his people. But it is a fundamental part of our Christian faith. In fact, our final goal as human beings is to share forever in the life of our Lord who has risen from the dead.

FOR REFLECTION AND DISCUSSION

What do I look forward to after death?

Why do I believe in resurrection and eternal life?

Thirty-third Sunday in Ordinary Time (A)

Proverbs 31:10–13, 19–20, 30–31

The book of Proverbs is one of the wisdom books of the Old Testament. It is a collection of maxims or aphorisms whose purpose is to provide guidance for successful living for the reader. Proverbs teaches how to appreciate life and how to live it to the fullest.

In its first chapter, Proverbs is attributed to King Solomon, the biblical wise man *par excellence.* However, the book seems to be a collection of material that comes from various places and various times. Scholars think that the final gathering of this mass of material into one book took place after the Israelites' return from exile, sometime early in the fifth century B.C.

This Sunday's reading from Proverbs is from the last chapter of the book. It is a passage describing the ideal wife. In the full Hebrew text, this section is an acrostic poem. That is, each verse begins with a different letter of the alphabet, starting at the beginning of the alphabet at the first verse and continuing with successive letters until the last letter and the end of the poem, twenty-two lines later. This is not an unusual form for Old Testament poetry, but the subject matter of poems written in this form often seems to be more determined by the alphabet than by the inherent thought structure of what is being said.

Our reading begins with a general statement about the value and excellence of "a worthy wife." She is the source of unending goodness and prosperity for the household. She is industrious, working hard to provide for the needs of her family. But she also extends herself for the poor. The passage ends with enthusiastic praise for this virtuous woman. It is not her beauty that is important, but her religious spirit. She deserves public recognition for what she does.

The ideal wife in ancient Israel was, therefore, industrious, charitable, prayerful. Her work was more than caring for the needs of her family. It was also the expression of her inner life, of her dedication to the Lord and the Lord's poor. She was a good wife because she was a holy wife.

This Sunday's Gospel (Matthew 25:14–30) talks about the need for God's servants to work, while the reading from Proverbs describes more extensively what virtuous work involves. This is a relationship between first and third readings that we have seen before. For example, last week the Gospel mentioned wisdom almost in passing and the First Reading described it in greater detail. On the thirtieth Sunday in Ordinary Time, Jesus spoke in general terms of love for neighbor and the reading from Exodus offered specifics about the practice of caring for our neighbor.

Work is part of our service of the Lord. That's the lesson of both Gospel and Old Testament reading on this Sunday. The servants in the Gospel who worked with their master's money are praised. The one who does not work is condemned. The ideal wife is one who works both for the well-being of her own family and for the good of the poor. She is to be praised because she fears the Lord.

Work is a necessary condition for our relationship with the Lord. We have to work if we are to be saved. It is not that our work earns us salvation or that God only loves us if we work hard at the responsibilities that we have received. It is rather that our work is an important aspect of our response to God's loving initiative in our regard. God approaches us with his offer of grace and salvation. We have to accept. One of the most important elements of our acceptance is our willingness to join our efforts to God's in caring for ourselves, for our loved ones, for the poor. Our willingness to work out the potential of God's gifts to us is a sign of our awareness of his generosity to us.

What this Sunday's overture reading says about the ideal wife applies to all God's servants. They are diligent about caring for their loved ones in the context of the home. They are generous about caring for the poor. It is important that they—we—be hard workers in the Lord's service. But even more important is that we be holy workers in the Lord's service. As followers of the Lord, our work is not supposed to be merely an economic exercise but also an exercise of our response to the Lord's love for us. We do not work just to earn a living, but to acknowledge the life that God has already given us.

FOR REFLECTION AND DISCUSSION

How is my relationship with God reflected in my work?
How do others benefit from my work?

Thirty-third Sunday in Ordinary Time (B)

Daniel 12:1–3

The book of Daniel is only used twice in the three-year Sunday cycle of readings, once on this Sunday and once again next Sunday.

Daniel is one of the younger books of the Old Testament. It seems to have been written during the persecution of King Antiochus Epiphanes between 167 and 164 B.C. This hellenistic Greek ruler was trying to force the Jews to conform to the religious practices of the pagans. The book of Daniel was written to offer encouragement to the Jews in their time of trouble.

The message of comfort is offered to the people through the character of Daniel, a wise, young Jewish man whose story is set at the time of the Babylonian exile, some four hundred years previously. In the first six chapters of Daniel we have several stories about Daniel and his friends. The point of these stories is that God cares for his own and that, with the help of God, Jews can stand up to the mightiest powers on earth. Then, in chapters seven to twelve, the text gives us a series of prophetic visions presented as coming from God through Daniel long ago during the time of the Babylonian captivity, but primarily intended for the Jews in Palestine in hellenistic times. At the end of the book, in a kind of appendix, are two more stories which serve to highlight the virtues of Daniel.

This Sunday's reading comes from the second main section of Daniel. Chapters ten through twelve are one long vision, and chapter twelve (from which our reading is taken) is not only the climax of this vision, but the peak point of the whole book.

God is telling Daniel about the future deliverance of the people from their tribulations. The chapters immediately prior to chapter twelve recount an ongoing battle in heaven between the heavenly princes Michael and Gabriel on one hand and the demonic powers of earthly kingdoms on the other. Now we hear of the final outcome. All the members of God's people whose names are written in the list of the predestined will be delivered from their tribulation. Some of the Israelites who have been killed by their enemies will rise from the dead to live in glory forever. Others, presumably the wicked, will rise from the dead into a state of everlasting horror and disgrace. Those who have provided teaching and leadership to others ("the wise") will shine with the brilliance of the stars in the heavens.

There are two aspects of this reading that call for comment. First of all, this section of Daniel is an apocalyptic or eschatological pronouncement. That is, it has to do with final things, with the end of time, with judgment, reward and punishment. This was a kind of writing and teaching that was common during the centuries just before and just after the time of Christ. Jesus sometimes taught in apocalyptic terms, as the gospel for this Sunday (Mark 13:24–32) demonstrates. The last book of the New Testament, Revelation, is also known as the Apocalypse because it is about deliverance from persecution and the end of the world.

The use of apocalyptic or eschatological teaching gives us to understand that the history of the world is not a haphazard series of disconnected events. On the contrary, there is a plan for the world, a plan that includes victory over the enemies of God, a plan that offers security and comfort to God's people, no matter how painful the tribulations in which they presently find themselves.

A second important aspect of this reading is its teaching about resurrection and eternal life. This was a teaching that was

not part of God's earliest revelation to his people. It was
something that God taught them only later, when the time was
ripe for them to understand it. This passage of Daniel seems to be
the earliest biblical passage that expresses unambiguously the
hope of individual resurrection. But even here, the text does not
say that everybody will rise to reward or punishment, but only
"some," apparently those who merit special attention because of
their virtue or their sinfulness. The resurrection of all the dead,
good and bad alike, would later become an important element in
the teaching of Jesus and a crucial element in the teaching of the
church. In fact, resurrection, i.e., the Resurrection of Christ, is a
key factor in all of Christian revelation.

This Old Testament reading introduces the eschatological
discourse that we hear from Mark's Gospel on this Sunday. It
gives some of the outlines of the cosmic dimension of God's plan
for humanity. It assures us that we will come out of our present
troubles and that God's ultimate purpose will be achieved at last.

FOR REFLECTION AND DISCUSSION

What basic convictions give shape and direction to my life?
Where do I look for comfort in times of trial?

Thirty-third Sunday in Ordinary Time (C)

Malachi 3:19–20a

This Sunday's reading is the shortest Old Testament reading in
the whole three-year cycle, only a verse and a half in length. It
comes from the book of Malachi. This book seems to have been
written about 455 B.C. by an author whose name we do not

know. "Malachi" means "my messenger" and the title of the book is taken from its first verse: "The word of the LORD to Israel by Malachi (my messenger)" (NRSV).

The Israelites had returned from exile and had rebuilt the temple (515 B.C.). After their initial enthusiasm, the Israelites' religious fervor seems to have cooled. The community seems to have been adrift. The priests had become careless about the ritual demands of the temple sacrifices, presenting sick or lame animals to God instead of the best. The people, too, seem to have become indifferent about the offerings that were expected of them. In addition, they readily entered into mixed marriages with foreigners. "What good is it to serve God, anyway?" they wondered. The prophet foretells the day of the Lord which would purify the priesthood, consume the wicked and bring about the triumph of the virtuous.

Our text is from the last part of the last chapter of Malachi. When the Lord is ready he will come like a fire, destroying and purifying. The day of the Lord would be like a field fire in a grain field. All that is there to start with is stubble, what was left behind after the harvest. This represents "the proud and all evildoers." Now comes the fire that will burn up the stubble along with any other remnants of the plant. Nothing will be left.

On the other hand, our text says, the good will experience another kind of warmth arising from "the sun of justice," i.e., from the loving care of the Lord for those who serve him. The text goes on to say (beyond the end of our reading) that the just will run around like calves let loose from the barn and will trample the wicked.

This text from Malachi seems to have been chosen to give a slightly more positive spin to the Gospel (Luke 21:5–19). In that reading from near the end of Luke's Gospel we hear Jesus' prophecy about the destruction of Jerusalem, indeed, about the destruction of the world. There will be persecution and tribulation before the Son of Man comes in power and glory. It is not until verse twenty-eight (not included in the Sunday reading) that Jesus tells his followers: "Stand up and raise your heads, because your redemption is drawing near" (NRSV).

Traditionally Christian spirituality has looked on the Last Judgment as a day of doom. Michelangelo's painting of it in the Sistine Chapel is certainly not cheerful! For centuries at Catholic funerals the mourners heard the grim verses of the *Dies Irae* (Day of Wrath) which described the end of the world and the judgment of God. This is understandable. There is plenty of sin to be dealt with. There are numberless sinners to be brought to punishment.

Yet there is another side to the Last Judgment. The author of 2 Peter (3:11 ff.) encourages his readers to conduct themselves in holiness, "waiting for and hastening the coming of the day of God" when there will be "new heavens and a new earth in which righteousness dwells" (NAB). This is reminiscent of Malachi's "sun of justice with its healing rays."

We are all sinners and we all deserve God's punishment to a greater or less extent. Yet we are also members of the household of the Christian faith, sharers in the life of the risen Christ. Part of what the final judgment involves is the fulfillment of all the wonderful things that Jesus had promised to those who love him, a whole new, definitive, unchanging creation in which those who love him will live with the Lord forever.

Often believers seek to know when the end will come. Jesus seems to discourage this sort of thing in this Sunday's Gospel. But maybe the real question is not when the Second Coming will occur—whether sooner or later—but rather how prepared will I be for it. Scripture teaches us that persons who disregard the will of the Lord should look forward to his coming with apprehension, while those who love the Lord should look forward with joy. The timing of Jesus' return in glory is of some importance. Of infinitely more importance is how each of us will stand when he comes.

FOR REFLECTION AND DISCUSSION

If Christ returned in glory today, would I be happy to stand before him?

Do I look on Christ's return in glory as far off or near?

PART SIX
Solemnities

Our Lord Jesus Christ the King (A)

Ezekiel 34:11–12, 15–17

This is the thirty-fourth Sunday in Ordinary Time. It is the last Sunday of the church's year and the Solemnity of Christ the King. There are, therefore several levels of significance to today's celebration. It is intended to remind us of the sovereignty of the risen Christ. It teaches us about the self-giving aspects of Christ's kingship. But most of all, it is an eschatological observance. This celebration highlights the last or final things: the end of the age, death, judgment, reward and punishment. Christ is king and, as such, is the final arbiter of all creation.

In year A the eschatological dimension of the feast of Christ the King is made very clear by the choice of the Gospel: Matthew 25:31–46, Jesus' discourse about the Last Judgment. The Old Testament reading is about judgment, also.

Chapters 33 to 37 of Ezekiel are a collection of prophecies of consolation for Israel. Ezekiel and other high-ranking Israelites had been deported to Babylon about 397 B.C., ten years before the final destruction of Jerusalem. Now word had come to the exiles of the capture of the city and, therefore, of the end of everything that the Israelites held sacred. Ezekiel speaks up to the exiles with the promise of renewal and transformation.

Chapter 34 is a parable about shepherds. At the beginning of the chapter the prophet speaks out against the shepherds of Israel, the leaders of the people who had misled the people and brought them to their present sorry state. God will punish the shepherds and take the sheep away from their care.

But now, as our reading begins, God promises to see to the well-being of the sheep. God himself will become the shepherd of the people. God will tend them and rescue them. God will seek out those who have strayed and take care of the sick and the injured.

But not all the sheep are equally worthy of God's care. Some members of the flock are arrogant and self-seeking, using what strength they have for their own selfish purposes. These members of the flock will be judged and marked out for destruction.

In the Gospel we see Jesus carrying out what Ezekiel had threatened. Both readings promise the separation of sheep and goats, the sentence of the Lord on the individual sheep.

These two readings from God's word remind us that the one who is ultimately in charge of the flock is the Lord, whether it be the Lord who takes over from unworthy shepherds the care of the exiled Israelite flock or the Lord who judges each individual member of the flock according to the way that each has treated the other members of the flock.

The Lord is kind and merciful. He looks after his flock with love. He protects the flock and its members from harm and heals them when they have suffered injury. God has always cared for his flock and he will continue to do so even after this world has reached its conclusion.

But the individual members of the flock have a share of responsibility, too. Each one of them contributes to his or her own state of health and energy. Each one of them contributes to the general state of the flock at large. The individuals may not lay all responsibility on the leaders of the flock. True, the leaders must stand before God and be judged for the way they have exercised their leadership, but the individuals must also give an accounting of the way in which they contributed to the life of the flock.

Christ the King is Christ the Judge. He loves his flock and cares for his flock, but he will not overlook the harm that can come to the flock through the misbehavior of its leaders or its members. Christ the Judge is kind and merciful. He knows that our sins are more often than not the result of our weakness. But he also knows that our sins are real and that our sins are destructive. He must take account of that as we stand before him to learn what his final disposition of us will be.

We all have reason to be grateful to Christ the King for the loving care that he has exercised and still exercises in our regard. And we all have reason to look with concern toward God's judgment because we are all sinners, because each of us, in one way or another, has harmed God's flock.

We mark the closing of the church's year with gratitude and with contrition.

FOR REFLECTION AND DISCUSSION

How does God watch over and care for me?

What are my sentiments as I look forward to God's judgment?

Our Lord Jesus Christ the King (B)

Daniel 7:13–14

This last Sunday of the church's year commemorates the last stage of creation, when God will be universally acknowledged as Lord and when the lordship of the risen Christ will embrace everything. The life and mission of Jesus, commemorated and relived in the long series of Sundays in Ordinary Time, comes to its conclusion in the celebration of the Kingship of Christ.

To introduce this theme, the lectionary gives us another Old Testament reading from the book of Daniel. This Sunday's reading, like last Sunday's, is from the second major section of Daniel, the section that gives us a long series of prophetic visions presented as coming from God to Daniel long ago.

Daniel has been having a prophetic dream in which four horrible beasts arose to threaten the people of God. Then the court of heaven is convened to deal with these threatening animals. To resist them, God sends forth his own champion.

This is where our reading begins. In the dream vision, the author sees the heavenly court. The Ancient of Days, God, is seated on his throne. God's great age is meant to symbolize wisdom, authority, prestige and power. Into the presence of this awesome personage comes one riding on the clouds of heaven. The clouds of heaven are mentioned most often in the Old Testament in the context of divinity. The one riding on the clouds of heaven, then, is one who is closely attached to God. He is a supernatural, heavenly figure. In contrast to the beasts, who symbolized the various enemies of God and the forces of chaos, this figure is "like a Son of man," i.e., in human form. The son of man receives power and dominion over all nations, a kingship that will not be destroyed.

The book of Daniel doesn't go on to say much more about this person, but it is clear that he is a heavenly figure who represents a supernatural power that is supporting the persecuted Jews of the second century B.C. His presence in the heavenly court is meant to teach that God's dominion will overcome every earthly power and that God's enemies will be overcome by a worldwide authority. The coming of this son of man symbolizes the ultimate and final establishment of the kingdom of God.

The term "Son of Man" is familiar to us from the Gospels. It is the phrase that Jesus applies to himself no less than seventy-eight times throughout the four Gospels. Our text from Daniel suggests that Jesus was a heavenly personage who would bring about the definitive reign of God.

But the term "son of man" is also used in some translations of the book of Ezekiel. There it is used more than ninety times by God to address the prophet. Apparently it was meant in that context to underline the contrast between the frailty and vulnerability of God's human spokesman and the divine majesty of God himself. It seems to stand for something like, "poor little creature."

When Jesus uses the phrase "Son of Man" to refer to himself, he seems to be alluding both to his heavenly credentials as an agent of the coming kingdom of God, but also to the reality of his human limitation. Jesus is one who rides on the clouds of heaven, but also one who is subject to all the weaknesses of humanity.

We see this mirrored in this Sunday's Gospel (John 18:33b–37). Pilate wants to know if Jesus is a king. Jesus answers that he is indeed a king, but that his kingdom is something other than the kind of kingdom that Pilate is thinking of. It is God's kingdom, one that is not of this world. Yet Pilate has Jesus put to death nonetheless. Jesus' human vulnerability is overpowered by the Roman's need for release from this troublesome person.

There is always a dimension of tension in Jesus. He is the Son of God, the agent of the Ancient of Days, the bringer of the kingdom of God, but he is also fully human, fully subject to pain and injury and even death.

This Sunday is the conclusion of the church's liturgical year. Over the past months the Scriptures have walked us through the public life and ministry of Jesus. Next Sunday marks the beginning of a new church year. On this day, therefore, the church's liturgy speaks to us what one might call the last word.

And that last word is that Jesus is in charge. No matter what our current circumstances, no matter what tribulations we may be suffering, the Lord reigns, the Lord is king. The Son of Man has "an everlasting dominion that shall not pass away" (NRSV).

FOR REFLECTION AND DISCUSSION

How has Christ expressed his kingship in my life?
Where/how do I ordinarily experience Christ's dominion?

Our Lord Jesus Christ the King (C)

2 Samuel 5:1–3

During these Sundays of Ordinary Time, our Gospels from Luke have been leading us through the public life of Jesus. One of the most common themes of his preaching was the kingdom of God or the kingdom of heaven. As the Gospel account of his public life draws to a close, and as we near the end of the church's liturgical year, it is appropriate that we give special attention to the Lord of that kingdom, to Christ the King.

The reading for year C's celebration of Christ the King is from the second book of Samuel and deals with the beginning of the reign of King David.

The first king of the tribes of Israel had been Saul. The people had clamored for a king to defend them from the Philistines and, through the agency of Samuel, the Lord gave them Saul. The young David had been one of Saul's outstanding warriors. But the relationship of Saul and David cooled over time. Saul developed deep personality problems and eventually was defeated by the Philistines. By that time, David had allied himself with the Philistines, although he was not with them in the battle in which Saul was killed.

After Saul's death the members of the tribe of Judah made David their king. (This occurred about 1000 B.C., surely one of the easiest dates to remember in all history!) There followed more than seven years of struggle between Judah (led by David) and the other tribes of Israel. Finally Saul's son and his primary military leader were assassinated and the leaders of the northern tribes came to David to ask him to be their king, too.

This is where our reading begins. The leaders of the north offer three reasons why David should agree to be their king: He is related by blood to their tribes; he had been a successful military leader; already the Lord had somehow made clear that David was his choice to be the people's leader. David agrees "and they anointed him king of Israel."

David ruled the dual monarchy of Judah and Israel for thirty-three more years. He managed to lead the tribes to common action. He extended the territory of the kingdoms. He led his people to an unprecedented level of power and prosperity. He was a man of great sins, but also one who was fundamentally faithful to the Lord and much loved by the Lord. In Psalm 89 God says about David, "Forever I will keep my steadfast love for him, and my covenant with him will stand firm." The years of David's rule (and those of his son Solomon) became the grand old times that the people of Judah and Israel looked back on with gratitude and nostalgia.

When the nation began to split apart and decline after the death of Solomon, God's promise of an eternal covenant with David became the basis of the people's messianic hope. They looked forward to a new king, like David, who would bring the people back to power and prosperity.

Many centuries later, people thought Jesus might be this messianic king. Jesus was very careful throughout his life not to allow people to call him messiah or king. The social and political position that the people thought he would assume was not what he had come for.

Yet he did preach about a kingdom, and was himself a king, but his kingdom was a different kind of kingdom than David's was, and he himself was a different kind of king than the people of his time looked for. His was not a kingdom of power and economic prosperity, but (in the words of this Sunday's preface) a kingdom of "truth and life…of holiness and grace…of justice love and peace." And of mercy.

In this Sunday's Gospel (Luke 23:35–43) we see Jesus being taunted for the hopes of the people in his regard, derided because he was thought to be the chosen one, the Christ of God, the king of the Jews. He was all that, of course, but not in the way that people thought. Even one of the criminals crucified with Jesus joins in the derision. The other criminal, however, seems to be more aware of what Jesus was really all about. "[R]emember me when you come into your kingdom." Jesus promises that they would be together that very day in Paradise.

So the successor of King David, the messianic savior, the anointed one proves himself to have access to and standing in the eternal kingdom of God. He can bring in whomever he chooses, even the worst sinners. He himself is a king there. He is a king of mercy. He is the king of Paradise.

FOR REFLECTION AND DISCUSSION

What does the kingship of Christ mean to me?

How have I experienced the power and the mercy of Christ?

Most Holy Trinity (A)

Exodus 34:4b–6, 8–9

On the Monday after Pentecost the church resumes Ordinary
Time, the season that does not recall any specific segment of
salvation history, as Advent/Christmas and Lent/Easter do, but
which rather recalls the mystery of Christ in all its aspects. One
might call Ordinary Time the season of ongoing salvation.
Ordinary Time runs from after Pentecost until the last day before
the first Sunday of Advent, when a new liturgical year begins.

But the first two Sundays of this season are not Sundays of
Ordinary Time. They are special solemnities that celebrate with a
particular explicitness the underpinnings and the outcomes of
salvation history. They have been called devotional or doctrinal
celebrations, or "idea feasts." These are the Solemnity of the Most
Holy Trinity and the Solemnity of the Most Holy Body and
Blood of Christ. In each of these observances, all three readings
for each of the three years of the lectionary cycle are chosen to
harmonize with the theme of the day. (Another such celebration
is the Solemnity of Our Lord Jesus Christ the King which falls
on the thirty-fourth, i.e., last, Sunday of Ordinary Time.)

Coming just after our annual paschal reliving of God's work
of salvation in Christ and of the coming of the Holy Spirit on
Pentecost, the feast of the Holy Trinity calls on us to reflect on
the foundation and goal of it all: God as Lord, God as three
Persons in eternal self-gift and communion, God as Trinity.

The Old Testament reading for this celebration comes from
Exodus, the book that tells the story of the Israelites' escape from
Egypt and their progress toward the Promised Land. The context
of our reading is the Israelites' sin of idolatry. They are in the
desert. Moses had gone up Mount Sinai to receive the tablets of

the law. He stayed longer than the people thought he would. They became afraid and, with Aaron's help, made an image of a golden calf for themselves that would symbolize God's power and protection. It became their god. Moses came down the mountain and saw what was going on. In his anger he threw down the stone tablets of the law that God had given him and destroyed the golden idol.

As our reading opens, we find Moses back on the mountain carrying two new stone tablets as God had commanded him. The law was to be written down again. But first God manifests himself to Moses.

God speaks out his name to Moses from the cloud: the Lord. Then God walks up and down before Moses repeating his name ("The LORD, the LORD...") and describing himself: merciful, gracious, patient, kind, faithful. And Moses responds. From his posture of worship he asks God to continue to be with the Israelites, to pardon their rejection of him, their sin of idolatry. And, although our text does not say so explicitly, the rest of Exodus shows that God answered Moses' prayer.

In this reading, God does more than tell Moses his name. He presents himself to Moses, offers himself to Moses as Lord and master, yet loving, kind and faithful. This is a mighty Lord, yet not distant and cold, but near and loving, in spite of the sinfulness of the people with whom he had involved himself. He was a God who would continue to travel with the people he had chosen for himself.

The God that manifested himself to Moses is the God that we reverence and adore. He is the Father who shares his Son with us. He is the Son who saved us through his life, death and resurrection. He is the Holy Spirit who continues to guide us toward our final goal, who travels with us in spite of our sinfulness.

It must have been hard for God to open himself up to us human beings. He had to do it a little at a time, first manifesting himself to Moses, not as a warrior god, not as a god of fertility, not as a god of death, but as a loving Lord who would walk with his people and bring them to the place he had in mind for them. Then, through Jesus, we are brought to know still more about God. God is not a solitary being, but a triune community of self-gift, knowledge and love. God wishes not only to share information about himself with us, but also his very life, grafting us into the community of Father, Son and Spirit.

This Sunday's reading, from one of the most ancient parts of the Old Testament, teaches us that God has wanted to be known and loved by us human creatures for a long time.

FOR REFLECTION AND DISCUSSION

How do I respond to the mercy and kindness of God?

How have I experienced God's company in my life's journey?

Most Holy Trinity (B)

Deuteronomy 4:32–34, 39–40

Eastertime ends with Pentecost. Ordinary Time resumes on the day after Pentecost, to run until the end of the liturgical year on the Saturday after the Solemnity of Christ the King. But the first two Sundays of this resumed Ordinary Time are Sundays of special observance: Trinity Sunday and Corpus Christi. It's as if the church wants to underline these two great realities of our faith before it gets back to merely "ordinary" observance of the unfolding of our faith.

The Solemnity of the Most Holy Trinity is not one of the church's ancient feasts. As a matter of fact, for a long time the apostolic see of Rome did not favor the celebration of a special feast of the Holy Trinity. Pope Alexander II, who died in 1073, said, "It is not the custom in Rome to set aside a special day for honoring the Most Holy Trinity, since, properly speaking, it is honored daily in psalmody by the singing of the 'Glory be to the Father.' " But the celebration became common in monastic liturgies, and, finally, Pope John XXII made the feast obligatory for the whole church in 1334. He assigned its observance to the Sunday after Pentecost where it has remained ever since.

The readings for Trinity Sunday have been chosen to illustrate the principal themes of the celebration rather than to harmonize with one another. For year B the First Reading is from the last part of chapter four of the book of Deuteronomy. In these verses the author is portraying Moses talking to the Israelites about the proofs of God's love that have been shown to them. In this account of how God had dealt with the Israelites, the text also teaches its readers something about the nature of the Lord.

"Has anybody ever heard of anything like this?" Moses asks. "God actually spoke to us amid the fire and thunder of Mount Sinai, and we have survived! God made us his own people by bringing us out of Egypt in the midst of miracles of his power! And now? Now we must acknowledge that our Lord God is the only God there is. We must follow his directions and obey his commands if we are to live peacefully and prosperously in the land to which God is bringing us."

There are three teachings about God inherent in this exhortation. First, there is the uniqueness of God. The God of Israel is not like the false gods of the Egyptians, a whole gathering of various powers each of which required special attention and devotion. No, God is one and there is no other god but the God that had manifested himself to the Israelites.

Second, this God is transcendent. That is, he is not a power that is rooted in our world so that we can relate to him as we relate to our fellow creatures. God is different from us, so different that even hearing his voice would destroy us unless God made special provisions for our safety.

Third, this God is also immanent. That is, despite his total difference from us, God has chosen to be part of what goes on in the world. God has chosen one particular people for his own. God has become involved in the affairs of that people. God expects to enter into a kind of dialogue with this people, a dialogue in which God will offer direction and his people will follow. God is a participant in what is going on here and now.

What God *did* for his first chosen people revealed something about God, and what God revealed about himself to them is also valid and true for us who are successors of that first chosen people. In his life and ministry, Jesus showed us still more about God. Jesus gave us the means to know God as Father, Son and Holy Spirit. But what Jesus taught us and showed us is founded on what God revealed to the Israelites in the desert.

God is one. God is totally different from us and is infinitely beyond us. Yet God is also concerned with us and involved with our human existence and our human history.

Each of those truths has consequences for our life. We must not pursue other gods such as power and comfort and success. The real God is one. And God is transcendent, totally different from us. We must therefore be careful not to scale God down to our own image and likeness. Yet we must also be careful to be attentive and responsive to God's overtures to us through Christ

Jesus and the Holy Spirit. God is immanent, part of what's going on in this world.

The God of Moses: unique, transcendent, immanent. That's what we recall and celebrate on this day.

FOR REFLECTION AND DISCUSSION
What does the transcendence of God mean to me?
What does the immanence of God mean to me?

Most Holy Trinity (C)

Proverbs 8:22–31

The church's annual reliving of the events of our redemption by Christ ends with Pentecost. On the day after Pentecost, Ordinary Time resumes, that long series of weeks in which the church walks again with Jesus through his public life. But the first two Sundays of Ordinary Time after the Easter season are preempted by special observances: Trinity Sunday and the feast of Corpus Christi. It's as if the church doesn't want to direct the attention of the faithful back to "ordinary" concerns without first calling them to give some special attention to the most fundamental realities that undergird and enliven our faith: the Trinity and the Eucharist. We can't understand redemption without the Trinity, and we can't live out our participation in redemption without the Eucharist.

The doctrine of the Holy Trinity—that there is one divine nature and three divine Persons—was not something that Jesus taught his disciples directly and explicitly. It was, rather, something that God led them to grasp through the events they experienced as they shared Jesus' public life and ministry and as they lived through the first years of the church.

Jesus spoke of God as his Father in a special way. Jesus promised to send the Paraclete. Finally the Holy Spirit comes upon the apostles at Pentecost. As the apostles reflected on all this, they began to see that God involved community and sharing and love in addition to being one, unique and totally different from creation. Eventually the church was able to articulate all this in its doctrine of the Trinity.

But even before the coming of Jesus there were some initial, tentative insights into the communitarian dimension of the one God. There were ways of speaking and things spoken about that stretched the boundaries of Old Testament theology. Later the Christian community would look on these expressions as previews of Christian revelation. One such context was the Old Testament concept of the wisdom of God and its relationship to Christian faith about the Trinity.

In the Old Testament, there is a whole series of books known as the wisdom books. Their purpose was to teach the Jewish reader how to live a successful life. These wisdom teachings range from pragmatic directions about how to get along with other people, at one extreme, to profoundly spiritual reflection about wisdom itself at the other.

The reading for this year's Solemnity of the Most Holy Trinity is one of these reflections about wisdom itself. It is from the book of Proverbs, a collection of wisdom sayings put together in the early part of the fifth century B.C. but containing material from many centuries before. In our reading the author personifies Wisdom as an attractive woman with a special relationship to God.

The reading is in two parts. In the first part we see Wisdom associated with God before the world came to be. She somehow constituted "the beginning of his ways," the idea and plan of everything that would come to be.

Next we see Wisdom cooperating with God in the creation of the world, acting as a kind of craftsman for God, bringing joy to God as she effortlessly and cheerfully brought God's ideas to completion.

This passage of Proverbs is a kind of hymn to Wisdom. Wisdom is personified as expressing the mind of God before the beginning of everything, as carrying out the mind of God as God presided over creation. Wisdom is presented as a person deeply rooted in and connected to the deepest depths of God.

Wisdom was one of those ideas that seemed to express certain aspects of Christ that would eventually be set forth as elements of the doctrine of the Trinity. Saint Paul in First Corinthians (1:24, NRSV) calls Christ "the power of God and the wisdom of God." In Colossians (1:15–17, NRSV) he calls the Lord Jesus Christ "the firstborn of all creation," in whom were created "all things in heaven and on earth....He himself is before all things..." The beginning of the Gospel of John ("In the beginning was the Word....All things came into being through him..." John 1:1–3 [NRSV].) seems to be a restatement of our Proverbs passage. The inspired writers, therefore, saw this Old Testament teaching about wisdom as preview of what the church was coming to understand and believe about the identity of Jesus and, eventually, about the nature of God's innermost life in the Trinity.

And that's why we read this hymn to Wisdom from Proverbs as part of our liturgical observance of the Trinity.

FOR REFLECTION AND DISCUSSION

What role does the Trinity play in my spirituality?
Where do I find wisdom?

Most Holy Body and Blood of Christ (A)

Deuteronomy 8:2–3, 14b–16a

Just as last Sunday's Old Testament reading dealt with the foundations of God's revelation of the Holy Trinity, so this Sunday's First Reading deals with the primary intimations of the Holy Eucharist.

This reading comes from the book of Deuteronomy. Deuteronomy is a kind of summary of the law that God had given to his chosen people. Deuteronomy consists of a series of discourses which are attributed to Moses at the end of the forty years' wandering in the desert. It portrays Moses reflecting on what had transpired between God and the people as the people stand ready to pass into the land that the Lord had promised them. Deuteronomy presents the last will and testament of Moses, his final exhortation to the people that God had brought out of Egypt.

This Sunday's selection from Deuteronomy is from the eighth chapter in which Moses is reflecting on the lessons that the people had been taught in their wanderings in the desert. The basic lesson is the lesson of dependence: God takes care of his people.

As the passage has been edited and is presented to us in the lectionary, we have two paragraphs, each structured like the other, each providing the same teaching.

Moses calls on the people to recall what God had done for them. God directed their journey out of Egypt and through the wilderness. They underwent all kinds of privation and affliction. God's purpose for permitting these trials was to test the people and to teach them that faithfulness to their Lord could be costly, painful and frightening. They even had to experience the lack of basic human needs like food and water.

But God came to their rescue. He miraculously provided water for them from the rock and manna to eat, a new kind of food "unknown to you and your fathers." This special food expressed God's care for his people. It demonstrated that God takes care of those he loves even when natural means seems to fail them. All it takes is God's will and God's command, issuing from God's mouth. God teaches them that their life depends not so much on what they can provide for themselves when things are normal (ordinary bread) as on the power of God's word. God's love provides for the people when human means fail.

These reflections on the manna in the desert offered to us today are obviously meant to teach us something about the Eucharist. There are two items that seem to call for our attention when we read this passage in the context of the Solemnity of the Most Holy Body and Blood of Christ.

The first is that the Eucharist, like the manna in the desert, is a gift from God that comes to us through the word and the will of God. We can't provide the Eucharist for ourselves. Only God can bring it to be. Only God can present it to us as our food for the life journey on which we are embarked. This reality is what we express when we profess that the Eucharist can only come to be through the action of an ordained priest. It is not that the priest is born a different kind of human being with powers that others do not have. It is rather that God has chosen to work through those who have been touched by the sacrament of Holy Orders. The power of the priest is the power of God, conferred on the priest through God's sacramental intervention.

The second element that calls for comment is the newness of the gift of manna and of the gift of the Eucharist. Twice in our reading we hear that the manna was unknown to "your fathers." The manna wasn't something that the people wandering in the desert had any right to expect. It wasn't part of their cultural inheritance. It was an unexpected gift of God to the people. The Eucharist is the same. Who could have imagined God giving us his own life under the appearances of ordinary human food? Who could have expected that God would nourish and energize us with a kind of food that is nothing less than his own being, his own energy, his own trinitarian community?

Moses' invitation to his people to recall God's gift to them of manna in the desert is an invitation to us to renew our appreciation of the gift of the Eucharist. Both are unexpected, unimaginable gifts; both come only through the power of God. Both call for gratitude.

FOR REFLECTION AND DISCUSSION

How does the Eucharist nourish me in my life's journey?
What would my life be like without the Eucharist?

Most Holy Body and Blood of Christ (B)

Exodus 24:3–8

Pope Urban IV established the feast of Corpus Christi to be observed by the whole Western church in 1264. This was apparently the first time that a pope used his authority to insert a new feast into the universal liturgical calendar.

According to the current general law of the church, Corpus Christi is a holy day of obligation to be observed on the Thursday after Trinity Sunday. However, because of local law in some parts of the world, including the United States, Corpus Christi is not observed as a holy day. When this is the case, it is observed on the Sunday after Trinity Sunday.

The First Reading for Corpus Christi in year B is taken from the book of Exodus, that portion of the Old Testament which recounts the escape of the Israelites from slavery in Egypt and the beginning of their journey to the Promised Land. The reading is concerned with the establishment of the covenant between God and the Israelites at Mount Sinai, and it invites us to give thought to the Eucharist as the expression of the covenant between God and his new chosen people in Christ.

Moses has been on Mount Sinai in conversation with God. Now, as our reading begins, he comes down from the mountain to see to the ratification of the covenant, i.e., the agreement that God invited the people to enter with him.

Moses tells the people what God expects of them. This would include the observance of the Ten Commandments and of the other fundamental directives that Exodus gives in chapters twenty to twenty-three. The people agree to abide by these laws. Moses then makes sure that all of God's commands will be known and preserved by writing them down. Then, at the foot of the mountain, he erects an altar, which represents God, and twelve stone shafts or slabs, which represent the twelve tribes of Israel.

Now Moses carries out the formal act of ratification of the covenant. Having arranged for sacrifices to be carried out, he takes some of the blood from these sacrifices and pours it on the altar. The rest he sprinkles on the people after he has read them the terms of the agreement one more time and after they have agreed once more to abide by what God commanded.

In Old Testament times, blood was thought to be where life resided. Consequently, to share blood was to share life, to become one with the person or thing from which the blood came. When Moses poured the blood of the sacrifices on the altar (which represented God) and sprinkled it on the people, it constituted a symbolic uniting between God and the people. God and Israel now form a single family. They share a communion of life. That communion of life would be expressed by Israel's observance of the terms of the covenant.

This Exodus event served as a preparation and background for another covenant between God and his people, the covenant that Jesus proclaims in the Gospel. Jesus gave his apostles a cup to drink from and said, "This is my blood of the covenant, which will be shed for many."

This covenant is constituted on the one hand by Jesus' pouring out of his own blood to the Father, i.e., by his life of service and dedication to the Father which finally brought him to death on the cross. On the other side, our side, the covenant is completed when we share in Christ's sacrifice by our participation in the Eucharist. We are united to the Father by sharing the blood of Christ. We participate in an identical life. We are bonded to the Father because we share the sacrifice that Jesus offered to the Father.

It is important to remember that this new covenant, like the former Sinai covenant, is not an affair of individuals. By the Sinai covenant, all the Israelites became the people of God. It wasn't just one or two tribes, or a handful of the people. Likewise, when we participate in the Eucharist, we are involved in an act that involves the whole new people of God. The sacrifice of Christ which we share, the pouring out of his blood in obedience to the Father, is something that involves all the members of Christ, all of those who share and have shared and will share in his divine life. The celebration of the Eucharist and the reception of Holy Communion is never an individual matter between God and me. It always involves all those who participate in the covenant that was brought about by the shedding of Christ's blood.

What dimensions of unity do I find in the Eucharist?
What difference does Christ's life make in my life?

Most Holy Body and Blood of Christ (C)

Genesis 14:18–20

Ordinary time goes on during the weeks after Pentecost, but on this Sunday there is yet one more "special" observance, the celebration of Corpus Christi, of the Body and Blood of Christ. Just as the church's liturgy last week reminded us that the Holy Trinity is the foundation for all human salvation, so this Sunday the liturgy highlights for us the centrality of the Eucharist, the power and the presence of the risen Christ in our ongoing life in the Lord.

Our First Reading for this year's celebration of Corpus Christi is taken from Genesis. It is one of the most mysterious and yet most rich passages of the Hebrew Scriptures.

Abram (whose name has not yet been changed by God to Abraham) has been pursuing a coalition of kings, robber barons who have kidnapped his nephew Lot and carried off Lot's possessions. Abram has defeated the kings, liberated his nephew and regained his possessions. On his way back home, Abram is met by Melchizedek, priest and king of Salem who brought out bread and wine and blessed Abram. It is not clear whether the offering of bread and wine was a ritual sacrifice or a step in the conclusion of a treaty or a simple offering of refreshment. In any case, Melchizedek blesses Abram in the name "of God Most High," the same God who had entered into a relationship with Abram, the God that Abram adored. In response, Abram gives

Melchizedek a tenth of everything he has acquired in his raid to save Lot. This tithe may be what was owed to Melchizedek as a priest or a gift that sealed a treaty. In any case we hear no more about Melchizedek in the story of Abraham. His appearance in the history of salvation is brief and mysterious.

Yet no appearance this brief and mysterious has elicited as much further reflection and teaching as these four verses of Genesis. Every subsequent epoch has found something of special significance in Melchizedek.

First of all comes Psalm 110 where the author speaks of the future messianic king as "a priest forever according to the order of Melchizedek" (NRSV). That is, the Davidic messiah still to come would be both priest and king. Abraham's obeisance to Melchizedek was to be a sign of the reverence that would be owed by the descendants of Abraham to later priest-kings of Jerusalem.

In the New Testament, Melchizedek appears in the Letter to the Hebrews, chapters five and seven. Here the author is dealing with the priestly ministry of Christ. He tells his readers that Christ is "a priest according to the order of Melchizedek" (NRSV) in that both Christ and Melchizedek are kings as well as priests. In addition, since neither the genealogy nor the death of Melchizedek is recorded in Scripture, his priesthood, like Christ's, is directly from God and does not come about through human descent as the levitical priesthood did. Likewise, the absence of data about birth and death suggest that the priesthood of Melchizedek, and of Christ, is an eternal priesthood. Melchizedek is, therefore, an anticipatory image of Christ as king, messiah, and priest engaged in offering an eternal sacrifice of himself to the Father.

But there is still more. Christian reflection subsequent to New Testament times looked on Melchizedek's offering of bread and wine as a symbol of the Eucharist. Melchizedek was not just an image of the priest-king-messiah, not just a foreshadowing of the priesthood of Christ, but also a figure of all those who, in times to come, would offer the sacrifice of Christ for Christ's people through the instrumentalities of bread and wine. This interpretation of our four verses of Genesis had been expressed numberless times and in numberless ways over the centuries in the context of the ordination of new priests for the service of the church. Every new priest has been saluted and congratulated in the words used by the Letter to the Hebrews, based on Psalm 110, and ultimately founded on the brief and mysterious narrative in Genesis: "You are a priest forever according to the order of Melchizedek" (NRSV).

All this reflects the church's conviction that the Eucharist was part of God's plan for the salvation of the world since the earliest times of God's relationship with human beings. Before Abraham was even Abraham, God was giving indications that something mysterious and awesome was connected with a priest's offering of bread and wine. On this feast of Corpus Christi we commemorate the mystery and awe of the Holy Eucharist in our own time and give thanks for God's plans for it long, long ago.

FOR REFLECTION AND DISCUSSION

To what extent is my personal history bound up with the Eucharist? How is my present life influenced by the Eucharist?

Assumption of the Blessed Virgin Mary (ABC)

Revelation 11:19a; 12:1–6a, 10ab

The choice of this reading for this liturgical observance is somewhat unusual. A long series from the book of Revelation is offered for the second readings on the Sundays of Eastertime in year C. But Revelation is never used for the First Reading for Sundays or Holy Days except for Assumption and All Saints' Day. The reading from Revelation that is used on All Saints Day is more or less the same reading that was used before Vatican II. The reading for the Assumption seems to have been chosen because it is traditionally applied to the Virgin Mary.

Revelation is a book of encouragement. It is addressed to Christians who were being rejected or excluded from the ordinary society of their time because of their unwillingness to take part in the religious activities (e.g., worship of the emperor) that were part of ordinary civic life. The encouragement that Revelation offers comes in the form of visions and narratives that deal with God's providence for the world, God's involvement in the present and God's plans for the future. It is a series of symbolic scenes that show the reader what God has in mind for those that he loves.

The reading prescribed by the lectionary for the Solemnity of the Assumption of the Blessed Virgin Mary is from a large segment of Revelation that is concerned with portraying the power of evil in opposition to God and his people. This whole part of Revelation deals with cosmic conflict.

The reading for Assumption Day is from the beginning of this section of Revelation. It gives us the general outlines of God's response to the powers of evil, of God's plan for salvation.

The lectionary reading is provided, first of all, with a more or less detached introduction which tells us that what follows is to be taken in the context of God's heavenly power now manifest to all. At the end of the reading is another detached sentence that expresses praise for what the Lord has done.

In between we have a vision of the basic work of God in the salvation of his people. First of all there is the glorious woman clothed with all the splendor of heaven. She is an image of God's people in the Old and New Testaments, the collective, symbolic mother of the Messiah. She gives birth in pain because she shares the inheritance of Eve.

Now there appears another "sign," another apparition that expresses some part of the reality at issue here. This sign is the huge red dragon, the symbol of evil, spectacular, powerful, ruler of the kingdoms of the earth. The dragon tries to devour the child that the woman is bearing. But the child, the messianic king who will "rule all the nations with an iron rod," ascends to heaven and is brought to the throne of God while the woman is taken to a place of protection in the desert.

The author of Revelation is using colorful images and scriptural allusions to remind his readers that a messiah has arisen from among the people of God, that the messiah has eternal, heavenly connections, and that God's people will be protected by the loving hand of God.

What does all this have to do with the assumption of the Blessed Virgin? It does not seem likely that the author of Revelation intended to signify Mary of Nazareth as the woman clothed with the sun. Most probably, the woman represents the people of God, the church. Yet Mary is not for that reason excluded here. Christians believe that the authors of the books of the Bible often said more than they were aware of and that the books of Scripture have depths of meaning that their first readers did not grasp.

The church teaches us that Mary is an image, a model of the church, that what she did is what the church does and vice versa. The church offers Christ to the world. So did Mary. The church only makes sense in light of Christ. So does Mary. We cannot properly venerate the Blessed Mother without including Christ and the church.

The dogma of the assumption teaches us that Mary, having completed her earthly life, was assumed into heavenly glory, body and soul. She was taken into eternal life with her Son to the fullest possible extent. In that context she represents the whole people of God. She is an image of the church as it will be when it comes to perfection.

FOR REFLECTION AND DISCUSSION

How do I experience the conflict of good and evil in my life?
How does devotion to Mary bring me closer to Jesus?

All Saints (ABC)

Revelation 7:2–4, 9–14

The book of Revelation is a book of encouragement addressed to Christians in a time of persecution. Through a series of visions and teachings from God the author leads his contemporaries to deepen their hope, to take reassurance of a future full of happiness, an eternal state of being loved and cared for by the Lord whose power will bring about ultimate victory.

The church presents readings from Revelation as second readings during Eastertime of year C. It is only on the feast of the Assumption of the Blessed Virgin and this feast of All Saints that Revelation provides the First Reading in a three-reading series. It seems significant that both Assumption and All Saints Day are concerned with heaven, since heaven is ultimately what Revelation is all about.

The verses that the lectionary presents for this feast come in the midst of the description of a long series of disasters that await the world. But our verses are a kind of interlude in the description of the disasters. They deal with God's elect. There are two distinct visions here.

In the first vision, God's messenger proclaims a moratorium on the execution of the catastrophes until God's elect could be identified and offered protection. They were to be marked in a special way that would distinguish them and protect them from the fate of the rest of the sinful world. The number of those so identified and marked is 144,000, the square of twelve (one of the perfect numbers and the number of the tribes of Israel) multiplied by a thousand. The issue here is not mathematical but theological. There is an immense community of faithful persons on earth whom God will protect as the world careens toward its end.

In the second part of our reading there is another vision, this time a vision of heaven. The author now sees "a great multitude which no one could count." This multitude is composed of people "from every nation, race, people, and tongue." They wear white robes and carry palm branches, symbols of victory. They are the women and men who have survived the time of trial and who have entered into definitive association with the Lamb. They are redeemed by his blood. All of heaven joins with them in offering praise and thanksgiving to God.

These two visions are about membership and multitude. The first vision deals with those who are members of God's people still on earth. They are vulnerable, but, because they belong to the Lord, they will be protected and preserved by the power of God. And their number is vast. It is not a mere handful of people who serve God on earth but a mystical immensity of 144,000.

If that number was unimaginably great, the number of those who praise God in heaven is greater still. It is a limitless gathering, "a great multitude that no one could count." Their commonality is the blood of the Lamb which has made them dear to God and has brought them together in the presence of the Lord forever.

It is clear how these verses fit in with the observance of All Saints Day. First of all, they are verses about hope. The saints in heaven once had to struggle on earth, even as we do. They are now in heaven, even as we long to be one day. A liturgical celebration of ultimate success on the part of those who have gone before is a celebration that offers hope to those who follow.

These verses are also about membership. Being protected by God on earth and being among the worshipers of God in heaven is not just a matter of relationship between individual persons and the Lord. It is a matter of being part of a community, of belonging to God's people.

Finally, these verses are about multitudes. They show us a multitude of holy persons striving, under God's protection, to be faithful on earth. They show us an even greater multitude of saints in heaven. God's love and care, God's salvation is not focused on some tiny group of the specially chosen. God's love and God's grace are extended to multitudes, multitudes on earth, multitudes in heaven. God is not a miser with his gifts.

The feast of All Saints invites us to renew our hope, our confidence that God's love will triumph in the end. It calls us to renew our dedication to membership in the people of God, which is the church. It reminds us that we are not alone in our struggles, but that there are countless multitudes of brothers and sisters both on earth and in heaven with whom we share God's love.

FOR REFLECTION AND DISCUSSION

What role does hope play in my life?

How many saints have I known?

Immaculate Conception of the Blessed Virgin Mary (ABC)

Genesis 3:9–15, 20

The Scripture reading from Genesis seems to have been chosen to provide contrast and background for the feast that the church celebrates on this occasion. On this feast we celebrate Mary's preservation from all separation from God, all stain of sin, from the first instant she came to be. The Old Testament reading tells us about how sin got started, about the origins of a state of sinfulness that all the rest of us share, about the initial sin, the original sin.

Chapter two of Genesis gives us an account of the creation of humankind. Man is formed out of the clay of the ground. God provides him with a whole world of plants and animals that he is to be in charge of. Then, in order to deal with man's loneliness, God provides him with a partner, the woman who would be bone of his bones and flesh of his flesh. They were given free run of the garden. The only exception was that they were not to eat of the tree that would give them the experience of evil.

Because of the temptation of the serpent, both the woman and the man disobeyed God's command. They ate the fruit that had been forbidden. They sought the experience of evil.

This is where our reading begins. God is still close to his human creatures and presents himself to them as he strolls in the garden in the cool of the evening. The man and the woman hide from God because they are now ashamed. They are no longer what they had been. God tries to elicit from them an acknowledgment of their guilt, but the man blames the woman and the woman blames the serpent.

Now comes God's punishment, beginning with the serpent.

(The punishment of the man and the woman are in the full text of chapter three, but they are not used in the liturgical reading.) The serpent will be different from other animals. It will crawl on its belly and eat dust. In addition to that, the serpent's evil-dealing plans will not be victorious in the story of God's creation. The offspring of the woman will crush the serpent's head, despite the serpent's continued attempts to destroy humanity.

At this point, our reading skips several verses, and comes to a conclusion with the verse about the woman being now called Eve, because she became the mother of all the living.

The account of the fall of humankind into sin that we have in Genesis has been the source of continued study and reflection over the centuries, both in Old Testament times and after the coming of Christ. Christian thinkers from the very beginning of Christianity have seen the conclusion of God's curse on the serpent as a promise: The offspring of the woman would eventually crush the head of the serpent, crush the power of evil. These words constitute God's first announcement of a redeemer. They are the first expression of God's good news for humankind. They constitute the first "gospel."

But the woman was to be involved in all this. She was to be the mother of all the living, and so the redeemer would be her offspring. Here again, Christian reflection has found greater meaning and depth in the Scripture than the literal meaning of the words seems to express. As Christian thinkers reflected on God's promise of a redeemer, they began to become conscious of the significance of another woman. This is the woman who would be the mother of the redeemer, and thus would be the mother of all those who found life and freedom in the redeemer. God foresaw a new Eve.

This new Eve is, of course, the Blessed Virgin Mary. Her acceptance of the mission that God proposed to her would open the gates of a new world, a new creation. Just as the first Eve, by her selfishness, led the way out of the first Eden, so Mary, by her generosity, led the way into the new paradise offered by Christ.

Mary was prepared for her unique mission by a special provision that God made for her. In view of the redemption that Jesus would bring about, Mary was preserved from ever sharing the state of separation from God that every other human being was afflicted with. All the other offspring of Adam and Eve would be born in a state of exclusion from the life of God that their first parents had shared in the beginning, all the others except Mary and her divine Son.

This day's Old Testament reading is about the beginning of the power of evil in God's creation. The feast that we celebrate deals with the beginning of the end of that power in our world and in our lives.

FOR REFLECTION AND DISCUSSION

What does Mary's sinlessness mean to me?
How and where do I see evil being overcome?